HUXFORD'S

COLLECTIBLE Advertising

AN ILLUSTRATED VALUE GUIDE

by
Sharon & Bob Huxford

COLLECTOR BOOKS
A Division of Schroeder Publishing Co., Inc.

ABJ-3856

The current values in this book should be used only as a guide. They are not intended to set prices, which vary from one section of the country to another. Auction prices as well as dealer prices vary greatly and are affected by condition as well as demand. Neither the Authors nor the Publisher assumes responsibility for any losses that might be incurred as a result of consulting this guide.

Cover photos courtesy of David Allen, Photographer, and Richard W. Oliver's Auction Gallery:

Campbell's Soups, sign, embossed tin, Pop Art graphics of the 60s by Standard Adv. Co., Coschocton, Ohio, 26x40", M, A, $85,000.00.

J.F. Cutter, tin sign, lithograph by Bachrach & Co., San Francisco, ca. 1895-1900, extremely rare in original frame, 15x22", $10,000.00.

French Dressing Satin Polish & Blacking, sign, tin, patriotic logo with man & boy giving ladies a shoeshine flanked by product, 1870s(?), 24x18", NM, A, $40,000.00.

Searching For A Publisher?

We are always looking for knowledgeable people considered to be experts within their fields. If you feel that there is a real need for a book on your collectible subject and have a large comprehensive collection, contact us.

COLLECTOR BOOKS
P.O. Box 3009
Paducah, Kentucky 42002-3009

Printed by IMAGE GRAPHICS, INC., Paducah, Kentucky

Introduction

The field of collectible advertising is vast and varied. Offering an almost infinite diversity of items, it has the obvious potential to appeal to nearly anyone, with any interest, within any budget. With this in mind, we have attempted to compile a guide that would be beneficial to all collectors of advertising memorabilia. This book includes five thousand descriptive listings and hundreds of photos. The format has been kept as simple as possible, and we've added an index to further facilitate its use.

Items are sorted primarily by alphabetizing the product name as worded on each specific sign, tray, tin, etc. For instance, you'll find listings for Pabst Blue Ribbon Beer, others under Pabst Brewing Co., still another under Pabst Malt Extract. Each variation indicates the primary, most obvious visual impact of the advertising message. There are some exceptions. Even though many examples of Coca-Cola advertising are simply worded 'Coke,' all have been listed under the title 'Coca-Cola.' The advertising message as it actually appears is given in the description. There are several other instances where this applies – Planters (Peanuts), Cracker Jack, and Pepsi-Cola, for example. When they seemed appropriate, cross references were added.

After the product (or company) name, the form of the item is given, i.e. sign, tin, mug, ash tray, etc. (Trays having 'deep dish' or rolled rims are so described; when the type of rim is not mentioned, you may assume it is the more common tray style.) Approximate date is given when that information was available. Following phrases describe graphics, colors, and sizes. When only one dimension is given, it is height; and height is first when two or more are noted. Often there is a detailed description of any damage; in lieu of specific details, condition is indicated by standard abbreviations: M for mint, NM for near mint, EX for excellent, VG for very good, G for good, and F for fair. See the section on 'Condition and Its Effect on Value' for more information.

Because our listings have been compiled from many sources, we have coded each line to indicate that the suggested value is (A), an auction result or a price actually realized by another type of sale, or (D), a dealer's 'asking' price. As everyone is aware, auction prices are sometimes higher than dealers' prices, but they are just as apt to be lower. At any rate, auction prices are legitimate prices for which merchandise actually changed hands and they have always been used by dealers as a basis for their evaluations. As you should regard any price guide, this one is offered as only an additional tool to be used alongside your personal observations of market dealings, show sales, and tradepaper ads.

Acknowledgments

We are indebted to the following galleries and dealers who have contributed catalogs, photographs, listings, and other information, all of which was vital to the production of this guide:

David Allen, Photographer

Noel Barrett Antiques & Auctions Ltd.
Carversville, Pennsylvania 18913

Cerebro
P.O. Box 1221
Lancaster, Pennsylvania 17603

Collector's Auction Services
327 Seneca St.
Oil City, Pennsylvania 16301-F

Dennis & George Collectibles
3407 Lake Montebello Dr.
Baltimore, Maryland 21218

Dynamite Auction Company
Franklin Antique Mall & Auction Gallery
280 Franklin Ave.
Franklin, Pennsylvania 16323

Henry F. Hain III Antiques & Collectibles
2623 N. Second St.
Harrisburg, Pennsylvania 17110
Eric Hardesty, Photographer

James D. Julia Inc.
Box 830
Fairfield, Maine 04937

Mike's General Store
52 St. Anne's Rd.
Winnipeg, Manitoba, Canada R2M 2Y3

Anthony J. Nard & Co.
US Route 220
Milan, Pennsylvania 18831

Nostalgia Galleries
657 Meacham Avenue
Elmont, New York

Richard W. Oliver Inc.
Plaza One, Route One
Kennebunk, Maine 04043

Richard Opfer Auctioneering Inc.
1919 Greenspring Dr.
Timonium, Maryland 21093

Mike Roscoe; Fred Smith
Lane St. Antiques
Blissfield, Michigan 49228

Condition and Its Effect on Value

Condition, possibly more than any other consideration, is very important when assessing the value of advertising collectibles. On today's market, items in good to very good condition are slow to sell unless they are extremely rare. Mint or near mint examples are high.

On the occasion when no condition is given in our listings, assume the item to be in excellent condition. Every effort has been made to describe any damage fully; so nearly every line has either specific mention of fading, rust, chips, etc. or a condition code. Tins are evaluated with original lids unless noted otherwise. Items that we found selling or offered for sale more than once are sometimes listed twice, when conditions varied.

The following criteria are generally used by most dealers and auction galleries when describing condition (corresponding numbers are sometimes used instead of letter codes; these are also given). Mint (M) (10) – Unused, absolutely no wear, like new. Near Mint (NM) (9) – Appears new, but on closer examination minor wear, a few very light scratches, or slight dullness can be seen. Excellent (EX) (8) – General appearance is very pleasing with only very minor dents, scratches, and loss of paint to distract. Very Good (VG) (7) – Still attractive to display, but with more defects than one in excellent condition; has some rust, pitting, and fading. Good (G) (6) – Used, faded; has paint wear, dents, scratches, and rust. Generally not collectible unless the item is especially hard to find. Fair (F) (5) – Has serious problems; heavily rusted, scratched, pitted; has little if any value.

To help you arrive at values for items in conditions other than those specifically given, we suggest the following guidelines. These are only general, and there are of course exceptions to the rule.

Using excellent as a basis, equate the same item in mint condition at 2X; NM at 1.5X; VG at -.5X; and G at -.75X. For instance, an item in EX condition at $100 used as a basis makes the same in M condition $200; NM, $150; VG, $50 (or less).

A Grof Distilling Co, sign, George Washington seated talking to child at outdoor gathering, 1906, 22x29" without frame, appears EX, A **400.00**

A&P Tea Co, calendar, 1903, cardboard, shopkeeper surrounded by products, people using products, full pad, framed, 19x15", EX, A **180.00**

A&P Tea Co, store dispenser, wood, lg red & gold logo, hinged lid, 30x19x18", G, A..............................235.00

A&P Tea Co, tin, pictures elderly woman within an oval, A&P's Teas & Coffees Have Been My Solace..., 1880s, slip lid, 11x7x7", EX, A **175.00**

A&P Tea Co, toy, horse & wagon by Marx, original box priced at $1.98, 16" long, A **35.00**

A&W Root Beer, mug, glass, 4", EX, D..............................**4.00**

A-1 Tire Co, playing cards, stylized logo on dark red with gold-black-gold border, Buy War Bonds, ca 1940s, complete, NM, D **8.00**

Aaron Burr Cigars, box label, inner lid, depicts Aaron Burr in profile in inset surrounded by moonlit night, 6x9", EX, D **40.00**

Abaco Cigars, box label, inner lid, Indian in profile blowing smoke rings, 6x9", EX, D **85.00**

Abaco Cigars, box top sheet, depicts Indian camp, 5x8", M, D **30.00**

Abbey Cigars, box label, inner lid, depicts house & carriage, 6x9", M, D..............................**2.00**

ABC Bohemian Beer, sign, celluloid with metallic corner pieces, patriotic eagle logo, American Brewing Co of St Louis, 7x9", EX, A **210.00**

ABC Brand Beer, sign, embossed die-cut tin, patriotic eagle with labeled bottle & nymphs atop, King of Bottled Beer, 14x10", VG+, A **2,000.00**

Abraham Lincoln Cigars, box label, outer, portrait of the president in profile, 5x5", EX, D **18.00**

AC Spark Plugs, bank, cast metal with wheels, horse in tub, EX, D **135.00**

AC Spark Plugs, sign, spark plug over red circle with product name in white, blue background, 1941, minor edge rust, 18x9", EX, A **70.00**

Ace High Motor Oil, tin, clouds with touring car, 3 logos below, sunburst on red, 1934-41, fading/no bottom, 1-qt, 6x4" diameter, EX, A **135.00**

Acme Boots, post card, 1950s, EX, D **3.00**

Acme Quality Motor Car Finishes, sign, tin, pictures a man painting a Model T with a paint chart below, 14x12", G, A **350.00**

Acme Quality Paint, sign, die-cut tin litho, Acme Quality on circle top, Paint on horizontal rectangular bottom, Authorized Dealer, EX, A **70.00**

Acorn Stoves & Ranges, match holder, die-cut tin, acorn figural with lettering, Over 1,000,000 In Use, 6x5", EX+, A **425.00**

Acorn Stoves & Ranges, match holder, die-cut tin, acorn figural with lettering, Over 1,000,000 In Use, heavily worn, 6x5", G-, A **110.00**

Acristo Cigars, box label, inner lid, depicts roses flanked by children, Habana, 6x9", M, D **9.00**

Acropolis Cigars, box label, inner lid, depicts cave men with clubs & ancient ruins, 6x9", M, D **10.00**

Adam Forepaugh Cigars, box label, inner lid, depicts this circus leader flanked by famous circus scenes, rare, 6x9", M, D **250.00**

Adam Hats, display, die-cut cardboard, Baby Snooks, Miniature Hat Box, hat missing, 17", VG, A..............................**25.00**

Adam Smith Cigars, box top wrap, wood grain with profile of Adam Smith, 5x8", VG, D..............................**10.00**

Adams Honey Chewing Gum, tin, pictures peacocks, flat, 1x9x6", G, D **50.00**

Adams Pepsin Gum, display & change tray, sections enclosed in frame with lettering, 3x16x12", G, A..............................200.00

Adams Pepsin Gum, display box, tin, green with hinged lid showing packs of Pepsin Gum, chips/rust, 6x7x5", G, A..............................**100.00**

Adams Pepsin Tutti-Frutti Chewing Gum, vendor, oak with tin insert, original key, 32", EX, A **1,200.00**

Adams Pure Chewing Gum, store container, glass jar, labeled front & decorative lid, ca 1915-20, 12x5x5", NM, A..............................**160.00**

Adams Pure Chewing Gum, store container, glass jar, lettering on front only, slip lid, minor fading to lettering, appears EX, A **110.00**

Adams Silver Roll Gum, store container, tin litho, unusual decor, dome lid with second interior lid seal, pedestal foot, rare, 8x5", VG, A **450.00**

Adams Spearmint Gum, display box, tin with vertical stripes, hinged lid, discoloration/bubbling/wear, 6x7x5", G, A...**135.00**

Admiral Gherardi Cigars, box label, inner lid, depicts portrait of the Admiral in inset surrounded by the Spanish-American War, 1892, 6x9", M, D **60.00**

Admiral Hopkins Cigars, box label, inner lid, depicts the Admiral, the American Revolution & ship, 1933, 6x9", M, D **45.00**

Admiration Cigars, box label, inner lid, depicts woman looking into hand mirror, 6x9", M, D.....................**6.00**

Admiration Cigars, sign, gutta percha, winking moon smoking cigar in embossed relief, 16x12", EX, A.............575.00

Admiration Iced Tea, cooler, 3-piece brown stoneware with pedestal, chipping to lid, D..........................**300.00**

Adriance, Platt & Co, poster, paper, view of Hudson river with insets of machinery, Enoch Bridges Agent, 28x22" without frame, VG, A.......................................**200.00**

Adriance Buckeye Harvest Machinery, poster, paper, depicts farm girl with insets of machinery, York Bros Agents, 1897, chips/creases/wrinkles, framed, 28x21", G, A **350.00**

Adriance Farm Machinery, match holder, tin litho, pictures a corn binder, company name on holder, Poughkeepsie NY, 5x3", EX, A **350.00**

Adriance Farm Machinery, match holder, tin litho, pictures a corn binder, plain black holder, paint chips, rare, 5x3", VG+, A **230.00**

Adriance Farm Machinery, sign, paper on cardboard, HS Graham Agent, pictures children on horse & machinery vignettes, 1902, framed, 28x21", G, A **225.00**

Adriance Farm Machinery, sign, wood, double-sided, Adriance on the diagonal, logo in upper left corner, 13x31", appears EX, A.......................................**110.00**

ADVO Gold Medal Coffee, tin, white with blue, red, & gold lettering & decoration, Crackers printed on back, press lid, round, EX, D **35.00**

AE Sonnedecker Coal, match safe, tin, EX, D **69.00**

Aero Mobiloil, tin, cream with Red Band lettered on red band, Gargoyle atop, 1935-45, no top, 5-qt, 10x7", VG, A...**100.00**

Aero Mobiloil, tin, white with Gargoyle atop gray band, Socony-Vacuum Oil Co Inc, 1932-38, 1-qt, 6x4" diameter, EX, A...**80.00**

Aetna Insurance Co, calendar, 1890, cardboard, some mounting holes, framed, 26x19", EX, A.........290.00

Aetna Insurance Co, ledger marker, tin, double-sided, black letters on green, silver on reverse, ca late 1800s, 12x3", G-, A **130.00**

Aetna Insurance Co, ledger marker, tin, pictures erupting volcano surrounded by lettered logo, Wells & Hope, ca 1890, 12x3", EX, A...**100.00**

Affectionate Cigars, box label, inner lid, depicts girl hugging older sister, 6x9", EX, D................................**25.00**

Africora Cigars, box label, inner lid, depicts woman walking through jungle, 6x9", M, D..............................**10.00**

Africora Cigars, box label, outer, depicts woman walking through jungle, 5x5", M, D....................................**2.00**

After Dinner Cigars, box label, outer, depicts men playing a game of cards, 5x5", M, D **16.00**

After Dinner Cigars, box label, outer, depicts 3 men being served at table, 5x5", M, D....................................**45.00**

After Glow Coffee, tin, red, gold, & black print, slip lid & bail, 4-lb, VG, D **42.00**

Agalion Motor Oil, tin, lion in inset atop gold & silver letters on red ground, screw lid & handle, 1926-30, bottom gone, 1-gal, 11", EX, A **375.00**

Agfa Photos, banner, canvas, orange, blue, & white with good hanger, made in Germany, 22x24", EX, D **75.00**

Aguila Cigars, box label, inner lid, depicts eagle perched on cigar, 6x9", VG, D **6.00**

Aim Hi Cigars, box label, inner lid, depicts bust-length portrait of Thomas Jefferson, 1924, 6x9", M, D **22.00**

Air Jamaica, playing cards, stylized bird logo, complete, NM, D...**10.00**

Air Race Motor Oil, tin, yellow airplane on cream background, Deep-Rock, ca 1935-45, no top or bottom/some rust, 1-qt, 4" diameter, G, A.............**30.00**

Airdale Cigars, box label, inner lid, depicts head of dog on yellow background, 6x9", M, D **18.00**

Airflite Motor Oil, tin, pictures red plane in blue sky below lg 3-color letters, 100% Paraffine Base, 1925-45, 2-gal, 12x9", EX, A **180.00**

Airline, crate label, California orange, depicts globe flanked by wings & stars, Fillmore Citrus Ass'n, 1940, 10x12", M, D **5.00**

AJ Stillwell Ham, sign, paper, some damage at bottom, wood frame, 16", VG, A..**150.00**

Akron Brewing Co, sign, decal process on wood, factory scene with triangle logo below, early, minor restoration/touch-up, 24x36", A.................................**125.00**

Akron Brewing Co, tray, stock image of girl with tiger, decorative border, Purity, white chipping/scratches, 14" diameter, VG, A...**85.00**

Akron Sewer Pipes, letter folder, tin litho, ca 1890s, 12", VG, D..**275.00**

Alabama Brewing Co, tray, pictures elegant woman dressed in red & labeled bottle, gold lettering on rim, Ideal Bottled Beer, round, EX, A...........................**375.00**

Alazan Cigars, box label, inner lid, pictures harem dancer, 6x9", M, D **3.00**

Albert Robin Cognac, sign, tin, bottle of product under lettering, British, vertical rectangle, appears EX, A **25.00**

Alcazar Cigars, box label, inner lid, race horse flanked with logo, 6x9", M, D **7.00**

Alcazar Cigars, tin, rare Liberty, slip lid, minor wear, 5x6", EX, A..825.00

Alexander The Great Cigars, box label, inner lid, depicts bust of Alexander the Great surrounded by battle scenes, 6x9", M, D...**16.00**

Algonquin Hotel Cigars, box label, inner lid, depicts the hotel & street scene, 6x9", M, D............................**125.00**

Alice Foote MacDougal Coffee, tin, black & yellow striped can with woman's silhouetted profile, slip lid, minor chipping, 1-lb, 6x4", EX, A....................**75.00**

Alka-Seltzer, display, die-cut stand-up, depicts Speedy, ca early 1960s, discoloration on hat/slight staining, 12", VG+, A..**125.00**

Alka-Seltzer, doll, cloth, Speedy, 1984 anniversary edition, 20", VG, D..**50.00**

Alka-Seltzer, tape holder & product display piece, tin with logoed sides, 11", EX, D **95.00**

All American Cigars, tin, All American arched above 3 portraits in circles, no lid, VG, A............................**60.00**

All American Motor Oil, tin, gold strip top & bottom with car, truck, & plane, shape of North America in center, 1925-45, 2-gal, 12x9", EX, A...................................**65.00**

All Jacks Cigarettes, sign, tin, depicts pack of All Jacks, Hard To Beat, ca 1940, 14x10", M, A.....................**33.00**

All Nations Tobacco, store bin, has red & black lettering on yellow background, 5¢, slip lid, 7x11x8", G, A......**350.00**

Allan Line New Steamers, sign, paper litho, steamship at sea with lettering below, heavy wear to letters, framed, 35x47", appears EX, A...**375.00**

Allen Square Cigars, box label, inner lid, depicts corner building & busy street scene, 6x9", M, D **100.00**

Allenhurst Famous Steak Dinners, sign, real horns mounted on die-cut wood, gold letters on black background, appears EX, A..**300.00**

Allens Red Tame Cherry, dispenser, glass potbelly with silver-plated brass faucet shaft on marble base, approx: 28x16", EX, A...**300.00**

Allens Red Tame Cherry, dispenser, oblong glass bulb on ornately embossed silver-plated base, lettering on bulb, 30x16" diameter, EX, A **675.00**

Allens Red Tame Cherry, dispenser, painted metal base with stoneware interior & glass top, faded letters on base/overall wear, 29x14x17", G-, A **65.00**

Allens Red Tame Cherry, sign, tin, colorful image, minor wear, framed, 28x18", VG+, A...........3,200.00

Allens Red Tame Cherry, soda bottle, glass with lettered logo on label, Cherryallen, milky haze interior, 11x3" diameter, EX, A **200.00**

Allens Root Beer Extract, sign, paper with metal strips, pictures woman distilling extract for cherubs, Donaldson Brothers, framed, 20x14", NM, A **650.00**

Alleppo Temple, sample tin, made for Edgeworth Cigarettes, temple pictured on front, Annual Meeting, 1909, EX, A **240.00**

Allied Radios, catalog, Chicago, 1930, EX, D **24.00**

Allyn & Blanchard Co, match holder, die-cut tin, man wearing a turban surrounded by ornate graphics, yellow & black, 7x4", VG+, A **200.00**

Almona Wafers, sign, Nat'l Biscuit Co, Uneeda Bakers, Nabisco product, ca 1910, rare, EX, A 65.00

Aloa Cigars, box label, outer, depicts pretty young lady, 1886, 5x5", M, D 15.00

Alouette Tobacco, tin, grouse, 9" diameter, D 35.00

Alphabetical, crate label, California orange, depicts little boy playing with stack of blocks, Villa Park Calif, 1930s, 10x12", M, D.................125.00

Alta Crest Farms, milk bottle, blue pyro, crown top, Pat 1929 on base, 1-qt, EX, D 70.00

Alta Ginger Ale, sign, tin, 20x14", NM, A 2,100.00

Amazon Insurance Co, letter folder, tin litho, ca 1890s, 12x3", VG, D.................150.00

Amber Soap, sign, embossed with Procter & Gamble's logoed man in the moon, flaking/dirt stains, 13x19" without frame, G-, A 70.00

America's Delight, crate label, Washington apple, depicts lg apple over orchard & mountains, North Pacific Sales Co, 1920s, 9x11", M, D 3.00

America's Pride Cigars, box label, inner lid, depicts Washington crossing the Delaware, 6x9", M, D 7.00

American Ace Coffee, tin, American Tea & Coffee Co, key-wind lid, wear, 3-lb, 8x6" diameter, VG, A ...350.00

American Ace Coffee, tin, shows aviator holding cup of coffee, key-wind lid, good sheen, scratches, 1-lb, 3x5" diameter, EX, A 120.00

American Airlines, playing cards, American Airlines DH-4, complete, NM, D 10.00

American Airlines, playing cards, green eagle on white encircled with gold on green, gold letters on white border, complete, NM, D 8.00

American Airlines, playing cards, light blue & red A's on white background, complete, NM, D 5.00

American Amoco Gas, sign, porcelain, double-sided, Courtesy Cards Honored Here, 1940s, 15x24", EX, A.................110.00

American Author Cigars, box label, inner lid, depicts portrait of Richard Harding Davis flanked by literature, 6x9", M, D.................55.00

American Author Cigars, box label, outer, depicts bust portrait of young man, 5x5", M, D 20.00

American Ball Nozzle, sign, paper, unusual image of firemen conquering a fire with a ball nozzle hose, 1895, framed, 12x16", EX, A.................200.00

American Beauties Cigars, box label, inner lid, depicts 2 women, patriotic theme, 1893, M, D.................16.00

American Belle Cigars, box label, outer, depicts Miss Liberty & Columbian Expo, 1904, 5x5", M, D.............45.00

American Brewing Ass'n, sign, tin litho, depicts 2 classical ladies in garden setting, Pilsener The Pure Beer, self-framed, 23", G, A.................300.00

American Brewing Co, tip tray, Indian princess seal for Liberty Beer, In Bottles Only, Rochester NY, 4" diameter, NM, A 130.00

American Brewing Co, tray, Indian princess seal for Liberty Beer, In Bottles Only, dirt spots/image wear/rim chips, 12" diameter, VG, A.................50.00

American Coach Oil, tin, stage coach graphic, Standard Oil Co, soldered, ca 1870-90, very rare, triangular shape, 1-qt, 7", VG, A 250.00

American Cough Drops, medicine bottle, thick flared rolled mouth, pontil scar, 5", EX, A 160.00

American Eagle Chewing Tobacco, tin, detailed pattern with girl & eagle logo on slip lid, scratches/chips/discoloration/dents, 5x6x4", G, A 100.00

American Express Co, sign, embossed tin, Established 1841, Money Orders, Foreign Drafts..., Hauesermann Co, ca 1913, 27x20", EX, A 600.00

American Family Soap, sign, die-cut tin figural, 20x19", VG+, A.................5,500.00

American Fence, sign, tin, pictures outdoor scene with fence, vertical, EX, A.................75.00

American Fire Insurance Co, ledger marker, tin litho, yellow with black lettering, late 1800s, 12x3", G, A .140.00

American Fletcher National Bank, playing cards, Reflecting The New Indy printed vertically on black background, AFNB, complete, NM, D **5.00**

American Girl Cigars, box label, inner lid, depicts portrait of a woman, 1896, 6x9", EX, D **18.00**

American Lady Coffee, tin, American Lady logo, slip lid, rare, 3-lb, 10x6" diameter, EX, A **500.00**

American Lady-American Gentleman Shoe, sign, textured surface, depicts mermaid looking at shoes from water's edge, Hamilton Brown Shoe Co, framed, 29x20", NM, A **2,600.00**

American Line, tip tray, pictures ship, Compliments of..., Philadelphia, Queenstown, Liverpool, crazing, 4" diameter, NM, A...**80.00**

American Line/Red Star Line, letter folder, die-cut tin, minor wear, 3x12", EX+, A **350.00**

American Locomotive Cranes, watch fob, D **60.00**

American Manure Spreader, match holder, tin litho, colorful image of horse-drawn wagon, American Harrow Co, Detroit Mich, 8x3", VG, A **275.00**

American Motors Co, playing cards, vertical blue print of AMC Pacer car, The First Wide Small Car, complete, NM, D **6.00**

American Pencil Co, display, cardboard, 3-dimensional roadster shape, 1692 & American Pencil Co NY printed on side, rare, EX, A **85.00**

American Perfect Beer, tip tray, man & woman toasting, American Brewing Ass'n, Houston Texas, 4" diameter, EX, A **300.00**

American President Lines, playing cards, white stylized eagle & 4 stars in center on orange, lettering on horizontal gold bands, complete, NM, D **10.00**

American Railway Express, sign, wood with gold letters, 1900-20, all original, 11x72", G, A........................**225.00**

American Rose Cigars, box label, inner lid, depicts woman in oval frame & roses, 1896, 6x9", EX, D **12.00**

American Soda Crackers, store bin, tin with paper label of Uncle Sam promoting product, general overall wear, 12x10x10", G-, A...**25.00**

American Steel Farm Fences, match holder, pictures wire fence, Best & Cheapest, Made In All Heights, fading to match striker/scratches, 5x4x1", G, A.....................**65.00**

American Stores, calendar, 1932, paper, children in colonial interior holding flag with 13 stars, full pad, framed, 31x18", VG, A **120.00**

American Sweeper Cigars, box label, inner lid, pictures eagle flying over United States with bag that says Expansion, 6x9", EX, D...**35.00**

American Tobacco Co, sign, paper, colorful image, 1899, sm edge tears, 26x18" without frame, EX+, A...**450.00**

American Tobacco Co, sign, paper, colorful image of a cowboy smoking cigar, minor edge tears, 26x18" without frame, NM, A...**300.00**

American Tobacco Co, sign, paper, colorful image of equestrian gentleman smoking cigar, scratches/edge tears, 26x18" without frame, NM, A **150.00**

American Tobacco Co, sign, paper, colorful image of gentleman holding cigar, minor creasing at edges, 26x18" without frame, NM, A...**50.00**

American Tobacco Co, sign, paper, depicts pub master smoking a cigar, 1899, 26x18" without frame, M, A .**50.00**

American Tobacco Co, tin, flaking to lid, rare, 4x5x1", G-, A..**525.00**

American Wringer Co, sign, embossed tin, lettering on product, No 514 Royal, Warranted For 5 Years, heavy background wear, framed, A **140.00**

American Writing Machine Co, ledger marker, tin litho, pictures calligraphy, red & blue on gray, ca late 1800s, color fading, 12x3", G, A **185.00**

Ammen's Powder, tin, paper label picturing baby's face, G, D..**10.00**

Amsterdamsche Munt Cigars, box label, inner lid, depicts Amsterdam Mint building, 6x9", VG, D.................**2.00**

Amsterdamsche Munt Cigars, box label, inner lid, depicts 3 Dutchmen smoking cigars, 6x9", M, D **12.00**

Amundson Florist, sign, tin with curled corners, stock image of Carnation Girl, Minneapolis Minn, minor wear/bends, 15" square, VG, A **225.00**

Andrew Johnson Cigars, box label, inner lid, brown, depicts portrait of Andrew Johnson, 1905, VG, D..**35.00**

Andy Gump Cigars, box label, outer, depicts Andy smoking a cigar, 5x5", M, D **125.00**

Angeles Brewing & Malting Co, tip tray, lettered logo in center, Seattle & Port Angeles, Washington Co, 4" diameter, NM, A **250.00**

Angeles Brewing & Malting Co, tip tray, depicts Washington state flag & labeled bottle, Seattle 1909, 4" diameter, NM, A..**400.00**

Angelus Marshmallows, pocket mirror, picturing cherubs, oval, EX, D...**50.00**

Angelus Marshmallows, tin, cream, gold, green, & red, 5-lb, round, EX, D **30.00**

Anheuser-Busch Brewing Ass'n, tray, colorful factory scene, Standard Adv Co, edge chips, oval, 16x19", NM, A...1,750.00

Anheuser-Busch Brewing Ass'n, tray, colorful factory scene with hops & eagle border, Standard Adv Co, scratches/wear/chips, oval, 16x19", VG+, A.........**800.00**

Anheuser-Busch Brewing Ass'n, tray, Victory with cherubs holding varieties of bottled products, decorative border, rare, oval, 14x17", EX, A....................**550.00**

Anheuser-Busch Brewing Association, sign, paper litho, 'Custer's Last Fight' & Anheuser-Busch Brewing Ass'n at bottom, 1905, rare, framed, 36x46", M, D **4,500.00**

Anheuser-Busch Inc, poster, paper, woman with outstretched hand & company's eagle perched on finger, frame has hops motif, 37x27", VG, A....................**950.00**

Anheuser-Busch Inc, sign, paper, 1 of 5 frontier images by August A Busch, 'Attack on an Immigrant Train,' 9x17" without frame, VG, A......................................**95.00**

Anheuser-Busch Inc, sign, paper, 1 of 5 frontier images by August A Busch, 'The Father of Water,' 9x17" without frame, VG, A...**110.00**

Anheuser-Busch Inc, sign, tin, Budweiser girl holding glass & bottle of beer, ca 1905-10, self-framed, 38x26", EX, A...**550.00**

Anheuser-Busch Inc, see also Budweiser

Anheuser-Busch Malt Nutrine, tray, ad copy on back, 1910, light rust, 10" diameter, VG, A 75.00

Anita Cigars, box label, outer, depicts woman with scarf, 5x5", EX, D **12.00**

Annie Laurie, crate label, California orange, girl in oval inset on plaid background, Strathmore Packing House, 1930s, 10x12", M, D...**8.00**

Ansel Briggs Cigars, box label, inner lid, portrait of the 1st Governor of Iowa (1846), 1906, 6x9", EX, D.........**35.00**

Ant Bernier Ltee Quebec Motor Oil, tin, American Packard car logo on red background, screw lid & handle, ca 1910-20, rare, 1-gal, 13", VG+, A...............**400.00**

Apache Trail Cigars, tin, shows Indian on horseback, Coast To Coast printed on slip lid, dents & scratches, 6x6x4", G-, A **125.00**

Apollo Cigars, box label, inner lid, depicts bust of Apollo, 6x9", EX, D **12.00**

Arabela Cigars, trolley sign, Arabela Cigars in fan-shaped graphic with lg cigar, 5¢, By Far The Greatest Value, 11x21", EX+, D...**50.00**

Ararat Smoking Tobacco, pack (full), pictures the sun, mountains, & fields, EX, D **20.00**

Arboleda, crate label, California lemon, depicts valley with stream in oval inset, Santa Barbara County Lemons, 1930s, 9x13", M, D...**2.00**

Archer Lubricants, tin, pictures Indian shooting arrow, Archer Petroleum Corp, ca 1950s, 1-qt, 6x4" diameter, EX, A...**55.00**

Arco Coffee, tin, key-wind lid, 1-lb, NM, D **45.00**

Arden Hard Candies, tin, depicts Christmas scene, 5-lb, EX, D..**25.00**

Argus Cigars, box label, outer, depicts Viking with green border, 5x5", EX, D **12.00**

Arm & Hammer, match safe, gutta percha, EX, D **50.00**

Arm & Hammer Baking Soda, booklet, 1933, 'Household Remedies,' 28 pages, VG+, D **8.00**

Arm & Hammer Baking Soda, booklet, 1938, 'Successful Baking For Flavor & Texture,' 7th editon, 38 pages, VG+, D **8.00**

Arm & Hammer Baking Soda, leaflet, 1933, 2-sided, 'A Friend In Need,' blue cover, 28 pages, EX, D **4.00**

Arm & Hammer Baking Soda, lunch box, tin, yellow, double handles, slip lid, EX, A **220.00**

Arm & Hammer Baking Soda, pamphlet, 1936, 'Good Things To Eat – Tested Recipes,' 116th edition, 32 pages, EX, D **10.00**

Arm & Hammer Baking Soda, pamphlet, 1939, 'Good Things To Eat,' 126th edition, 15 pages, VG+, D ...**10.00**

Armour & Co, puzzle, paper over cardboard, people in tent enjoying live animal displays, chipping/soiling, 28x20", VG+, A **175.00**

Armour's Star Ham, floor display, die-cut cardboard litho of Easter bunny holding wrapped ham, Fixed Flavor, 59", appears EX, A................................**130.00**

Arnholdt-Schaefer Co, tip tray, girl holding roses in center, Philadelphia's Largest Brewery Bottlers, rare, 4" diameter, EX, A................................**65.00**

Around The World Motor Oil, tin, product name on red above earth encircled by cars, Atlas Oil Co, screw lid & handle, 1925-45, 2-gal, 12x9", EX, A **100.00**

Arrow Beer, sign, paper, late re-issue of striking nude girl, Matchless Body, wear/overstrips top & bottom, framed, 25x14", VG, A **45.00**

Arrow Beer, sign, paper, striking nude girl, Matchless Body, framed, 25x14", EX, A **250.00**

Arrow Collars, sign, cardboard, pictures handsome young man with head turned to right, appears EX, A.....**270.00**

Arrow Lubricant, tin, blue & white-gray stripes end in chevron band top & bottom, logo in lg oval, ca 1940, 1-qt, 6x4" diameter, EX, A................................**50.00**

Arrow Motor Oil, tin, depicts arrow logo in yellow circle, screw lid & handle, ca 1915-25, 5-gal, 17x14" diameter, VG, A **250.00**

Arrow Shirts, sign, cardboard, depicts windblown couple in rowboat, framed, 29x23", EX, A **75.00**

Arthur Honan, catalog, 1950, dolls & toys, 172 pages, EX, D................................**35.00**

Arthur M Butts Wagons, Harnesses, Automobiles..., tip tray, shows bird dog Champion Tony's Gale in field with lettering, decorative border, fluted corners, 3x5", VG, A................................**15.00**

Artie Cigars, sign, tin, Artie atop bridge parapet looking over city, TJ Dunn & Co Makers, nicks/scratches, framed, 10x14", VG+, A **500.00**

Artie Cigars, sign, tin, playing children flanked by lettering, Geo F Ditmann B&S Co, ca 1890-1900, flaking, wood frame, 9x20", EX, A **350.00**

Artola Cigars, box label, inner lid, depicts woman on blue & orange background, 6x9", EX, D **9.00**

Ashland Flying Octanes, globe, glass cover, white with red, green, yellow, & gold lettering, Ethyl Corporation, 1930s, 16" diameter, VG, A................................**350.00**

Astor Wine Co, shot glass, Astor Wine Co, Mail Order House, San Francisco & Hornbrook Calif in lg letters on 6 lines, EX, D................................**35.00**

Ath-Lo-Pho-Ros Ointment, display, 3-piece die-cut cardboard, street scene, Searles Remedy For Rheumatism, Neuralgia..., 18x29" overall, EX, A **170.00**

Atkins Saws, sign, tin, pictures saw with lettering atop, Use Atkins Silver Steel Saws, ca 1900-05, wood frame, 9x18", EX+, A................................**200.00**

Atlantic, pump sign, porcelain, Atlantic in lg letters between 2 lines top & bottom, 1953-66, flaking/bend, 9x13", VG, A................................**45.00**

Atlantic, pump sign, porcelain, red with blue Atlantic on white band, angle lines above & below, 1966-69, 5x9", M, A................................**30.00**

Atlantic Imperial, sign, gold-plated metal shield, Atlantic in white & blue on red, embossed script Imperial, 1957-66, scuffs, 12x9", A................................**75.00**

Atlantic Kerosene, pump sign, porcelain, D **70.00**

Atlantic Motor Oil, banner, cloth, Aviation motor oil with airplane on cans, Made From Pennsylvania Crude, some wear, rare, 36x60", VG, A **225.00**

Atlantic Motor Oil, tin, embossed ribbing, depicts red airplane on blue arrow, ca 1935-45, minor dents, 1-qt, 4" diameter, VG, A................................**75.00**

Atlantic Refining Co, pump sign, porcelain, navy letters in white circle with arrows, scalloped orange edge, 1910-20, 9" diameter, NM, A................................**350.00**

Atlantic Stove Co, salesman's sample, heater & furnace, marked #24, rare, 7", G, A **300.00**

Atlantic White Flash, gas globe, milk glass with white letters on red & blue, lens & casing joined by metal ring, 1930-40, 17" diameter, M, A **300.00**

Atlantic White Flash, sign, porcelain on metal, Atlantic & lettered circle atop long vertical line, 3 colors, 1940s, holes/flaking, 42x15", A **40.00**

Atlas Beer, master pitcher, depicts eagle over Western hemisphere, EX, D................................**150.00**

Atlas Underwear Co, paperweight mirror, unusual graphics with a man posing in underwear, Richmond Union Suits, 4" diameter, VG+, A **90.00**

Atlas Van Lines, doll, cloth, Atlas Annie, in original bag, 1977, 16", M, D **15.00**

Auborn Wagon Co, sign, paper, amusing scene of husband & wife outpacing racing trotters, overall wear, 20x26", VG, A **275.00**

Auctioneer Cigars, box label, inner lid, depicts giant standing over tobacco, 6x9", M, D **45.00**

Augustiner Bottled Beer, sign, touch-ups, framed, 15x15", G+, A **175.00**

Aultman-Taylor Thresher & Mounted Horse Power, sign, paper, farm scene with vignettes of animals & figures in each corner, Shober litho, matted & framed, 17x37", EX, A **1,350.00**

Aunt Jemima, apron, 1950s, Aunt Jemima Pancake Jamboree lettered in red on yellow canvas-type material, adult size, EX, D **85.00**

Aunt Jemima, cornbread pan, EX, D **165.00**

Aunt Jemima, doll, 1905, cloth, Diana, 15", EX, D....**130.00**

Aunt Jemima, doll, 1940s, oilcloth, Uncle Mose (Aunt Jemima's husband), 13", EX, D **70.00**

Aunt Jemima, mask, ca 1905, rare, EX, D **465.00**

Aunt Jemima, place mat, 1955, Aunt Jemima's face surrounded by The Story Of Aunt Jemima, Yesterday, Today, & Now, 10x14", D **25.00**

Aunt Jemima, puzzle, ca 1906, EX, D **375.00**

Aunt Jemima, recipe book, 1906, rare, EX, D **375.00**

Aunt Jemima, restaurant table card, 1953, depicts Aunt Jemima's face in die-cut relief, ...Time For Aunt Jemima Pancakes, M, D **25.00**

Aunt Jemima Flour, sign, die-cut cardboard litho, colorful image, minor damage, framed, 17x8", EX, A **1,050.00**

Aunt Jemima Pancakes, banner, Aunt Jemima & plate of pancakes, Coming...Aunt Jemima Serving Her Famous Pancakes, Sat Nov 4, 1946, 32x52", M, A..............**425.00**

Aurora Cigars, box label, outer, depicts woman in clouds, 5x5", EX, D..**7.00**

Aurora Coffee, pail, tin, paper label showing the goddess of morning with 4 horses, original lid & bail, 1-lb, 5x5" diameter, G, A **150.00**

Austin's Dog Bread, display, die-cut cardboard with original package, depicts dogs in front of sign, In Use Over Fifty Years, M, A **20.00**

Austin's Dog Bread, sign, tin litho, seated woman feeding biscuits to canines, Don't All Speak At Once, ca 1918, self-framed, 38x26", G, A..................**1,450.00**

Austin's Gun Powder, sign, colorful graphics, Champion Duckling Powder, wear on lettering, original marbleized frame, 11x24", G+, A **1,000.00**

Auto Doctor, vendor, wood case with reverse-painted beveled mirror, 27x12x5", EX, A **10,000.00**

Auto-Lite Spark Plugs, sign, tin with mounting flange, 2-sided, Cleaning Service, Motor Tune Up, 4-color, 1940, 11x11", NM, A......................................**110.00**

Autobacco Tobacco, tin, portrait of driver in circular inset, some fading mostly on back/color distortion/minor scratches, 5x6x4", G, A..............................**35.00**

Autocrat Coffee, tin, paper label shows steaming cup & lettering, Brownell & Field Co, slip lid, paper loss, 1-lb, 5x4" diameter, VG, A..............................**20.00**

Autocrat Whiskey, tray, depicts monk & gentleman playing cards, Edwin Schiele & Co, rim wear, oval, 14x17", A **160.00**

Automotive Electric Association Authorized Service, sign, die-cut tin with 18 add-ons listing brands & services available, 1930-40, add-ons: 11" wide, 72" overall, NM, A......................................**600.00**

Avenue, crate label, California orange, depicts tree-lined street, Victoria Ave Citrus Ass'n, Riverside, 1920, 10x12", M, D **5.00**

Avis, playing cards, white Avis printed vertically on 16 red vertical rectangles, Avis Features GM Cars, complete, NM, D **5.00**

Avon Club Coffee, tin, paper label shows couple on horseback with distant clubhouse, overall wear, 1-lb, 6x4" diameter, G-, A **200.00**

Aw Stevens & Son Threshers, Engines, & French Burr Mills, sign, paper, depicts various scenes of farm machinery, Gies litho, framed, 30x24", NM, D..**1,000.00**

Ayer's Cathartic Pills, sign, tin, cherubs holding up pill on red background, minor wear, rare, 20x14" without frame, G+, A **2,100.00**

Ayer's Cherry Pectoral, sign, tin, woman holding a baby & cherries, For The Cure Of Coughs, Colds, Asthma..., rare, framed, 20x14", G, A..................**1,200.00**

Ayer's Hair Vigor, poster, paper litho, depicts girl with long flowing hair, gold letters on flower petals, walnut frame, 19x16", NM, D.........................**600.00**

Ayer's Hair Vigor, sign, glass, early sepia photo on hand-lettered glass with color-enhanced imaging, image touch-up, approx: 13x11", G-, A.................**170.00**

Ayer's Hair Vigor, sign, tin, long-haired girl, Restores Gray Hair To Its Natural Vitality..., 1880-85, rare, original frame, 26x12", VG, A....................**2,200.00**

Ayer's Pills, sign, paper, pictures 2 Indians with bottle of pills in scroll inset, Ayer's Pills, Universally Popular, framed, 42x30", EX, A...........................**7,500.00**

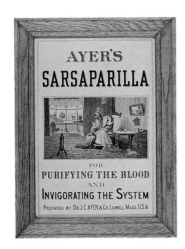

Ayer's Sarsaparilla, sign, tin, Wells & Hope litho, ca 1880, rare, framed, 20x14", NM, A 10,500.00

Azalea, crate label, Florida citrus, bunch of azaleas, WH Clark Fruit Co, Jacksonville Fl, 1940s, diagonal corners, 9x9", M, D.................................**65.00**

Azurea Talc, tin, rare, NM, A...................150.00

❧ B ❧

B Denton Healing Balsam, medicine bottle, 8-sided, aqua, applied mouth, pontil scar, 4", EX, A...................**35.00**

B&L Tobaccos, see Buchanan & Lyall's Tobaccos

B-1 Lemon-Lime Soda, sign, tin, depicts bottle of soda at left with round logo to the right, Plus Vitamin B1, 30x54", A.................................**30.00**

B-1 Lemon-Lime Soda, sign, tin, shaped like a soda bottle, A.**50.00**

Babbitt's Best Soap & Soap Powder, sign, pictures little girl with lilies, 1895, Donaldson Art Sign Co litho, foxing/creases across middle, 28x14", A....................**300.00**

Babbitt's Cleanser, doll, composition & cloth, Babbitt, 1916, 15", EX, D **250.00**

Babbitt's Cleanser, sign, split image, ca 1920, framed, 12x22", EX, A.....................................200.00

Babbitt's Cleanser, sign, product in center, hands working on either side, Use It Every Day, Monday To Saturday, framed, 11x21", EX, A.............................**110.00**

Babbitt's Soap, sign, paper, little girl on tricycle, sign is selling litho of the little girl for 10 soap wrappers, 1892, 28x14", EX, A.....................................**400.00**

Baby Label Brand Honey Bread, tin, depicts baby in highchair, lettering above & below, Matthaei Bread Co, 20x16", EX, A.......................................**75.00**

Baby Ruth Candy Bars, display holder, full-color tin litho, EX, D.................................**125.00**

Baby Ruth Candy Bars, display holder, pictures candy bar on front, 5¢, paint loss on front/overall chipping/general wear, 10x5x6", G-, A........................**25.00**

Baby Ruth Candy Bars, puzzle, 45-piece die-cut cardboard, double-sided, 2 kids under umbrella eating candy while dog watches, 1930s, 6x8", A..............**12.00**

Bachelor Cigars, display case, wood with slanted front & taller back for product display, Canada's National Smoke, 12x10x8", NM, D.......................**280.00**

Bachelor Cigars, poster, paper, 2 racing trotters in hot pursuit, A Whirlwind Quarter, 1903, water stain, framed, 30x24", EX, A.........................**250.00**

Baffin Cigars, box label, inner lid, depicts bust of Artic explorer & ship, 6x9", EX, D.................**15.00**

Bagdad Tobacco, pocket tin, short, EX, D..............**135.00**

Bagdad Tobacco, pocket tin, short, G, D **100.00**

Bagley's Buckingham Bright Cut Plug Smoking Tobacco, pocket tin, logo with floral & decorative border, Trial Package, appears VG, A **90.00**

Bagley's Buckingham Tobacco, sign, die-cut cardboard litho, double-sided, framed, 15x8", VG+, A..........**350.00**

Bagley's Burley Boy Tobacco, lunch box, tin, Burley Boy logo, Pipe or Cigarette, hinged lid & wire handle, horizontal rectangle form, VG+, A **500.00**

Bagley's Burley Boy Tobacco, pocket tin, depicts young boy in boxing stance in circle, Pipe or Cigarette, spotting/chipping, 4x4x1", G-, A...................**265.00**

Bagley's Burley Boy Tobacco, tin, Burley Boy logo, Pipe or Cigarette, rare, EX+, A.....................................**700.00**

Bagley's Old Colony Mixture Tobacco, pocket tin, double-sided, portrait of a woman, Colony Mixture, slip lid, 5x3", EX, A.......................................**70.00**

Baid & Peters Tea, bin, house-shaped tin with glass windows, unique hinged door, chimney intact, some damage, 8x9x6", G+, A **250.00**

Bailey & Farrell Bathroom Fixtures, catalog, 1921, EX, D ..**75.00**

Baker's, see also Walter Baker & Co

Baker's Breakfast Cocoa, tip tray, serving girl logo above 'New England Homestead,' narrow rim, minor chipping/wear, 6" diameter, EX, A................................**150.00**

Baker's Coconut, leaflet, 1956, 'Cut Up Cakes,' D **3.00**

Balcony Cigars, box label, inner lid, depicts 2 men drinking, 6x9", EX, D **16.00**

Bald Eagle Cigars, box label, inner lid, depicts eagle perched on rock, 6x9", M, D **15.00**

Baldwin Dry Air Refrigerator, sign, tin litho, logo flanked by various animals, ca 1885, minor surface discoloration/background rubs, 3x10", VG+, A **425.00**

Ballantine & Sons Ales & Beers, tip tray, lettered logo center on 'barrel-end' background, Newark NJ, 5" diameter, NM, A **35.00**

Ballantine's Brews, sign, tin litho, depicts musketeer seated at table enjoying a brew & smoking a pipe, self-framed, 31", G, A **425.00**

Ballard's Obelisk Flour, match holder, tin, minor fading, rare, EX, A **325.00**

Ballard's Obelisk Flour, pocket mirror, Egyptian scenes, 2", D **25.00**

Baltimore Bargain House, poster, paper, view of early Baltimore Emporium, Strictly Wholesale To Merchants Only, framed, 28x25", EX, A................................**500.00**

Baltimore Telegram, sign, paper, colorful vignettes of people reading newspaper, The Great Southern Weekly, ca 1890, framed, 10x13", VG, A...........**1,600.00**

Bambino Smoking Tobacco, pocket tin, pictures Babe Ruth, EX, A **1,000.00**

Banjo Tobacco, sign, paper, 2 Black ladies dance to Black man's banjo music, David Dumlop, Petersburg Va, USA, framed, 16" long, M, A..**220.00**

Bank Note Cigars, box label, inner lid, pictures brown note resembling currency, 6x9", M, D....................**6.00**

Bank Roll Cigars, tin, shows wad of cash, scroll lettering, slip lid, hairline scratches/chips, VG, A **110.00**

Banner Buggies, match holder, tin litho, pictures encircled portrait of Russell E Gardner, The Standard of the World, 5x3", EX, A..**275.00**

Banquet Hall Bouquet Cigars, sign, cardboard, politicians at table drinking Moet & Chandon Champagne & smoking cigars, 1894, framed, 27x33", G, A..................**225.00**

Bantam Cigars, box label, inner lid, depicts 2 mad cocks ready to fight, 6x9", EX, D **25.00**

Bantam Mints, vendor, slot machine-type, 5¢, original working condition, 21x14", A..................................**775.00**

Bar BQ Coffee, tin, slip lid, 1-lb, EX, D......................**40.00**

Barbour's Peanut Butter, pail, tin, depicts landscape with cows, logo above, slip lid & bail, VG, A................**95.00**

Barbour's Salted Peanuts, tin, red, yellow, & black letters, Goody-Goody Brand, GE Barbour Co, Canada, slip lid, 10-lb, 11x8" diameter, G+, A **150.00**

Barker's Horse & Cattle Powder, poster, paper litho, pictures farm animals with woman & child running from a bull, framed, 20x15", EX, A.....................................**525.00**

Barker's Horse & Cattle Powder, sign, paper, farm animals startled by train, Thos Hunter litho, stains/tears, rare, 22x29" without frame, G-, A **800.00**

Barker's Horse & Cattle Powder, sign, paper over canvas, farm animals startled by train, flaking/paper loss/breaks/wear, rare, framed, 27x33", G-, A **200.00**

Barnsdall Motor Oil, tin, refinery in black, B in square & product name in red on cream background, 1932-35, 1-qt, 6x4" diameter, EX, A..**145.00**

Barrett Cigars, tin, portrait image on wood-grained background, slip lid, 5x6x4", VG+, A...........................**270.00**

Barrington Hall Coffee, tin, Baker-ize above oval picturing Barrington Hall, 1-lb, EX, A..............................**30.00**

Bartel Perfection Work & Play Clothes, sign, cardboard, 4 boys & man in coveralls at work & play, logo lower right, Stands The Wear & Tear, 20x27", EX, A **210.00**

Bartels, tray, deep-dish, Bartels on white background, ca 1935, oval, 13x15", NM, A......................................**15.00**

Bartels Beer, sign, reverse-painted glass, C Shonk litho, 18" diameter, NM, A 500.00

Bartels Beer, sign, tin, gentleman having a beer with dinner, lettered logo atop, ca 1905-10, minor rust, self-framed, 24x20", EX, A **450.00**

Bartels Beer, sign, tin, lettered logo in blue & white, C Shonk litho, rim chips/dents, 18" diameter, EX, A.**85.00**

Bartels Beer, tray, deep-dish, early diamond logo, background/rim wear, 13" diameter, VG, A..................**175.00**

Bartels Beer, Ale & Porter, tray, deep-dish, lettering on white background, ca 1935, minor background touch-up/restoration, oval, 13x15", EX, A **15.00**

Bartels Best Beers, tray, pictures girl in center, lettering on decorative border, Tuscarora Advertising Co, minor rubs/chips, 17x12", VG, A....................................**160.00**

Bartels Brewers & Bottlers, sign, paper, pictures Uncle Sam looking out window at brewery, logo, ca 1906, matted & framed, 20x15", EX, A **1,500.00**

Bartels Brewing Co, calendar, 1913, paper, pictures young girl in profile, full pad, water stains/creasing, matted & framed, 25x16", VG, A **525.00**

Bartels Brewing Co, charger, pictures bowl of flowers in center, lettered logo on reverse, sm image scratches, 18" diameter, EX, A **35.00**

Bartels Brewing Co, charger, pictures floral bouquet laying on ledge, lettered logo on reverse, 18" diameter, NM, A **20.00**

Bartels Brewing Co, charger, pictures young girl in turbaned scarf, lettered logo on reverse, overall wear, 18" diameter, VG, A **50.00**

Bartels Brewing Co, charger, young girl wearing a bonnet, lettered logo on reverse, 18" diameter, EX, A **75.00**

Bartels Brewing Co, sign, paper, colorful factory scene, overall water staining, framed, 40x28", VG, A ...**1,100.00**

Bartels Brewing Co, sign, paper, factory scene within an oval, framed, 11x14", VG, A **75.00**

Bartels Brewing Co, tray, deep-dish, crown logo above Bartels in lg letters, lettering below, decorative rim, 12" diameter, NM, A **150.00**

Bartels Brewing Co, tray, deep-dish, soldier toasting with mug of beer, overall wear, 12" diameter, G, A.......**30.00**

Bartels Brewing Co, tray, Fibrotta fiberboard, embossed crown logo on red background, ca 1890, 12" diameter, EX, A **20.00**

Bartels Brewing Co, tray, nickel-plated, Bartels 25th Anniversary, ca 1890, 15" diameter, EX, A............**115.00**

Bartels Crown Beer, tray, pictures knight holding a stein, Nachtwachter, Bartels Brewing Co, background scratch, 12" diameter, NM, A..**150.00**

Bartels Crown Beer, Old Devonshire, tray, white lettering on wood-grain background, ca 1930, 13" diameter, NM, A **15.00**

Bartels Lager, Ale & Porter, tip tray, pictures knight holding a stein, Bartels Brewing Co, Syracuse NY, 4" diameter, NM, A...**85.00**

Bartels Old Devonshire, Crown & Root Beer, tray, pictures young girl surrounded by flowers with lettering below, edge chips, 12" diameter, NM, A **145.00**

Bartels Pure Beers, tip tray, lettered logo, commemorating Wilkes-Barre Centennial Jubilee & Old Home Week, May 1906, 4" diameter, EX, A **55.00**

Bartholomay Brewing Co, match safe, silverplated, 3", VG, D **110.00**

Bartholomay Brewing Co, sign, paper, girl on winged wheel in the clouds, printed by Hyneman & Schmidt, wear, matted & framed, 35x24", G, A **400.00**

Bartholomay Brewing Co, sign, tin, self-framed, 20x16", EX, A..1,400.00

Bartholomay's Beers, Ales & Porter, tip tray, deep-dish, girl on winged wheel in the clouds, Beers, Ales, & Porter In Kegs & Bottles, 4" diameter, M, A **100.00**

Bartholomay's Beers, Ales & Porter, tip tray, deep-dish, girl on winged wheel in the clouds, In Kegs & Bottles, rim chips, 4" diameter, G+, A **30.00**

Bartholomay's Beers, Ales & Porter, tray, girl on winged wheel in clouds, lettered rim, minor background circling/rim chips, 12" diameter, EX, A **85.00**

Bartholomay's Rienzi Beer, tip tray, pictures cavalier riding a horse, Rienzi Beer In Bottles, background scratch, 4" diameter, NM, A...**150.00**

Bartholomay's Rochester, sign, Victorian lady tasting Bohemian Beer, Troutmann, Bailey & Blampey litho, tear at base/right side, 31x21", EX, A....................**500.00**

Bartholomay's Tam O' Shanter Ale, tip tray, pictures a Scotsman holding a glass of beer, image scuffs/rim chips, 4" diameter, EX, A **75.00**

Barton & Guestier Olive Oil, sign, tin litho, ad copy & logos flanked by bottles of olive oil, self-framed, horizontal rectangle, appears EX, A **100.00**

Basket, crate label, California lemon, basket of lemons, Lemon Cove Association, 1930s, 9x13", M, D **2.00**

Bat Chewing Tobacco, tin, depicts Philly baseball logo on plug, black, red, & yellow, minor creases on lid, 7x7x3", D **35.00**

Batavia Peanut Butter, tin, no lid, 6", D.....................**30.00**

Battle Ax Tobacco, sign, hanging cardboard litho, framed, on the bias: 12x12", G, A **250.00**

Battle Royal Cut Plug Tobacco, pocket tin, sailing ship in circular inset with anchor motif in blue & white, flat, appears EX, A **80.00**

Battleship Coffee, tin, pictures battleship, ca 1920, 3-lb, G+, A **50.00**

Battleship Coffee, tin, ship on 1 side, 'Loaf Sugar' on other, for use as canister, 9" diameter, NM, D........**28.00**

Bauer & Black Baby Talc, tin, depicts circus animals on parade, EX+, A...**90.00**

Bay State Fertilizer, trade card, potato man facing right, NM, D **8.00**

Bayle Peanut Butter, pail, depicts Boy Scouts & Girl Scouts on this unusual container, press lid & bail, overall wear, 4x4", VG, A...**400.00**

Bayonne Motors, key chain, with tube to hold license, ca 1940s, EX, D **16.00**

Bayuk Cigars, tin, embossed, 6x5", VG, D **25.00**

Bazooka Bubble Gum, doll, stuffed cotton, Bazooka Joe, 1973, EX, D **15.00**

Beacon Oils, sign, die-cut porcelain shield with logo in center, green, cream, & red, 1930-40, minor fading, 10x9", VG, A..**215.00**

Bear Creek, crate label, pear, depicts face of lg brown bear with logo above, Bear Creek Orchards, Medford Oregon, 1930, 8x11", M, D...**50.00**

Beard Cinnamon, keg, wood, camel scene & lettering on paper label, label creased/minor paper loss/tears, 10-lb, 11x9" diameter, G-, A.......................................**200.00**

Beardsley Mfg Co, ledger marker, has a ruler in light green on reverse, rare, EX, A.......................................**425.00**

Beaver Line of Steamships, sign, paper litho, steamship at full sail, Liverpool, Canada, & United States, framed, 31x24", A...**600.00**

Beaver Peanut Butter, pail, tin, beaver logo, side gradually narrows toward top, press lid & bail, overall wear, unusual, 4x4", G, A...**500.00**

Beaver Peanut Butter, pail, tin, beaver surmounting billboard surrounded by maple leaves, press lid & bail, some wear, 4x4", VG, A.................................**375.00**

Beck's Bottled Beer, tip tray, pictures patriotic eagle on shield with barrel, Buffalo's Best, Mangus Beck Brewing Co, NY, 4" diameter, NM, A.............................**65.00**

Beech-Nut Candy, display, tin, 3-tiered, Fruit Drops, Candy Drops, Mints, missing marquee, overall wear, 12x10x15", G-, A...**95.00**

Beech-Nut Chewing Gum, display & stand, some wear, 15x10x10", VG, A..325.00

Beech-Nut Chewing Gum, display box, cardboard, logoed sides & top, 6" long, G, A **40.00**

Beech-Nut Chewing Gum, display rack, tin, little girl holding stick of gum, Peppermint Flavored Chewing Gum 5¢, rare, 14" with lid open, EX, A **700.00**

Beech-Nut Chewing Tobacco, sign, die-cut cardboard litho, framed trapezoid, 26x18", VG+, A **250.00**

Beech-Nut Chewing Tobacco, sign, die-cut tin, figural package in bright reds & blues, Lorillard's, Extra Picked, ca 1910-20, 15x11", M, A **110.00**

Beech-Nut Chewing Tobacco, sign, die-cut tin litho, package of product, scratches/rust/holes, 18", A............**30.00**

Beech-Nut Chewing Tobacco, store bin, slant front pictures yellow, red, & blue package, Quality Made It Famous, hinged lid, 9x10x8", G+, A **225.00**

Beech-Nut Cigars, tin, pictures a beechnut, slip lid, scratches/chips/edge wear, 6x5" square, G, A.......**90.00**

Beech-Nut Cough Drops, display, vertical tin dispenser for 5¢ packages of cough drops, minor chipping/wear, 11x3x5", EX, A **65.00**

Beech-Nut Mints, display box, tin, slant front with sides showing 5¢ Beech-Nut Mints, scratches/edge wear/soiling, 8x10x9", EX, A **110.00**

Beech-Nut Mints, sign, paper, girl serving mints to 2 men in study, logoed top & bottom, oval logo inset, restored, framed, 28x18", F, A **100.00**

Beech-Nut Packing Co, card game, Going To Market, 52 cards with various logos plus 1 instruction card, 1915, 3x4", D **115.00**

Beeman's Pepsin Gum, sign, tin, portrait of man against green background, Chew Beeman's Pepsin Gum, Good For Digestion, 9" diameter, G, A **110.00**

Beeswing Tobacco, tin, pictures bee on lid, overall scratches, 5x3x1", D **30.00**

Behr Stains & Varnishes, sign, tin, orange, black, & white, CP Signs Co litho, rusting on corner edges/few scratches, 18x24", A........................25.00

Beiser & Fisher, spirit bottle, pig figural, amber, foot crack/haze, 10", A **200.00**

Bell Roasted Coffee, pocket mirror, bell form, edge stains, 2" diameter, D..**20.00**

Bell Telephone Co, hanging shade, milk glass, Bell System rope image, American Telephone & Telegraph Co, globe: 12", fitter ring: 4", EX, A **450.00**

Bella De Cuba Cigars, box label, inner lid, depicts woman playing guitar, 6x9", M, D **22.00**

Belle of Saginaw Whiskey, shot glass, Dittmar, Cooper & Co, Saginaw Mich, scarce, VG, D...........................**17.00**

Belle Rose Cigars, box label, outer, depicts woman with autumn leaves in background, 5x5", EX, D.............**9.00**

Bellmore Whiskey, tray, depicts man in spectacles, C Shonk litho, 12" diameter, G-, A...........................**45.00**

Belmont Tobacco, pocket tin, cube-cut with crossed pipes over shield, Montreal Canada, overall wear, 4x3x1", G, A..**300.00**

Belvadere Cigars, box label, outer, depicts couples dining, 5x5", G, D **3.00**

Bemis Brothers Bag Co, calendar, 1908, cloth with top metal strip, shows first 12 Presidents of the US, red, white, & blue, 14x10", VG, A.................**90.00**

Ben Hur Cigars, box label, outer, pictures Ben Hur in chariot pulled by 4 white horses, 3x5", M, D..........**2.00**

Ben Hur Cigars, sign, paper on cardboard, Gustav A Moebs & Co, 22x32", VG, A.................400.00

Ben Hur Cigars, sign, quartered oak veneer board, Ben-Hur 5¢ Cigar over 3 wise men conversing, Wise Men Make..., 1904, 21x15", G+, A.................**150.00**

Ben Hur Horse Blankets, sign, tin, horse looks into store window at horse products & mannequin, edge wear/scratches, self-framed, 17x20", EX, A.........**875.00**

Ben Hur Tea, tin, double-sided, chariot scene on front, shows medals on back, Ceylon Tea, press lid, 7x7", G, A.................**125.00**

Ben West Cigars, box label, inner lid, depicts portrait of Ben West, 6x9", M, D.................**35.00**

Benedict English Peas, display, tin, figural can of product picturing a bowl of peas, Better Quality, ca 1915-25, 14x9" diameter, EX, A.................**100.00**

Bengel Ranges, clock, neon, depicts yellow & black tiger on a red & white background, octagon shape, appears EX, A.................**125.00**

Benjamin Moore & Co Paints & Varnishes, sign, lighted, elongated, appears EX, A.................**70.00**

Bennett Coffee, tin, early, round, appears EX, A......**140.00**

Berina Malted Milk Food, sign, porcelain, depicts Scotsman looking over valley & lg box of product, For Energy & Strength, 24x60", D.................**400.00**

Bering Cigars, tin, paper label picturing Admiral Bering, VG, D.................**60.00**

Berlin Iron Bridge Co, calendar, 1897, cardboard, multiple images of bridges & factory, by Kellogg & Bulkeley Co, 14x11", VG, A.................**80.00**

Berlin Machine Works, sign, tin litho, depicts factory at night, Beloit Wisconsin USA, background scratches, 24x39" without frame, EX+, A.................**900.00**

Berma Coffee, tin, cream & black on red, product name above plantation & mountains beyond, Grand Union Co, NY, screw lid, 1-lb, EX, A.................**38.00**

Bernard Fischer Whiskey, tray, elderly gentleman imbibing glass of whiskey, Bellmore Whiskey, C Shonk litho, ca 1910-20, 12" diameter, EX, A.................**200.00**

Best Strike, crate label, apple, depicts baseball pitcher at left of logo, Pajaro Valley Apples, Watsonville Cal, 1920, 9x11", M, D.................**45.00**

Besty Ross Cigars, box label, inner lid, depicts Betsy Ross in an oval flanked by her home & the Liberty Bell, 6x9", M, D.................**4.00**

Betteryet Salted Peanuts, tin, orange & blue with 2 boys facing each other holding giant peanuts, press lid, 5-lb, EX+, A.................**375.00**

Betty Crocker, book, 1959, hard-bound, 'Betty Crocker's Guide To Easy Entertaining,' 1st ed, 178 pages, D ..**15.00**

Betty Crocker, booklet, 1948, 'Betty Crocker Chiffon Cake Recipes & Secrets,' 19 pages, VG, D.................**6.00**

Betty Crocker, booklet, 1969, 'Let's Eat Outdoors, Recipes & Ideas,' 27 pages, VG, D.................**3.00**

Betty Crocker, cookbook, 1958, hard-bound, 'Dinner For Two,' 1st ed, 207 pages, D.................**8.00**

Betty Crocker, cookbook, 1965, 'Dinner In A Dish,' 152 pages, D.................**7.00**

Betty Crocker, leaflet, 1959, 'Frankly Fancy Foods,' 26 pages, D.................**5.00**

Between The Acts Little Cigars, trolley sign, cardboard, man in top hat lighting cigar with woman gazing at him, 11x20" without frame, G, A.................**45.00**

Beverwyck Beer & Ales, display, die-cut cardboard, features man pouring a glass of beer & round logo, separation to cardboard, 32", A.................**5.00**

Beverwyck Beer & Ales, tray, deep-dish, depicts Billy Beaver as marching drummer, Join The Beverwyck Parade, 14" diameter, A.................**15.00**

Beverwyck Famous Lager, tip tray, pictures factory scene with horse-drawn wagons, minor rim dents/chips, rare, 4" diameter, EX, A.................**185.00**

Bewley's, cookbook, 'Bewley's Best Bakes Better,' 8x6", EX, D.................**10.00**

BF Goodrich, playing cards, blue-gray BF Goodrich printed on white logo, white Industrial Products on blue-gray, complete, NM, D.................**5.00**

Bickmore Gall Salve, tin, hand-painted image of an old work horse, D.................**9.00**

Bicycle Playing Cards, display, oversized box & 2 boxes of playing cards, Bicycle logo, When You Play With...You Hold Good Cards, 12", EX, A.................**45.00**

Biere Fontenac White Cap Ale, sign, captain & sailor standing by porthole enjoying White Cap Ale, logo at left, framed, 17x34", appears EX, A.................**280.00**

Bieren Roman, sign, embossed tin, brewery atop lettering, German, 1935, minor paint loss, 14x20", G, A......**30.00**

Big Bear Cigars, box label, inner lid, depicts black bear, 6x9", VG, D.................**35.00**

Big Ben Cigars, box label, outer, depicts white rooster in circular inset, 5x5", M, D.................**20.00**

Big Ben Clocks, sign, embossed tin litho, pictures alarm clock, National Alarm, minor fading/soiling/scratches, self-framed, 13x19", A.................**200.00**

Big Ben Smoking Tobacco, sign, paper, tobacco tin at left of stallion & rider, Union Made, Save B&W Coupons, 14x20, appears EX, A.................**120.00**

Big Chief Seltzer, siphon bottle, glass with tube, nozzle, & valve, trademark label w/Indian, marked top, EX, D **215.00**

Big Elm Dairy Co, milk bottle, green, 1-pt, EX, D ...**175.00**

Big Game, crate label, pear, ball player at left of stadium in lg football, Bartlett Pears, Walnut Grove Cal, 1930, 8x11", M, D **10.00**

Big John Tobacco, carton label, pack of product at right of Big John Tobacco, The Mild Cut Plug Tobacco, horizontal, appears EX, A **50.00**

Big Sister Peanut Butter, pail, shows witch on broom & children riding peanut, slip lid & bail, some damage, 4x4" with bail, G, A **375.00**

Big Wolf Cigars, box label, inner lid, pictures angry wolf showing his teeth, 6x9", M, D **4.00**

Big Wolf Cigars, box label, outer, pictures angry wolf showing his teeth, 5x5", M, D **2.00**

Bigger Hair Tobacco, canister, cardboard, paper label of Black woman with nose ring & earrings, slip lid, 7x5" diameter, EX, A **115.00**

Billings-Chapin Paints, match holder, tin, dripping paint brush lying on top of paint can, wear to match striker/rust/chips, 5x4", G, A **65.00**

Billings-Chapin Paints, match holder, tin litho, colorful image of paint can, 5x4", EX+, A **275.00**

Binghamton OK Ice Cream, sign, embossed tin, OK Binghamton..., 'Its Right,' framed, 36x24", VG, A **175.00**

Binghamton OK Ice Cream, tip tray, shows young girl eating dish of ice cream, company name & product on rim, oval, 16x13", EX, A **800.00**

Birchola, dispenser, ceramic potbelly, original pump, rare, 15x9" diameter, EX, A **900.00**

Bison Motor Oil, tin, black with black bison on yellow oval, Motor Oil on yellow banner, ca 1925-45, 2-gal, 12x9", G+, A **90.00**

Bisonoil, tin, shows a red & black bison, 100% Pure Pennsylvania Motor Oil, ca 1935-45, back scratches, 1-qt, 4" diameter, NM, A **85.00**

Black & Decker Mfg Co, sign, tin, Electric B&D Tools in center, hexagonal, appears EX, A **85.00**

Black & White Scotch Whiskey, sign, cardboard, cute image of 2 Scotty dogs playing tug-of-war, original mat & frame, 21x24", G+, A **85.00**

Black Cat Cigarettes, tin, black cat on lid, 4x3x2", D.**45.00**

Black Cat Polish, match holder, tin, Shoes & Stoves, Bright Black, Lasting Luster, Nonsuch Mfg Co, Toronto Canada, rare, 6x4", G, A **150.00**

Black Eagle Beer, sign, tin over cardboard, man with glass of beer, elements of image in color float on black background, 19x13", G+, A **375.00**

Black Fox Cigars, tin, seated fox on red background, London & Canada, some wear to slip lid, 5x5" diameter, G, A **250.00**

Black Label Beer, tumbler, glass, black & white label on red, 6", D **14.00**

Black Label Whiskey, sign, tin over cardboard, men conversing, elements of image in color float on black background, scratches, 19x13", G+, A **250.00**

Black Oak Tobacco, poster, depicts drummer with marching infantry behind, Virginia USA, framed, vertical rectangle, M, A **25.00**

Blackhawks Blood & Body Tonic, tin, paper label, 5x2", EX, D **28.00**

Blacklegoids Antraxoides, sign, paper litho, 2 cowboys injecting medicine into bucking horse, Park Davis Co, ca 1905, 28x20", G, A **250.00**

Blanke's Coffee, store bin, tin, horsewoman on front flanked by Always Uniform, Always The Best, hinged lid with ball knob, 24", G-, A **160.00**

Blanke's Exposition Brand Coffee, store bin, tin, 'MOJAV' stenciled on hinged lid, logoed sides with decorative borders, CF Blankes Tea & Coffee Co, EX, A **450.00**

Blatz Beer, counter display, white metal figural, depicts can, bottle, & keg playing baseball, 16", G, A......**120.00**

Blatz Beer, display, metal figural, man with logoed barrel body holding mug of beer, Blatz On Draft on base, 16", appears EX, A **80.00**

Blatz Beer, sign, oilette, by R Bohanek, overall crazing, 20x28", G, A **350.00**

Blatz Beer, sign, red & blue neon, no transformer, A .**90.00**
Bliss Coffee, tin, key-wind lid, 1-lb, EX+, D **30.00**

Bliss Native Herbs, match holder, tin, minor rust, rare, VG+, A **200.00**
Blue Beacon Coal, sign, embossed tin, pictures a lighthouse & bold letters, Your Guide To Fuel Economy, Donaldson Art Co litho, 14x20", A **450.00**
Blue Bird Cigars, box label, outer, depicts bluebird perched on a tree stump, 5x5", VG, D **8.00**
Blue Bird Handkerchiefs, display box, metal with slant glass front showing 4 different boxes, bends/scratches, 7x11", EX, A...**95.00**

Blue Bird Ice Cream, sign, 2-sided porcelain with cord hanger, ca 1915, 28x20", EX, A **2,800.00**
Blue Boar English Blend Cigarettes, package, sealed, M, D..**26.00**
Blue Boar Rough Cut Tobacco, sign, die-cut tin litho stand-up, depicts Blue Boar tin with hunter & dogs after wild boar, 14", G+, A....................................**230.00**
Blue Bonnet Margarine, doll, cloth with yarn hair, Miss Blue Bonnet, original bag, 1980s, 10", EX, D **12.00**
Blue Coat Cigars, box label, inner lid, depicts Civil War soldier with rifle, 1913, 6x9", EX, D **38.00**
Blue Goose Cigars, box label, inner lid, depicts goose flying over trees, 6x9", M, D **45.00**

Blue Jay Cigars, tin, shows blue jay on ground, slip lid, some paint loss/dents/scratches, 6x6x4", G-, A **85.00**
Blue Ribbon Baking Powder, sign, tin, yellow, red, & blue on white, shows product, Double Action on blue band below, round corners, 20x27", VG, A............**35.00**
Blue Ribbon Bourbon, sign, oilette, hillbillies hard at work distilling bourbon, minor color loss/tear in middle, 28x38", G, A **70.00**
Blue Ribbon Cigars, display, folding cardboard, green & white with Blue Ribbon logo, appears EX, A........**35.00**
Blue Ribbon Coffee, store bin, logoed canister with hinged lid & ball knob, A......................................**65.00**
Blue Ribbon Fountain Specialties, flyer, 4 pages of soda fountain supplies, 12x9", VG, A **35.00**
Blue Ribbon Malt Extract, doll, uncut cloth, Lena, 1930, 14", EX, D **175.00**
Blue Ribbon Tea, tin, red, green, yellow, & black with ribbon on front & back, Winnipeg, Edmonton, Calgary..., scratches/rust, 3-lb, D **65.00**

Blue Sunoco, pump sign, die-cut porcelain, letters on yellow diamond, red arrow over elongated blue diamond, 1957-74, 22x19", VG, A.......................**75.00**
Blue Sunoco 200 X, pump sign, die-cut porcelain, blue diamond & red arrow on elongated yellow diamond, ca 1957-61, scuffs, 21x15", A **120.00**
Blue Tiger Chewing Tobacco, store container, cardboard, picturing a tiger, 5 Cent Packages, creasing/minor chipping, 11x8x6", VG, A **225.00**
Blue Tiger Chewing Tobacco, store container, tin, picturing a tiger, 5 Cent Packages, slip lid, 12x8" diameter, G-, A...**110.00**
Blue Wing Whiskey, tray, pictures dead game, CH Wittenberg Co, St Louis Mo, multiple scratches in center, oval, 17x14", G, A **155.00**
Blue-Jay Corn Plasters, display, die-cut tin box, pictures woman applying plaster to foot, some damage, 13x10x5", G, A **105.00**
Bluette Cigars, box label, outer, depicts young woman, 5x5", VG, D...**9.00**
Blush Pink Cigars, box label, outer, depicts woman in pink dress, 5x5", EX, D..**16.00**

Board of Trade Cigars, box label, inner lid, depicts building & street scene on left with Board Of Trade on right, 6x9", M, D..**90.00**

Bob White Mixture Tobacco, tin, depicts bird, horizontal rectangle form, worn, rare, A **140.00**

Bob'Link Cigars, mirror, counter top, Smoke Bob'Link Cigar etched on mirror, ebony Eastlake frame marked Fitzpatrick & Draper..., EX, A **200.00**

Bohemian Export Bottled Beer, see Union Brewing Co

Bokar Coffee, bank, tin, EX, D **12.00**

Bokar Coffee, tin, screw top, vertical, VG+, D **45.00**

Bon Ami Powder, thimble, porcelain, Bon Ami... on diagonal blue band, chick hatches from egg, Hasn't Scratched Yet, gold bands, EX, D **15.00**

Bond Street Tobacco, canister, cardboard, 1940s, appears EX, D..**25.00**

Bond Street Tobacco, pocket tin, NM, D **20.00**

Bonded Motor Oil, tin, product name over oil well, scenes of summer & winter with cars & houses at bottom, 1925-45, 2-gal, 12x9", VG, A.............................**80.00**

Bone, Eagle & Co Cough Drops, tin, picturing trademark for Black variety, slip lid, overall fading/scratches/chips, 8x5" square, G, A **90.00**

Bone, Eagle & Co Cough Drops, tin, picturing trademark for Menthol variety, slip lid, slight color fading/chips/scratches, 8x5" square, G+, A **80.00**

Bone, Eagle & Co Cough Drops, tin, picturing trademark for Menthol variety, slip lid, some denting, overall scratches, 8x5" square, G-, A **65.00**

Bone, Eagle & Co Cough Drops, tin, picturing trademark for Red variety, slip lid, minor scratching/chipping, 8x5" square, VG, A...**110.00**

Bonita Coffee, tin, paper label picturing logo woman, Coffee & Chicory Compound, ca 1906, slip lid, denting/wear, 1-lb, 6x4", G, A.................................**55.00**

Bonnie-B Hair Nets, display case, 6-sided, wood base, mirrored front with Pricilla Dean on panels, ca 1921, general wear, 14x14x11", G, A..............**170.00**

Bonpland's Fever & Ague Remedy, medicine bottle, aqua, applied mouth, pontil scar, 5", EX, A **30.00**

Boone Cola, sign, cardboard, Daniel Boone on bottle, 15x5", EX, D..**35.00**

Boone Spring Distillery, shot glass lettered with company name & address, traces of gold on rim/some worn letters, VG, D **29.00**

Boot & Shoe Worker Union, pocket mirror, EX, D...**30.00**

Booty, crate label, Florida citrus, pirate & chest of oranges on beach, WH Clark Fruit Co, 1930s, diagonal corners, 9x9", M, D **24.00**

Borax, sign, tin litho, Borax Is King, 30", G, A.............**5.00**

Borden, belt buckle, solid brass, Elsie, 2x3", M, D **40.00**

Borden, booklet, 1920(?), 'Borden's Eagle Brand Book Of Recipes,' 32 pages, VG+, D **15.00**

Borden, booklet, 1952, 21 'Non-Such Mince Meat Recipes for Winter, Summer, & Fall,' 31 pages, VG, D **6.00**

Borden, booklet, 1978, 'Bouillon Is Basic,' Wyler's Bouillon, 32 pages, VG, D.......................................**3.00**

Borden, doll, plush with vinyl head, Elsie The Cow, 12", G, D..**28.00**

Borden, foldout, 1947, 'Easy New Ways To Make Every Meal More Nourishing...,' 8 pages, VG, A..............**4.00**

Borden's Condensed Milk, sign, cardboard litho, little girl in witch hat surrounded by kittens & spilled saucer of milk, ca 1893, 15x11", G, A **450.00**

Borden's Ice Cream, sign, Enjoy Borden's Ice Cream in gold letters on simulated wood ground, It's Real Food on red ground, 13x22", EX, D **135.00**

Borden's Malted Milk, store container, glass jar, diamond-shaped paper label insert on front, embossed lettering on metal lid, appears EX, A.................................**350.00**

Borden's Milk, trade card, girl drinking glass of milk with pug dog in lower right, NM, D.................................**8.00**

Borden's Process Cheese Food, box, wood, red & green logo & lettering, 1950s, 4x12x4", EX+, D **18.00**

Born Steel Range, match holder, tin, pictures a woman cooking, HD Beach litho, 5x4", G, A **275.00**

Boschee's German Syrup, sign, tin, depicts sailing ship on rough coastal sea, product names printed on cliff, framed, 20" long, VG, A.................................**2,000.00**

Boschees German Syrup, sign, tin, Wells & Hope litho, minor in-painting on some of the gold lettering, 27x18", VG+, A..**1,900.00**

Boston Belting Co, paperweight, glass, 3", G, D.......**10.00**

Boston Belting Co, sign, paper, factory & multiple vignettes of rubber gathering, Vulcanized..., original mat, framed, 25x21", VG, A...................................**250.00**

Boston Belting Co, sign, paper, factory & multiple vignettes of rubber gathering, Vulcanized Rubber Goods, 19x14" without frame, G, A **150.00**

Boston Confectionary Co, pail, tin, 'Three Little Pigs' pictorial, slip lid & bail, rare, bucket shape, EX, A ...**190.00**

Boston Garter, display cabinet, tin, man demonstrating & holding product, overall wear, 13x15x3", G, A **155.00**

Boston Herald Newspaper, pocket mirror, pictures colorful image of newsboy selling newspapers, 2" diameter, NM, A **50.00**

Boston Herald Newspaper, tip tray, running newsboy hawking newspaper, HD Beach litho, ca 1905, overall soiling/edge chips, 4" diameter, G, A **50.00**

Boston Herald Newspaper, tip tray, running newsboy hawking newspaper, HD Beach litho, ca 1905, 4" diameter, NM, A...**80.00**

Boston Motorist, booklet, 1933, 15 pages, EX, D.......**13.00**

Bostonia Cigars, box label, inner lid, depicts Boston skyline & ships, 1896, 6x9", EX, D **35.00**

Bouer & Black Elastic Stockings, display, papier-mache leg on pedestal with stocking, 31", A **100.00**

Bouquet Cigars, box label, inner lid, depicts woman toasting with glass & holding bouquet, 6x9", M, D.......**32.00**

Bouquet Cigars, sign, tin, depicts pretty girl in flowered hat, 10¢, MH Higgens Maker, Scranton, self-framed, oval, 19x13", NM, A...**475.00**

Bour Quality Coffee, store bin, tin, dark green with gold lettering, slanted lid, ca 1910, VG, A **110.00**

Bower & Bartlett's Favorite Boston Coffees, store bin, tin, Blue Ribbon logo, hinged lid is broken off from top/scratches, 18x19x15", G, A 195.00

Bower & Bartlett's Red Shield Brand Coffee, store bin, ca 1930s, 17x20x13", M, A **600.00**

Bowes Peanut Butter, pail, tin, lettered image, Bowes Co Ltd, Toronto Canada, original slip lid & bail, minor chipping, 1-lb, 4x4", EX, A **500.00**

Bowes Seal Fast Special Spark Plug Service, sign, die-cut tin, spark plug on left, Expert Spark Plug Service, Seal Fast, 1940, scuffs/scratches, 20x26", VG, A...........**220.00**

Bowl of Roses Tobacco, tin, colorful image of a gentleman in a leisure chair smoking pipe in front of a fireplace, 4x3" diameter, EX, A **175.00**

Boyce Motometer, sign, embossed tin figural, bends/surface darkening, 19", G, A **650.00**

Boydell Bros Paints, match holder, tin, VG+, A.......**350.00**

Boye Needle Co, display, Needles, Shuttles, Bobbins For Your Machine, disk shape, 15" diameter, EX, A...**100.00**

Boye Needle Co, sign, tin litho, colorful image with lettering flanked by mother & children, The Boye Hand Sewing Needle..., 5x18", A................................**300.00**

BP Gas, pump sign, porcelain, D **45.00**

Brach's Candy, doll, cloth, Bracho Clown, 17", G, D ...**8.00**

Brading Brewing Co Ltd, sign, paper, elk trademark with bottles & glasses of beer, Ottowa Canada, ltd ed, wrinkled/stained, framed, 40x30", A **950.00**

Bradley Fertilizer, poster, paper litho, pictures the factory in North Weymouth Mass, water marks on bottom border, framed, 28x42", VG, A...................................**475.00**

Brainerd & Armstrong Co Crown Braid, cabinet, oak, 2 drawers with porcelain knobs, drawers painted with carved-out letters, 22x14x13", NM, A...................**400.00**

Braniff International, playing cards, white line down center on orange with Braniff... printed vertically on either side, complete, NM, D **8.00**

Brave Joan Cigars, box label, outer, depicts Joan of Arc in armor, 5x5", VG, D **14.00**

Breakfast Call Coffee, tin, screw top, vertical, EX, D **50.00**

Bregner & Engel Brewing Co, sign, paper, couple at seaside table with bottles of Tannhaeuser Beer, some wear, matted & framed, 31x25", EX, A **600.00**

Breidt City Brewery, tray, American Maid removing bottles of beer from cooler, lettering on decorative rim, image touch-up, 11x13", G, A **85.00**

Brents Pills, sign, metal, wording changes depending on position from which it is viewed, rare, 4x19", appears EX, A **950.00**

Bri-Nee's Fresh Roasted Peanuts, tin, man rowing peanut-shaped boat, Teasingly Salty, 10-lb, VG+, D **75.00**

Briar Pipe Tobacco, sign, tin, pictures gentleman smoking a pipe, Spaulding & Merrick, Chicago, spotting/chipping/soiling, 14x10", G, A **95.00**

Bridal Brand Coffee, tin, grower with donkeys laden with coffee, embossed rim (may not be original), unusual, scratches, oval, 6x4x5", VG, A **275.00**

Brigg's Smoking Tobacco, container, wood, barrel-shaped, 7", G, A **10.00**

Brigg's Smoking Tobacco, pocket tin, EX, D.............**25.00**

Brillo Pads, sign, die-cut cardboard, depicts box of Brillo pads atop front view of skillet being hand-scrubbed, 17x15", EX, A...**100.00**

Broadway Brewing Co, bottle, depicts embossed buffalo, EX, D **20.00**

Broadway Perfectos Cigars, box label, inner lid, depicts knight on horseback above clouds, 6x9", EX, D ...**45.00**

Brockway Motor Trucks, sign, tin, photo of 1920s truck on embossed panel surrounded by blue embossed letters, white background, 20x28", VG, A.................**750.00**

Bromo Seltzer, dispenser, bottle supported by chrome holder on cobalt blue glass base dispenses into glass marked Bromo Seltzer, A **200.00**

Bromo Seltzer, dispenser, glass, plastic, & metal, cobalt blue bottle on dispensing apparatus, ca 1920, 15x6" diameter, NM, A **100.00**

Brook Farms, milk bottle, embossed baby's face, 1-qt, M, D...**70.00**

Brooklyn Rye, sign, pictures woman in sheer negligee holding product, Made Famous By Public Favor, 32x23", NM, A **2,500.00**

Brooks & Co Varnishes, calendar, 1881, paper, Black people in 12 comical scenes prepared on 1 mat, each sheet: 7x5", 25x26" overall, EX+, A **350.00**

Brooks Glace & Soft Cotton, cabinet, wood with glass inserts, 2-drawer, ca 1900-10, 7x21", EX, A **275.00**

Brooks Spool Cotton, cabinet, wood, 4-drawer, labels on sides, 22x14x13", NM, A **300.00**

Brotherhood Overalls, pocket mirror, bare-breasted woman in overalls, The Best Thing In Overalls, Dover NJ, round, appears EX, A..**75.00**

Brotherhood Tobacco, sign, paper on cardboard, rare, original frame, 43x33", EX+, A....................4,500.00

Brown & Sharpe Tools, catalog, 1920, 609 pages, 4x6", EX, D..**20.00**

Brown Shoe Co's Star-Five-Star Shoes, match holder, tin litho, rare, 9x5", VG, A 325.00

Brown's Hungarian Flour, pocket mirror, 2", G, D .**30.00**

Brown's Iron Bitters, calendar, 1888, revolving, Burren Giles NY litho, EX+, D **70.00**

Brownie Brand Peanuts, tin, Palmer Cox 'Brownies' on label, United Fig & Date Co, press lid, scratches/dents, 10-lb, 9x8" diameter, G, A..**50.00**

Brownie Laundry Wax, display, cardboard box for laundry wax with slanted glass front, Palmer Cox 'Brownies' on paper label, 6x10x7", G, A **25.00**

Brubaker Mfg of Taps & Dies, calendar top, paper, shoulder-length portrait of woman in oval, trimmed/some wear, matted & framed, approx: 21x17", G, A **80.00**

Bruinoil Bruin Gasoline, sign, 2-sided die-cut tin with mounting flange, 1920s, oval, NM, A............1,600.00

Brunswick-Balke-Collender Co, sign, cardboard, depicts billiard experts from around the world, tears/paper loss/soiling, framed, 31x41", G-, A........................**400.00**

Brush, King of Wizards, poster, paper litho, magician & his assistant, School of Occidental & Oriental Magic, ca 1910, framed, 31x24", NM, A **425.00**

Brynhilda Cigars, box label, inner lid, pictures woman within an oval surrounded by flowers & medallions, 6x9", M, D..**12.00**

BSC & Co Coffee, pail, tin, 5-lb, VG, D......................**120.00**

Buchanan & Lyall's Tobaccos (B&L), sign, paper on cardboard, 1886 fire scene, framed, 23x39", VG, A.....300.00

Buchanan & Lyall's Tobaccos (B&L), sign, paper on cardboard, 1895 fire scene, framed, 23x30", G+, A.........**275.00**

Bull Durham Tobacco, display, cardboard box picturing a bull, plus 18 pouches of tobacco, EX, A **35.00**

Bull Durham Tobacco, sign, Black father & son on a hunting trip, Standard Of The World For Three Generations, framed, 26x18", G-, A **500.00**

Bull Durham Tobacco, sign, cardboard, bullfighting scene, waterstaining/creasing/chipping, original frame, 33x52", G, A **450.00**

Bull Durham Tobacco, sign, cardboard, depicts woman smoking pipe at the General Store, 1880-1900, edge stain, 10x25" without frame, A **300.00**

Bull Durham Tobacco, sign, paper, black & white scene titled 'My Mother In Law,' Duck of Durham, 1920, framed, 14x11", NM, A **45.00**

Bull's Head Motor Oil, tin, bull's head on light blue-green ground, Globe Solvents Co, screw lid & handle, ca 1925-45, 2-gal, 12x9", VG, A **85.00**

Bull's Head Motor Oil, tin, dark green background, screw lid & handle, ca 1915-25, 2-gal, 11", EX, A 150.00

Bullock Ward & Co, match holder, tin litho, colorful factory image, Our Factory Area 30,000 Square Feet, 5x3", G+, A **200.00**

Bulwark Cut Plug Tobacco, tin, pictures man looking across water through a telescope, horizontal rectangle with square corners, appears EX, A **25.00**

Bumble Bee Tuna, doll, inflatable plastic, Yum Yum Bumble Bee, 24", EX, D **5.00**

Bunker Hill Breweries, button, pin-back, celluloid, full-color, NM, D **35.00**

Bunker Hill Breweries, tray, bulldog with collar initialed PB, image scratch, 12" diameter, NM, A 350.00

Bunker Hill Coffee, tin, pictures famous Boston obelisk, key-wind lid, slight chipping/scratches/slight denting, 1-lb, 6x4", VG, A **75.00**

Bunnies Salted Peanuts, tin, bunny in top hat with 5¢ package, press lid, GE Barbour Co, Canada, good sheen, minor wear, 10-lb, 11x8", EX, A **400.00**

Bunnies Salted Peanuts, tin, bunny in top hat with 5¢ package, press lid, GE Barbour Co, Canada, 10-lb, 11x8", G, A **150.00**

Burger King, doll, cloth, 12", G, D **13.00**

Burger King, doll, cloth, 24", EX, D **16.00**

Burgermeister Beer, bank, can shape, paper label pictures Burgie Man, EX, D **11.00**

Burgermeister Beer, opener, D **10.00**

Burgermeister Cigars, box label, outer, depicts bust of man & flowers, 5x5", M, D **2.00**

Burkhardt's, see also GF Burkhardt's Lager Beer

Burkhardt's Beer, tip tray, 1 of only 2 known with lettered logo, One Bottle, Like The Other, 4" diameter, EX/, A **50.00**

Burkhardt's Beer, tray, woman at piano serenading 2 men drinking beer, leaf border, image scratches/rim chips, 14" diameter, G, A **300.00**

Burley Boy Tobacco, see Bagley's

Burnham's Wild Cherry Phosphate, pitcher, embossed ceramic, minor scratching towards spout area, 9x5" diameter, VG, A **60.00**

Buster Brown, display, die-cut tin stand-up figures, Buster's hat & face discolored, 33", VG+, A **3,500.00**

Buster Brown, display, silk-screened die-cut fiberboard, 3-D images of Buster & Tige, Buster: 68x31x31", Tige: 28x23x23", VG, A **425.00**

Buster Brown All Spice, tin, paper label pictures Buster & Tige, press lid, sm puncture hole at top near rim, round, VG, A **25.00**

Buster Brown Blue Ribbon Shoes, pocket watch, ca 1925, rare, A **340.00**

Buster Brown Bread, match holder, die-cut tin litho, colorful image of cartoon characters featuring Buster Brown, rare, creases, 7x2", VG, A **1,000.00**

Buster Brown Cigars, tin, 5x5" diameter, VG, A...650.00

Buster Brown Shoes, display, die-cut tin figural, Buster with arms above head straddling Tige, lettering along bottom, EX, A **1,000.00**

Buster Brown Shoes, sign, embossed tin, pictures Buster & Tige, Brown's Shoes Are 5 Star Best, Advertised To The Nation..., 14x20", EX, A **800.00**

Buster Brown Shoes, sign, hand-painted tin, Buster Brown Shoes flanked by a winking Buster & smiling Tige, 12x58", appears EX, A **500.00**

Butler Oil Sales Co, tin, pictures bear holding barrel, Bruin Petroleum Products, screw lid & handle, ca 1917, 1-gal, 11", G+, A **200.00**

Butter-Nut Coffee, tin, paper label, 1-lb, EX, D **42.00**

Butterwick, see E Butterwick

Byron Weston Ledger & Paper Co, sign, paper, view of the Massachusetts factory, water stain/minor foxing, framed, 30x38", VG, A **65.00**

∽∾ C ∽∾

C Pfeiffer Brewing Co, tip tray, labeled bottle in center, Detroit Mich, rim chips, 4" diameter, NM, A **60.00**

C Pfeiffer Brewing Co, tip tray, lettered logo in center, Famous Beers, white background flecks & other minor flecks, 4" diameter, NM, A **45.00**

C Schmid & Sons Beer, opener, D **10.00**

C&H Sugar, doll, cloth, Hawaiian Girl, 1973, 16", worn, G, D **10.00**

CA Jackson Tobacco, sign, tin, factory flanked with war scenes & 1868 factory view, Petersburg Va, ca 1878, gold leaf frame, 30x40", VG+, A **7,000.00**

CA Lammers Bottling Co, tray, pictures the Denver brewery, 13" diameter, VG+, A **325.00**

Cabin Boy Cigars, box label, inner lid, depicts cabin boy & clipper ship, 6x9", M, D **30.00**

Cabinet Cigar Co, sign, cardboard, pictures Washington & his cabinet, taped tears/breaks, 18x22" without frame, G-, A **60.00**

Cable Cabinet Cigars, box label, inner lid, depicts 7 famous men, 6x7", M, D **75.00**

Cadette Baby Talc, tin, designed as toy soldier, appears EX, A **65.00**

Cal-Crest, crate label, California lemon, depicts lg lemon on stem with logo above, Evans Bros, Riverside Cal, 1940s, 9x13", M, D..**2.00**

Calabash Tobacco, pocket tin, embossed lettered logo on colorful tin, Montreal Canada, overall wear, 4x4x1", G+, A..**225.00**

California Beauty, crate label, pear, lg pear & roses, CM Otoy Co, Fresno Calif, 1930s, 8x11", M, D...............**5.00**

California Dream, crate label, California orange, depicts gold peacock, Bradford Bros Inc, Placentia Calif, 1920, 10x12", M, D **18.00**

California Insurance Agency, sign, paper, wounded bear surmounting burning San Francisco, original frame, 20x13", NM, A.....................................750.00

California Nugget Tobacco, tin, unusual pillow shape, minor chipping/slight dents/general wear, 2x3x3", G+, A..**105.00**

California Perfume Co, ad, pictures dental products, ca 1915, matted & framed, horizontal rectangle, A **85.00**

California Perfume Co, tin, suitcase shape with Jack & Jill Jungle Jinks motif, some scratching/slight chipping, 1x6x4", VG, A **45.00**

CALSO Supreme Gas, pump sign, porcelain, D **196.00**

Calumet Baking Powder, display, 4-shelf unit, oak, Calumet burned into wood top, 45x32", EX, A....**220.00**

Calumet Baking Powder, regulator clock, wood with reverse painted glass panel, 35x5x17", G, A..450.00

Calumet Insurance Co, sign, reverse painting on glass, Indian logo on black background, Chicago, image wear, framed, 24x23", A......................................**220.00**

Calvano Cigars, box label, outer, pictures Spanish man smoking a cigar, 5x5", M, D..........................**2.00**

Camel, crate label, California orange, depicts camel & Arab on sand dune, Orange Heights Orange Ass'n, 1930, 10x12", M, D **30.00**

Camel Cigars, tin, slight rust, 6x5x2", G, D **45.00**

Cameo Cigarettes, sign, front & back views of 4 men in top hats & tuxedos dancing, We Went For The Best & Got It, vertical rectangle, A..................................**381.00**

Cameron & Cameron Best Tobacco, tin, depicts trademark on blue & gold can with rounded corners, slip lid, scratches/rust/dents, 5x6x4", G, A................**125.00**

Campbell Brand Coffee, pail, tin, depicts desert scene with camels & Arabs, slip lid & bail, 4-lb, 8x8" diameter, EX, D **56.00**

Campbell Brand Coffee, pail, tin, shows figures with camels, Campbell Holton & Co, slip lid & bail, slight wear, 4-lb, 8x8" diameter, EX, A **105.00**

Campbell Soup Co, doll, Campbell Kid, 50th birthday, 1955, 9", EX, D **42.00**

Campbell Soup Co, doll, cheerleader, 1957, EX, D **40.00**

Campbell Soup Co, doll, vinyl, Wizard of O's, 8", some wear, VG, D...**18.00**

Campbell Soup Co, puzzle, frame tray, 30-piece die-cut cardboard, depicts Campbell Kids jumping hurdles, 10x13", EX, A **12.00**

Campbell Soup Co, thimble, porcelain, Franklin USA, EX, D **16.00**

Campbell's Condensed Vegetable Soup, sign, curved porcelain, superb color & graphics, 2 dings in lettering, NM, A 3,100.00

Campbell's Soups, display, revolving (electrical), Campbell Kid with bowl of soup, Ready In A Jiffy, ca 1950, rare, appears EX, A **550.00**

Campbell's Soups, sign, embossed tin, patriotic image of flag made up of soup cans, some crazing/scratches, rare, framed, 28x39", EX, A **4,000.00**

Campbell's Soups, sign, embossed tin, Pop Art graphics of the 60s by Standard Adv Co, Coschocton, Ohio, 26x40", M, A **85,000.00**

Campbell's Varnish Stains, display case, wood & embossed tin, tiered, with Victorian interior scenes, chips/dents/rust, 16x20x8", G+, A **1,700.00**

Canada Dry, clock, plastic face with metal frame, Canada Dry logo in center, 16" square, VG, D...................**35.00**

Canada Dry, dispenser, frosted reservoir on green & black milk glass base, 5¢ A Glass, cracked, EX, A..........**70.00**

Canada Dry, display, 3-tiered metal, Serve Yourself Canada Dry Beverages, Gingervating Sparkling Water Club Soda, 55", A **35.00**

Canada Dry, display, 3-tiered wire, Serve Yourself..., Sparkling Water, A Club Soda, 53", A **35.00**

Canada Dry, sign, cardboard, fizzing glasses atop, bottles below, Ginger Sparkling Ale, Lemon-Lime Rickey, vertical rectangle, A...**40.00**

Canada Dry Ginger Ale, sign, wall hanger, heavy cardboard, colorful image of an old bottle & hamburger platter, dated 1964, 12x13", D **18.00**

Canada Straight Cut Plug Tobacco, tin, picturing a beaver, orange & blue, 9" diameter, D **20.00**

Canadian Club Cigars, box label, inner lid, depicts maple leaf on gold label, 6x9", M, D..................................**4.00**

Canadian Club Cigars, sign, cardboard, pictures 2 men conversing with lettering aside, open box of cigars below, heavy wear, 16x11", A **25.00**

Canadian Club Cigars, sign, paper, 3 men enjoying cigars, boxes of product, 5¢, Made Clean In Factories..., framed, vertical rectangle, M, A...........................**25.00**

Canadian Club Cigars, sign, 2-sided hanging cardboard, Canadian Club over maple leaf, 5¢ Cigar, Different From All Others, 7" diameter, EX, D **10.00**

Canadian Club Whiskey, pitcher, ceramic, EX, D **10.00**

Canadian Pacific Railway Co's Pacific Service, sign, pictures ship at full sail, framed, 33x47", A **400.00**

Canby, playing cards, Aura Roberts, 68 cards with instructions, 1938, original box, M, A **10.00**

Candee Rubber Co, sign, die-cut cardboard, hanging cords simulate hammock, 12x17", EX, A **2,100.00**

Cannon Ball Cigars, sign, tin litho, pictures an Indian maiden referred to as Joneta, Sold By Lapeer Mercantile Co, 1910, 14x12", A **260.00**

Cannstatter Park, sign, chromolitho, turn-of-the-century amusement park, matted, 29x18", EX, A.............**140.00**

Canova Coffee, tin, paper label, 1-lb, EX, D **36.00**

Capital Airlines, playing cards, white logoed center with red, blue, & black lettering on black edged in gold, Viscount, complete, NM, D..................................**10.00**

Capitan Parlube Motor Oil, tin, blue & pink car on mountain road under product name, Beckett Bros, screw lid & handle, 1925-45, 12x9", EX, A **170.00**

Capitol Motor Oil, tin, white with blue capitol dome over product name in red, red & blue letters & logo, 1929-35, 2-gal, 11x7", EX, A **50.00**

Captain Alvarez Cigars, box label, inner lid, pictures a Spanish cavalier, 6x9", M, D **3.00**

Caravan Cork Tip Cigarettes, tin, flat, red, holds 50 cigarettes, Canada, VG+, D **15.00**

Caravan Plain Cigarettes, tin, flat, green, holds 50 cigarettes, VG, D.................................**12.00**

Card Seed Co, display rack (with many packets of seed), wire, ca 1925, 8x14", EX, A..................**80.00**

Cardinal Beer, tip tray, pictures young girl with roses, The Beer With The Real Hop Flavor, rim wear/chips, 4" diameter, EX, A **75.00**

Cardinal Cut Plug Tobacco, pocket tin, yellow with cardinal on blue square, VG+, A **650.00**

Cardinal Cut Plug Tobacco, sample tin, yellow with cardinal on blue square, VG+, A **425.00**

Carey's Roofing, sign, tin with embossed display of product, Magnesia Flexible Cement, Famous For Durability, edge chips, 10x14", VG, A **170.00**

Cargray Gas, pump sign, porcelain, EX, D **150.00**

Carhartt, window decal, red, white, & blue with heart-shaped background, From Mill To Millions, Overall, Trousers..., 6x9", NM, D **5.00**

Carling's Ale, sign, tin, depicts 9 'Bobbies' drinking, Nine Pints Of The Law, 12x19", NM, A.....................**95.00**

Carlisle Rye, shot glass, clear letters on frosted pennant design, early, minor rim imperfections, EX, D **15.00**

Carnation Gum, sign, tin, self-framed, 14x14", appears VG, A 600.00

Carnation Malted Milk, store container, embossed tin canister, lettered front, slip lid with knob, 8", A........**180.00**

Carnation Malted Milk, store container, milk glass canister, lettered front with carnation flower logo, slip lid with knob, 8", EX, A.................................**85.00**

Carolina Gem Long Cut Tobacco, tin, black spot on top, square, VG, D.................................**25.00**

Carson Pirie Scott & Co, shoe horn, NM, D **10.00**

Carter's Ink, sign, embossed tin on wood, bookkeeper within an oval, After All, No Ink Like Carter's, ca 1900, 25x19", NM, A **1,350.00**

Carter's Overalls, sign, tin, blue & red with white lettering, depicts train in center, Union Made, lg chip, 6x15", VG, A **150.00**

Cartier's Watch & Ring House, clock, regulator style, oak with glass front, gold lettering on black background, paint chips on bottom glass, NM, A.....................**425.00**

Cascade Beer, tray, Union Brewing & Malting Co, rare, 12x17", G-, A..550.00

Cascarets Laxative, pocket mirror, shows angel boy on potty, pinpoint bumps/rust, 2" diameter, G, A **25.00**

Case, sign, porcelain/neon, eagle atop lettered globe, blue neon tube outline, 1930, 40x18", NM, A..............**700.00**

Cash Value Chewing Tobacco, pack (full), pictures money bag, EX, D **20.00**

Castle Blend Coffee, tin, oval image of Windsor Castle on colorful can, Montreal, Quebec, St John NB, Canada, some wear, 5x4" diameter, G, A **350.00**

Castle Brand Pure Whiskies, paperweight, glass, depicts castle & lettering in full color, rounded corners & edge, ca 1900, 4x3", EX, A **35.00**

Castle Steel Distributors, playing cards, black castle logo encircled in white on orange background with white border, complete, NM, D **7.00**

Cavalier King-Size Cigarettes, poster, cavalier & lg pack of cigarettes, lettering above, 20x28", EX, D **22.00**

CD Kenny, figurine, ceramic, Indian in canoe, EX, D.**15.00**

CD Kenny, pail, depicts milkmaid on front, Kenny's Maid Coffee, sm amount of paint on 1 side, EX, A.......**200.00**

CD Kenny, plate, tin, depicts Santa & sleeping child, 10", M, D **175.00**

CD Kenny, tip tray, depicts girl with roses, Drink & Enjoy Kenny's Teas & Coffees, 1910, minor dents/wear, 4" diameter, A **45.00**

CD Kenny, tip tray, pictures seated Victorian lady, 4" diameter, EX, D **100.00**

CD Kenny, tray, holly band around little girl with necklace & doll, 1910, scratches/crazing, 10" diameter, A **25.00**

Centennial Beer, calendar, 1937, gentleman holding beer while pointing to advertisement on wall, full pad, framed, 31x19" overall, NM, A **300.00**

Central Brewing Co, tip tray, horse's head logo, Highest Grades of Pure Lager, Ales, & Porter, 1 of 3 known, rim chips, 4" diameter, EX, A **375.00**

Central Brewing Co, tray, pictures factory scene, 14x17", NM, A **1,300.00**

Central Brewing Co, tray, factory scene with boats in foreground, inset of horse's head upper left, some wear, oval, 14x17", EX, A...**600.00**

Central City Cigars, box label, inner lid, depicts building & busy street scene, 6x9", M, D **150.00**

Central Hudson Line, poster, paper litho, pictures ship Benjamin B Odell, Sunset Fleet To..., artist signed WG, 1918-20, NM, A **140.00**

Central Hudson Line, poster, pictures couple with camera & binoculars at ships rail, artist signed WG, 1918-20, 45x30", NM, A.......................................**190.00**

Central Union Tobacco, pocket tin, NM, D **325.00**

Central Union Tobacco, sign, cardboard litho, pictures 2 men with 1 pointing to Central Union tobacco sign, framed, 11x14", VG, A **150.00**

Century Bottled Beer, tip tray, Phil Schneider Brewing Co arched above couple toasting, product name on rim, 4" diameter, M, A......................................**150.00**

Cer-ola Beverages, sign, cardboard, bottle & glass of Cer-ola on tray with couple under beach umbrella, made by Kolb, Bay City Mich, M, A.................................**40.00**

Ceresota Flour, cookbook, 1930s, soft-bound, logoed cover, 32 pages, Consolidated Milling Co, spine wear/stains, 9x5", VG+, D...**18.00**

Ceresota Flour, match holder, die-cut tin, Ceresota boy slicing bread, barrel holder, 5x2", VG+, A............**325.00**

Ceresota Flour, match holder, die-cut tin, Ceresota boy slicing bread, flour box holder, 5x2", NM, A **600.00**

Ceresota Flour, match holder, tin, Ceresota boy slicing bread, horizontal holder, 5x3", VG+, A **525.00**

Ceresota Flour, sign, die-cut cardboard litho, Ceresota boy slicing bread, Prize Bread Of The World, framed, 13x9", EX, A **350.00**

Ceresota Flour, sign, embossed tin, Ceresota boy slicing bread, Made By Consolidated Milling Co, rare, framed, 29x22", G+, A.................................**7,500.00**

Certo, leaflet insert, 'Certo Recipes For Making Jams & Jellies,' 31 pages, 1937, D...**4.00**

Challenge Cigars, box label, outer, pictures Spanish soldiers in an Indian camp, 5x5", M, D **10.00**

Champion Cigars, box label, outer, depicts knight on horseback on shield inset, 5x5", M, D **46.00**

Champion Coal, sign, porcelain, logoed center, It's The Best, Subway Coal & Ice Co, rust around nail holes, horizontal rectangle, A **60.00**

Champion Ginger Ale, sign, tin, blue, green, & white lettering on orange & green, 20" long, G, A..............**35.00**

Champion Spark Plugs, board game, Champion Road Race, cardboard, with 6 cut-out race cars & instructions, 18x12", D **45.00**

Champion Spark Plugs, display, painted tin, spark plug shown on 2 sides, globe on front For Best Possible Service..., 1930-40, 14x36", EX, A.............................**225.00**

Champion Spark Plugs, playing cards, white on red & black logos superimposed over repeated gold world graphics, white border, complete, NM, D **5.00**

Champion Spark Plugs, sign, embossed tin, Champion superimposed over spark plug logo, More Power, More Speed, 1920-30, 14x30", EX, A.............................**110.00**

Champion Spark Plugs, sign, tin, 3-color, ca 1930-40, minor scuffs, 12x26", EX+, A.......................210.00

Champlain Ale & Porter, tray, enamel, decorative logoed center, lighter banded rim, 12" diameter, G, A.......**50.00**

Charles Denby Cigars, display, die-cut cardboard, bellboy displaying product, All Time Favorite, For Smoking Pleasure, 11x6", appears EX, A.............**60.00**

Charles Denby Cigars, sign, cardboard, bellboy displaying product, First Call For The Leader In Cigar Value, framed, 11x14", appears EX, A.............**80.00**

Chas D Kaier Co Ltd, match holder, tin litho, pictures 3 bottles & a glass, Brewers & Bottlers, Mahanoy City Pa, 5x3", VG+, A.........................**325.00**

Chas Ehlermann Hop & Malt Co, sign, tin, portrait of founder & factory, 1860-1890, Souvenir 40th Year, self-framed, fading/scratching, 26x18", G, A.400.00

Chase & Sanborn's Famous Boston Coffees, sign, baked enamel with mounting flange, We Sell..., horizontal rectangle, EX, A.....................**180.00**

Chase & Sanborn's Seal Brand Coffee, string holder, tin, sign with wire basket string holder inserted in top, dents/chips, 10x14x4", G, A.............**750.00**

Chase's Ice Cream, container, cardboard, depicts girl on skis, 1923, half-pint, NM, A......................**10.00**

Chateau Frontenac Coffee, tin, inset view of Frontenac surrounded by leaves, original slip lid, wood knob, some wear, 1-lb, 8x4" diameter, G-, A....................**35.00**

Chatfield & Woods, playing cards, gold edges, 52 cards with 2 jacks, M, D....................................**8.00**

Cheasepeake & Ohio Railroad, playing cards, 2 decks with Chessie, boxed, NM, D......................**10.00**

Cheer Detergent, doll, vinyl, new, 10", EX, D...........**18.00**

Cheerios, bee, 14", EX, D **25.00**

Chekola, crate label, pear, stone litho, depicts Congdon Orchards, North Yakima WA, 1915, 8x11", M, D...**16.00**

Chero-Cola, sign, paper, girl with soft drink wearing advertising pin, framed, 24x15", VG+, A **600.00**

Cheroots, sign, paper, girl with fan, 9x7", NM, D **35.00**

Cherry Blossom Soda, sign, die-cut tin, double-sided teeter-totter with boy & girl sipping product, Milford Spring Bottling Co, 7x12", F, A............................**175.00**

Cherry Chick, dispenser, embossed porcelain potbelly, cherries & leaves, green base, gold print & banding, brass pump, rare, EX, A.........................**2,000.00**

Cherry Phosphate-Grape Phosphate, sign, cardboard litho, basket of grapes & cherries, J Hungerford Smith Co, original decorative frame, 23x16", VG, A **310.00**

Cherry Smash, dispenser, ceramic potbelly, cherry logo, Our Nation's Beverage, original pump, hairlines/chip, 16x9", F, A **350.00**

Cherry Smash, dispenser, ceramic potbelly, original pump, some gold leaf loss, 16x9", EX, A.....1,300.00

Cherry Smash, dispenser, lettered logo on cranberry glass, metal mount for counter top, nickel-plated lid, 15x10", EX, A **525.00**

Cherry Smash, dispenser, lettered logo on cranberry glass, metal mount for counter top, lid missing, 15x10", VG, A **105.00**

Cherry Smash, dispenser, porcelain potbelly, ca 1915, rare, 12x10", EX, A 1,400.00

Cherry Smash, menu board, tin, round top with vertical rectangle bottom attached by chains, Drink Cherry Smash, A True Fruit Blend, A **150.00**

Cherry Smash, sign, paper litho, man in colonial dress, Drink Cherry Smash, sm holes, framed, 26", G, A.**160.00**

Cherry Smash, syrup bottle, white & red fired-on label on both sides, no top, 12", NM, A **205.00**

Chess Cigars, box label, outer, depicts colonial couple playing chess, 5x5", M, D **30.00**

Chester Whiskey, shot glass, lettering on the diagonal, Cahnmann & Co, Sole Distributors, 1804 Amsterdam Ave..., partial gold rim, VG, D **20.00**

Chesterfield Cigarettes, ash tray, tin, football stadium encircles entire tray, They Satisfy in center, 1930-50, minor scuffing, 6" long, A **20.00**

Chesterfield Cigarettes, thermometer, tin, embossed pack of Chesterfields, They Satisfy, 6x13", EX, A **110.00**

Chesterfield King Cigarettes, door plate, tin litho, pictures large pack, More Than Ever They Satisfy, 1945-55, 9x4", VG, A **60.00**

Chevrolet, brochure, 16 full-color pages of the complete 1958 line including Corvette, slight water stain, 11x12", A **12.00**

Chevrolet, catalog, 1937(?), 12 full-color pages, slight stain, 9x9", A **22.00**

Chevrolet, key chain, brass, commemorating 50th Anniversary, 1", VG, D **23.00**

Chevrolet, mask, Chevrolet Man, die-cut paper, NOV 7 appears on hat, ca 1940s, slight bend on nose, 11", EX, D **35.00**

Chevrolet, poster, fold-out, depicts complete 1952 line in full color, opens to 21x29", EX, A **10.00**

Chevrolet, poster, fold-out, depicts full line of 1954 models in color, opens to 15x21", EX, A **22.00**

Chevrolet, poster, showroom, 27x60", VG, A **20.00**

Chevrolet, sign, porcelain, Chevrolet For Economy & Transportation, EX, D **625.00**

Chevrolet, wall clock, neon illumination, electric, second hand, 6" deep, 20" diameter, EX, A **450.00**

Chevron, sign, porcelain, Chevron Low Lead, D **12.00**

Chic-Mint Gum, vendor, cast iron & pressed steel, product label on glass dome, coin trap in base, 12x6x8", EX, A **450.00**

Chicago Combination Lock Co, lock, brass, stamped on front, 3", EX, D **80.00**

Chicago Cubs Chewing Tobacco, tin, patriotic eagle logo, Chicago Cubs, NM, A **180.00**

Chicago Tribune, playing cards, black depiction of newspaper building on white edged in gold & red, lettering below, complete, NM, D **5.00**

Chickencock Pure Rye Whiskey, tin, depicts rooster against colorful background, 8", EX, A **80.00**

Chickering & Sons Piano Fortes, sign, reverse-painted glass, medallion-type symbol in center with lettering, Boston, New York, framed, 43" long, VG, A **750.00**

Chief Okee Cigars, box label, outer, depicts Indian Chief, 1912, 5x5", M, D **32.00**

Chief Paint, sign, depicts head of Indian in headdress, 12x28", NM, D **38.00**

Chief Two Moon Bitter Oil, display, cardboard with 3 sections depicting Chief's laboratory & a bus with various medicinals, 39x52", EX, A **150.00**

Chippewa Ice Cream, sign, tin on wood, double-sided, shows Indian Chief, All-Ways-Good, Chippewa Model Dairy Co, horizontal rectangle, VG, A **275.00**

Chiquez Le Tebac Stag, calendar, 1918, framed, 39x22", EX, A **140.00**

Chiquita Bananas, doll, 1974, 16", EX, D **18.00**

Chiquita Bananas, leaflet, 1951, 'Chiquita Banana Presents 18 Recipes,' 18 pages, D **6.00**

Chock's Vitamins, doll, man, 1970, 20", EX, D **20.00**

Chocolat Revillon, clock, EX, A **475.00**

Chocolate Cream Coffee, playing cards, gold Chocolate Cream Coffee on medium blue with decorative gold & white border, complete, NM, D **4.00**

Chocolate Cream Coffee, tin, key-wind lid, 1-lb, appears NM, D **45.00**

Choice Family Tea, store bin, tin, depicts stenciled flowers & bee, general wear, 14x11x11", G, A **125.00**

Chore Girl, doll, stuffed, 16", 1970, EX, D **20.00**

Chr Heurich Brewing Co, tray, shows Lady Liberty & factory surrounded by stylized eagle & border, overall wear, rare, 13" diameter, VG, A **500.00**

Chr Heurich Brewing Co, see also Maerzen-Senate Beer

Christian Feigenspan Brewing Co, tray, pictures long-haired girl in profile, PON, Newark NJ, ca 1900, minor scratches, 13" diameter, NM, A..............**100.00**

Christian Moerlein Brewing Co, sign, paper, depicts various products, National Export & Barbarossa Bottled Beer, Cincinnati USA, framed, 18", G, A..............**100.00**

Christie's Biscuits, cabinet, 16 tin litho fronts with glass viewing windows in wood case, tins faded & worn, 54x47x13", EX, A..............**1,400.00**

Christin's Waters, tray, shows dog spraying cat from seltzer bottle with dancing bottles around perimeter, good color, 13" diameter, G-, A..............**190.00**

Christo Ginger Ale, dispenser, barrel form with silver-like bands, Drink 5¢, with pump, appears EX, A..............**525.00**

Christy Girl Cigars, box label, inner lid, bust of a woman in a red dress, 6x9", M, D..............**5.00**

Chrysler Motors, Polaroid lenses for viewing 3-D movie 'In Tune With Tomorrow' shown at 1939 World's Fair, cardboard, NM, D..............18.00

Chuck E Cheese Pizza, doll, plush, Chuck E Cheese with his telescope, 12", G, D..............**18.00**

Chum's Liquor, tip tray, man seated at table enjoying product with dog at side, minor chips & scratches, 4" diameter, EX, A..............**165.00**

CHYP Inter-Collegiate Mixture Tobacco, tin, pictures sporting motif, square, minor chipping/slight denting, 2x5x3", VG, A..............**150.00**

Cincy Chewing & Smoking Tobacco, package, red, white, & blue, sealed, M, D..............**30.00**

Cincy Stoves, bank, cast iron with light blue porcelain enamel, nickel grill, 4", EX, D..............**45.00**

Circus Club Mallows Candy, tin, monkey, green hat-form lid, 7x3" diameter, hat: 4" diameter, EX, A.......270.00

Circus Club Mallows Candy, tin, bear, hat-form lid, 7x3" diameter, hat: 4" diameter, G, A..............**75.00**

Circus Club Mallows Candy, tin, elephant, hat-form lid, 7x3" diameter, hat: 4" diameter, G, A.......**350.00**

Circus Club Mallows Candy, tin, dog, hat-form lid, 7x3" diameter, hat: 4" diameter, VG, A..........**325.00**

Circus Club Mallows Candy, tin, cat, hat-form lid, 7x3" diameter, hat: 4" diameter, EX+, A..............**175.00**

Citadel Tobacco, tin, multiple images of Citadel & soldiers, rare, ovoid, 7x5x4", G+, A..............**800.00**

Cities Service Koldpruf Anti-Freeze, tin, Cities Service logo, penguin on white across bottom, ca 1957-65, 1-qt, 5" diameter, EX, A..............**40.00**

Cities Service Oils, pump sign, porcelain, letters arch above central logo, Once-Always, ca 1927-36, flakes/scuffs, 10" diameter, A..............**170.00**

City of New York Insurance Co, sign, embossed tin, oval insert with Manhattan skyline, Fire, Cash Capital 1,000,000, some wear, framed, 19x27", VG+, A..**575.00**

CJ Fell & Brother Spice Co, sign, paper, flags & factory scene within Victorian framework flanked by list of products, ca 1910-20, 24x18", EX, A..............**600.00**

CL Centlivre Brewing Co, poster, paper, colorful factory scene with portrait in lower left, Henderson Litho Co, framed, 25x38", EX+, A..............**350.00**

Clabber Girl Baking Powder, booklet, 1934, 'Clabber Girl Baking Book,' 15 pages, D..............**6.00**

Clairol, doll, vinyl, Misty, new, 12", D..............**25.00**

Clark & Sons Liquor Merchants, poster (possibly a calendar), paper, woman in Victorian garden setting, minor wear, matted & framed, 35x25", VG+, A..............**400.00**

Clark's Mile End Cotton Thread, sign, paper roll-down, depicts Victorian woman with parasol, original metal strips top & bottom, 1890s, 23x15", EX, A..............**45.00**

Clark's Mile End Spool Cotton, sign, paper roll-down, depicts mother holding daughter up on rail, 1890, creasing/scratches/tear, framed, 29x17", A..............**50.00**

Clark's ONT Spool Cotton, cabinet, oak case with 2 lettered glass drawer inserts, case relacquered/top insert cracked, 8x22x16", VG, A..............**225.00**

Clark's ONT Spool Cotton, sign, cardboard, pictures cowboy on horseback roping a bull, framed, horizontal rectangle, appears EX, A..............**220.00**

Clark's ONT Spool Cotton, sign, paper, 'My Mama Wants A Spool Of ONT,' 21x16" without frame, EX, A...1,500.00

Clark's ONT Spool Cotton, sign, paper roll-down, 'The First Lesson,' Use Clark's ONT Spool Cotton, metal strips, minor edge damage, 27x15", G, A **50.00**

Clark's ONT Spool Cotton, sign, tin, John Clark Jr & Co, Best Six Cord Spool Cotton, Thos Russell, Sole Agent, 14x20" without frame, VG, A................**155.00**

Clark's ONT Spool Cotton, thimble, porcelain, logo superimposed over scene of girl hanging clothes on line, gold bands, Franklin USA, EX, D **15.00**

Clark's ONT Spool Cotton, trade card, 2 boys flying a kite, NM, D **4.00**

Clark's Peanut Butter, pail, tin, shows scenes of moose hunting, Indians, beavers & dog sled, slip lid & bail, rare, 4x4", EX, A..................**1,050.00**

Clark's Teaberry Gum, display, glass pedestal dish, appears M, A **50.00**

Clark's Teaberry Gum, display shelf, etched glass, holds gum packages, minor chip on upper right edge/discolored brackets, 5x16x4", VG+, A **75.00**

Clark's Teaberry Gum, ruler, ca 1937, D.................**2.00**

Class Cigars, tin, embossed, 5x6x4", EX, D.............**100.00**

Claus Lipsious Lager Beer, sign, wire on wood background, mug of beer in center of star, faded letters/worn, 36x36", A **800.00**

Clavecin, Catel & Farcey, playing cards, 52 cards with 1 joker, ca 1960s, M, D **15.00**

Clayton & Russell's Ginger Cordial, sign, reverse-painted glass with gold leaf product name with filigree border, 8x15", EX, A.................**125.00**

Clayton & Russell's Stomach Bitters, sign, paper litho, nude bearded man logo, Good Appetite, Good Digestion, & No Malaria, very rare, 40x27", A **2,200.00**

Clements Electric Vacuum Cleaners, thimble, aluminum, company name on worn red band, D **3.00**

Cleveland-Akron Bus Co, sign, celluloid, pictures early bus, 12x7", EX, A..............................**115.00**

Cleveland-Thurman Democratic Cigars, box, pictures Cleveland & Thurman in ovals surrounded by flags on inside of lid, appears EX, A **80.00**

Clicquot Club Beverages, sign, tin, 12x30", EX, A......**50.00**

Clicquot Club Ginger Ale, ad, child in fur-hooded coat with glass of product, Aged 6 Months, ca 1925, matted, horizontal rectangle, A **40.00**

Climax Brand Soda Bicarbonate, barrel with cover, 2 round paper labels depicting running ostrich, minor fading/puckering, 22", EX, A.....................**40.00**

Climax Plug Tobacco, sign, paper, depicts traveler sleeping on cliff ledge dreaming of nymph, Chew Climax Plug printed on cliff, 24x12", A............................**380.00**

Climax Plug Tobacco, sign, paper, framed, 34x19", appears EX, A..............................**1,200.00**

Climax Stoves, tray, pictures trademarked flaming warrior, The Taplin, Rice-Clerkin Co, Akron Ohio, some wear, 13" diameter, VG, A **55.00**

Clipper, crate label, Florida citrus, sailing ship in front of setting sun, Keen Fruit Corp, 1920s, diagonal corners, 9x9", M, D **3.00**

Clix Cigarettes, sign, cardboard, woman in plumed hat against blue background, A Blend That Suits, paper abraded in 2 areas, 28x16", A.........................**160.00**

Close-Up Toothpaste, Dumbo the Elephant, vinyl, 1974, 8", EX, D **25.00**

Close-Up Toothpaste, Mickey Mouse, vinyl, 8", appears EX, D................................**22.00**

Cloth of Gold Cigarettes, sign, paper roll-down, pretty girl holding a fan, printed by Julius Bien & Co, framed, 29x13", NM, A............................**200.00**

Club House Cigars, box label, inner lid, depicts palm trees against sunset, 6x9", M, D **4.00**

Club House Cigars, sign, depicts woman at boat helm with lettering above, printed in gold monochrome, approx: 19x14", A..............................**475.00**

Club Manhattan Cocktails, sign, tin, seated gentleman with cocktail & cigarette, C Shonk litho, ca 1894, original gold leaf frame, 15x11", EX+, A **375.00**

Clubb's Perique Mixture Tobacco, tin, picturing 3 portraits within a club logo, Toronto Canada, some wear, 4x7x2", G+, A **35.00**

Clysmic Table Water, playing cards, special aces & photo jacks, 52 cards with 1 joker, original box, VG, D...**18.00**

Clysmic Water, tip tray, pictures young girl with bottle & elk by stream, oval, 6", VG, A **75.00**

Co-Re-Ga Denture Adhesive, tin, for dental plates, free sample, EX, D **8.00**

Coca-Cola, ad, 1905, from back cover of magazine, man, child, & 4 ladies waiting behind counter, matted & framed, 10x14", VG+, A **110.00**

Coca-Cola, ad, 1906, depicts couple golfing, Adds Refreshing Relish To Every Form Of Exercise, matted, vertical rectangle, EX, A.................................**100.00**

Coca-Cola, ad, 1906, magazine, girl in buggy, EX, D..**23.00**

Coca-Cola, ad, 1906, Massengale, depicts fancy lady & maid, good color, 14x10", EX+, D.....................**100.00**

Coca-Cola, ad, 1910 (June), both covers of 'The Housewife' magazine, depicts 2 women & dog at soda fountain, 16x23", G, A...**170.00**

Coca-Cola, ad, 1915, depicts side view of seated girl, Drink Coca-Cola, Order It By The Case, framed, 19x14", NM, A..**145.00**

Coca-Cola, ash tray, 1936, brass, Coca-Cola 50th Anniversary, D 50.00

Coca-Cola, ash tray, 1960s, metal wood grain, Enjoy That Refreshing New Feeling, D **4.00**

Coca-Cola, bang gun, 1950s, Dayton Coca-Cola Bottling Co, D..**10.00**

Coca-Cola, bank, 1950s, dispenser form, battery operated, no glasses (on back cover), EX, D.....................**500.00**

Coca-Cola, banner, 1930s, Drink Coca-Cola In Bottles, Get A Large Toy Balloon Free With Each Bottle, 12x18", D **12.00**

Coca-Cola, banner, 1950s, Santa with dog, When Friends Drop In, Stock Up For The Holidays, 20x11", D....**20.00**

Coca-Cola, blotter, 1904, period lettering, Drink Coca-Cola, Delicious + Refreshing, 5¢, ink/dirt smudge/creasing, 4x9", VG, A **45.00**

Coca-Cola, blotter, 1906, logo in period border, Restores Energy & Strengthens The Nerves, NM, D **100.00**

Coca-Cola, blotter, 1938, cardboard, depicts a policeman drinking a Coke, 4x8", NM, D **20.00**

Coca-Cola, blotter, 1942, girl on stomach with hand under chin, logo inset at head, I Think It's Swell, rectangle, NM, D **8.00**

Coca-Cola, blotter, 1944, cardboard, 3 girls at the fountain, 4x8", NM, D **6.00**

Coca-Cola, blotter, 1951, cardboard, Sprite boy & bottle of Coke, Delicious & Refreshing, 4x8", NM, D.............**5.00**

Coca-Cola, blotter, 1953, Sprite boy in the snow with a bottle of Coke on left, Good! on right, NM, D **4.00**

Coca-Cola, blotter, 1955, 2 couples enjoying party with bottles of Coke, French-Canadian, NM, D **20.00**

Coca-Cola, blotter, 1956, cardboard, depicts a hand holding a bottle of Coke, Friendliest Drink On Earth, 4x8", NM, D...**6.00**

Coca-Cola, blotter, 1958, hand holding Coke superimposed over the earth, Friendliest Drink On Earth, rectangle, NM, D...**6.00**

Coca-Cola, blotter, 1960, pictures bottle of Coke on chart, Over 60 Million A Day, Refreshing New Feeling, NM, D **6.00**

Coca-Cola, book cover, Coke bottle with button logo plus 3 scenes on front, back has safety 'ABCs,' EX, D...**12.00**

Coca-Cola, book matches, 1960s, Santa with elves, Promote Coca-Cola, D **16.00**

Coca-Cola, bookmark, 1900, celluloid, depicts black & white image of Hilda Clark within a heart, red letters, 3x2", EX, A................................275.00

Coca-Cola, bookmark, 1904, paper, Lillian Nordica in front of dressing screen, Drink Coca-Cola 5¢, filigree border, vertical, A...**275.00**

Coca-Cola, bookmark, 1906, celluloid, owl-shaped, What Shall We Drink, Drink Coca-Cola 5¢, 3", EX, A....**300.00**

Coca-Cola, bottle, straight-sided glass, Westminster Md, slightly foggy, 1-qt, D...................................**110.00**

Coca-Cola, bottle, 1960s, clear, No Refill, 10-oz, M, D **12.00**

Coca-Cola, bottle carrier, 1931, cardboard, depicts Santa, Delicious & Refreshing, wear, 8x7x5", G-, A **95.00**

Coca-Cola, bottle carrier, 1939, cardboard, red & white with logo, 7", EX+, D **40.00**

Coca-Cola, bottle carrier, 1939, 6-pack, red, white, & green Christmas motif, VG, D **30.00**

Coca-Cola, bottle carrier, 1940s, wood, natural & red, Drink Coca-Cola In Bottles, NM, D **65.00**

Coca-Cola, bottle carrier, 1940s, wood, yellow & red, EX+, D..**50.00**

Coca-Cola, bottle covers, 1960s, cloth, Hi-Jaks, in original package, D..**13.00**

Coca-Cola, bottle opener, Lion's Head, Drink Goldelle Ginger Ale on reverse, G, D **90.00**

Coca-Cola, bottle opener, 1920s, bottle shape, Perfection, appears EX, D **20.00**

Coca-Cola, bottle opener, 1930s, metal spoon, Greenwood Miss, D **45.00**

Coca-Cola, bottle opener, 1940s, chrome corkscrew, 5", NM, D...**50.00**
Coca-Cola, bottle opener, 1950s, bottle shape, EX+, D..**10.00**
Coca-Cola, bottle opener, 1960s, Drink Coca-Cola, D...**2.00**
Coca-Cola, bottle opener/ice pick, metal with circular handle, pick end has hook opener, VG+, D **60.00**
Coca-Cola, calendar, 1904, paper, woman with glass in front of folding screen, decorative border, January pad, 15x8", M, A **4,200.00**
Coca-Cola, calendar, 1914, paper, depicts Betty wearing bonnet, July pad, edge tear/creasing, 31x13" without frame, EX, A **675.00**
Coca-Cola, calendar, 1921, girl in white & blue dress seated in garden holding glass, full pad, matted & framed, 31x17", EX, A **610.00**

Coca-Cola, calendar, 1933, depicts 'The Village Blacksmith,' full pad, some wear, 30x17", EX, A 325.00
Coca-Cola, calendar, 1937, paper, colorful image of a young boy & dog going fishing, full pad, matted & framed, 25x13", EX, A **500.00**
Coca-Cola, calendar, 1948, metal, red button atop vertical oblong with rounded corners, Have A Coke, May cover sheet, 19x8", NM, D **195.00**
Coca-Cola, calendar, 1962, die-cut metal, red & green on white with fishtail logo atop, May pad, 13x10", appears NM, D **175.00**
Coca-Cola, calendar, 1969, depicts couple at table, full pad, D..**35.00**
Coca-Cola, calendar top, 1918, paper, 2 women holding bottle & glass on beach, pad missing, discoloration/creases, 28x13", A...**400.00**
Coca-Cola, calendar top, 1927, girl standing sideways facing front with glass of Coke, 8" tear, matted & framed, D **140.00**
Coca-Cola, can, 1980s, aluminum, red & white, 4-oz Free, Max Headroom on back, 16-oz, NM, D..................**3.00**
Coca-Cola, carton topper, 1958, Have A Party From Your Pantry, Drink Coca-Cola, D..**5.00**
Coca-Cola, carton topper, 1958, You'll Want Plenty of Coke, Chick-n-Que, D **8.00**

Coca-Cola, chalkboard, 1950s, tin with rounded corners, lettered oval insert atop, Have A Coke at bottom, 26x18", G, D..**50.00**
Coca-Cola, channel card, 1953, cardboard, red, white, & yellow, Drink Coca-Cola, Goes Good With Food, 7x22", NM, D **35.00**
Coca-Cola, channel card, 1959, cardboard, steak dinner & glass of Coke, Steak Plate, 7x24", NM, A...............**30.00**
Coca-Cola, channel card, 1960s, cardboard, depicts mountains & glass of Coke, Ham & Cheese & Coke, 7x24", NM, D..**30.00**

Coca-Cola, checkers, 1940s, Dragon, Coca-Cola logo on each checker, complete, D 55.00
Coca-Cola, clock, 1910, boudoir, wooden, Drink Bottled Coca-Cola, rare, 3" diameter, D...........................**800.00**
Coca-Cola, clock, 1939, wood & glass, numbered 1-12 on white ground, red center, Drink Coca-Cola In Bottles, 16x16", NM, D **425.00**

Coca-Cola, clock, 1950s, counter top, metal & glass, 9x20", EX, A...395.00
Coca-Cola, clock, 1950s, metal & glass light-up, red, green, & white with gold bottle, 15" diameter, NM, D ..**425.00**
Coca-Cola, clock, 1950s, plastic light-up, red with white letters & border, Have A Coke Here (with arrow), 16" diameter, NM, D **450.00**
Coca-Cola, clock, 1960s, metal & glass, even numbers on white ground, fishtail logo, green strips, original box, 15x15", D **125.00**
Coca-Cola, clock, 1960s, metal & glass light-up, red & white with fishtail logo, 12x11", NM, D **160.00**
Coca-Cola, clock, 1974, plastic, Betty, D....................**50.00**

Coca-Cola, clock, 1980 Sessions, wood with glass face, white, red, & light oak stain, limited edition, 25x17", NM, D **450.00**

Coca-Cola, coaster, 1939, cardboard, red, yellow, & white, shows silhouette of a girl, Drink Coca-Cola Ice Cold, 3" diameter, M, D **5.00**

Coca-Cola, coaster, 1950s, cardboard, white, green, & red, Sprite boy & bottle of Coke, Have A Coke, octagonal, 4" diameter, M, D **5.00**

Coca-Cola, coaster, 1950s, green & white, Please Put Empties In The Rack, D...**3.00**

Coca-Cola, coaster, 1970s, paper, Tiffany design, 4", D ..**1.00**

Coca-Cola, cooler, metal, embossed side panels & tall legs with wheels, 2 Coke bottles on 2 sides, logo on others, 32x22x17", NM, A 1,250.00

Coca-Cola, cooler, vinyl, white on red, Drink Coca-Cola, Enjoy That Refreshing New Feeling, sm tears, 11x9x6", VG+, A **25.00**

Coca-Cola, cooler, 1940s, 72", NM, D...................**1,200.00**

Coca-Cola, coupon, 1920s, cardboard, 2-sided, 2x3", NM, D **12.00**

Coca-Cola, coupon, 1930s, complimentary, 65th anniversary, D **5.00**

Coca-Cola, coupon, 1950s, cardboard, shows 6-pack, Save This Valuable Coupon, 3x4", NM, D **5.00**

Coca-Cola, cribbage board, 1940s, wood, beige & red, complete with box & instructions, 3x10", NM, D...**60.00**

Coca-Cola, crystal radio, 1950s, red, has earphone & alligator clip, minor wear, very rare, 3x2x2", EX, D **575.00**

Coca-Cola, cup, plastic, miniature, EX, D.....................**2.00**

Coca-Cola, darts, streamlined, 1950s, in original box, EX, D...**85.00**

Coca-Cola, display, 1950s, die-cut cardboard, easel-back, children at refrigerator, For Santa, 9x14", D.........**135.00**

Coca-Cola, display, 1950s, die-cut porcelain on metal stand holding Slow School Zone sign, Canadian, 60", NM, D **1,895.00**

Coca-Cola, display, 1971, die-cut cardboard, depicts Santa in front of Christmas tree holding Coke & sack, 26x17", NM, D..**18.00**

Coca-Cola, display dispenser, 1940s, 3-piece rubber with Coke glass inserted in bottom, red paint restored, decals worn, 19", D..**495.00**

Coca-Cola, display for bags, metal, Sprite boy & white lettering on red background, 17x36", A.........220.00

Coca-Cola, display rack, folding wire that holds 6-packs of Coke, rounded logoed top, 47", EX, A....................**70.00**

Coca-Cola, display stand, steel with circular sign at top, Take Home A Carton, 25¢, some wear, 56x16" diameter, G, A **100.00**

Coca-Cola, doll, 1960s, Santa holding a bottle of Coke, 19", EX+, D...**85.00**

Coca-Cola, door plate, 1930s, red, yellow, & white porcelain, Prenezux Coca-Cola, Canadian, horizontal, 4x7", EX, D..**75.00**

Coca-Cola, door plate, 1938-40, red, yellow, & white porcelain, Thanks Call Again For A Coca-Cola, Canadian, 12x4", D..**190.00**

Coca-Cola, dry server, 1929, with 2 bottles, The Pause That Refreshes, 3x6", D **3.00**

Coca-Cola, Expresso Snack Bar by Schuco, Coca-Cola logo, in original box, rare, M, A **240.00**

Coca-Cola, fan, 1956, cardboard on wood stick, hand holding bottle, logo on back, 12x8", NM, D **28.00**

Coca-Cola, fan pull, 1957, double-sided Santa form, Family Size, Serve Coca-Cola, D...**13.00**

Coca-Cola, glass, 1923-27, modified flare-shape, etched logo with syrup line, 4", M, A **35.00**

Coca-Cola, glass, 1941-46, bell shape, etched logo with 'Trade-Mark' underneath, 4", M, A **20.00**

Coca-Cola, gum box, wood, faded image of Coca-Cola Gum printed in a key shape on side of box, overall wear, 6x13x6", G, A **275.00**

Coca-Cola, handkerchief, Kit Carson on red, D..........**65.00**

Coca-Cola, holder for auto, 1950s, cardboard, diagrams how & where to hang it, Drink Coca-Cola, Drive Refreshed, D **20.00**

Coca-Cola, ice bucket, 1960s, Drink Coca-Cola In Bottles, D..**10.00**

Coca-Cola, ice pick, 1950s, in original box, Delicious & Refreshing, Compliments Of Coca-Cola Bottling Co, EX, D..**10.00**

Coca-Cola, knife, 1972, truck shape, Fleet Management Seminar, Have A Coke & A Smile, D......................**10.00**

Coca-Cola, lamp shade, 1918, leaded glass with fringed brass, Property Of The Coca-Cola Company..., 16" diameter, EX, A..4,500.00

Coca-Cola, lighter, bottle form, bottle separates in middle to show lighter, M, D....................................**14.00**

Coca-Cola, match striker, 1938-39, porcelain, Drink Coca-Cola, Strike Match Here, touch-ups, 4x4", D........**155.00**

Coca-Cola, match striker, 1938-39, porcelain, Buvez Coca-Cola, Frottez Allumettes Ici, 4x4", D **90.00**

Coca-Cola, matchbook, 1930s, Refresh Yourself, A Pure Drink of Natural Flavors, D **15.00**

Coca-Cola, menu board, Coke bottle & Drink Coca-Cola atop menu, Delicious Refreshing, Good With Food, horizontal rectangle, EX, A.....................................**240.00**

Coca-Cola, message pad cube, 1983, formed like case of Coke, 4x6", D..**5.00**

Coca-Cola, miniature carton with 6 black bottles, 1970s, It's The Real Thing, D **3.00**

Coca-Cola, miniature case, 1960s, yellow with 24 gold bottles, D..**15.00**

Coca-Cola, miniature case, 1970s, red with 24 black bottles, D **10.00**

Coca-Cola, mobile, 1950s, double-sided with red dangling disc, Extra Refreshment, 19" diameter, D **150.00**

Coca-Cola, money clip, 1949, brass with red plastic logo, EX, D..**22.00**

Coca-Cola, music box, 1950s, cooler form (same as radio), some wear, D **1,600.00**

Coca-Cola, napkin, 1911, rice paper, red, white, & blue, lady in fancy dress, matted, 16x16", NM, D..........**125.00**

Coca-Cola, napkin, 1912, rice paper, red, white, & blue, logoed, framed, on the bias: 15x15", NM, D **110.00**

Coca-Cola, needle case, 1924, cardboard, depicts woman with hand on hip enjoying Coke, great color, 3x2", NM, D..**60.00**

Coca-Cola, notebook, 1987 Coca-Cola Advertising Schedule, spiral-bound, D **8.00**

Coca-Cola, pedal car, 1940-50, metal & rubber wheels, very red with white lettering, restored, 19x36", M, A..1,200.00

Coca-Cola, pen & pencil set, 1965, 50th anniversary of Coca-Cola Bottling, Frankport Ind, in plastic case, appears EX, D...**15.00**

Coca-Cola, pencil, Bullet, Drink Coca-Cola, D..............**5.00**

Coca-Cola, pencil, 1940s, mechanical, bottle-shaped metal clip, in original box, D **20.00**

Coca-Cola, pencil, 1950s, mechanical, goldtone, top has floating bottle, D **18.00**

Coca-Cola, pencil holder, 1960s, red on white ceramic, urn shape, shows some wear, 8x4", EX+, D **190.00**

Coca-Cola, pencil sharpener, 1960s, D **8.00**

Coca-Cola, picnic cooler, 1940s, cardboard, red & beige, Drink Coca-Cola, 10x10", EX, D **65.00**

Coca-Cola, placemats, 1950s, set of 4 different 'Around The World' depictions, D **10.00**

Coca-Cola, plate, 1905, shows bare-breasted woman, marked Vienna Art Plates/Western Coca-Cola Bottling Co..., 10" diameter, NM, A **300.00**

Coca-Cola, playing cards, WWII era, 3 silhouetted airplanes, box depicts nurse with Coke, NM, A **110.00**

Coca-Cola, playing cards, WWII era, 3 silhouetted airplanes, box depicts nurse with Coke, VG, A **50.00**

Coca-Cola, playing cards, 1943, box depicts stewardess & Coke bottle with wings, NM, A......................95.00

Coca-Cola, playing cards, 1943, box depicts stewardess & Coke bottle with wings, VG, D **50.00**

Coca-Cola, playing cards, 1943, depicts girl in circular inset with leaves & Coke bottle, NM, A..........................**95.00**

Coca-Cola, playing cards, 1963, white & red, depicts a bottle Coke, Things Go Better With Coke, complete, 3x2", NM, D...**35.00**

Coca-Cola, playing cards, 1963, depicts lady with tray of Cokes, in original box, D..**45.00**

Coca-Cola, playing cards, 1974, Drink Coca-Cola on stained-glass graphics, original box, VG, D **5.00**

Coca-Cola, pocket mirror, 1908, Victorian woman drinking from glass with fountain in background, rare, oval, 3x2", EX, A...**700.00**

Coca-Cola, pocket mirror, 1910, depicts girl with wide-brimmed hat facing left, oval, 3x2", EX+, A **220.00**

Coca-Cola, pocket mirror, 1911, woman in floral hat facing right, edge discoloration/sm crack/soiling, oval, 3x2", G, A..**75.00**

Coca-Cola, pocket mirror, 1916, Elaine, bumping to surface, oval, 3x2", EX, A..**275.00**

Coca-Cola, pocket mirror, 1920, Golden Girl, creases in celluloid, oval, 3x2", EX, A..........................550.00

Coca-Cola, post card, 1930s, depicts Weldmech Coca-Cola truck, D **5.00**

Coca-Cola, post card, 1940s, International truck, D.......**6.00**

Coca-Cola, post card, 1950s, commemorates 65th Anniversary with coupon depicting Free 6 Bottles, shows wire-handled carton, D...**5.00**

Coca-Cola, post card, 1973, Bobby Allison Coca-Cola race car, D **4.00**

Coca-Cola, poster, cardboard, Sprite boy peeking around glass of Coke, Refresh Yourself, 5¢, FW Woolworth Co, 14x11", VG, A **50.00**

Coca-Cola, poster, 1936 reproduction, cardboard, dog entertaining boy, clown, & girl, rectangular logo upper right, 18x27", NM, D...**26.00**

Coca-Cola, poster, 1946 reproduction, cardboard, sunbather being handed a Coke, round logo on right, 11x27", NM, D **28.00**

Coca-Cola, poster, 1960s, depicts boy & girl sitting facing each other, The Pause That Refreshes, 36x20", D..**35.00**

Coca-Cola, poster, 1960s, girl exercising, Refreshing New Feeling, 36x20", D...**35.00**

Coca-Cola, poster, 1960s, depicts girl with sailor hat, Things Go Better With Coke, original aluminum frame, 18x30", D **50.00**

Coca-Cola, poster, 1970s, depicts Santa at the fireplace, Keep Up The Tradition, 18x24", D **15.00**

Coca-Cola, poster, 1976, depicts Santa with a note, Coke Adds Life To Holiday Fun, 10x24", D **10.00**

Coca-Cola, push bar, Coca-Cola, Enjoy Here, rare, 3x30", D **160.00**

Coca-Cola, push bar, 1930s, red & white porcelain, Drink Coca-Cola, 16x4", D **200.00**

Coca-Cola, push bar, 1940s, Coca-Cola, Buvez Glace, edge chips, 3x30", D **54.00**

Coca-Cola, push bar, 1940s, red, yellow, white porcelain with black ends, Coca-Cola Iced Here, Canadian, minor chips, 3x30", D **110.00**

Coca-Cola, radio, cooler form, works well, minor paint chips, D..1,100.00

Coca-Cola, radio, 1980s, AM/FM, shaped like a bottle, 8", NM, D **22.00**

Coca-Cola, record album, 1971, 'The Shadow,' D **20.00**

Coca-Cola, record carrier for 45 rpms, 1960s, red & white vinyl with plastic handle, Hi Fi Club, index & 12 sleeves, 9x8", EX, D **30.00**

Coca-Cola, ruler, 1930s, wood, Good Rule, D **3.00**

Coca-Cola, sales training kit, 1940, case with record, incomplete film strips & lesson chart, hinged lid, 20" long, G, A **70.00**

Coca-Cola, sales training kit, 1955, case with records & film strips, 19" long, VG, A..**50.00**

Coca-Cola, school box, pictures bottle of Coke & insets of Safety depictions, Safety ABCs, Always Be Careful, 8x10", EX+, D **10.00**

Coca-Cola, school-teaching kit, 1970s, Man & His Environment, D **20.00**

Coca-Cola, score pad, 1940s, American Women's Volunteer Service, D **10.00**

Coca-Cola, seltzer bottle, blue, with spigot, EX, A....**350.00**

Coca-Cola, service pin, metal, green & black, 25-year pin, 1", M, D **125.00**

Coca-Cola, sign, cardboard, bathing beauty with beach umbrella, some breaks/overall wear/minor touch-ups, 38x21", G, A 405.00

Coca-Cola, sign, cardboard with beveled edge, woman skier drinking Coke, 2 skiers behind, red disc logo, So Delicious, 20x36", A 165.00

Coca-Cola, sign, die-cut cardboard, hand-painted lady's face with actual scarf, minor edge damage/crazing to face, 21", A.....................................100.00

Coca-Cola, sign, die-cut ribbon with V-cut ends, red lettering on yellow background, Sign Of Good Taste, 45" long, A...70.00

Coca-Cola, sign, drug store, enamel, 2-sided, yellow & green with white on red letters, Art Deco motif on sides, 63x42", EX, A 600.00

Coca-Cola, sign, masonite, red lettering on white background, Drink Coca-Cola, approx: 8x31", VG+, D.**41.00**

Coca-Cola, sign, plastic with metal case, electric, works, Drink Coca-Cola, 34" long, VG, A 75.00

Coca-Cola, sign, stand-up, metal ring quartered by rods frames yellow circle with girl tennis player, lg racket, 3-D ball, early, A 250.00

Coca-Cola, sign, tin, Take A Case Home Today! $1.00 Plus Deposit in white circular inset, Coca-Cola at bottom, NM, A 30.00

Coca-Cola, sign, tin litho, oval, 10", G, A 5,700.00

Coca-Cola, sign, tin litho, red square logo at left, Coke Adds Life To Everything Nice at right, raised border, 18x36", G, A...45.00

Coca-Cola, sign, wood, Navy cruiser against mariner's compass & Coca-Cola symbol, Heavy Cruiser, crack at lower right, 9x25", G+, A 140.00

Coca-Cola, sign, wood with 2 round hangers at top, pictures bottle of Coke & Refreshing at left, Drink Coca-Cola at right, 8x31", A 110.00

Coca-Cola, sign, 1908, cardboard, Victorian woman in red hat drinking Coke, may be cut from larger sign, matted, 8x6", EX, A...................................525.00

Coca-Cola, sign, 1910-1914, embossed tin, C Shonk litho, 19x27", EX, A 1,900.00

Coca-Cola, sign, 1920s, die-cut cardboard, woman with a glass of Coke, trimmed/creased/touched up, 15x10", VG+, D 30.00

Coca-Cola, sign, 1920s-30s, reverse-painted glass, 12" diameter, EX, A 350.00

Coca-Cola, sign, 1923, embossed tin, pictures Coke bottle & logo, long scratch in center, 11x35", A 180.00

Coca-Cola, sign, 1927, 5-color metal, raised border, Drink Coca-Cola, 11x31", D 425.00

Coca-Cola, sign, 1928, cardboard, bathing beauty in robe holding glass of Coke, overall wear/some restoration, 32x22", G-, A 300.00

Coca-Cola, sign, 1930, cardboard stand-up, bathing beauty in cap & cape, restoration/inpainting/overall wear, 18x10", G, A 660.00

Coca-Cola, sign, 1930s, cardboard, hanging, Trink Coca-Cola, Eisekuhlt, German, oval, 8x12", D 85.00

Coca-Cola, sign, 1930s, cardboard, red, white, & yellow, Ice Cold Coca-Cola As Always 5 Cents, framed, 12x18", NM, D..**80.00**

Coca-Cola, sign, 1930s, embossed metal, Dasco 5-color, Drink Coca-Cola, 6x18", D....................................**225.00**

Coca-Cola, sign, 1930s, porcelain, decorative edge at top, Fountain Service, Drink Coca-Cola, Delicious & Refreshing, 45x60", EX, A **450.00**

Coca-Cola, sign, 1930s, porcelain, red, yellow, black, & green, Drink Coca-Cola, edge chips/surface scratches, 10x30", EX, A..**350.00**

Coca-Cola, sign, 1933, embossed metal, December bottle, Ice Cold Coca-Cola Sold Here, 28x19", D.............**600.00**

Coca-Cola, sign, 1936, cardboard, Sundblom litho, framed, 27x18", EX, A......................................225.00

Coca-Cola, sign, 1936, tin, red, white, & green, Drink Coca-Cola, bottle of Coke at left, 12x36", EX+, D**375.00**

Coca-Cola, sign, 1939, cardboard, bathing beauty seated on diving board with a Coke, water stains/creases/paper loss, 50x30", G, A **125.00**

Coca-Cola, sign, 1939, porcelain, red, yellow, white, & green, Drink Coca-Cola, Sold Here Ice Cold, Canadian, 12x19", NM, D **525.00**

Coca-Cola, sign, 1939, porcelain, red, yellow, white, & green, Drink Coca-Cola, Sold Here Ice Cold, Canadian, chips, 12x31", VG, D **175.00**

Coca-Cola, sign, 1940, electric, metal with glass front, Serve Yourself in green on white above Drink Coca-Cola, 10x16", EX, A **550.00**

Coca-Cola, sign, 1941, tin, man & woman sharing a Coke at right, Drink Coca-Cola at left, 29x66", A...........**140.00**

Coca-Cola, sign, 1946, metal, bottle with 16" metal disc on top, 40x16", D **400.00**

Coca-Cola, sign, 1946, porcelain, red, yellow, & white, Coca-Cola, Ice Cold, rounded corners, Canadian, chips, 20x28", EX+, D **135.00**

Coca-Cola, sign, 1948, tin, bottle of Coke with Drink Coca-Cola above, Canadian, 53x17", NM, D **325.00**

Coca-Cola, sign, 1948, tin, red & yellow on white, Drink Ice Cold Coca-Cola In Bottles, minor paint chips, 11x24", EX+, D **75.00**

Coca-Cola, sign, 1949, cardboard, woman in white dress holding bottle of Coke, embossed medallion on frame, 26x41", G, A..**150.00**

Coca-Cola, sign, 1950, cardboard, double-sided with girl on 1 side & party goers on the other, wood frame, 28x20x3", EX, A **175.00**

Coca-Cola, sign, 1950s, cardboard, cheese & red disc, Drink Coca-Cola In Bottles, Cheese Treats, 18x24", D **30.00**

Coca-Cola, sign, 1950s, cardboard, depicts hamburgers, hot dogs, & Cokes, Family Favorites, 18x24", D...........**30.00**

Coca-Cola, sign, 1950s, cardboard, depicts plates, napkins, Cokes..., Drink Coca-Cola In Bottles, Picnic Needs, 18x24", D **30.00**

Coca-Cola, sign, 1950s, cardboard, depicts woman drinking a Coke, So Delicious, 20x36", EX, D....................**220.00**

Coca-Cola, sign, 1950s, cardboard, 3-D with easel-back, lady on work break with a Coke, Be Really Refreshed, 15x18", D **60.00**

Coca-Cola, sign, 1950s, die-cut porcelain, Coke bottle, sm chip, 16", EX+, D..**175.00**

Coca-Cola, sign, 1950s, lighted counter, Pause, Please Pay When Served, D **650.00**

Coca-Cola, sign, 1950s, masonite, Take Home A Case Today, $1.00 Plus Deposit, 14x12", D....................**50.00**

Coca-Cola, sign, 1950s, metal, bottle shape, 16", D...**100.00**

Coca-Cola, sign, 1950s, metal, flanged, red & white, Drink Coca-Cola, Ice Cold, 22x18", NM, D **350.00**

Coca-Cola, sign, 1950s, metal, Fountain Service, Drink Coca-Cola, 12x30", VG, A **150.00**

Coca-Cola, sign, 1950s, metal, green, red, & white, Pick Up 6, For Home Refreshment, 16x50", NM, D **275.00**

Coca-Cola, sign, 1950s, metal, white, yellow, & red, tipped Coke bottle in white circle, Have A Coke above, 54x15", EX+, D **85.00**

Coca-Cola, sign, 1950s, metal, white on red button, Drink Coca-Cola In Bottles, sm chip by edge, 24" diameter, NM, D..**275.00**

Coca-Cola, sign, 1950s, metal, 2-sided, shows early soda fountain dispenser, round corners, rust/discoloration, 24x24", VG, A **175.00**

Coca-Cola, sign, 1950s, tin, pictures girl with bottle, denting/chipping/overall wear, 32x56", G, A **100.00**

Coca-Cola, sign, 1950s, tin, red on white button, Drink Coca-Cola In Bottles, 24" diameter, NM, D **225.00**

Coca-Cola, sign, 1950s, tin, red with white Drink Coca-Cola Ice Cold lettering at left, Coke bottle at right, 20x28", NM, D..**150.00**

Coca-Cola, sign, 1950s, tin, red with white Drink Coca-Cola lettering at left, bottle of Coke at right on white, 11x28", NM, D **135.00**

Coca-Cola, sign, 1950s, tin, white on red button, Drink Coca-Cola, paint flecks, 12" diameter, EX+, D **100.00**

Coca-Cola, sign, 1950s, white, gray, & red aluminum button arrow, Drink Coca-Cola, button: 12" diameter, arrow: 21", NM, D **250.00**

Coca-Cola, sign, 1950s, white & brown aluminum button, depicts hand holding bottle of Coke, 16" diameter, NM, D..**85.00**

Coca-Cola, sign, 1950s, white metal button, depicts hand holding bottle, 16" diameter, D **175.00**

Coca-Cola, sign, 1950s-60s, plastic light-up with metal back frame, Drink Coca-Cola, some edge scratches, 15" diameter, D..**170.00**

Coca-Cola, sign, 1950s-60s, red button with white lettering, Drink Coca-Cola, 54" diameter, EX, A **160.00**

Coca-Cola, sign, 1950s-60s, tin, red button, Coca-Cola superimposed over a bottle of Coke, rust/dents, 25" diameter, G-, A **45.00**

Coca-Cola, sign, 1951, paper, red & yellow on green, depicts basket of food & 6-pack of Coke, Good With Food, 11x24", NM, D..................**65.00**

Coca-Cola, sign, 1953, cardboard, red, white, & yellow, Drink Coca-Cola, Goes Good With Food, 7x22", NM, D **35.00**

Coca-Cola, sign, 1954, cardboard, fits in case, Eddie Fisher On Radio, 12x20", D **75.00**

Coca-Cola, sign, 1954, cardboard, 3-D, depicts Coke bottle & snacks, Stock Up Now, Take Some Home, 33x35", D **100.00**

Coca-Cola, sign, 1955, cardboard, yellow, red, & green, Sprite boy with bottle of Coke, Now! Family Size Too!, 20x36", NM, D **80.00**

Coca-Cola, sign, 1958, cardboard, aluminum frame, 36" long, G+, A..................60.00

Coca-Cola, sign, 1959, metal, depicts red fishtail logo with Coke bottle at right on white background, 12x31", NM, D..................**125.00**

Coca-Cola, sign, 1960s, cardboard, easel-back, depicts girl & boy under mistletoe, Things Go Better With Coke, 16x27", D **20.00**

Coca-Cola, sign, 1960s, die-cut cardboard, bottle cap, white on red, Drink Coca-Cola, sm hole punched on side, 13", NM, D **65.00**

Coca-Cola, sign, 1960s, glass with decal, red fishtail Drink Coca-Cola logo, 21x28", EX, A **120.00**

Coca-Cola, sign, 1960s, metal, fishtail logo & bottle, Coca-Cola, Sign Of Good Taste, 28x11", D..................**125.00**

Coca-Cola, sign, 1960s, metal, red fishtail logo with Ice Cold above & bottle of Coke at right on white background, 20x28", NM, D **150.00**

Coca-Cola, sign, 1960s, metal, 2-sided, Refreshing New Feeling, Drink Coca-Cola, fishtail logo on other side, 11x17", D **125.00**

Coca-Cola, sign, 1960s, tin, bottle in white inset on right, Enjoy Coca-Cola on left in white letters, scratches, 32" long, VG, A..................**45.00**

Coca-Cola, sign, 1960s, tin, paper Coca-Cola cup with logo, Ice Cold, Prepared By The Bottlers Of Coca-Cola, scratches, 28", VG, A **75.00**

Coca-Cola, sign, 1963, tin, self-framed, 53", VG, A........**80.00**

Coca-Cola, sign, 1964, metal, red, green, & white, Things Go Better With Coke at left, Coke bottle at right, 24x24", NM, A **135.00**

Coca-Cola, sign, 1964, metal, round logo at left, Coke bottle in center, Things Go Better With Coke at right, 11x31", NM, A..................**125.00**

Coca-Cola, sign, 1970s, cardboard, Coke, Planters, Van-Camp, Coke Adds Life To The Great American Get Together, 18x24", D **15.00**

Coca-Cola, sign, 1970s, metal, Enjoy Coca-Cola, Coke Adds Life To Everything Nice, 35x17", D **30.00**

Coca-Cola, sign, 1970s, metal, Enjoy Coke, Have A Coke & A Smile, horizontal, 17x35", D..................**30.00**

Coca-Cola, sign, 1970s, metal, Enjoy Coke, Have A Coke & A Smile, vertical, 35x17", D..................**30.00**

Coca-Cola, sign, 1985, red, white, & black, Drink Coca-Cola In Bottles, 4x17", M, D **14.00**

Coca-Cola, sign for building, 1950s-60s, Drink Coca-Cola, 48" diameter, A..................**150.00**

Coca-Cola, sign for drink rack, red, yellow, & white with arrow pointing down, Take Home A Carton 25¢, 18" diameter, G, D **46.00**

Coca-Cola, sign for drink rack, 1940s, metal, white, yellow, & red, Take Home A Carton, rim wear, 12" diameter, EX+, D **95.00**

Coca-Cola, sign for drink rack, 1960s, metal, fishtail logo, Coca-Cola, Sign Of Good Taste, Big King Size, 17x10", D..................**75.00**

Coca-Cola, sign for pole-type drink rack, 1940s, red, white, & yellow, Enjoy A Coca-Cola, Take Home A Carton 36¢, 16x12", G-, D **19.00**

Coca-Cola, siren whistle, 1930s, tall thimble shape, D ..**50.00**

Coca-Cola, siren whistle, 1940s, wood, red & yellow, Drink Coca-Cola, 2x1", NM, D **25.00**

Coca-Cola, snack bowl, 1930s, ceramic, green, D.....**450.00**

Coca-Cola, straw box & straws, 1940s, cardboard, red & green, depicts a Bottle of Coke with a straw, 10x4", EX, D..................**40.00**

Coca-Cola, syrup bottle, applied label with red lettering on white background, missing cap, 12", F, A **45.00**

Coca-Cola, syrup can, white background with red logoed disc, A **125.00**

Coca-Cola, syrup can, 1930s, EX, A 100.00

Coca-Cola, syrup jug, 1960s, glass, green, red, & white, label slightly worn on edges, 1-gal, EX+, D **15.00**

Coca-Cola, tally card, 1940s, tray of Cokes & red disc on tally side, birds on back, Richmond Coca-Cola Bottling Works, D...**35.00**

Coca-Cola, thermometer, 1930s, die-cut tin bottle with white lettering, good color, rust spots on white areas, 17", EX, A...**100.00**

Coca-Cola, thermometer, 1936, tin, red with gold Christmas bottle, 16x7", D.....................................**175.00**

Coca-Cola, thermometer, 1941, tin, 16x7", NM, A .160.00

Coca-Cola, thermometer, 1944, masonite, green, yellow, red, & brown, depicts a bottle of Coke, Thirst Knows No Season, 17x7", NM, D **275.00**

Coca-Cola, thermometer, 1950s, die-cut metal, brown bottle with white lettering, good color, 17", NM, D **75.00**

Coca-Cola, thermometer, 1950s, metal, white on red, Sign Of Good Taste, good shine, no bulb, rounded oblong: 30x8", EX+, D **85.00**

Coca-Cola, thermometer, 1950s, metal & glass, round dial type, white on red ground, Drink Coca-Cola, 12" diameter, NM, A...**110.00**

Coca-Cola, thermometer, 1956, in the form of a gold bottle, in original box, 9x2", M, D **45.00**

Coca-Cola, thermometer, 1959, bottle shape, 29", D ..**100.00**

Coca-Cola, thermometer, 1960s, plastic, red & white with red down sides, Coca-Cola, 17x6", D.....................**50.00**

Coca-Cola, thimble, 1920s, aluminum, Drink Coca-Cola on red band, EX, D...**25.00**

Coca-Cola, tip tray, 1905, pictures girl with glass, Delicious, Refreshing, minor staining/overall wear, 4" diameter, VG, A **200.00**

Coca-Cola, tip tray, 1907, decorative border, dents/wear, oval, 6x4", G, A **400.00**

Coca-Cola, tip tray, 1910, pictures girl in wide-brimmed hat, decorative border, oval, 6x4", EX, A **275.00**

Coca-Cola, tip tray, 1912, pictures girl holding glass, fading/scratching/sm rust spot, oval, 6x4", G-, A........**80.00**

Coca-Cola, tip tray, 1913, pictures girl in wide-brimmed hat holding a glass, oval, 6x4", VG+, A.....................**200.00**

Coca-Cola, tip tray, 1914, depicts Betty in bonnet, some scratching/fading, oval, 6x4", G, A....................**175.00**

Coca-Cola, toy dispenser, Item No 16, Toy Coke Dispenser & Four Miniature Glasses printed on side of original box, EX, A...**35.00**

Coca-Cola, toy top, 1970s, plastic, Coke Adds Life To...Fun Times, D...**3.00**

Coca-Cola, toy truck, 1940s, Canadian, Lincoln-type, 8 original wood cases, decals, rust marks on grill, 16" long, EX, D...**550.00**

Coca-Cola, toy truck, 1940s, Japan, friction-type, tin with decals, scarce, 4", VG, D.....................................**90.00**

Coca-Cola, toy truck, 1940s, Marx, yellow with decals, 20" long, EX, A **300.00**

Coca-Cola, toy truck, 1940s vintage, red with 12 wood block cases of Coca-Cola (a rare feature), paint loss, 5x16x5", G+, A 450.00

Coca-Cola, toy truck, 1960, Matchbox, yellow, regular cases, very minor scratches, EX, D.........................**37.00**

Coca-Cola, toy truck, 1960s, Buddy L logo on door, tin, yellow, some scratches/rust, VG, A **180.00**

Coca-Cola, tray, 1903, Hilda Clark holding fan & glass, overall fading/spotting/minor color loss, 10" diameter, G-, A..**300.00**

Coca-Cola, tray, 1904, depicts Lillian Nordica with a glass, overall dirt/minor scuffing/chipping, rare, oval, 13x11", EX, A......................................2,350.00

Coca-Cola, tray, 1909, girl holding glass with festive scene in background, cocoa beans on border, minor wear, oval, 13x11", VG+, A...**800.00**

Coca-Cola, tray, 1913, pictures young girl with glass of Coke, Delicious & Refreshing, overall fading, oval, 16x13", A **210.00**

Coca-Cola, tray, 1914, depicts Betty in a bonnet, color fading/scratches, 13x11", G-, A.............................**60.00**

Coca-Cola, tray, 1914, depicts Betty in a bonnet, Passaic Metal Ware Co, 13x11", EX+, A.............................**300.00**

Coca-Cola, tray, 1916, Elaine seated on a box holding glass of Coke, 19x9", EX, A **230.00**

Coca-Cola, tray, 1916, Elaine seated on a box holding glass of Coke, 19x9", G-, D.......................................**160.00**

Coca-Cola, tray, 1922, Summer Girl holding glass of Coke, HD Beach Co litho, 13x11", NM, A **500.00**

Coca-Cola, tray, 1924, girl standing sideways looking to the front holding a Coke, hole in rim/overall wear, 13x11", G-, A **85.00**

Coca-Cola, tray, 1925, girl in fox stole & hat in profile holding glass of Coke, 13x11", VG, A **175.00**

Coca-Cola, tray, 1926, minor background scuffing/chips, 13x11", EX, A.........................325.00

Coca-Cola, tray, 1927, couple given curb service, rust spotting/rim chips, 11x13", G+, A **120.00**

Coca-Cola, tray, 1927, pictures soda fountain clerk with 3 glasses, slight rust spotting to image/rim, 13x11", VG+, A..**200.00**

Coca-Cola, tray, 1929, pictures seated girl in yellow bathing suit, surface scratches/rim chips, 13x11", EX, D **235.00**

Coca-Cola, tray, 1930, bathing beauty in red cap with Coke bottle, minor image/rim chips, 13x11", EX, A **170.00**

Coca-Cola, tray, 1930, telephone girl, Meet Me At The Soda Fountain, minor rim wear, 13x11", A....................**200.00**

Coca-Cola, tray, 1930s, woman with her jacket partially on, rim chips, 13x11", NM, D.......................................**265.00**

Coca-Cola, tray, 1931, seated boy & dog, rim chips/ scratches, 13x11", EX+, D **400.00**

Coca-Cola, tray, 1932, seated girl drinking a Coke, 2 scratches in suit, 13x11", NM, D **425.00**

Coca-Cola, tray, 1933, Frances Dee in bathing suit sitting on a ledge holding a Coke, 13x11", G, A **150.00**

Coca-Cola, tray, 1934, Maureen O'Sullivan & Johnny Weissmuller seated back to back, 11x13", M, A.................**1,250.00**

Coca-Cola, tray, 1935, Madge Evans standing by armchair holding a glass of Coke, minor discoloration, 13x11", EX+, A...**170.00**

Coca-Cola, tray, 1937, bathing beauty in cape running on beach holding a bottle of Coke in each hand, 13x11", M, A **160.00**

Coca-Cola, tray, 1937, bathing beauty in cape running on beach holding bottle of Coke in each hand, overall wear, 13x11", VG, A...**70.00**

Coca-Cola, tray, 1938, colorful image of a woman sitting pretty, surface scratches/rust, 13x11", VG, D **65.00**

Coca-Cola, tray, 1938, French, colorful image of a woman sitting pretty, minor rim chips, 13x11", NM, D.....**130.00**

Coca-Cola, tray, 1939, girl sitting on diving board holding bottle of Coke, edge wear/chipping to image, 13x11", VG, A **170.00**

Coca-Cola, tray, 1940, colorful image of a woman enjoying a Coke while fishing, some fading/surface marks, 11x13", EX, D...**85.00**

Coca-Cola, tray, 1941, ice skater seated on a log with a Coke, surface rubs/minor chips, 13x11", EX+, A .**115.00**

Coca-Cola, tray, 1942, NM, A.................................210.00

Coca-Cola, tray, 1948, smiling blonde lifting bottle to her mouth, minor wear/rust, 13x11", NM, A..............**100.00**

Coca-Cola, tray, 1950s, girl in hat rests chin on her left hand & holds Coke bottle in right, 13x11", M, A ..**70.00**

Coca-Cola, trolley sign, Santa Claus with a Coke & children unwrapping presents, fold marks, A....................**140.00**

Coca-Cola, trolley sign, framed, EX, A 700.00

Coca-Cola, trolley sign, girl holding 5¢ glass on green background, Drink Coca-Cola, Delicious & Refreshing, 11x21", NM, A **1,800.00**

Coca-Cola, wallet, 1920s, leather, brown, inside says Drink Coca-Cola, Delicious & Refreshing, 9x4", NM, D ..**50.00**

Coca-Cola, wallet, 1960s, pigskin, light tan with gold embossed image of bottle & logo, NM, A...............**18.00**

Coca-Cola, watch fob, 1905, embossed brass, girl with product, Drink Coca-Cola in Bottle, 5¢, mfg by Schwabb, Milwaukee, VG, A **250.00**

Coca-Cola, whistle, 1950s, plastic, Merry Christmas, Coca-Cola Bottling, Memphis Tenn, D............................**13.00**

Coca-Cola, writing tablet, 1930s, Pure As Sunlight, D .**12.00**

Coca-Cola, writing tablet, 1940s, silhouette girl, sports around disc, D **6.00**

Coca-Cola, writing tablet, 1960s, depicts Flags Of The Nations, D **2.00**

Coca-Cola, writing tablet, 1970s, depicts Wildlife Of The United Nations, D **2.00**

Coca-Cola, Yo-Yo, 1960, red & white plastic, modeled as a bottle cap, D **10.00**

Cocoa Wheats, doll, 1949, Gretchen, rare, EX, D........**35.00**

Coffee Exhibit, tin, key-wind lid, 1-lb, D **45.00**

Coiner Cigars, box label, outer, pictures eagle perched on top of earth, 5x5", M, D **8.00**

Col-Tex, pump sign, porcelain, D **95.00**

Colchester Tennis Shoes, sign, paper, rare, framed, 28x11", G+, A **5,500.00**

Colgan's Taffy Tolu Chewing Gum, store container, glass jar, embossed letters with whimsical clown figural lid, ca 1910-20, 11x5x5", NM, A.............................**175.00**

Colgan's Taffy Tolu Chewing Gum, vendor, glass & metal with original marquee & side glass decal, 2 Sticks Every 5th Penny..., some wear, 15x6x8", G+, A..........**2,600.00**

Colgate, sample cosmetic box, with various Colgate & Cashmere Bouquet toiletries, Colgate's Week-End Package, 1920s, EX, D **80.00**

Colgate's Baby Talc, tin, product name above baby in oval, ca 1910, shaker top, NM, A........................**85.00**

Colgate's Cashmere Bouquet Toilet Soap, magazine ad, little girl washing her hands with Colgate, advertising below, Maxfield Parrish drawing, 15x10", A **20.00**

Colgate's Talc Powder, sign, cardboard, blue lettering on pale blue & white striped background, Soothing, Cooling, Sanative, 11x61", A **25.00**

College Flags Cigars, box label, inner lid, depicts 12 different school flags, 6x9", M, D...........................**35.00**

College Ribbon Cigars, box label, inner lid, ornate non-pictorial on green background, 6x9", D, M **3.00**

Collins & Co Axes, sign, ca 1910, 21x11", EX, A........**65.00**

Collins & Co Liquor Dealers, match safe, silverplated, embossed flowers at edges, Christmas 1904, minor dents/stress mark at spring, A **30.00**

Colman's Mustard, sign, mirror, depicts man's portrait in center with 2 boxes of product, lettering above & below, vertical rectangle, A **50.00**

Colonial Club Cigars, sign, cardboard, woman in wide-brimmed hat, 5¢ Cigar, appears trimmed top & bottom, 22x17" without frame, EX, A **190.00**

Colonial Club Cigars, sign, metal, double-sided, 5¢, horizontal rectangle, EX, A..**30.00**

Colonial Orator Cigars, box label, inner lid, depicts portrait of Patrick Henry, 1900, 6x9", M, D **12.00**

Columbia Batteries, display, tin & wood litho, oversize battery, 25", EX, A **1,000.00**

Columbia Batteries, sign, double-sided & flanged, devil shielding his face from Columbia dry cell battery, 1910-15, 14x18", EX+, A **800.00**

Columbia Batteries, sign, tin, red & black on white with 2 different dry cell batteries, Electrical Supplies, FA Carter..., 12x35", NM, A...................................**75.00**

Columbia Bikes, sign, paper roll-down, colorful image of woman on 3-wheeled bicycle, creasing, rare, 28x13", VG, A **1,700.00**

Columbia Brewing Co, tray, colorful patriotic image, Tacoma Wash, 10" diameter, EX+, A **550.00**

Columbia Export Beer, tray, colorful image of the Henry Weinhard City Brewery of Portland Oregon, oval, 14x16", EX, A **500.00**

Columbia Export Beer, tray, colorful image of the Henry Weinhard City Brewery of Portland Oregon, Columbia Export on rim, oval, 14x16", G-, A **350.00**

Columbia Grafonola, sign, tin, couple with Non-Set Automatic Stop Modern Phonograph, Don't Get Up, It Stops Itself, 18x24", EX, A................................**275.00**

Columbia Mill Co, match holder, embossed die-cut tin figural of patriotic woman & product, rare, 6x2", EX, A...**650.00**

Columbia Records, thermometer, tin, 78 rpm record at top, Columbia Records On Sale Here, music note & microphone at bottom, 61", G, A **500.00**

Columbian Beer, sign, embossed tin with hanging chain, labeled bottle flanked with logo, Tennessee Brewing Co, 14x10", EX+, A.................................**300.00**

Columbian Fruit Tuxedo Pepsin, display case, wood frame with glass sides & rounded glass front with lettering, EX, A...**750.00**

Columbian Rope Co, thermometer, litho face with brass holder, 8" diameter, A...**20.00**

Columbus Brewing Co, tip tray, Christopher Columbus in center, Select Pale Beer, minor rim wear/chips, 4" diameter, NM, A **100.00**

DISTRIBUTING SHIP CARGO OF STANDARD BUGGIES COAST OF AUSTRALIA

Columbus Buggy Co, poster, paper, matted & framed, 24x34", NM, A 6,750.00

Comet, crate label, California lemon, comet zooming over orchard with 3 lg lemons, Central Lemon Ass'n, 1930, 9x13", M, D **40.00**

Comet Cut Plug Tobacco, lunch box, tin, paper label with stars & comet motif, slip lid with latch & bail, overcoat/overall wear, 5x8x5", G-, A **225.00**

Comfort Powder, tin, pictures a baby, press lid, lg cylinder, EX, A 275.00

Comfort Powder, tin, pictures a baby, press lid, sm cylinder, G, A **80.00**

Commodore Cigars, sign, paper, gentleman in fez smoking a cigar with dog at his feet, Forbes Co litho, framed, vertical rectangle, G, A.............................**200.00**

Comrad Coffee, tin, slip lid, 1-lb, VG+, D **65.00**

Conant Co Pumps, calendar sign, paper, display of company's product with lady in oval inset, full pad, soiled/creases, 47x17", VG, A **100.00**

Condor Coffee, tin, image of condor & palm trees, slip lid, Montreal, Toronto, overall wear, rare, 7x4" diameter, G, A **350.00**

Conestoga, crate label, vegetable, depicts oxen-drawn wagon, Western Vegetables, Watsonville Calif, 1940s, 9x6", M, D **3.00**

Congo, tray, Serve Cold Congo, Haberle-Crystal Bottling Dept, Syracuse NY, minor scuffs/chips, 12" diameter, EX, A **40.00**

Congress Beer, match holder, tin, pictures open case of Congress Beer with logo atop, Haberle Brewing Co, Syracuse NY, 5x5x3", G-, A **170.00**

Congress Beer, match holder, tin, pictures open case of Congress Beer with logo atop, Haberle Brewing Co, Syracuse NY, 5x5x3", NM, A................................**425.00**

Congress Beer, menu board, tin, lists several kitchen items, overall dirt/scrapes, 12x6", EX, A...............**150.00**

Congress Beer, sign, embossed brass & reverse painting on glass, eagle logo on black background, Haberle Brewing Co, 15x20", NM, A **450.00**

Congress Beer, sign, porcelain, white lettering on blue background, Haberle Brewing Co, Syracuse NY, overall wear, 14x20", G, A **175.00**

Congress Beer, sign, Vitrolite, colorful eagle logo, Haberle Brewing Co, Syracuse NY, matted & framed, 25x18", NM, A.................................**1,000.00**

Congress Beer, tray, brass rim, porcelain center, eagle logo, People's Choice, Old Reliable, Haberle Brewing Co, 12" diameter, NM, A **325.00**

Congress Beer, tray, brass rim, porcelain center, eagle logo, People's Favorite, Old Reliable, Haberle Brewing Co, 15" diameter, M, A..**575.00**

Congress Beer, tray, capitol building on light blue background, Haberle Brewing Co, Syracuse NY, ca 1935, 13" diameter, NM, A 100.00

Congress Beer, tray, Congress on the diagonal, eagle logo above, letters restored, oval, 8x11", G, A..............**40.00**

Congress Beer, tray, deep-dish, capitol building on navy blue background, lettering on rim, ca 1940, 12" diameter, NM, A..**55.00**

Congress Beer, tray, nickel-plated, capitol building logo, 7x10", VG, A..**25.00**

Congress Beer, tray, nickel-plated, embossed rim, eagle logo, Congress Beer above, Haberle Brewing Co below, oval, 12x16", VG, A............................**30.00**

Congress Beer, tray, nickel-plated, embossed rim, eagle logo, Congress Beer above, Haberle Brewing Co below, 12" diameter, EX, A....................**25.00**

Congress Beer, tray, logoed center on wood grain, 11x13", EX, A **65.00**

Congress Beer, tray, logoed center on wood grain, 12" diameter, NM, A..**45.00**

Congress Beer, tray, 12" diameter, NM, A..................**35.00**

Congress Beer/Derby Cream Ale, tray, deep-dish, Congress Beer on gold ground divided by Derby Cream Ale on red ground, 12" diameter, NM, A ...**30.00**

Congress Beer/Derby Cream Ale, tray, lettering on wood-grained background, Haberle-Congress Brewing Co Inc, 13" diameter, NM, A............................**20.00**

Congress Beer/Derby Cream Ale/Black Bass Ale, tray, deep-dish, lettering on red-gold-red banded background, 12" diameter, M, A............................**25.00**

Congress Perfectos, box label, inner lid, depicts view of Capitol, bill, & seal, 1896, 6x9", VG, D..................**24.00**

Congress X-tra Fine Beer, sign, self-standing tin, pictures glass & labeled bottle, Haberle-Congress Brewing Co, Syracuse NY, ca 1930, 5x14", G, A........................**55.00**

Congress Yeast Powder, cookbook, paperback, 'Congress Yeast Powder Cookbook,' 80 pages, 1899, D..........**8.00**

Connecticut Mutual Life Insurance Co, sign, tin, Victorian building in round insert, Hartford, Organized 1846, ca 1882, 24x18" without frame, EX, A..................**650.00**

Conoco Gasoline, sign, porcelain, depicts Colonial sentry with gun & Ethyl logo in center, ca 1926-29, 25" diameter, NM, A **2,300.00**

Conoco Motor Oil, tin, minuteman with rifle on cream background, Continental Oil Co, screw lid & handle, ca 1915-25, 1-gal, 11", VG+, A..................**700.00**

Conrad Pfeiffer Beer, tray, depicts 3 monks working, decorative border, some pitting, round, EX, A............**25.00**

Consolidated Ice Co, hand mirror, round with embossed handle, backside shows arctic scene with lettering above, ca 1910, 9", EX+, A..................**65.00**

Consolidated Ice Co, hand mirror, scene of polar bear & Eskimo, D **150.00**

Consumer's Brewing Co, tip tray, factory scene in center, Columbia Special Dark Triple X, 4" diameter, NM, A..**250.00**

Consumer's Brewing Co, tray, portrait & lettering in center, Consumer's Beer, Ask Father, Hillsgrove, Warwick..., 14" diameter, EX, A **45.00**

Consumers Best Peanut Butter, pail, tin, depicts fairies beside a peanut, Packed For Consumers Wholesale Grocers, original lid & bail, 14-oz, NM, A.........**5,000.00**

Continental Cubes Pipe Tobacco, pocket mirror, beautiful lady in long dress, gloves & feathered hat by package of product, oval, M, A....................**375.00**

Continental Cubes Pipe Tobacco, pocket mirror, pictures woman atop canister of pipe tobacco, Latest & Best Process, minor wear, oval, 3x2", EX, A..................**250.00**

Continental Fire Insurance Co, sign, shows Indians & buffalo flanked by company's buildings, New York, J Ottmann litho, framed, water stains, 34x69", A....**750.00**

Continental Fire Insurance Co, sign, tin, minor scratches to image, self-framed, 30x20", G+, A 1,250.00

Converse Footwear, catalog, 1955, EX, D..................**25.00**

Cook Brewing Co, see FW Cook Brewing Co

Coon Skin Cigars, box label, outer, Coon Skin printed on coon skin at left with woman peering out window, 5x5", M, D..**250.00**

Coors Beer, bank, aluminum can figural, M, D............**5.00**

Coreco Motor Oil, container, glass jar with embossed lettering & yellow label with lettering, metal screw lid, 1940s, 6x4" diameter, NM, A..................**25.00**

Coreco Motor Oil, tin, blue & white letters on golden yellow, round logo in center, screw lid & handle, 5-gal, 17x15" diameter, VG, A **120.00**

Conoco Harvester Oil, tin, screw lid & handle, ca 1915-25, minor dents, half-gal, 7", VG+, A 650.00

Cork Distilleries Co Ltd, sign, tin, framed, 13x17",
A 50.00

Corliss-Coon Better Collars, display case, oak with glass
front depicting 4 white collars, 23x9", EX, A........**300.00**

Corner Stone Coffee, tin, logoed paper label, Java, slip
lid, paper loss primarily to edge/stains/discoloration, 1-
lb, 6x4", G-, A 20.00

Corona Crown, crate label, California orange, depicts
crown on blue background, Orange Heights Orange
Ass'n, 1930s, 10x12", M, D 3.00

Cortez Cigarettes, sign, die-cut cardboard, For Men Of
Brains, 12x17", G, A 225.00

Corticelli Spool Silk, cabinet, walnut, 7 drawers,
17x22x16", A...160.00

Corticelli Spool Thread, cabinet, walnut, 5 drawers with
glass fronts, raised side panels with gold lettering, 1
missing glass, 13x21x16", EX, A 275.00

Cortwright Rye, back bar bottle, with sterling bottle tag
lettered Mountain, no cap, D.................................35.00

Corylopsis of Japan Talcum Powder, tin, embossed, pictures Oriental girl serving tea, shaker top, made by
Riker Hegeman, 9", EX, A 65.00

Cotes Bakery, marble, D..**250.00**

Cott Soda, sign, tin, ca 1950s, EX, A 50.00

Cottage Peanut Butter, tin, yellow, blue, red, & white, Mfg
by AO MC Coll & Co, Vancouver Canada, paint
flakes/scratches, D 45.00

Cottolene Shortening, cookbook, '52 Sunday Dinners,'
192 pages, 1915, D 8.00

Cottolene Shortening, leaflet, 'Cottolene Recipes,' 1905,
D...**15.00**

Couch & Four Tobacco, pocket tin, NM, D.............**350.00**

Counsellor Cigars, display, cardboard, free-standing tri-
fold, A **110.00**

Countess Cookies, tin, pictures children at play, Bond
Bakers, slip lid, rare, 1-lb, M, A **80.00**

Country Club Cigars, tin, picturing people at various
sports, slip lid, chips/spots/discoloration to lid, 6x4"
diameter, G, A..**250.00**

Country Club Cigars, tins, pictures people at various
sports in club setting, 5¢, minor chipping/slight edge
wear, 6x5" square, EX, A **300.00**

Country Club Coffee, tin, pictures clubhouse, slip lid, colors bright & shiny, some denting/scratching/chipping,
1-lb, 6x4", G+, A **80.00**

Country Gentleman Pipe & Cigarette Tobacco, package,
cloth sack, sealed, paper has some rips/creases, D ..**6.00**

Country Kitchen Restaurants, doll, cloth, Country Boy,
1975, 24", EX, D **15.00**

Court House Mixture Tobacco, tin, shows Pittsburgh
courthouse on lid with decorative border, curved corners, paint loss/chips/crazing, 2x6x4", G-, A **100.00**

Cousin Kate Cigars, box label, outer, depicts young
woman, 5x5", VG, D **9.00**

Covered Wagon Cigars, box label, inner lid, colorful
image of cowboys & wagon train, M, D **20.00**

Covered Wagon Cigars, box label, outer, colorful image
of cowboys & wagon train, 5x5", M, D..................**4.00**

Cox's Gelatine, cookbook, 1914, paperback, 'Cox's Manual
Of Gelatine Cookery,' 64 pages, D.........................**8.00**

Cox's Gelatine, leaflet, 1933, 'Cox's Delicious Recipes,' 30
pages, D **4.00**

Cox's Gelatine, sign, cardboard, Brownies carrying
gelatin mold to children, checkered border, ca
1920, A **180.00**

Cracker Jack, canister, tin, Cracker Jack candy corn crisp,
10-oz, EX, D...**75.00**

Cracker Jack, canister, tin, Cracker Jack coconut corn
crisp, 10-oz, EX, D...**65.00**

Cracker Jack, dealer incentive, cart, 2 movable wheels,
wood dowel tongue, Cracker Jack, EX, D.............**33.00**

Cracker Jack, dealer incentive, halloween mask, paper,
Cracker Jack, 10" or 12", EX, D **15.00**

Cracker Jack, dealer incentive, jigsaw puzzle, Cracker Jack or Checkers, 1 of 4 in envelope, 7x10", EX, D **35.00**

Cracker Jack, dealer incentive, match holder, hinged, engraved gold-tone case, Cracker Jack, 3x2", EX, D **650.00**

Cracker Jack, dealer incentive, pencil top clip, metal & celluloid, oval boy & dog logo, EX, D......**125.00**

Cracker Jack, dealer incentive, 1907, post card, pictures a bear, 1 of 16, EX, D......**22.00**

Cracker Jack, display, 1923, popcorn box, Cracker Jack, no contents, EX, D **65.00**

Cracker Jack, doll, 1974, sailor (official doll by Vogue), 15", EX, D......**35.00**

Cracker Jack, popcorn box, 1920s, red scroll border, Cracker Jack, EX, D......**85.00**

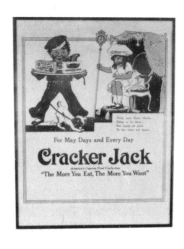

Cracker Jack, poster, framed, 21x17", A......**200.00**

Cracker Jack, premium, baseball & bat, wood, Hillerich & Bradsby, full-size, EX, D **125.00**

Cracker Jack, premium, book, jester on cover, pocket-size, EX, D......**42.00**

Cracker Jack, premium, book of riddles, sailor boy & dog on cover, pocket-size, EX, D **35.00**

Cracker Jack, prize, baseball score counter, 4" long, EX, D......**85.00**

Cracker Jack, prize, die-cut tin boy & dog complete with bend-over tab, EX, D **110.00**

Cracker Jack, prize, fold-out hat, paper, More You Eat, More You Want, early, EX, D **70.00**

Cracker Jack, prize, horse & wagon, die-cut tin litho, Cracker Jack & Angelus, 2", EX, D......**41.00**

Cracker Jack, prize, pistol, soft lead, inked, Cracker Jack on barrel, early, rare, 2", EX, D **180.00**

Cracker Jack, prize, rocking horse, cast metal, no rider, 3-D, inked, early, 1", EX, D......**9.00**

Cracker Jack, prize, 1914-23, horse & wagon, die-cut tin litho, gray with red, Cracker Jack, 3", EX, D **250.00**

Cracker Jack, prize, 1920s, miniature book, drawing with tracing paper, EX, D **110.00**

Cracker Jack, prize, 1928, button, cast metal stud back, crossed bat & ball, EX, D......**78.00**

Cracker Jack, prize, 1928, miniature book, 'Birds We Know,' EX, D **45.00**

Cracker Jack, prize, 1930, miniature book, 'Twigg & Sprigg,' EX, D **75.00**

Cracker Jack, prize, 1931, badge, cast metal 6-point star, silver, Cracker Jack Police, 1", EX, D **35.00**

Cracker Jack, prize, 1931, badge, silver, metal shield, Jr Detective, 1", D......**35.00**

Cracker Jack, prize, 1931, sled, tin-plated, 2" long, EX, D......**20.00**

Cracker Jack, prize, 1933, disguise glasses, paper, hinged, with eyeballs, EX, D......**6.00**

Cracker Jack, prize, 1933, disguise glasses, paper, hinged with cellophane lenses, extremely rare, EX, D......**65.00**

Cracker Jack, prize, 1933, top, golf game, paper with wooden stick in center, EX, D......**35.00**

Cracker Jack, prize, 1936-46, comic character, tin, oval stand-up, 1 of 10, EX, D **65.00**

Cracker Jack, prize, 1937, miniature book, 'Bess & Bill on Cracker Jack Hill,' 1 in series of 12, EX, D **75.00**

Cracker Jack, prize, 1939, iron-on transfer, patriotic figure, EX, D......**32.00**

Cracker Jack, prize, 1939, iron-on transfer, sports figure, EX, D......**32.00**

Cracker Jack, prize, 1939, movie, Goofy Zoo, turn the wheels & it changes animals, EX, D **12.00**

Cracker Jack, prize, 1946, magic game book, erasable slate, series of 13, EX, D **27.00**

Cracker Jack, prize, 1947-49, decal, cartoon or nursery rhyme figure, EX, D **26.00**

Cracker Jack, prize, 1948, spinner, plastic, various colors, 10 designs, EX, D **2.00**

Cracker Jack, prize, 1949, clicker, aluminum pear shape, 'Noisy Cracker Jack Snapper,' EX, D......**25.00**

Cracker Jack, prize, 1950-53, whistle, plastic tube with animals on top, 1 of 6, 1", EX, D......**9.00**

Cracker Jack, prize, 1954, disc, embossed plastic, comic character, 1 in series of 12, EX, D **12.00**

Cracker Jack, prize, 1956, disc, embossed plastic fish plaque, EX, D **9.00**

Cracker Jack, prize, 1961, magnifying glass, plastic, many designs & shapes, EX, D **1.00**

Cracker Jack, prize, 1964, pinball game, plastic, lever shoots balls, score in holes, EX, D **2.00**

Cracker Jack, prize, 1965, booklet of stickers, wisecracks, & riddles, Borden, EX, D **1.00**

Cracker Jack, prize, 1966, palm puzzle, balls roll into holes, plastic dome, EX, D......**1.00**

Cracker Jack, prize, 1967, sand picture, paper, sand pours for action, series of 14, EX, D **9.00**

Cracker Jack, shipping crate, wood, Cracker Jack, early, lg, EX, D **150.00**

Crawford's Cherry-Fizz, dispenser, white porcelain potbelly with white porcelain knob on pump, appears EX, A......**2,800.00**

Cream City Sash & Door Co, calendar, 1919, cardboard, Santa's elves riding wagon with shutters & doors past the factory, full pad, 16x12", EX, A......**500.00**

Cream of Milk Talcum, tin, pictures baby on swan, Toilet & Nursery, rare, EX, A......**80.00**

Cream of Wheat, cereal bowl, yellow ceramic, depicts early locomotive marked 20th Century with Cream of Wheat Chef above, crazing, EX, D......**145.00**

Cream of Wheat, doll, cloth, Rastus, 1922, 16", G, D .**200.00**

Cream of Wheat, note reminder, leather, VG, D **25.00**

Cream Supreme Ice Cream, tray, pictures woman eating dish of ice cream, Lake Shore Ice Cream Co, round, appears EX, A **240.00**

Creator's Pop Corn, box, cardboard, girl enjoying box of popcorn on orange & blue, 1929, 7x5x2", D **12.00**

Cremo Cigars, trunk, metal over wood, has directions in 5 languages, 2 side vents, early, rare, 16x19x29", appears EX, A **160.00**

Crescent Flour, push plate, embossed tin, pictures sack of flour, ca 1930, 10x4", M, A.................................**110.00**

Crescent Tool Co, sign, wood litho, 9 wrenches flanked by logos, lettering above & below, A Size For Every Purpose, framed, 26x25", EX, A **140.00**

Creysyl Gas, sign, porcelain pump, D **175.00**

Crisco, booklet, 1925, '199 Selected Recipes' by Sarah Field Splint, 64 pages, VG, D.................................**14.00**

Crisco, booklet, 1934, '24 Pies Men Like,' 28 pages, 3x5", G, D **7.00**

Crisco, booklet, 1967, 'Better Baking,' 16 pages, 9x11", G, D.................................**5.00**

Crispo Graham Dainties, container, royal blue & white stripes, hinged lid, square, VG, D **28.00**

Crispy Sodas, container, red & white stripes, hinged lid, square, VG, D.................................**18.00**

Crompton Velveteen, ad, pictures bust-length portrait of woman in lg decorative hat, matted & framed, vertical rectangle, A **15.00**

Crosman Bros Seeds, sign, paper, smiling farmer with pipe standing next to big cabbage, New Crop, Rochester NY, image: 24x17", EX, A.................**325.00**

Cross Counry Motor Oil, tin, orange with lettered blue banner superimposed on US map, ...Sears Roebuck Co, 1915-25, 5-gal, 15x9", VG, A **35.00**

Cross-Cut Cigarettes, box, cardboard, image of men sawing, 8 photo cards of females inside, slip lid, tears/stains/creases, 3x2x1", EX, A **75.00**

Cross-Cut Cigarettes, folding chair, wood, 2 women on paper labels on front & back of chair, label discoloration/chips, 33x17x20", G-, A **125.00**

Crow-Mo Smoker's Tobacco, lunch box, shows crowing rooster on brown box, slip lid, wire handle, slight chips/scratches/dents, 4x7x5", G, A.................**250.00**

Crown Beer, see Bartels Crown Beer

Crown Beverage, menu board, cardboard with logo at top & menu below, vertical rectangle, EX, A.................**30.00**

Crown Derby Tea, store bin, tin, stenciled letters, Fancy Orange Pekoe Black Tea, overall wear, 20x15x15", G-, A **60.00**

Crown Diamond Paints, sign, porcelain flange, red, black, yellow, & gray on white, crown logo bordered by lettering, 16" diameter, EX+, D **125.00**

Crown Gasoline, globe, 1-piece crown figural, traces of original red decoration, 16", EX, A 185.00

Crown Quality Ice Cream, sign, die-cut tin ice cream freezer, Anderson & Patterson Mfgrs, EX, A..**155.00**

Cruiser Motor Oil, tin, cruise ship scene on white overlaying a black diamond, yellow & black lettering, 1935-45, 1-qt, 4" diameter, EX, A **140.00**

Crush, sign, embossed tin, Ask For A Crush Carbonated Beverage, Flavor Sealed In The Brown Bottle, 19x27", VG, A.................................**45.00**

Crush, sign, tin, yellow, white, blue on orange, Ask For A Crush, Natural Flavor! Natural Color!, 4x26", appears EX, D **65.00**

Crystal Spring Brewing Co, match striker, stoneware, 5x7", EX, A.................................**325.00**

Crystal Spring Brewing Co, sign, paper, elf riding on barrel of Bock Beer pulled by a ram, Louis Porr litho, matted & framed, 33x24", VG, A **500.00**

Crystal Spring Brewing Co, tray, pictures 2 girls holding a jug, C Shonk litho, overall scratches/chips, 12" diameter, EX, A.................................**200.00**

Crystal Spring Brewing Co, tray, porcelain center, brass rim, no graphics, 12" diameter, VG, A **50.00**

Crystal Spring Brewing Co, tray, porcelain center, brass rim, rare, 15" diameter, NM, A.................**550.00**

Crystal Spring Brewing Co, tray, porcelain center with brass rim, Superior Stock Lager, Syracuse NY, 12" diameter, NM, A **300.00**

CS Oswald General Merchandise, sign, cardboard litho with canvas-like finish, framed, 15x20", VG+, A..**300.00**

Cuban Cousin Cigars, box label, inner lid, depicts woman holding Cuban flag, 6x9", M, D.................**35.00**

Cudahy's Diamond C Ham, Bacon, & Lard, sign, embossed tin, pictures woman slicing ham, Kaufmann & Strauss litho, ca late 1800s, heavy restoration, framed, 32x26", A.................................**650.00**

Culture Tobacco, pocket tin, G, D............110.00

Cunard Line, sign, pictures ship flanked by logo on dark blue border, Cunard Line Travellers' Cheques Cashed Here, 7x10", VG+, A............325.00

Cupid's Best Cigars, box label, inner lid, depicts Cupid giving cigar box to woman, 6x9", EX, D............25.00

Cupid's Best Cigars, box label, outer, depicts Cupid giving cigar box to woman, 5x5", M, D............12.00

Curlox Hair Nets, display case, wood with glass front displaying product, decaled labels on sides, cracking/staining, 13x19x11", VG, A............85.00

Curly Head Cigars, box label, inner lid, depicts a boy holding a box of cigars, 6x9", EX, D............35.00

Curtis & Moore's Crushed Fruits, tray, pictures girl & horse with saddle & bridle equipment border, Charles Ehlen, 1905, rubs/soiling, 17x14", G, A............40.00

Curtze Coffee, display case, shaped glass & textured metal with lighted top, frosted glass says Signal Blend, 29x14x16", EX, A............150.00

Custom House Cigars, box label, inner lid, depicts government building, 6x9", EX, D............100.00

Custom House Cigars, tin, depicts Custom House & street scene, Club Perfectos, slip lid, minor paint drools/chips, 6x6" diameter, VG, A............165.00

Cutter Cigars, box label, outer, depicts yacht in full sail with US flag, 1887, 5x5", VG, D............32.00

Cycling News, sign, cloth, brick red & black illustration of bicycle riders, The Scorcher, All The Cycling News, 1890s, 24x18", VG, A............75.00

Cyclone Twister Cigars, sign, cardboard, EX, A.....55.00

Cyrus Noble Whiskey, sign, cardboard litho, pictures the product, distillery, & founder, WJ Van Schuyver & Co, stains, framed, 14x11", G-, A............225.00

❧ D ❧

D'Eaux Gazeuses Factory, tray, deep-dish, factory scene, Elzear Fortier Limite, Quebec, lettering on rim, 12" diameter, EX, A............80.00

Dad's Root Beer, sign, depicts bottle cap, ca 1940s, 29", NM, A............115.00

Dad's Root Beer, sign, tin, product name center, You'll Love...Tastes Like Root Beer Should, red, yellow, blue, & black, 48" wide, EX, A............150.00

Daddy's Choice Coffee, tin, girls head pictured as if bursting through label, 1-lb, NM, A............430.00

Daggett & Ramsdell's Cold Cream, display, tin, colorful image of a dark-haired girl resting her head on a table, HD Beach Co litho, 10x10", EX, A............450.00

Daily Habit Cigars, box label, inner lid, depicts a parrot on perch over a plantation field, 6x9", M, D............16.00

Daily Habit Cigars, tin, depicts a parrot on a perch over plantation field, The Cigar Of Merit, slip lid, overall wear, 5x6" diameter, G, A............155.00

Daisy, crate label, California orange, single daisy, Covina Orange Growers Ass'n, 1930s, 10x12", M, D............3.00

Daisy Darlings Cigars, box label, outer, depicts 2 women cheek-to-cheek, 1887, 5x5", EX, D............15.00

Dalecarlia Cigars, box label, outer, pictures 2 Scandinavian women, 1896, 5x5", D, M............22.00

Dallas Brewery, tip tray, labeled bottle in center, Home Beer, Dallas Tex, 4" diameter, NM, A............250.00

Dalley's Prime Coffee, tin, pastoral scene with extract & jelly containers on back, original slip lid, wood knob, 1-lb, 8x4" diameter, G-, A............75.00

Damschinsky's Hair Dye, country store display poster showing strands of real hair, natural & with dye, 19x14" without frame, EX, A............60.00

Dan Patch Cut Plug Tobacco, lunch box, tin, shows man on surrey, hinged lid with clasp, original wood handled bail, 4x7x5", G+, A............275.00

Dan Patch Cut Plug Tobacco, lunch box, tin, shows man on surrey, slip lid, 2 movable handles, overall wear, 4x7x5", G, A............90.00

Dan Patch Cut Plug Tobacco, tin, shows man on surrey on yellow background, slip lid, 3x6x4", A............50.00

Dan Patch Rye, sign, reverse painting on glass, 24x34", NM, A............3,500.00

Dandro Solvent, sign, tin, hand holding product, You Too Can Have Beautiful Hair..., black background, self-framed, 10x13", EX, A............80.00

Daniel Webster Flour, sign, tin, red & black lettering on yellow background, framed, 14x39", EX, A............130.00

Danville Stove Works, sign, tin litho, some blemishes, 28", G, A............475.00

Darby & Joan Tobacco, sign, canvas & paper, elderly couple seated at a table holding hands, Mfg By Chas W Allen, Cincinnati, rectangular, A............120.00

Darby's Swan Tolu, tin, for medicinal candy, black on red with square edges & corners, chips/scratches/dents, 2x4x4", VG, A **35.00**

Darlene Ice Cream, sign, embossed tin, blue & red lettering on white horizontal oval doily on lavender ground, 24x44", M, A **40.00**

Darlene Ice Cream, sign, 2-sided embossed tin, blue & red lettering on white horizontal oval doily on lavender background, 23x30", M, A **45.00**

Daukes Ale, sign, paper, man holding glass of ale, Guinness Stout & Bass Ale, overall darkening due to age, 24x18", VG+, A **450.00**

Dauntless Coffee, tin (full), paper label picturing a little boy dressed up like a knight, 1-lb, EX, A **80.00**

David Stevenson Brewing Co, calendar, 1900, depicts men toasting around a table with factory view above, full calendar, 28x20", appears EX, A **1,000.00**

David Stevenson Brewing Co, calendar, 1907, depicts factory scene above tavern scene, used pad with 1908 calendar beneath, 29x20", NM, D **1,600.00**

David Stevenson Brewing Co, tray, picturing the brewery in New York City, 1918, 13" diameter, VG, A 850.00

Davids' Inks, ledger marker, tin, black & green, depicts stacked bottles of ink with rope border & round logo atop, vertical, EX, D **250.00**

Davis Ice Cream, dish, porcelain, pictures woman eating bowl of ice cream, Davis Quality, Ridgeway's, ca 1920, 7" diameter, M, A **200.00**

Davis' Maryland Rye, tray, a maiden & cherub, Ask For..., decorative border, oval, 17x14", NM, A **225.00**

Day & Night Tobacco, sign, paper, provocative woman with revealing image in mirror, 1904, matted & framed, 27x18", overall, VG, A **1,700.00**

De Laval, sign, tin, We Use De Laval, Better Farm Living, Better Farm Income, circular logo bottom center, rectangular, A **30.00**

De Laval Cream Separator, sign, tin, blue with yellow border & lettering, ca 1920s, 12x16", EX, A **15.00**

De Laval Cream Separator Co, letter opener, brass, 1878-1928, D **38.00**

De Laval Cream Separator Co, match holder, embossed die-cut tin cream separator, 6x4x1", NM, A **220.00**

De Laval Cream Separators, broom holder, tin, lettering & graphics picturing 2 separators, in original envelope, 4x4", NM, A **115.00**

De Laval Cream Separators, cabinet for tools & parts, wood, embossed tin front, shows separator, The World's Standard, some wear, 26x18x11", G, A ...**400.00**

De Laval Cream Separators, calendar, 1904, colorful image of a little boy & girl in cornfield with the months as the border, framed, 18x12", VG, A **250.00**

De Laval Cream Separators, calendar, 1908, colorful image of girl hugging a cow within an oval, minor creasing, framed, 20x13", VG, A **325.00**

De Laval Cream Separators, calendar, 1910, elegant woman within an oval, lettering atop, December pad, framed, 21x13", EX, A **350.00**

De Laval Cream Separators, calendar, 1916, little boy & girl with flowers on a crate, Do You Like Butter?, full pad, framed, 24x12", EX+, A **230.00**

De Laval Cream Separators, calendar, 1917, young girl & her dog seated in a landscape, full pad, framed, 24x12", EX+, A **275.00**

De Laval Cream Separators, calendar, 1918, depicts woman standing with horse, full pad, some stains/creases, matted & framed, 24x12", EX, A ...**400.00**

De Laval Cream Separators, calendar, 1919, full pad, tape residue on pad, framed, 24x12", EX, A ..400.00

De Laval Cream Separators, calendar, 1928, pictures a child in a carriage pulled by a goat, framed, 22x12", EX, A **170.00**

De Laval Cream Separators, calendar, 1929, pictures boy & girl with dog & kite under a tree, Norman Rockwell, EX, A **350.00**

De Laval Cream Separators, calendar, 1931, colorful image of separator on blue background, framed, 53x20", EX, A **350.00**

De Laval Cream Separators, perpetual calendar, 1810-1920, tin litho with paper rolls to reveal months, pictures woman & separator, 6x7", G+, A **265.00**

De Laval Cream Separators, sign, paper, shows milkmaid using No 15 separator, 1914, matted & framed, 42x25", VG, A **750.00**

De Laval Cream Separators, sign, tin, ca 1907, 41x30", NM, A..**4,000.00**

De Laval Cream Separators, sign, tin, milkmaid with cow surrounded by vignettes of cows & separators, ca 1907, 31x20" without frame, VG+, A **1,300.00**

De Laval Cream Separators, tip tray, lady & child with separator, The World's Standard, HD Beach Co litho, ca 1905, 4" diameter, G, A **35.00**

De Laval Cream Separators, tip tray, mother & son with separator, The World's Standard, HD Beach Co litho, ca 1905, 4" diameter, NM, A **150.00**

De Laval Cream Separators & Milkers, sign, porcelain, red, white, & blue, Agency lettered above Cream Separators & Milkers, 20x30", VG, A............................**100.00**

De Laval Milker, sign, tin, black letters on bright yellow background, We Use The De Laval Milker, 12x16", appears EX, A **35.00**

Dean's Peacocks Prophylactics, tin, lg peacock on lid, Reservoir Ends, flat, rectangular, EX, A..................**55.00**

Deer Park Beer, tip tray, deep-dish, depicts a deer, Purity & Strength, Ale, Porter, crazing background/rim wear, 4" diameter, VG, A **165.00**

Deer Park Brewing Co, tray, encircled 12-point buck in center, Lager above, Ale & Porter below, company name on rim, 12" diameter, NM, A **200.00**

Deer Run Whiskey, sign, tin with embossed edge & hanging cord, lg buck in a mountainous landscape, Aug Baetzhold, 12" diameter, EX+, A **250.00**

Deerfoot Rye, tray, deep-dish, sprinting Indian outpacing the white man, The Winning Whiskey, James Olwell Co, NY, 12" diameter, NM, A...............................**750.00**

Defender Motor Oil, tin, dark blue, WWI sentry guarding tents under product name, Pennsylvania Petroleum Products, 1925-45, 2-gal, EX, A **50.00**

Defender Motor Oil, tin, WWII sentry guarding tents under product name, Pennsylvania Petroleum Products, 1940-50, 2-gal, 12x9", VG, A...................**20.00**

Defiance Tick Mitten Co, pocket mirror, factory scene on yellow, red, blue, & white background, ca 1920s, 3x2", VG, D **20.00**

Del Monte, doll, plush, Sweet Pea, has original tag, 9", G, D **12.00**

Del Monte, poster, paper, 35x25", EX, A **100.00**

Delaware Cigars, box label, inner lid, depicts Washington crossing the Delaware & Indians, 6x9", VG, D.......**28.00**

Delaware Punch, sign, cardboard, Delicious Delaware Punch above bottle, ...3-Panel Punch Bowl Bottle, tin frame, 60x21", NM, D.....................................**225.00**

Delicious Coffee, tin, decorative label with lettering, slip lid, chipping, 1-lb, 6x4" diameter, G, A **40.00**

Della Rocca Cigars, can label, pictures a bust portrait of a young woman with gold flowing hair, M, D.........**14.00**

Denison, Prior & Co Brokers Insurance, sign, somber-faced girl in elegant dress, flowers draped over shoulder, fiery red ground, framed, 27x19", EX, A **950.00**

Denniss's Pig Powders, sign, tin, Denniss's Lincolnshire, Prevent & Cure Disease In Pigs & Poultry, lg pig on right, 25¢ per doz, 10x14", VG, A **180.00**

Densmore Cigars, box label, inner lid, depicts view of park with fountains & stairs, 6x9", M, D.................**35.00**

Dental Sweet Snuff, sign, cardboard, couple seated on ground by car, product logo lower left, How Did You Know I Use... 12x16", G, A......................................**35.00**

Dentyne Gum, display, die-cut tin, girl holding package of Dentyne with space below for box of gum, ca 1915-20, 7x4", NM, A...**45.00**

Detmer Woolens, display box, heavy cardboard, when opened reveals pictures of stores & people wearing woolens, opened: 21x29x21", VG, A **75.00**

Detroit Stove Works, sign, tin, pictures factory for Jewel Stoves & Ranges, Largest Stove Plant In The World, self-framed, 13x37", G, A **150.00**

Detroit-Bohemian Beer, match holder, tin litho, pictures Brownies with a case of beer, C Shonk litho, 5x5", G-, A..**140.00**

Devilish Good Cigar, sign, tin, cigar box with 3 boys shown on lid flanked by lettering, 5¢, None Better, 1890, round corners, 10x14", NM, A **200.00**

Devlish Good Cigar, sign, open box of product, None Better, 5¢ Cigar in bottom right corner, flaking on margins, horizontal rectangle, A **80.00**

Devoe Paints & Varnishes, sign, 2-sided die-cut tin in 2 parts, flanged, lg oval with kneeling Indian attached with chain, 1925, 25x15", A **650.00**

Dexter Cigars, sign, porcelain, white & orange on blue, RG Sullivan's on sm wavy banner over lg Dexter with Cigar at right, 3x18", F, A **30.00**

Diamond Brand Children's Shoes, whirlygig, cardboard & wood, pictures colorful airplane, Weatherbird & Peters Co, 1950s, minor bends, EX, D **14.00**

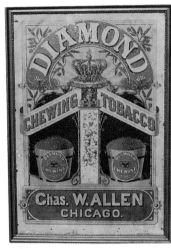

Diamond Chewing Tobacco, sign, tin, early, nail holes/flaking, 20x14", G, A 350.00

Diamond Dyes, cabinet, wood, embossed tin front, kids jumping rope, mansion beyond, Standard Package Dyes.., 1910-15, 25x16x9", EX, A **1,200.00**

Diamond Dyes, cabinet, wood, embossed tin front, kids playing with balloon, Standard Package Dyes..., ca 1912, 25x16x9", EX, A **900.00**

Diamond Dyes, cabinet, wood, embossed tin front, woman dying clothing, It's Easy To Dye With Diamond Dyes, 30x23x10", VG, A **800.00**

Diamond Dyes, cabinet, wood, tin front, court jester entertaining, 28x21x11", EX, A.............................**400.00**

Diamond Dyes, cabinet, wood, tin front, rare, 20x17", VG, A 950.00

Diamond Dyes, cabinet, wood, tin front, depicts the evolution of women, Fancy Colors, Domestic & Fancy Dying, 30x23x10", G+, A **650.00**

Diamond Dyes, cabinet, wood, tin front, fairy surrounded by vignettes, For Domestic & Fancy Dying, 31x24x10", EX, A...**2,500.00**

Diamond Dyes, cabinet, wood, tin front, pictures kids playing with ribbons in landscape, It's Easy To Dye With..., 30x23x10", EX, A **2,000.00**

Diamond Dyes, sign, cardboard, parrot suspended from wire surrounded by circular logo, Easy To Use, 45 Colors, 13x9" diameter, NM, A **700.00**

Diamond Dyes, sign, double-sided, promotes colorful dyes on 1 side & paints on reverse, diamond-shaped metal frame, EX, A **130.00**

Diamond Dyes, sign, embossed tin, depicts girls of different ethnics, All American Girls Use Diamond Dyes, wood frame, 30" long, G-, A **260.00**

Diamond Dyes, sign, paper with metal stand, shows various wool colors, A **70.00**

Diamond Dyes, sign, tin, signed Bessie Pease Gutmann, ca 1911, 11x17", VG, A **1,400.00**

Diamond Hammer Drive Anchor, paperweight, D .**18.00**

Diamond Matches, match box, tin, family reacts to match dispenser, You Chillun Keep Back Deah..., hinged lid, 2x5x2", VG, A **200.00**

Diamond Matches, vendor, steel, Diamond Book Matches 2 for 1¢, heavy paint wear, 13x5", F, A **50.00**

Diamond Matches, vendor, 1¢, molded steel, round slanted top on base, working condition, 14x11x8", VG, A **135.00**

Diamond Tobacco, thermometer, tin litho, 2 tobacco pails with lettered banners surrounding a crown atop, ca 1885, rare, 10x5", G-, A **80.00**

Diaparene Baby Wipes, baby, vinyl, wearing diaper, EX, D...**20.00**

Dibbit's Toffees, store bin, tin, 2 parrots perched on limb on decorative background, hinged lid, some wear, 12x11x7" diameter, VG, A **300.00**

Dick Bros Quincy Beer, tip tray, labeled bottle on black background, Drink & Enjoy..., minor scuffs, 4" diameter, EX, A **70.00**

Dick Custer Cigars, box label, inner lid, cowboy with a pistol surrounded by ornate graphics, Holds You Up lettered below, 6x9", M, D.................**10.00**

Dickens Ale, tray, 2 men toasting with ale, Syracuse Brewery Inc, 12" diameter, VG, A.................**65.00**

Diehl Brewing Co, tray, alluring woman in gown with arms reaching toward lg bottle in mountainous landscape, 12" diameter, VG, A.................**35.00**

Diesel, gas globe, milk glass with letters & No 2 in blue, metal base, crown shape, 1940-50, 17x17", A.......**600.00**

Dill's Best Slice Tobacco, tin, flat, 4x3", VG, D...........**8.00**

Dill's Best Slice Tobacco, tin, flat, 7x5x1", VG, D......**20.00**

Dill's Best Smoking Tobacco, tin, round, EX, D........**20.00**

Dill's Pipe Cleaners, package, half-full, pictures Dill's tins, G, D.................**10.00**

Dingman's Soap, sign, cardboard, crawling baby usually seen for Ivory soap, 13x15" without frame, VG+, A.........**150.00**

Diplomat Cigars, box label, inner lid, depicts man in filigree inset with Diplomat lettered on the diagonal, 6x9", M, D **40.00**

Dixie Jumbo Salted Peanuts, tin, depicts boy trying to eat giant peanut with Dixie lettered on peanut, press lid, 10-lb, EX, A.................**250.00**

Dixie Kid Cut Plug Tobacco, can, cardboard, paper label shows baby, screw lid, discoloration/paper loss, 5x5" square, G-, A **550.00**

Dixie Kid Cut Plug Tobacco, lunch box, tin, shows baby, He Was Bred In Old Kentucky, flat lid, wire handle, good sheen, 4x8x5", VG, A **250.00**

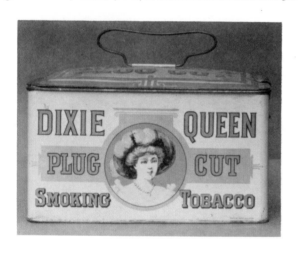

Dixie Queen Plug Cut Smoking Tobacco, lunch pail, appears EX, A.................160.00

Dixie Smoking Tobacco, tin, barrel-shaped with press lid & ring handle, discoloration/chips, 4x3" diameter, appears G, A.................**120.00**

Dixon's American Graphite Pencils, sign, paper, pictures little girl holding comical drawing of a pencil, Jos Dixon Crucible Co, framed, 29x15", VG+, A........**450.00**

Dixon's Carburet of Iron Stove Polish, poster, colorful girl wearing paper hat on deep red background, fold marks, framed, 30x13", VG, A **550.00**

Djer Kiss Talc, tin, G, D.................**12.00**

Do-U-No Cigars, canister, wood, paper label of 2 boys smoking cigars, 1 with newspapers, 1 in top hat & coat, ovoid, 3x5x5", G, A.................**250.00**

Dobler Brewing Co, tray, pictures profiled Asti girl, 13" diameter, EX, A.................**50.00**

Dobler Lager, tray, pictures horses pulling 3 beer wagons with product name & circular logo above, oval, 13x16", EX, D.................**400.00**

Dobson Carpets, sign, cardboard, view of factory with insets of mills, cracking/soiling, original frame, 28x38", G, A.................**90.00**

Dockash Stove Factory, match holder, tin litho, pictures Scranton factory in gold color on simulated wood background, 5x3", G, A.................**60.00**

Doctor's Blend Cut Plug Tobacco, tin, lid pictures doctor measuring medicines on balance beam, Montreal Canada, some wear, 3x5x4", VG+, A.................**75.00**

Dodge & Plymouth, calendar, 1954, pictures Boy Scouts by Norman Rockwell, C&F Motor Sales, full pad, vertical, appears EX, A.................**25.00**

Doe Wah Jack, mug, pictures Indian, inscribed Compliments of Beckwith Estate 1907, D.................**85.00**

Doger Cola, sign, die-cut tin, bottle form, 6", D........**300.00**

Dogs Head Bottling Co, pot lid, porcelain, bulldog logo on bright blue, WT Copeland & Sons, ca 1915-20, 6" diameter, EX, A **75.00**

Dold Niagara Hams & Bacon, sign, tin, litho, 17x13", EX, A.................500.00

Dolly Madison Ice Cream, sign, die-cut cardboard standup, shows Dolly Madison with different flavors of ice cream before her, 37x27", EX, A **25.00**

Dolly Madison Ice Cream, sign, die-cut cardboard standup, shows White House with carriage & lg dish of chocolate ice cream, 41x26", NM, A.................**15.00**

Dolly Madison Ice Cream, sign, embossed tin, cameo flanked by Deliciously Different with Dolly Madison above & Ice Cream below, 21x33", M, A **35.00**

Dolly Madison Selected Ice Cream, playing cards, Dolly Madison Quality Checked Selected Ice Cream in blue, red, & white graphics on yellow, complete, M, D ...**5.00**

Domestic Sewing Machines, thimble, sterling silver, product name imprinted on band, EX, D **40.00**

Domino Sugar, bear, plush, new, lg, EX, D **25.00**

Domino Sugar, box, blue metal with Domino logo on inside of lid, hinged lid & clasp, A.................**10.00**

Domino Sugar, sign, colorful image of a bag of sugar, basket of grapes, & homemade jams, Save The Fruit Crop, ca 1918, 11x21", EX, A **350.00**

Don Rodrigo Cigars, box label, inner lid, depicts Columbus trading with an Indian, 1920, 6x9", M, D **50.00**

Donald Duck Coffee, bank, tin, sample size, rare, appears EX, A **200.00**

Donald Duck Orange Juice, can, no lid, rare, EX, A .**35.00**

Doral Cigarettes, change receiver, G, D....................**10.00**

Dotterweich Brewing Co, tip tray, glass & labeled bottle in center, Beer, Ales, & Porter, Olean NY, rare, 4" diameter, G-, A **45.00**

Double-Kay Salted Nuts, dispenser, 3 glass jars on porcelain stand, lettering on jars & stand, minor overall wear, 17x21x10", VG, A **100.00**

Dougherty's Mince Pie, sign, This Boy Wants A Piece Of lettered over 2 boys, minor pitting, A...................**300.00**

Douglass Cough Drops, store bin, wood with glass window, oval portraits with silhouette lettering on sides, overall wear, 5x9x7", G-, A.....................................**100.00**

Dr Bell's Pine Tar Honey, stickpin, Cures Colds, D ..**12.00**

Dr Chase's Nerve Food, thermometer, tin, round logo with product name & picturing Dr Chase, lists other products, both ends rounded, VG, A **50.00**

Dr D Jaynes Expectorant, poster, pictures woman in laced bodice & cape, Remedy For Worms, Debility, & Dyspepsia, 29x13", VG, A **425.00**

Dr D Jayne's Expectorant, sign, paper, depicts the doctor, The Strength Giver For Grown People & Children..., framed, 33", VG, A **500.00**

Dr D Jayne's Tonic Vermifuge, sign, reverse-painted glass, ca 1870, framed, 12x15", NM, A 1,100.00

Dr Daniels' Animal Medicines, cabinet, wood, tin front, 3 horses' heads in blue circle on off-white background, lettering above & below, 28x22", G+, A **4,700.00**

Dr Daniels' Canker Remedy, tin, portrait of Dr Daniels & lettering surrounded by decorative border, decorative slip lid, rare, round, appears EX, A.....................**130.00**

Dr Daniels' Dog & Cat Remedies, cabinet, tin, rare, 20x14x5", VG, A **4,500.00**

Dr Daniels' Horse, Cat, Dog Medicines, sign, embossed tin, Use Dr AC Daniels' Horse Cat Dog Medicines For Home Treatment, 18x28", NM, A............................**75.00**

Dr Daniels' Horse/Dr True's Elixir, display box, 2-tiered with leather cover, all sides promoting Horse Medicines & Dr True's Family Elixir, 38x30", EX, A **4,700.00**

Dr Daniels' Medicated Dog & Puppy Bread, calendar top, 1913, pictures little girl feeding her dogs, framed, 20x14", EX, A...**500.00**

Dr Daniels' Veterinary Medicines, cabinet, wood, embossed tin front, Dr Daniels with products & pricing chart, Veterinary Medicines, 27x20", G-, A **525.00**

Dr Daniels' Veterinary Medicines, display, cardboard, 2-sided illustration relating to varieties of medicines, tears/chips/creases, 23x40", VG, A **550.00**

Dr Daniels' Veterinary Medicines, mirror, celluloid, pictures lady with horse & dog standing inside gate, proprietor's name & address, 2" diameter, NM, A **130.00**

Dr Daniels' Warranted Veterinary Medicines, cabinet, wood, embossed tin front, shows Dr Daniels with products display below, 1900-10, 29x22x8", EX, A...**2,600.00**

Dr DeWitt's Household Remedies, sign, cardboard, interior surrounded with vignettes of antidotal cures, WJ Parker & Co, framed, wear, 24x30", G-, A **2,600.00**

Dr Drake's Glesco Cough & Croup Remedy, sign, embossed tin over cardboard, colorful image of parents watching baby sleep, Lessner Medicine Co, 14x12", EX, A..**1,100.00**

Dr Haile's Ole Injun System Tonic, sign, paper litho, Indian in headdress, Kidneys, Liver & Stomach, in cut-down frame, 1940, 13x20", VG, A **50.00**

Dr Hand's Remedies For Children, sign, paper, children playing in chicken lot, list of remedies on side of house, matted & framed, 22", VG, A....................**625.00**

Dr Haynes Arabian Balsam, sign, little girl listening to a watch, 1885, brass bound, rare, 16x11", A **375.00**

Dr Hess Instant Louse Killer, sign, circle inset of Dr Hess upper left, ad copy in rectangular inset at right, product & chicks below, 27x20", G, A..................**40.00**

Dr Hess Poultry Pan-A-Ce-A, sign, depicts mother hen & chicks eating, Raise All The Chicks You Hatch..., restoration at center creases, 26x21", G, A **35.00**

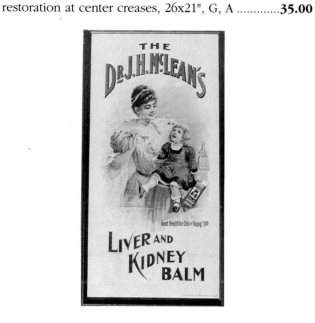

Dr JH McLean's Liver & Kidney Balm, sign, paper, Forbes litho, 1896, framed, 85x47", EX, A ..4,500.00

Dr JH McLean's Liver & Kidney Balm, sign, red, black on white, depicts box of product & lettering, The Peerless Remedy For Diseases..., 18x46", NM, D................**125.00**

Dr JH McLean's Strengthening Cordial & Blood Purifier, sign, red & black lettering on yellow, An Unfailing Remedy For Weakness, Nervous Debility..., rectangular, EX+, D...**75.00**

Dr JT Claris, cabinet, oak with glass front, 20x16x7", appears EX, A...**225.00**

Dr Kellogg's Asthma Remedy, tin, pictures Dr Kellogg at work, lettering above, press lid, vertical with rounded corners, 5", G, A..**75.00**

Dr LeGear's Stock & Poultry Remedies, sign, tin with cardboard backing, pictures Dr LeGear, The Horse Owned By Dr LD LeGear Medicine Co..., self-framed, 14x18", G, A..**100.00**

Dr Lesure's Famous Remedies, cabinet, wood, embossed tin front, wood knob, 26x21x6", EX, A...............**2,200.00**

Dr Lesure's Warranted Veterinary Medicines, cabinet, wood with glass door & 3 shelves, stenciled lettering, includes box of product, 28x21x7", EX, A **550.00**

Dr M McHenry's Soothing Syrup..., broadside, To All Who Use..., Stomach Bitters, Oil For Burns, & Popular Liniments, framed, 11x14", M, A...........................**120.00**

Dr Meyer's Foot Soap, poster, paper, pictures a variety of people & package of foot soap, Relieves All Foot Troubles, 38x25", NM, A..**150.00**

Dr Miles Heart Cure, display, die-cut figure of little girl, with 2 extra outfits & a hat, 1890, EX, A **190.00**

Dr Miles Nervine, display, cardboard, pictures pretty girl pouring a dose flanked by 2 happy customers, 36x51", VG, A **240.00**

Dr Morse's Indian Root Pills, display, cardboard stand-ups, Indian grinding roots, teepees in background, plus 3 die-cuts of Indians, G, A....................................**485.00**

Dr Morse's Indian Root Pills, sign, die-cut cardboard Indian in canoe on lake, EX, A **20.00**

Dr Nebb's Talcum, tin, baby, shaker top, EX, D........**65.00**

Dr Pepper, calendar, 1949, full pad, NM, D **50.00**

Dr Pepper, calendar, 1960, 75th anniversary, EX, D ..**35.00**

Dr Pepper, clock, electric, Drink A Bite To Eat, Drink Dr Pepper, Good For Life, Warren Telechron Co, 15" diameter, EX, A 235.00

Dr Pepper, clock, logo under clock face, glass front, 15" square, EX, D..**85.00**

Dr Pepper, door pull, metal, bottle form, VG, D.........**45.00**

Dr Pepper, fan, cardboard, pictures a 6-pack of Dr Pepper, green & red, VG, D...**50.00**

Dr Pepper, menu board, tin, Dr Pepper logo atop board, vertical, EX, D **35.00**

Dr Pepper, radio, can figural, D **40.00**

Dr Pepper, seltzer bottle, Cheerio-Memphis, D.........**150.00**

Dr Pepper, sign, late 1890s, cardboard, framed, 15x11", EX, A 4,200.00

Dr Pepper, sign, porcelain, white & black lettering on red background with green border, 27" long, G+, A..**130.00**

Dr Pepper, sign, 1950s, metal, Drink Dr Pepper, 12x32", EX, D..**30.00**

Dr Pepper, syrup dispenser, lime green with nickel-plated spigot, scratches/light pitting, 16", G, D **80.00**

Dr Pepper, thermometer, tin, bottle shape, early, 26", NM, D..**150.00**

Dr Pepper, thermometer, tin, Dr Pepper logo above with Hot or Cold lettered below, 27x8", NM, D **65.00**

Dr Russell's Pepsin Calisaya Bitters, sign, paper, rare, matted & framed, 22x15", EX, A **3,000.00**
Dr Sayman's Toilet Talcum, container, cardboard & tin, depicts portrait of the founder with product name atop, shaker top, round, M, A **75.00**
Dr Scholl's Absorbo Corn & Bunion Pads, display case, tin, depicts a foot in each corner, lettering in center, overall chips/scratches, 15x12x7", VG, A **150.00**

Dr Scholl's Zino-Pads, display, glass in wood & metal case with back light, some wear, 5x13", G, A .**60.00**
Dr Shoop's Health Coffee, match holder, tin litho, pictures Dr Shoop, CH Custer, Middleburg Pa, 5x3", appears EX, A..........................**120.00**
Dr Shoop's Lax-ets, match holder, Only 5¢ Per Box, rectangular, appears EX, A **250.00**
Dr Shoop's Restorative, sign, embossed tin, portrait of Dr Shoop & list of cures, ca 1905, minor rust, framed, 10x7", EX, A **675.00**
Dr Swett's Root Beer, dispenser, ceramic, with pump, rare, EX, A...4,000.00
Dr Swett's Root Beer, pocket mirror, celluloid, pictures labeled bottle, 3" diameter, VG, A **130.00**
Dr Swett's Root Beer, sign, cardboard, pictures boy in front of man's silhouette holding a mug of root beer in circular inset, 18x14", G, A **40.00**

Dr Swett's Root Beer, sign, die-cut tin bottle, Priced at 5¢, Delicious, Refreshing, EX, A..................................**600.00**
Dr Swett's Root Beer, sign, embossed tin, features the great Dr Swett's ad of age & youth, HD Beach Co litho, framed, 9x24", EX+, A...**550.00**
Dr Swett's Root Beer, sign, tin over cardboard, features image of age & youth, red, blue, & gold with sandpaper like finish, 6x9", VG, A...............................**200.00**
Dr Swett's Root Beer, sign, 2-sided die-cut tin, blue & gold stein with intricate scenes, lettering on top & bottom rims, rare, 6", NM, D **200.00**
Dr Thomson's Sarsaparilla, cabinet, oak with slant front, frosted letters on glass, Thomson's Flavoring Extracts Are The Best, 29x20x18", EX, A **550.00**
Dr WL Johnson's Crackers, container, tin litho, Noah's Ark figural with animals looking out windows, Educator Ark, 1 of 3 known, 5x11", EX, A **1,600.00**

Drako Brand Coffee, tin, rare, 1-lb, 6x4", G, A.....250.00
Dread-Nowt Razor Blades, vendor, porcelain front & sides, cast iron mechanism, ship logo, British Made, Shave Sir?, 2 D Each, 20x11x5", VG A **425.00**
Dream Girl Talcum, tin, shaker top, EX, D **43.00**
Droste's Cocoa, tin, bright colors, sq, 1-lb, 6", M, D...**20.00**
Drum Major Marshmallows, tin, depicting drum major, slip lid, Toronto Canada, slight overall wear, 5x11" diameter, EX, A **45.00**
Drummer Boy Smoking & Chewing Tobacco, pack (full), pictures Drummer Boy, G, D **25.00**
Drummer's Choice, tip tray, depicts labeled bottle, Drink Drummer's Choice, Cape Ice Brewery Co, minor background wear, 5" diameter, EX, A..........................**120.00**
Dry Slitz Cigars, thermometer, enameled, 2 for 5¢, The Leader for 35 Years, works, minor discoloration to background, 39x8", G, A **155.00**
Du Bois Brewing Co, tip tray, lettered graphics in center, Du Bois Budweiser, Hahne's Export, 4" diameter, NM, A...**95.00**
Du Bois Brewing Co, tip tray, logoed image of The American Maid, Du Bois Budweiser, Du Bois Wurzburger, 5" diameter, NM, A **170.00**

Du Pont, playing cards, gold logo on dark blue background with double gold border, complete, D **3.00**

Du Pont, sign, paper, pictures 2 men duck hunting in a boat, several creases/tears, 23x15", G-, A **45.00**

Du Pont, sign, paper, 2 images, cavalryman shooting buffalo, 2 setters pointing, original ad mat, framed, 15x34", VG, A...**75.00**

Du Pont Ballistite Smokeless Powder, sign, paper, 1913, metal frame, 30x20", G-, A.....................725.00

Du Pont Gunpowder, tin, paper label depicts lettered logo, Delaware, flat lid, scratches/dent, 6", G, A ...**30.00**

Du Pont Powders, sign, pictures hunting dog with duck in his mouth, Shoot Du Pont Powders lettered in lower right corner, 1904, 30x20", A **400.00**

Du Pont Powders, sign, tin, father & son with dogs in field, Generations Have Used It, scratches/chips, self-framed, 33x23", G, A...**275.00**

Du Pont Smokeless Powder, calendar, 1901, paper, signed EH Osthaus, framed, 28x14", EX+, A...1,400.00

Du Pont Smokeless Powder, sign, paper litho, cut-away view of interior of US Armored Cruiser, Tennessee, ca 1905, minor tears, 26x48", VG+, A **450.00**

Du Pont Smokeless Powder, sign, paper litho, depicts US Armored Cruiser, Tennessee, ca 1905, minor tears, 26x48", VG+, A..**300.00**

Du Pont Sporting Powders, envelope, colorful image of bird on railing, Sporting Powders, right side torn off, 4x7", G-, A **30.00**

Du Pont Sporting Powders, sign, hunter & dogs surrounded by other generations of hunters, 1917 around hunter in center, 31x20", G, A **350.00**

Dubuque Packing Plant, playing cards, depiction of South San Francisco Plant in red graphics on white with gold & red border, complete, D...............................**5.00**

Duenning Construction Co, watch fob, nickel plated, EX, D **38.00**

Duesseldorfer Beer, tray, pictures bald baby, gold lettering on rim, round, EX, A **750.00**

Duffy's Pure Malt, mirror, celluloid, chemist testing product, lettering around border, 2" diameter, VG, A ..**13.00**

Duffy's Pure Malt, mirror, celluloid, chemist testing product, lettering around border, oval, 3", EX, A.............**5.00**

Duffy's Whiskey, sign, tin, chemist with bottle of pure malt whiskey, overall darkening/minor scratches, self-framed, 28x22", VG, A **300.00**

Duke's Cameo Cigarettes, sign, hanging paper litho, elegant woman with curly hair, framed, triangular, 19x14", EX, A **290.00**

Duke's Cameo Cigarettes, sign, paper litho, curly-haired girl in a bonnet holding sign, product name above, Duke Sons & Co below, vertical, M, A **2,000.00**

Duke's Mixture, poster, cardboard, original frame marked Duke's Mixture, 27x21", G+, A 600.00

Duke's Mixture Smoking Tobacco, sign, paper rolldown, pictures pretty farm girl holding a sign, framed, 42x15", VG, A **75.00**

Duke's Pharmacy, clock, calendar drop regulator, Roman numerals, case appears reconditioned/retouched face, 31x16x6", A **500.00**

Dunham's Cocoanut, thermometer, etched brass, ca 1888, replaced paper dial, working condition, 12" diameter, VG, A **250.00**

Dunlap's Seeds, poster, paper litho, girl seated among variety of vegetables, Good Harvest From Good Seed, framed, vertical, EX, A **160.00**

Dunlop Bicycles, sign, chromolitho on rag paper, French lettering, 5 cyclists riding forward on arrow pointing backward, 48x32", EX, A **350.00**

Duplex Gear Grease, tin, yellow with early car & lady left of center, Pierce Arrow Motor Car, Enterprise Oil Co, 1910-15, 5-lb, 7", VG, A **140.00**

Duplex Marine Engine Oil, tin, light aqua with motor boat under product name, Enterprise Oil Co Inc, Buffalo NY, 1915-25, 5-gal, 14x9", VG+, A **400.00**

Duplex Motor Oil, tin, Made Expressly for Pierce Arrow, #350 on front, dented, 1-gal, 5x5x10", G, A **200.00**

Duplex Motor Oil, tin, yellow with picture of lady in car, Pierce Arrow Motor Car on slug plate, 1915-25, 5-gal, 15", VG, A **350.00**

Duplex Outboard Special Motor Oil, tin, light blue with product name at top, dark blue bottom with 2 fishermen in red & blue boat, 1940-50, NM, A..............**850.00**

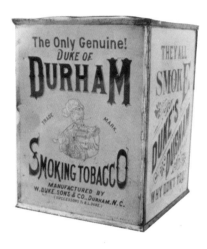

Durham Smoking Tobacco, store bin, very early Hines & Ginna (precedes Ginna & Co), 15x11x11", G+, A 700.00

Durham Tobacco, pouch (empty), cloth, VG, D **5.00**

Durham Tobacco, pouch (full), cloth, VG+, D **10.00**

Durham Tobacco, sign, cardboard, man yelling over counter at another man, 'This Is The Best, Do You Understand?,' framed, 14x11", G+, A **600.00**

Durlex Motor Oil, tin, woman driving Pierce Arrow car in oval, Enterprise Oil Co Inc Established 1884, ca 1910, 1-gal, 15x7", G, A..**75.00**

Dutch Boy (Atlantic White Lead) Paint, string holder/sign, die-cut tin, bucket holds string, 30x14", VG+, A.......................................2,000.00

Dutch Boy Paints, display, cardboard triptych, pictures the famous Dutch boy with lettering atop, That Room Of Your Dreams..., EX, A..**80.00**

Dutch Boy Paints, lamp, plaster figural, depicts seated Dutch boy with arm outstretched, working condition, some wear, A..**125.00**

Dutch Boy Paints, match holder, embossed die-cut tin, Dutch boy with can, overall fading/chipping, 7x3x1", G-, A **165.00**

Dutch Boy Paints, match holder, embossed die-cut tin, Dutch boy with can, 7x3x1", EX, A.....................**400.00**

Dutch Boy Paints, sign, die-cut cardboard, pictures the famous Dutch boy & several pieces of furniture, Quick Lasting Beauty!, EX, A **60.00**

Dutch Boy Paints, sign, lighted, Dutch Boy Paint in lg letters, horizontal rectangle, A..................................**140.00**

Dutchess Trousers, sign, embossed tin, black & yellow, product name above detailed warranty, ...From $2-$5, For Sale By..., 24x20", NM, A..................................**95.00**

DW Herb, match holder, tin litho, colorful image of man hunting on water, Dealer in General Merchandise, 5x3", VG, A **300.00**

DW Hoegg Canned Goods, sign, paper litho, pyramid of cans surrounded by lobster & assorted typography, ca 1885, ornate frame, 28x22", NM, A **750.00**

Dwinell-Wright Co Boston Coffee, store bin, tin front with paper label showing the factory, Largest & Most Complete Coffee Roasting..., dents, A **180.00**

Dwinell-Wright Co Boston Coffees, box, wood with 2 paper labels, 1 showing logo & lettering, 1 showing the factory, 16x15", EX, A 200.00

Dwinell-Wright Co Celebrated Boston Roasted Coffee, store bin, tin, slant front, hinged lid, white lettering on blue with black & gold graphics, logo on lid, 20x19", VG, A **230.00**

DY-O-LA Dyes, cabinet, wood with tin front, 17x13", applies G, A..**70.00**

Dynafuel, pump sign, die-cut porcelain diamond with Dynafuel extending beyond perimeters, 1940s, minor rust/flakes, 8x12", A...**130.00**

❧ E ❧

E Butterwick & Co, Quarterly Report Of New York Fashions, Fall 1870, park scene with ladies by arched pavilion, framed, 28x32", VG, A.....................................**125.00**

E Fleckenstein Brg Co, sign, wood grain with tin center picturing 3 men eating & drinking, 2 circular logos atop, self-framed, 19x13", NM, A..........................**500.00**

E Robinson's Sons Pilsener Bottled Beer, tip tray, label on maroon background, product name surrounds rim, minor edge scrapes, 4" diameter, EX, A.................**45.00**

E Robinson's Sons Pilsener Bottled Beer, tray, deep-dish, colorful factory scene, C Shonk litho, 12" diameter, EX, A **350.00**

E Robinson's Sons Pilsener Bottled Beer, tray, rolled rim, colorful factory scene, Haeusermann MM Co litho, 12" diameter, EX, A **400.00**

E Robinson's Sons Pilsener Bottled Beer, tray, rowboat scene in center, product name around rim, 12" diameter, VG+, A **300.00**

E-J Workers Coffee, tin, namesake on inset with scrolled design, Johnson City, Endicott, West Endicott, 1-lb, 6x4" diameter, VG, A.......................................**75.00**

Eagle Beers, tip tray, deep-dish, bottle of Peerless Lager, Made In Utica NY below, rare, 4" diameter, EX, A **75.00**

Eagle Beers, tray, deep-dish, pictures bottle of Peerless Lager on wood grain background, scuffs/rim chips, 12" diameter, VG+, A **50.00**

Eagle Brand Coffee, tin, pictures logoed eagle, chips/scratches/overall crazing, 1-lb, 6x4", G, A....**50.00**

Eagle Brand Dry Cleaner, tin, American Shoe Polish Co, 5x3", EX, A...**125.00**

Eagle Brewing Co, see Lembeck & Betz

Eagle Head Cigars, box label, inner lid, Eagle Head lettered over eagle & mountains above with tropical scene below, 6x9", M, D **35.00**

Eagle Lock Co, cabinet, wood & glass with 3 shelves, lettered graphics, ca 1920, 20x16x12", EX, A............**135.00**

Eagle Lye, match holder, tin litho, colorful image of product, Established 1870, Purest & Best, heavy wear on box, 5x3", G, A...**80.00**

Eagle Run Beer, tip tray, pictures cherub riding an eagle, Pure & Aged, Fuhrmann & Schmidt, Shamokin Pa, rare, 4" diameter, NM, A..**210.00**

Eagle Snacks Honey Roasted Peanuts, bear, original box, M, D **25.00**

Early Times Distillery Co, plaque, sculptured plaster of loaded wagon & still in back woods of Kentucky, color enhancements, framed, 3x28x23", G, A.................**90.00**

Early Times Kentucky Straight Bourbon Whisky (sic), playing cards, a fifth of Early Times on yellow background, Just Mention My Name, complete, D **8.00**

Eau Claire Club Cigars, box label, inner lid, depicts brick building & street scene, 6x9", EX, D.....................**100.00**

EB Lamme Clothing, sign, tin, pictures man standing to the left of product name, Bozeman lettered below, 7x14", EX+, D **50.00**

Ebling's Beer & Ale, tray, deep-dish, pictures illustrated woman holding a glass of beer, 1934, rust spotting/overall chipping, 13" diameter, VG, A......**40.00**

Ebling's Celebrated Beers, tray, factory scene with red buildings & busy street scene flanked by bottles, Celebrated Beers, 11x13", NM, A **1,300.00**

EC Atkins Silver Steel Saws, watch fob, D **38.00**

Eclipse Coffee, tin, desert scene with Arabs & camels, slip lid, round, EX+, A..**175.00**

Eddie Cantor Cigars, box, portrait of Eddie Cantor on front & inside lid, Now 2 For 5¢, EX, A.................**80.00**

Edelweiss Beer, sign, die-cut tin, red-haired girl on a swing beside a labeled bottle holding a glass of beer, 16", appears EX, A **5,750.00**

Edelweiss Beer, tip tray, Peter Schoenhofen Brewing Co lettered on rim, 14" diameter, EX, A **175.00**

Edgeworth Smoking Tobacco, display, die-cut cardboard trifold, product flanked by 2 amused men, Edgeworth banner above, 33x42", G, A...................................**65.00**

Edgeworth Smoking Tobacco, display, die-cut cardboard trifold, product flanked by 2 amused men, Edgeworth banner above, 33x42", EX, A...................................**125.00**

Edison Bulbs, display, tin litho, decorated on all sides, 18x20x8", EX, A **200.00**
Edison Mazda Auto Lamps, display, 2-piece cardboard, auto & bulbs, in original mailer, 24x24", M, A **90.00**
Edison Mazda Auto Lamps, tin, picturing a lamp, For Your Car, 3x2x2", G, D **25.00**

Educator Cakelets, lunch box, tin, pictures Peter Rabbit & other story heroes, hinged lid & wire handle, rare, 3x6x4", EX, A...**170.00**
Edward G Robinson Pipe Mixture, pack (full), pictures Edward G Robinson, EX, D **20.00**
Edwin Cigars, tin, paper label with warehouse, cigars, employees, etc, New York, Connecticut, 1920s, round, EX, D **20.00**

Edwin J Gillies & Co, display cabinet for Fruit Extracts, wood with glass front, 3 shelves, 43x24", EX, A ...**375.00**
Egg Baking Powder, pocket mirror, child in hat holds cake to left of product name, round, NM, A **70.00**
Egyptian Deities Cigarettes, sign, tin, Egyptian still life with pack of cigarettes, Plain End Or Cut Tip, self-framed, overall wear, 21x15", G, A **120.00**
Egyptienne Luxury Cigarettes, sign, framed, 18x12", EX, A **675.00**
Egyptienne Straights Cigarettes, sign, depicts girl's face in a black bonnet on red background, product & lettering below, framed, 20x18", appears EX, A **280.00**
Egyptienne Straights Cigarettes, sign, depicts girl's face in a black bonnet on red background, product & lettering below, framed, 36x25", appears EX, A **500.00**
Ehlermann Hop & Malt Co, see Chas Ehlermann

Eichler Brewing Co, tray, pictures an elderly man with beer glass & newspaper, Pilsener And Real German Beers, minor image wear, oval, A.........................**325.00**

Eight O'Clock Coffee, bank, tin, tan & black on red, 4", D **8.00**
El Barb Cigars, tin, paper label of Arabian knight & white horse, has original contents, paper loss/wrinkles/stains, 6x4" square, VG, A **55.00**
El Camino, crate label, California orange, monk with oranges in front of archway, El Camino Citrus Ass'n, 1920s, 10x12", M, D...**25.00**
El Caso Cigars, box label, inner lid, boats in moonlit harbor bordered with flowers, 1895, 6x9", M, D.........**45.00**
El Corsicano Cigars, box label, outer, depicts Napoleon on white horse, product name above, 5x5", M, D.**18.00**
El Dallo Cigars, sign, paper, pictures an open box of cigars flanked by lettering, Special Wrapping Prevents Breaking, framed, 14x18", A **30.00**
El Leon Cigars, box label, inner lid, depicts lion with paw on shield, 6x9", M, D **35.00**
El Macco Cigars, sign, tin, oval image of an elegant couple with man lighting cigar, minor fading/chips, self-framed, 24x20", G, A...**150.00**

El Paterno Cigars, sign, embossed tin litho, self-framed, 26x18", VG, A...**700.00**

El Poeta Cigars, box label, inner lid, depicts famous authors, 6x9", M, A **25.00**

El Poeta Cigars, box label, inner lid, depicts image of Henry Longfellow at desk, 6x9", VG, D **30.00**

El Premio Cigars, box label, outer, depicts street scene with trolleys, 5x5", M, D **85.00**

El Principal Cigars, sign, die-cut cardboard, 2 cigar boxes on blue background, 10¢ to 3 for 50¢, The Taste Pleases..., 38x25", EX, A...................................**20.00**

El Ricardo Havana Cigars, tip tray, colorful image of a Spanish gentleman, ca 1910, 4" diameter, EX, A..**125.00**

El Trelles Tobacco, tin, intact label, EX, D................**20.00**

Elastica Floor Finish, sign, tin, pictures man & product, The Man Who Knows... above, Standard Varnish Works below, self-framed, 10x17", EX, A **375.00**

Electric Mixture Tobacco, tin, pictures 4 bathing beauties by Hasker & Marcuse Mfg Co, slip lid, lg chip on side/minor fading/wear, 2x5x3", G-, A **100.00**

Elephant Salted Peanuts, container, embossed glass jar, shows an elephant with product name above & below, ball shape, M, A **450.00**

Elephant Salted Peanuts, tin, logoed paper label, press lid, overall scratching/some denting, 10-lb, 11x8" diameter, G, A..100.00

Elgin Watches, sign, decal on wood, depicts Tom Sawyer-type boy holding watch, My Elgin's All Right below, ca 1900, worn, 22x15", A..**140.00**

Elk Speed Pure Rye, sign, tin litho, running elk, 1905, HD Beach litho, self-framed, 26x38", VG+, A **650.00**

Elliott Ear Protector, sign, celluloid, centered ear graphic flanked by list of cures with lettering above & below, rectangular, appears EX, A **40.00**

Ellwood Steel Fences, match holder, tin, pictures a fence, white lettering on red background, Old Reliable, A Perfect Hinge..., VG, A **60.00**

Elm Cigars, tin, embossed image on wood-grained background of elm tree & house inserts, slip lid, chips/spots, 5x5" diameter, G, A...........................**125.00**

Emblem Cigars, box label, outer, depicts eagle on American shield, 5x5", EX, D **24.00**

Emmerling's Grossvader Beer, sign, tin, ca 1913, framed, 20x28", NM, A **1,700.00**

Emmerling's Grossvader Beer, tray, German couple enjoying mugs of beer & bratwurst, Das Schmeckt Gut, lettering on decorative border, 10x13", EX, A......**175.00**

Empire Brewing Co, sign, tin, depicts 5 potential customers with factory in background, overall wear, self-framed, 23x29", G-, A...**250.00**

Empire Drill Co, sign, paper litho, young boy & girl under a parasol in a country scene, early, framed, 29x22", appears EX, A...**475.00**

Empire Liniment, sign, paper, comical image of pigs causing bicycle wreck, The World's Greatest Household..., framed, approx: 31x25", A......................................**550.00**

Empire Motor Oil, tin, Crew Levick Delaware in black diamond on red ground, Empire arched above, 1915-25, half-gal, 6", NM, A **35.00**

Empire Rye, shot glass, Empire Rye, Melchers' Best etched in lg letters, rare, M, D **20.00**

Empire Soap Co, sign, dated 1887 with Library of Congress stamp, framed, 27x19", EX, A.........550.00

Empire State Motor Oil, tin, red with lettered green banners around Empire State Building, airplane flying past, 1960s, 2-gal, 12x9", VG, A **35.00**

Empress Chocolates, sign, celluloid, pictures empress with regal robes & crown, ca 1906, minor rubbing/breaks at corners, 18x14", VG.................**275.00**

EN-AR-CO Motor Oil, sign, tin, 2-sided, lg image of boy holding chalkboard with product name, 3-color, 1940s, 40" diameter, NM, A...**450.00**

EN-AR-CO Motor Oil, tin, boy holding chalkboard with product name, National Refining Co in black, yellow ground, 1915-25, 1-gal, 11", G+, A **75.00**

EN-AR-CO Motor Oil, tin, green & yellow eagle on yellow logo, National Refining Co, Cleveland Oh below, 1915-25, 5-gal, 15x9", VG, A **50.00**

EN-AR-CO Motor Oil, tin, Special For Ford... in black letters on yellow background, 5-gal, 15x9", VG, A .**185.00**

Engesser Brewing & Malting Co, sign, tin, factory scene, early, rare, corners damaged, matted & framed, 20x27", A..**4,250.00**

Engle Spring Gun, sign, paper litho, pictures man giving shooting lessons flanked by 5 hunting scenes, early, rare, framed, 21x14", EX, A **900.00**

English Pug Smoking Tobacco, tin, pictures pug dog & pipe, Spaulding & Merrick, square corners, minor distortion/chipping/denting, 1x5x3", VG, A **95.00**

Enna Jettick Shoes, thimble, aluminum, Enna Jettick Shoes $5.00 on worn blue band, D............**3.00**

Ensign Perfection Cut Tobacco, pocket tin, 1 word of product name on each of 3 pennants, EX, A **375.00**

EO Webber Lumber, match holder, tin, black with silver lettering, Compliments of EO Webber, Marysville Kansas, 5x5", VG+, A **110.00**

Epco Cigars, box label, outer, pictures woman by a lake, 3x5", M, D............**2.00**

Epicure Tobacco, pocket tin, EXT, D **310.00**

Epicure Tobacco, pocket tin, G, D **150.00**

Equitable Life Assurance Society of the US, ledger marker, double-sided tin, red with black lettering, Policies Incontestable..., late 1800s, 12x3", VG, A......**175.00**

ER Heller Milling Co, flour sack, paper, depicts rooster pulling child on a wagon, 20x10", A............**18.00**

Erickson's Pure Rye Whiskey, sign, tin litho, depicts sinking ship with whiskey bottles afloat, product name in red across sky, 23x33", appears EX, A............**300.00**

Erie Brewing Co, tip tray, Purity, Age, Strength lettered around logoed center, Beer, Ale, Porter on rim, edge chips, 4" diameter, NM, A **60.00**

Erie Brewing Co, tray, woman resting on a tiger in center, circular logo upper left, lettering on decorative border, 14" diameter, VG, A **125.00**

Escapernong Wine, sign, depicts Uncle Sam & Liberty toasting a lg bottle of wine, company name on decorative frame, 18x26", EX+, A **6,750.00**

Eskimo Pie, ice cream cooler, cylinder shape with cast Eskimos as feet, original glass liner & lid, some wear, 16x9", G+, A 450.00

Eskimo Smoking Tobacco, tin, husky dog in front of igloos in gold on brown can, original slip lid, Montreal Canada, 6x4" diameter, G+, A **250.00**

Esterbrook's Oval Pointed Pens, sign, hanging, celluloid over cardboard, pictures ink pen with product name above, Smooth As Velvet below, 8x12", VG, A ...**275.00**

Ethyl Gasoline Corporation, pump sign, porcelain, sunrays as backdrop for lg Ethyl Anti Knock Compound logo, 1940, minor wear, round, VG, A **40.00**

Eureka Cigars, box label, outer, pictures roses & red lettering, 1908, 5x5", M, D............**2.00**

Eureka Coffee, tin, logoed inset surrounded with floral design, Ross Weir & Co, NY, slip lid with knob, overall wear, 1-lb, 7x4", G, A **40.00**

Eureka Mower Co, sign, paper, pictures a farmer on horse-drawn equipment, appears trimmed, framed, 26x20", G, A............**175.00**

Eureka Spool Silk, spool cabinet, wood, 3 drawers with glass fronts, several spools of thread, EX, A........**400.00**

Eureka Spool Silk, spool cabinet, wood, 5 drawers with glass fronts, some separation of top boards, 22x16", G, A............**150.00**

Eve Tobacco, tin, pictures nude with tobacco leaf, Cube Cut, slip lid, 4x4", EX, A............**50.00**

Even Steven Cigars, tin, shows man with cigar leaning over banner, slip lid, minor scratches/chips/edge loss/dents, 5x3", EX, A **225.00**

Ever-Ready Safety Razors, clock, pictures man shaving, split at 12 o'clock/discoloration to lacquer, 22x18" diameter, G, A **550.00**

Ever-Ready Safety Razors, clock, pictures man shaving, 22x18" diameter, NM, A 2,000.00

Ever-Ready Shaving Brushes, counter display, tin with glass front, pictures man shaving, ca 1910-20, rare, 10x16", EX, A 1,350.00

Eveready Batteries, bank, vinyl, black cat figural, new, 1981, EX, D............**15.00**

Eveready Flashlight, sign, double-sided die-cut, flashlight figural with mounting bracket, by Brilliant Mfg Co, Philadelphia, 11x4", VG, A **375.00**

Eveready Flashlight & Batteries, thimble, plastic, red logo on cream background, EX, D............**3.00**

Eveready Flashlight Batteries, counter display, 3-D, hinged front, Need A New Flashlight Lamp? lettered on storage drawer in base, 1940s, 18", NM, A..200.00

Eveready Flashlight Batteries, dispenser, slanted front holds 24 batteries, logo on hinged stand-up top, sides & front lettered, 16", appears EX, A **80.00**

Everett Piano Co, sign, paper, factory scene with figures & horse-drawn wagons carrying pianos, 22x38" without frame, G-, A **200.00**

Everett Piano Co, sign, paper, printer's proof, factory scene with figures & horse-drawn wagons carrying pianos, 28x44", appears EX, A...............................**700.00**

Everhardt & Ober Brewing Co, sign, paper, colorful image of brewing company & factory, logo & company name across bottom, 32x46", EX+, A **400.00**

Eversweet Deodorant, tip tray, pictures lady, D......**125.00**

Everyday Cut Plug Tobacco, tin, depicts woman's profile in circle, man in lower left corner, rounded corners, chips/scratched, rare, 1x5x3", VG, A **315.00**

Evinrude, playing cards, Evinrude printed on patriotic emblem in lower right corner on blue with white border, complete, M, D **17.00**

Evinrude, sign, tin, moonlit fishing scene with boat motor at left, First In Outboards, Stuart's Outboard Service, 1930, 14x26", A..**380.00**

Ex-Cel-Cis Talc, tin, G, D **15.00**

Ex-Lax, door plate, Pull lettered over box of product, Get Your Box Now, vertical, M, D **250.00**

Ex-Lax, sign, product name in center on white background, Patent Medicines For Children & Grown-ups, ca 1930, framed, 12x23", A **65.00**

Excelsior Brewing Co, tray, pictures factory scene with lettered rim, Pilsener & Real German Lager, rare, round, EX, D **275.00**

Excelsior Brewing Co, tray, girl in sailor suit holding glass flanked by labeled bottles, company name below, rare, oval, EX, A..**650.00**

Excelsior Life Insurance Co, ledger marker, tin, double-sided, lists officers on front & medical examiners on back, 1880-90, 13x3", NM, A...................................**25.00**

Excelsior Motor Oil, tin, touring car scene, ca 1915-25, 1-gal, 11", EX, A **1,000.00**

Exide Batteries, sign, embossed tin, orange & white lettering on black, 14x40", appears EX, A........................**35.00**

Extons Oyster & Butter Crackers, tin, glass front, lg gold letters on red, Established 1847, Celebrated Crackers..., lift top, rectangular, EX, A **750.00**

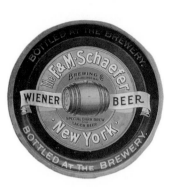

F&M Schaefer Brewing Co Weiner Beer, tray, barrel logo, EX, A **190.00**

F&M Schaeffer Brewing Co Weiner Beer, tray, logoed barrel, Est 1842, Bottled At The Brewery lettered above & below, oval, 14x17", VG+, A **325.00**

Fab Detergent, Americana Doll, plastic, 1957, 8", appears EX, D...**20.00**

Factory 100 Cigars, box label, inner lid, factory scene with store front & trolley, 1947, 6x9", EX, D..................**85.00**

Fairbank's Gold Dust Washing Powder, see Gold Dust

Fairmont Tobacco, pocket tin, rub marks on lid, NM, D **225.00**

Fairy Soap, sign, cardboard, little girl atop lettering, horizontal creasing/tears/stains, rare, 11x21", A **50.00**

Fairy Soap, sign, metal, double-sided, early, 18x12", NM, A 6,500.00

Fairy Soap, sign, paper, little girl telling another girl 'Why Don't You Wash With Fairy Soap?,' matted & framed, 21", EX, A...**400.00**

Fairy Soap, tip tray, little girl sitting atop a bar of soap, Have You A Little Fairy In Your Home?, 1915-20, 4" diameter, EX+, A **55.00**

Falstaff Beer, can, cone top, G, D 45.00
Falstaff Beer, charger, depicts medieval men & women, Lemp Brewing Co, ca 1910, hole at center/faded, 24" diameter, A 12.00
Falstaff Beer, charger, man in medieval dress holding stein, minor chips/scratches, 16" diameter, VG, A .35.00
Falstaff Beer, charger, woman in medieval dress holding a glass, minor chips/scratches, 16" diameter, VG, A .35.00
Falstaff Beer, goblet, heavy glass, M, D 12.00

Falstaff Bottled Beer, sign, tin litho, framed, 23x31", NM, A 3,200.00
Famous Beer, tip tray, deep-dish, product name in lg script in center, 4" diameter, NM, A 30.00
Famous Biscuit Co, display bin, glass front, clean, rectangular, A 25.00
Fanny Farmer Candy, doll, little girl with cloth body & molded plastic face, 10", G, D 20.00
Farewell Feeds, salt & pepper shakers, ceramic, pipe-smoking farmers, logo on back of each, EX, D ...150.00

Farm House Peanut Products, store container, tin, press lid, 50-lb, 13x13" diameter, VG, A.........150.00
Farran-Oid Fan Belts, case, tin litho, decorated front with open shelves on back, scratches/surface damage, 30x53x17" diameter, A 100.00
Farrell & Co Safes, ledger marker, double-sided, monochrome, pictures a Champion Safe, ca late 1800s, 12x3", G, A...............125.00
Fashion Cut Plug Tobacco, lunch box, tin, depicts well-dressed couple with landscape beyond, wire handle, hole in lid/overall wear, 4x8x5", G-, A 125.00

Fast Mail Tobacco, pocket tin, pictures train on front by J Bagley, extremely rare, EX, A 1,725.00
Father John's Medicine, display, die-cut paper over wood, depicts bust of Father John with lettering on base, paper missing on shoulder, 72", A 45.00
Father John's Medicine, sign, oval portrait depicting Father John, The Greatest Body Builder, No Drugs, ca 1920, horizontal, framed, EX, A...............120.00
Fatima Turkish Cigarettes, match holder & ash tray, porcelain, pictures veiled woman & Turkish symbols, ca 1915-20, 4x6", NM, A...............55.00
Fatima Turkish Cigarettes, pack (empty), G, D 2.00

Fatima Turkish Cigarettes, sign, tin, ca 1905-10, self-framed, 19" diameter, EX, A 450.00
Fatima Turkish Cigarettes, sign, tin, veiled woman holding pack of cigarettes, 20 For 15 Cents below, ca 1905-10, self-framed, oval, 23x17", EX, A 750.00
Fauerbach Beer, sign, tin, Fauerbach lettered on diagonal band with Since 1848 & logo above, Beer lettered below, 36x48", G+, D 110.00
Faultless Starch, thimble, porcelain, blue Faultless atop red star burst, gold bands, Franklin USA, EX, D ...15.00

Faultless Wonder Nipples, display, embossed glass in oversize form of baby bottle, lid simulates bottle nipple, rare, 13x6" diameter, NM, A...............1,500.00

Faust Blend Coffee, coffeepot, ceramic, pictures devil on black background, EX, D..............................285.00

Favorite Range, sign, lady seated at table with her head down, Ruined...Buy Her A Favorite Range, rectangular, NM, A..............................120.00

Fay's Corset Shop, sign, lg A on left, lg Y on right of company name, horizontal rectangle, A.....................40.00

Federal Oil Co, tin, orange lettering, 1917, half-gal, 6", EX+, A.............................185.00

Federal Sugar Refining Co, sign, canvas, factory scene with company name & address below, Julius Bien litho, 24x39", appears EX, A..............................900.00

Feen-A-Mint Laxative, display, tin with wood base, pictures girl holding product, oval mirror inset atop, 1910-20, 16x8x6", EX+, A..............................350.00

Feen-A-Mint Laxative, display, tin with wood base, pictures girl holding product, oval mirror inset atop, 1910-20, scratches, 16x8x6", G, A..............................160.00

Fehr's Beer, tray, depicts King & Queen with product name arched above & below in lg letters, 16" diameter, appears EX, A..............................100.00

Fehr's Famous FFXL Beers, tray, 13" diameter, appears EX+, A..............................400.00

Fehr's Malt Tonic, match holder, die-cut tin litho, figural bottle, some fading/rust, 6x2", G, A.....................250.00

Feigenspan Beer, opener, D..............................10.00

Feigenspan Breweries, tip tray, pictures young girl in profile, Compliments Feigenspan Breweries lettered below, 4" diameter, NM, A..............................75.00

Feigenspan Breweries, tray, pictures young girl in profile, Compliments Feigenspan Breweries lettered below, 1910, 13" diameter, G, A..............................25.00

Feigenspan's Amber Ale, sign, die-cut porcelain, red, white, & blue, PON Trade Mark & product name lettered above & below, 24x18", G-, A.....................200.00

Felix Potin Chocolat, sign, paper on composition board, 25x18", EX, A..............................600.00

Fenix Self-Rising Flour, thimble, aluminum, product name on dark blue band, EX, D..............................5.00

Ferris Corsets, display, 2-sided die-cut tin, 3-quarter female wearing corset, slight fading/scratching/denting, 43x18x14", G, A..............................1,200.00

Ferris Waists, sign, tin litho, mother reading to her children, Ferris Good Sense lettered below, ca 1900, self-framed, 22x16", VG, A..............................800.00

Ferris Waists, sign, tin litho, self-framed, 23x17", EX+, A..............................4,500.00

Fiddle Faddle Carmel Corn, bear, with fiddle, plush, original box, M, D..............................20.00

Fidelio Brewery, tray, deep-dish, tavern scene with men seated around a table being served, ca 1936, image wear, 12" diameter, VG, A..............................45.00

Fidelity & Casualty Co, ledger marker, tin, yellow with black & red lettering, 1891 calendar on reverse, Ginna & Co litho, 12x3", VG, A..............................120.00

Film Cigars, box label, inner lid, depicts people at the movies in silhouette, 6x9", M, D **28.00**

Filmkote 22's, sign, cardboard trifold, pictures man instructing 2 boys at target practice, Peters Cartridge Co below, 28x35", EX, A..**55.00**

Finck's Overalls, sign, embossed tin, 12x24" without frame, VG, A **150.00**

Finck's Overalls, sign, porcelain, pig logo, Detroit Special lettered above, Try a Pair, The Man Who... below, rectangular, EX, A..**150.00**

Fine Point Cigars, box label, inner lid, depicts couple lighting up from the same cigar, 6x9", M, D..........**35.00**

Finest Golden Spring Whiskey, shot glass, product name etched in thin letters with entwined GB monogram above, EX, D...**16.00**

Finlay Brewing Co, tip tray, circular logo on leaf pattern, Finest Beers, Toledo O lettered above & below, rim chips, 4" diameter, EX, A **200.00**

Finlay Brewing Co, tip tray, woman holding oversized bottle, company name & Toledo O lettered above & below, rim chips, 4" diameter, EX, A **75.00**

Firemen's Insurance Co, sign, metal, depicts fireman at left & lg lettering at right with geometric border, Newark NJ, pitting, 12x18", G, A............................**25.00**

Firestone Spark Plugs, case, display & storage, tin, pictures lg spark plug, blue & black letters upper left, 1940-50, 15x20", VG+, A.....................................**175.00**

Firestone Tires, calendar for JW Richley Automobile Co, 1917, pictures man helping 3 women out of a car, full pad, framed, 36x17", VG+, A...............................**1,100.00**

Fisk Tires, display rack, Time To Re-Order Fisk in raised letters, 1940, scuffs/scratches, 6x15" with tire, A...**160.00**

Fisk Tires, figure, nickel-plated white metal boy holding tire & candle holder, wooden base, 18", EX, A ...**750.00**

Fisk Tires, light, plastic figure of boy holding tire, Fisk on base, interior illumination, 12", EX, A..................**475.00**

Fisk Tubes & Tires, sign, porcelain, 60", D **225.00**

Fitzgerald Bros Brewing Co, tray, deep-dish, 2 women flanking seal with factory in background, lettering below, image chips, 12" diameter, G, A **300.00**

Flaked Rice, giveaway doll, cloth, My Name Is Flaked Rice, Canadian, ca 1890, slight stain/light wear, 25x12x4", VG, A **350.00**

Flaroma Coffee, tin, trademark on red background, minor chipping, 1-lb, 6x4" diameter, VG+, A **55.00**

Flat Iron Plug Tobacco, sign, cardboard, girl's face in lg oval with sm eye above, 4 girls in squares vertically at left, 1900-10, 21x15", VG, A...............................**140.00**

Flavor, crate label, California orange, valley of orchards with mountains, Orange Heights Orange Ass'n, 1940s, 10x12", M, D **3.00**

Fleer's Gum, vendor, 1¢, oak & brass, tin litho front with lettered graphics, ca 1898, overall dirt/paint chips, 15x10", VG, A...**1,250.00**

Fleer's Guru-Kola Gum, sign, tin, filigree border, overall wear, 10x14", G+, A **6,500.00**

Fleet-Wing Motor Oil, tin, Certified lettered in blue over orange bird, product name on orange band below, cream ground, 1945-50, 1-qt, VG+, A **25.00**

Fleetwood Motor Oil, tin, dark blue with white lettered banner over plane superimposed on white circle, 1925-45, 2-gal, 12", EX, A **150.00**

Fleischmann's, booklet, 1916, 'Dainty Dishes Made With Freihofer's Bread Raised With Fleischmann's Yeast,' 32 pages, 7x5", VG+, D **12.00**

Fleischmann's, booklet, 1917, paperback, 'Fleischmann's Recipes,' 48 pages, D **9.00**

Fleischmann's, booklet, 1924, 'Fleischmann's Recipes,' 48 pages, D **6.00**

Fleischmann's, calendar, 1906, cardboard, depicts horse-drawn wagon, July pad, minor edge tears/wrinkling, 14x10", EX, A **110.00**

Fleischmann's, door push, porcelain, D **250.00**

Fleischmann's Yeast, sign, tin with hanging chain, nail holes/1 dent, 14x20", VG+, A **1,700.00**

Flick & Flock Cigars, tin, pictures 2 dogs, slip lid, rare, minor scrapes, rare, elongated, VG, A **175.00**

Flint's Cigar Store, match safe, tin, EX, D..................**25.00**

Flor de Kearney Cigars, box label, inner lid, depicts bust portrait of Civil War officer flanked by eagle & soldier on horse, 6x9", M, D **75.00**

Floressence Violette Talc, tin, Art Nouveau, G, D.....**15.00**

Florsheim Shoes, sign, lighted, dome shape, A..........**90.00**

Flyer 5¢ Cigars, sign, cardboard litho, plane above globe flanked by Paris & NY scenes, World's Greatest..., 1930, framed, 8x20", EX, A.......................................**85.00**

Foley's Kidney Pills, container, glass jar, product name on paper label insert, appears EX, A **200.00**

Folger's Coffee, lighter, Zippo, within presentation case, D **40.00**

Forbes Coffee, thimble, aluminum, black band with company name & product, EX, D **4.00**

Ford, catalog, 'Big 52 Ford,' color illustrations of the complete line of Ford, 30 pages, 12x9", EX, A **10.00**

Ford, sign, porcelain, double-sided, Property of Ford Motor Co on back, 24", EX, A 250.00

Ford, table lamp, wicker base, Buy a Ford lettered on lampshade, shade revolves in response to heat of bulb, 15", EX, A **475.00**

Ford Anti-Freeze, tin, yellow with navy blue borders, Ford emblem at top, Contains Corrosion Inhibitor below, 1930-40, 1-gal, 11", VG+, A **65.00**

Ford Motor Co, puppet, Ford logo, wearing straw hat, 1975, EX, D **15.00**

Fore 'n Aft Tobacco, sign, paper, depicts bearded man on ship in a red logoed sweatshirt smoking a pipe, framed, vertical rectangle, EX, A...**180.00**

Forest & Stream Tobacco, pocket tin, double-sided, depicts 2 men & dog fishing from canoe, Montreal & Granby Canada, slip lid, 4x3x1", G+, A **550.00**

Forest & Stream Tobacco, tin, depicts fisherman in canoe with dog, minor scratches/chips at embossed rim/some denting, 4x4" diameter, VG, A...........................**575.00**

Forest & Stream Tobacco, tin, depicts man fishing in stream, original embossed slip lid, Montreal & Granby Canada, 6x4" diameter, VG, A **425.00**

Forest & Stream Tobacco, tin, depicts man fishing in stream, original embossed slip lid, Montreal & Granby Canada, 3x4" diameter, VG, A **275.00**

Forest & Stream Tobacco, tin, depicts man fishing in stream, original pictorial slip lid, Montreal & Granby Canada, 3x3" diameter, VG, A **350.00**

Forest & Stream Tobacco, tin, inverted image of man in stream, original embossed slip lid, Montreal & Granby Canada, 6x4" diameter, G+, A **200.00**

Forster's Peanut Butter, pail, circular logo, slip lid & bail, EX+, A **55.00**

Fort Garry Tobacco, tin, pictures fort at Hudson Bay with Indians in foreground, Canada, overall wear, 5x4x3", VG, A **125.00**

Fort Pitt Coffee, tin, fort pictured, Young-Mahood Co, press lid, light wear, 3-lb, 8x6" diameter, VG, A .**350.00**

Fort Western Coffee, tin, shows coffee cup & Indian in canoe passing Fort Western on the Kennebec River, Augusta Maine, 1-lb, 6x4", VG, A.........................**125.00**

Foss & Deering Mustard, pail, black & yellow, Portland Me lettered below product name, press lid & bail, quarter-lb, NM, A...**155.00**

Foss & Deering Mustard, pail, black & yellow, Portland Me lettered below product name, press lid & bail, lid has plating loss, half-lb, NM, A **180.00**

Foster Hose Supporters, sign, celluloid, woman superimposed over corset with supporters, The Name Is On The Buckles, overall wear, 17x9", VG, A **125.00**

Foster Hose Supporters, celluloid, woman superimposed over corset with supporters, The Name Is On The Buckles, 17x9, NM, A.....................400.00

Fostoria Undermuslin Co, tip tray, pictures young woman with flower in her hair, company name above, ca 1908, 4" diameter, NM, A **105.00**

Fountain Fine Cut Tobacco, tin, fountain with classical figures, lettering above & below, Penn Tobacco Co..., slip lid, round, appears, EX, A **150.00**

Four Roses Smoking Tobacco, pocket tin, green, appears NM, D...**750.00**

Four Roses Smoking Tobacco, pocket tin, pictures 4 red roses on cream circle, EX+, A **650.00**

Four Roses Tobacco, poster, cardboard litho, pictures elegant women in centers of 4 roses, original frame, 12x16", EX, A...**325.00**

Fowler's Cherry Smash, see Cherry Smash

Fowler's Root Beer, dispenser, white ceramic potbelly, red lettering, 5¢, The Best, original pump, crack in base, VG+, A **800.00**

Fox Trot Panatelas, tin, running fox on yellow background, 3 for 5¢, embossed rim, minor chipping mostly to rim, rare, 6x5" diameter, VG, A **700.00**

FR Penn Tobacco Co, sign, embossed tin, rare, 10x13", A **1,150.00**

Francis Lee Cigars, tin, portrait of Lee (1734-1797), signer of Declaration of Independence, slip lid, chips/dents, 6x6" diameter, VG, A **340.00**

Francisco Auto Heaters, sign, tin, automobile on a snow-covered road with logo superimposed on the hood, Summer Here All The Year, 18x40", EX, A........**1,100.00**

Frank Fehr Brewing Co, sign, tin, elderly man sleeping in chair with woman holding beer over his head, None Purer..., 1905-10, 28x22, EX, A **400.00**

Frank Jones Portsmouth Ales, tip tray, lettered logo in center, Look For This Sign, Accept No Substitute lettered around rim, 4" diameter, VG, A **40.00**

Miller's Blacking, display box, inside lid label depicts Uncle Sam shaving by his reflection in polished boots, minor wear, 3x11x9", EX, A **350.00**

k's Fruit & Beverages, tray, depicts branch of cherries in center with lettering on rim, horizontal rectangle, EX, A **15.00**

k's Kutlery Kuts, playing cards, USPC, 52 cards with 1 Joker & 2 extra cards, ca 1900, original box, M, D ...**30.00**

klin Caro Gum, container, glass jar, embossed lettering on lid & bottom, ca 1915, 12x5x5", NM, A.....**100.00**

klin Life Insurance Co, doll, cloth, Ben Franklin, in original bag, 13", M, D **18.00**

ser's Axle Grease, sign, tin, pictures 2 teams & wagons, 1 has wheel missing, American Art Works litho, self-framed, 25x38", G-, A **750.00**

sier Thornton Reliable Remedies, sign, paper, pictures Dr Thornton & nurse surrounded by veterinary remedies with lettering above, matted & framed, 26x22", NM, A **260.00**

red Bauernschmidt's American Brewery, tray, picturing the Baltimore brewery, 14x17", EX, A **950.00**

Fred Oppermann Jr Brewery, sign, paper, portrait superimposed on turtle shell, EX, A...............**850.00**

Fred Roebuck Liquor, tray, stock image of Griselda, touch-up to girl's face/overall scratching/rim chips, 13" diameter, G, A **40.00**

Fred Sehring Brewing Co, tip tray, labeled bottle on black background, Joliet's Popular Beer lettered above, rare, 4" diameter, NM, A......................................**70.00**

Fredericksburg Bottled Beer, display, die-cut tin stand-up, glass & labeled bottle figural, San Jose Calif, surface rust on edges, 6x10", G, A.....................**325.00**

Fredericksburg Bottled Beer, tip tray, pictures hooded little girl in center, Bottled Beer, Always Good lettered on border, 4" diameter, EX, A **300.00**

Fredericksburg Brewery, tray, minor touch-up on decorative rim, 13" diameter, EX+, A **650.00**

Fredericksburg Lager Beer, tray, pictures hooded little girl flanked by logo, lettering on decorative border, some fading, 14" diameter, G+, A **500.00**

Free Lance Cigars, sign, hanging, cardboard, box label in center, Smoke A Free Lance And Be Convinced, rectangular, appears EX, A......................................**35.00**

Freedom Motor Oil, tin, bulldog standing on the word Freedom above FC on banded label, Motor Oil lettered below, ca 1935-45, 1-qt, VG, A......................................**20.00**

Freedom Motor Oil, tin, stylized Nouveau vine motif in silver around FOWCO logo, silver & black lettering, ca 1915-25, 1-gal, 9", EX, A **100.00**

Freedom Perfect Motor Oil, tin, bulldog above blue letters on yellow circle, Vacuum Process below, screw top, 1932-40, 1-qt, 6x4" diameter, EX+, A **100.00**

Freedom Perfect Motor Oil, tin, bulldog above blue letters on yellow circle, Vacuum Process below, 1935-45, no top, 5-qt, 10x7" diameter, EX+, A **80.00**

Freihofer's Quality Cakes, display cabinet, metal & glass, 2 shelves, A Cake For Every Taste, Pound, Sponge, Fruit, product name above, 22", EX, A **100.00**

French Auto Oil, tin, letters superimposed on arrow above race car at track, all in lg yellow circle, 1915-25, 1-gal, 11", VG+, A..**1,200.00**

French Dressing Satin Polish & Blacking, sign, tin, patriotic logo with man & boy giving ladies a shoeshine flanked by product, 1870s(?), 24x18", NM, A **40,000.00**

Freshpak Coffee, tin, building with product name above & below, slip lid, 1-lb, round, appears EX, A **40.00**

Fresno Brewing Co, tray, deep-dish, island maiden with ukulele, California, overbubbling to image colors/rim chips, 13" diameter, G, A **150.00**

Frigidaire, tape measure, celluloid, retractable, text on back, 1" diameter, D **30.00**

Frigidtest Anti-Freeze, tin, arctic scene with polar bears & icebergs, plane flying past sun, ca 1940, no top, 1-qt, EX, A **160.00**

Frisch's Big Boy, ash tray, glass, orange graphic of Frisch's boy holding up a Big Boy hamburger on clear background, 3" diameter, D **30.00**

Frishmuth's Whittle Cut Tobacco, tin, flat, blue & red on green, Will Not Bite The Tongue below logo, I Am Good & Try Me vertically on sides, 4x5", EX, A.....**30.00**

Frontenac Beer, sign, pictures girl in a tree with a baseball scene beyond, vertical rectangle, EX, A...............**400.00**

Frontenac Beer, tray, colorful frontal view of factory & street scene, lettering on rim, Canada's Best, Montreal, 12" diameter, VG+, A **80.00**

Frontenac Export Ale, sign, tin, 8x26", EX, A **130.00**

Frontenac White Cap Ale/Special Lager Beer, tray, porcelain, White Cap Ale arched above Frontenac, Special Lager, Canada, minor scratches, 13" diameter, EX+, A **35.00**

Frontier Cigars, box label, inner lid, depicts 2 hunters with downed buck in snow scene, cabin beyond, 6x9", EX, D...**125.00**

Frontier Mixture Tobacco, tin, soldier riding towards small outpost, medallions on back, British-American Tobacco Co, 4x3" diameter, G+, A........................**110.00**

Frostie Root Beer sign, die-cut cardboard, animated figure holding sign with silhoutted figures, Everybody Loves Frostie, 13x21", D..**25.00**

Fru-Tola, syrup dispenser, glass bulb atop round metal base, metal lid, 18", appears EX, A **110.00**

Fruits & Flowers Smoking Tobacco, sign, paper litho, water stained, gilt frame, 32x24", EX, A 550.00

Fruits of California, sign, paper litho, colorful image of eagle stealing can of fruit from bears, San Jose Fruit Packing Co, 14x10", M, A **1,350.00**

Fry's Extract, clock, figure-8 shape with Why Not Try This bordering raised extract bottle on bottom circle, 28", VG, A **470.00**

Frye's Western Cigars, box label, outer, pictures a man with a moustache, mountains in the background, 5x5", M, D...**8.00**

Full Dress Cigars, box label, inner lid, depicts man in formal attire smoking a cigar, 6x9", M, D...................**35.00**

Fuller Brush Co, doll, boy, stuffed, 8", M, D..............**20.00**

Fulton's Chocolates, sign, die-cut, man with box of chocolate & 2 women behind lg logo, light blue background, framed, 20x33", appears EX, A **260.00**

FW Cook Brewing Co, glass, etched factory scene, NM, A..**55.00**

FW McNess Breakfast Cocoa, sample tin, EX, A........**45.00**

✎ G ✎

Gail & Ax Chesapeake Tobacco, tin, rare Ginna litho, slip lid, chips/dents, 4x7x5", G-, A **800.00**

Gail & Ax Navy Tobacco, label, pictures 3 sailing frigates, product name above, 1886, dirt smudges/creases, matted & framed, 9x11", VG, A **50.00**

Gail & Ax Navy Tobacco, lunch box, tin, logoed sailor on lid with silver background, slip lid with fasteners, 5x8x5", G, A...**75.00**

Gail & Ax Navy Tobacco, sign, embossed tin litho, framed, 20x14", VG, A 1,400.00

Gail & Ax Virginity Smoking Tobacco, tin, double-sided, pictures the factory & 'The Virgin,' Gail & Ax, slip lid, major lid damage/chips/dents, 4x7x4" G, A.........**400.00**

Gale Manufacturing Co, match holder, tin litho, colorful factory image, Makers of Agricultural Implements, Albion Mich, 5x3", G, A **135.00**

Galenol Motor Oil, tin, yellow with arched Galenol over 100% Pure logo, Friction's Moremost Foe, scratched letters, 1915-25, 1-gal, EX+, A **65.00**

Galion Iron Works, watch fob, 3 machines, D...........**28.00**

Gallaher's Rich Dark Honeydew Tobacco, tin, depicts 2 men enjoying a smoke with servant & billiards player behind, rounded corners, 4x7", appears EX, A **95.00**

Gallaher's War Horse Tobacco, sign, embossed tin litho, 2 armored soldiers on chargers at battle, Plug Smoker's Favourite below, paint rubs, 20x14", A.................**300.00**

Gallant Knight Cigars, box label, inner lid, depicts a Knight flanked by logo, 6x9", M, A **6.00**

Galliker Ice Cream, tray, pictures mother & her 2 children having a dish of ice cream, Galliker's Quality on decorative rim, round, EX, A **260.00**

Galveston Brewing Co, tip tray, labeled bottle in center, High Grade, The Beer That's Liquid Food, minor rim scratches, 4" diameter, NM, A...............................**250.00**

Game Cock Rye, charger, tin, dead game & bottle of whiskey, John Miller & Co below, C Shonk litho, fading/scratches, 24" diameter, G, A **125.00**

Game Fine Cut Tobacco, store bin, tin, shows 2 game cocks on floral field, Jon J Bagley & Co, slip lid, crazing/chips, 8x7x12", VG, A.....................................**375.00**

Gander Cooking & Salad Oil, sign, tin litho, woman at table being served, goose on window sill, Makes Good Things To Eat, framed, 19" long, G-, A.................**475.00**

Garcia Lopez Cigars, box label, inner lid, depicts man flanked by 2 white statues, 1882, 6x9", M, D **5.00**

Garcia Roses Tobacco, box label, inner lid, depicts a basket of roses, 6x9", M, A **7.00**

Garfield Tea, sign, tin, depicts bust portrait of a bearded man, Cures Constipation & Sick Headache, dings/scratches, 27x19", A **850.00**

Garland Stoves & Ranges, match holder, cardboard litho, plus 1904 calendar pad, 7x4", VG+, A ..**250.00**

Garland Stoves & Ranges, match holder, die-cut tin, Ginna & Co litho, 7x4", VG+, A **500.00**

Garland Stoves & Ranges, pin holder, tin litho, Somers Bros, early, EX, D..**48.00**

Gayrock Clothing, sign, embossed tin, framed, 39x29", EX+, A...**1,300.00**

Geisecke Shoes, match holder, tin litho, colorful logo with key atop, Key Brand, St Louis, All Ways Best, 6x4", VG, A..**175.00**

Geiser Mfg Co, sign, paper, oval factory scene with farm implements above & below, vignettes in bottom corners, 26x15", EX, A......................................**1,400.00**

Gem Damaskeene Razors, clock, wood with original pendulum, working condition, 28x23", VG, A **1,700.00**

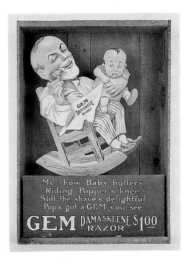

Gem Damaskeene Razors, display, cardboard with clockwork mechanism, 1910-20, original crate, rare, 29x21", NM, A..**3,250.00**

Gem Damaskeene Razors, display, die-cut cardboard, pictures open shaving box with razors, color touch-up, 21x23", G, A **100.00**

Gem Damaskeene Razors, display, tin with beveled mirror inset, papa & baby sitting on razor atop, product below, 1910-20, 19x11", NM, A...........................**1,100.00**

General Accident Automobile Insurance, sign, reverse painting on glass, pictures touring car, silver lettering, original frame, 23x31", EX, A **9,500.00**

General Electric, ash tray, heavy white ceramic, embossed figural fluorescent bulb with platinum ends, Power Groove, M, D **50.00**

General Electric, calendar, 1932, depicts Maxfield Parrish's 'Solitude' atop, GE emblem in center, in original envelope, 19x9", M, A......................**310.00**

General Electric, doll, cloth, Mr MaGoo, 11", EX, D ..**16.00**

General Electric, tape measure & sewing caddy, blue & white plastic figural canister vacuum with metal trim, 3", EX, A......................**45.00**

General Electric, trade card, pictures blue tinted irons with astronomical background, horizontal, D........**10.00**

General Foods, cookbook, hard-bound, 'All About Baking,' 144 pages, 1935, D......................**8.00**

General Foods, cookbook, hard-bound, 'All About Home Baking,' 144 pages, 1933, D......................**6.00**

General Foods, recipe booklet, 'A Calendar Of Desserts,' 1940, 48 pages, VG, D **5.00**

General Mills, doll, Boo Boo Ghost, 1975, 8", EX, D .**10.00**

General Mills, doll, Count Chocula, 1975, EX, D........**20.00**

General Mills, doll, Slippin' Sam, D......................**15.00**

General Steedman Cigars, box label, inner lid, depicts General Steedman's portrait with his name above & below, 6x9", M, D......................**35.00**

General Wm J Palmer Cigars, box label, inner lid, depicts a bust portrait of General Palmer & a train scene, 6x9", M, D **4.00**

Genese Lager Beer, sign, tin, C Shonk litho, self-framed, 14x22", EX, A......................275.00

Genuine Pollack Experts, sign, cardboard, depicts riverboat & city at river's edge with box of Genuine Pollack Experts, framed, 30x21", EX, A......................**60.00**

Geo Ehret's Extra, tray, logoed star flanked by Hellgate Brewery, overall touch-up, oval, 17x14", G, A **25.00**

Geo J Renner Brewing Co, tray, elderly gent pouring glass of beer flanked by lettering, Just Like Our Grandfathers Brewed below, round, M, A **360.00**

Geo Ringler & Co Brewery, calendar poster, paper, factory view with product & hops in foreground, some wear, matted & framed, 33x24", VG+, A..............**850.00**

Geo Zett Brewery, calendar, 1905, paper, scene of 'The Lorelei' luring the troops to destruction, full pad, matted & framed, 21x14", VG, A **750.00**

Geo Zett Brewery, tray, deep-dish, brass, lion logo in center, Bavarian Lager, Syracuse NY lettered below, 12" diameter, EX, A......................**35.00**

Geo Zett Brewery, tray, green & red with lion logo in center, Lager, Ales, & Porter lettered below, lacquer shrinkage, 13" diameter, VG, A **100.00**

Geo Zett's Ale, tray, lion logo on wide band in center, product name in lg letters above & below, ca 1935, oval, 15x13", VG, A......................**40.00**

Geo Zett's Bavarian Beer, calendar, 1911, paper, pictures returning soldiers, Kaufmann & Strauss, full pad, some creasing, 18x20", EX, A......................**155.00**

Geo Zett's Bavarian Beer, calendar, 1912, paper, soldier on furlough with friends, Kaufmann & Strauss, full pad, matted & framed, 18x20", VG, A......................**90.00**

Geo Zett's Bavarian Beer, tray, colorful image of cavalier lifting glass of beer & holding flag with product name, 13" square, EX, A......................**225.00**

Geo Zett's Par-Ex Beer, calendar, 1915, paper, German-type brewery scene, Kaufmann & Strauss litho, full pad, matted & framed, 18x20", EX, A......................**110.00**

Geo Zett's Par-Ex Beer, tray, deep-dish, Dutch girl carrying basket of Par-Ex beer bottles, It Beats The Dutch below, 12" diameter, NM, A......................**150.00**

Geo Zett's Par-Ex Beer, tray, deep-dish, pictures girl holding dove, Kaufmann & Strauss litho, ca 1904, 12" diameter, NM, A......................**160.00**

Geo Zett's Par-Ex Beer, tray, deep-dish, pictures girl resting on a tiger, Kaufmann & Strauss litho, ca 1904, edge chips, 12" diameter, NM, A......................**225.00**

Geo Zett's Par-Ex Beer, tray, deep-dish, 12" diameter, EX, A......................145.00

George Lawrance Co Dog Chains & Leads, sign, tin, pictures dog's head with product & company name below, Established 1857, square, A......................**90.00**

George Washington Cut Plug Tobacco, lunch box, red, blue, & silver with bust of George Washington, wire bail with wood handle, good color, 5x8", EX, A....**70.00**

George Washington Instant Coffee, tin, EX, D........**30.00**

Gerber, playing cards, Gerber baby logo in white circle on red background with white border, Gerber in white, complete, D......................**7.00**

Gerber, spoon, stainless steel, Gerber 50 Years Of Caring, 1928-1978, 6", G, D......................**12.00**

German American Brewing Co, tip tray, deep-dish, factory scene in subtle sepia tones, Maltosia Pure Malt lettered below, rare, 4" diameter, NM, A **250.00**

German American Brewing Co, tip tray, Maltosia logo shield in center, Our Beer Is Sterilized Not Pasteurized lettered below, 4" diameter, NM, A......................**30.00**

German American Brewing Co, tray, depicts 2 bottles over Leda riding swan among hops & grain, lettering on rim, square, EX+, D 275.00

German American Insurance Co of New York, sign, depicts German & American ladies shaking hands in center oval with lettering above & below, cream background, EX, A ....,.............350.00

Germania Brewing Co, sign, paper litho, artist painting a ram for Buck Beer, Comptom & Sons, ca 1890, framed, tear/restoration, 38x25", EX, A........1,000.00

Germania Brewing Co, tip tray, elk's head in center, Chammer's High Grade Bottled Beer, minor chips, 4" diameter, NM, A 130.00

Germania Brewing Co, tip tray, pictures dainty little girl with roses in her hair, Chammer's High Grade Bottled Beer, 4" diameter, NM, A 200.00

Germania Brewing Co, tip tray, pictures girl holding roses, Chammer's High Grade Bottled Beers, 4" diameter, NM, A.....................65.00

Germania Lager, tray, ca 1890, 19x15", G-, A.......150.00

Gevaert Roll Film, display rack, tin, colorful image of the product, 11x15x5", EX, A.......................50.00

GF Burkhardt's Lager Beer, sign, tin litho, early, framed, 17x14", EX+, A......................800.00

Ghiradelli's Chocolate & Cocoa, sign, tin litho, scratches, rare, self-framed, 28x22", VG+, A...................8,000.00

Giant Salted Peanuts, pail, depicts club-toting giant surveying circus parade, slip lid & bail, overall wear, rare, 4x4", G, A 125.00

Giant Salted Peanuts, tin, depicts club-toting giant with castle beyond, Superior Peanut Co, Cleveland O, press lid, 10-lb, 11x8", VG, A.........................150.00

Giant Salted Peanuts, tin, press lid, 10-lb, 11x8" diameter, EX+, A.........................650.00

Gibson's Lozenge, tin, lettered & floral decoration on medicinal tin, Gibson's Cough Lozenge, Manchester England, 9x6x6", VG+, A 250.00

Gibson's Whiskey, sign, depicts Art Nouveau nudes & lg whiskey bottle, ca 1895-1905, framed, 16x11", appears EX, A 1,550.00

Gilbert Raes Aerated Waters, sign, embossed tin, 3 labeled bottles above factory scene, Baldridge Works Dunfermline, Hunt & Frenkel litho, 28x20", A 900.00

Gillies Coffee, lunch pail, lid with ring handle, wire bail, fading, 5x5" diameter, G, A 50.00

Gillies Coffee Co Tea, tin, company name on diagonal above Tea, 233 to 239 Washington St NY, wire ring handle, square, EX, A 280.00

Gimball Printing Co, match safe, nickel with celluloid insets, NM, D 45.00

Ginger-Mint Julep, dispenser, barrel shape with metal bands & spigot on top, painted oval on side with lettering, 14", appears EX, D.................................**35.00**

Girard Cigars, sign, tin over cardboard, man smoking cigar, elements of image in color float on black background, 19x13", G+, A.................................**325.00**

Girard Educators Cigars, tin, shows portrait of founder of Girard College, slip lid, minor denting/slight chipping, 6x6" diameter, EX, A.................................**75.00**

Glendora Coffee, sign, tin, 14x9", NM, A.................................**80.00**

Glendora Coffee, tin, sample, EX, D.................................**25.00**

Glennen's Beer, tray, shows Indian hunting buffalo, lettering on rim, hairline scratching/fading/rim chips, 13" square, VG, A.................................**300.00**

Glicks Cabaret Mints, tin, pictures a ballerina, slip lid, round, A.................................**15.00**

Globe Chalk, box containing 3 white chalks, ca 1920s, EX, D.................................**3.00**

Globe Dyes, cabinet, wood case with gallery top & circular paper inset displaying colors, worn finish/inset, 29x16x10", VG, A.................................**100.00**

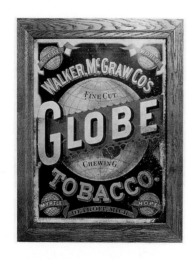

Globe Fine Cut Chewing Tobacco, sign, tin, rare, framed, 23x17", EX, A.................................1,450.00

Globe Sales & Service, sign, globe in black with yellow letters & red lightning bolt, Battery Station, 1920-30, 42" diameter, VG+, A.................................**185.00**

Globe-Wernicke Sectional Bookcases, tip tray, couple constructing & filling bookcase, 1913, minor scratches/flaking, EX+, A.................................**20.00**

Gluek Beer, sign, curved Vitrolite, logoed star with product name above & below, 23x16", M, A.................................**700.00**

GO Blake Whiskey, tray, colonial aristocrat enjoying pipe, book, & whiskey, HD Beach Co litho, ca 1910-20, 12" diameter, NM, A.................................**150.00**

Gobblers' Cigars, tin, picturing full-feathered turkey, The Latest Smoke, slight fade/minor spotting/sm dents, 5x5" diameter, G-, A.................................**300.00**

Goebel Beer, tip tray, deep-dish, blue & white, Dutch girl with baskets & sailboat beyond, minor rim chips, 4" diameter, NM, A.................................**60.00**

Goebel Beer, tip tray, deep-dish, blue & white, Dutchman with a boat, minor rim chips, 4" diameter, NM, A.**40.00**

Goebel Beer, tip tray, deep-dish, blue & white, 2 Dutch girls carrying a basket, minor rim chips, 4" diameter, NM, A.................................**60.00**

Goebel Beer, tip tray, Dutch gentleman having a brew, Detroit USA, background chips/edge wear, 4" diameter, EX, A.................................**55.00**

Goebel Beer, tray, Dutch gentleman flanked by product name, decorative border, Detroit USA, 12" diameter, G, A.................................**175.00**

Goebel's Malt Extract, tip tray, little girl teaching at blackboard, Detroit USA, rare, 4" diameter, EX, A.................................**250.00**

Goff's Angora Braid, sign, paper, shows seated woman with fan, top appears trimmed/surface crazing/wear, 14x10" without frame, G, A.................................**50.00**

Gold Buckle, crate label, California orange, orchards encircled by belt, East Highlands Of The Citrus Belt, 1930s, 10x12", M, D.................................**4.00**

Gold Coin Stoves & Ranges, sign, tin, lettered graphics, Stoves & Ranges Exchanged For Greenbacks, ca 1880s, 6x7", EX, A.................................**170.00**

Gold Dust & Fairy Soap, fan, cardboard, round hand fan with Gold Dust twins overlooking 1904 World's Fair, creasing/chips, 12x8" diameter, EX, A.................................**70.00**

Gold Dust Scouring Cleanser, tin, Gold Dust twins pictured over product name on paper label, EX, A....**65.00**

Gold Dust Washing Powder, sample box (full), pictures Gold Dust twins, EX, D.................................**25.00**

Gold Dust Washing Powder, shipping box, cardboard, depicts multiple images of twins, some surface damage/chipping/rubbing, 12x19x14", G-, A.................................**95.00**

Gold Dust Washing Powder, shipping box, wood with paper label on 1 side depicting twins, stamped lettering on other sides, early, 9x30x12", VG, A.................................**165.00**

Gold Dust Washing Powder, sign, paper, 26x13", appears EX, A.................................5,500.00

Gold Medal Braid Co, cabinet, wood with 3 drawers lettered in gold leaf, Golden Fleece 61 Roll Braid, replaced knobs, 13x24x18", EX, A.................................**325.00**

Gold Medal Camp Furniture, sign, tin litho, family fishing & camping, Haeusermann, self-framed, overall chipping, 14x19", VG, A.................................**650.00**

Gold Medal Flour, broom holder, wood with tin front insert, Use Gold Medal Flour, Washburn-Crosby Co, 41", appears EX, A.................................**150.00**

Gold Medal Flour, cookbook, 1904, D **20.00**

Gold Medal Flour, cookbook, 1917, paperback, 74 pages, D...**18.00**

Gold Medal Flour, cookbook, 1955, paperpack, 'Jubilee Recipes,' D **9.00**

Gold Medal Flour, sign, hold-to-light, product name arched above factory scene, Washburn Crosby, framed, 24x34", appears EX, A **1,100.00**

Gold Pheasant Cigars, box label, inner lid, depicts pheasant next to tree stump, 1936, 6x9", M, D **35.00**

Gold Seal Boots, tin, embossed depiction of a rubber boot & lettering, American Art Works litho, overall wear, framed, 20x14", G+, A **195.00**

Gold Shore Cut Plug Tobacco, tin, red & gold lettering on white, Smoking Or Chewing, hinged lid, rectangular, A **40.00**

Gold Shore Tobacco, pouch (empty), cloth, EX, D **5.00**

Gold Shore Tobacco, tin, depicts flying horse, Cut Plug Tobacco, Smoking Or Chewing, hinged lid, dents/flaking, rounded corners, 4x6", A **60.00**

Golden Grain Tobacco, pouch (full), cloth, G, D **10.00**

Golden Leaf Motor Oil, tin, royal blue with yellow letters & gold-yellow leaf in center, ca 1935-45, 1-qt, 6", EX+, A **25.00**

Golden Link Flour, tip tray, Always Good, blue & white, 1910-20, light wear, 4" diameter, EX, A **20.00**

Golden Orangeade, sign, cardboard litho, oranges surrounding a glass, J Hungerford Smith Co, original decorative frame, 23x16", VG, A **325.00**

Golden Rod Ice Cream, sign, die-cut cardboard, young girl in sailor top holding ice cream cone, Keeps Youth In Health, 27x17", EX, A **70.00**

Golden Shell Auto Oil, tin, Golden Shell lettered above embossed shell, yellow & black lettering on orange, 1915-25, 1-gal, 11", NM, A **800.00**

Golden Shell Motor Oil, tin, Golden Shell lettered on lg red shell with orange highlights on orange ground, 1935-45, 5-qt, 10x7", EX, A **60.00**

Golden Shell Motor Oil, tin, seashell in center with Golden Shell lettered above & Auto Oil below, ca 1935-45, minor dents, 1-qt, EX, NM **85.00**

Golden Vine Brand Salted Peanuts, tin, lettered gilt & black geometric inset on yellow background, logoed center, press lid, round, 12", EX, A **90.00**

Golden Wedding Whiskey, sign, tin over cardboard, 2 men conversing, elements of image in color float on black background, 20x14", G-, A **175.00**

Goldstein's Sons, thermometer, painted wood, Metals Smelters & Refiners, Philadelphia Pa, arched top with metal hanger, 15x4", VG, A **28.00**

Good & Plenty Candy, beanbag doll, vinyl face & hands, Choo-Choo Charlie, 10", EX, D **18.00**

Good Roads Farm Machinery Co, sign, paper, factory scene with horse-drawn & steam equipment on street, 12x12" without frame, EX, A **225.00**

Good Year Service Station, sign, porcelain, yellow & green letters on purple, lg tire revolving around Earth, chipping, approx: 24x74", VG, A **170.00**

Good Year Tires, sign, 2-sided with flange, Service Station, Good Year Tires, green with orange striped border, 1915-25, 12x23", EX, A **300.00**

Good-Will Soap, sign, paper roll-down, original metal strips, 29x14", G, A **145.00**

Good-Will Soap, wagon, wood, 27" long x 14" wide, appears EX, A **12,000.00**

Goodell Auto Oil, tin, silver with potted tree logo, product name in green letters on circle, ca 1917, half-gal, 6", EX+, A **175.00**

Goodrich, corner sign for rubber footwear, tin, 2-sided, A Step Forward! Goodrich 'Hipress' Rubber Footwear Here, scratches, A **250.00**

Goodrich Tires, ash tray, tire, D **12.00**

Goodrich Tires, sign, metal, red G flanked by red diamonds between Good Rich lettered in white vertically on blue ground, 77x18", EX, A **230.00**

Goodwill Shoes, knife, Holliston Mass, Germany, 3", appears G, D **75.00**

Goodyear, Camelback & Repair Materials, manual, painted tin, shows clock face to tell when garage men will be back, Goodyear logo, yellow & blue, octagon, 8", D **23.00**

Gopher Distributing Co, shot glass, ...Liquors, Direct To Consumers At Wholesale, 124 E Third St, St Paul Minn etched in lg letters, sm nick, D **14.00**

Gorton, leaflet, 1906, 'Codfish Recipes,' D **4.00**

Gorton's Cocoanut, tin, Ginna litho, minor scratches, 11", A..............................**1,700.00**

Goshen Club Cigars, box label, inner lid, depicts interior view of men's club, 1917, 6x9", M, D **100.00**

Gottfried Kreuger Brewing Co, tip tray, foaming stein in center, High Grade Beer, minor scarring in image, 4" diameter, EX, A **45.00**

Gotzian & Co Hiawatha Shoes, sign, tin, Indians at campsite flanked by sm print, unusual graphics below, creases/surface damage, 10x14", G-, A.................**110.00**

Governor Coffee, tin, pictures Edward Tipten, 1st Governor of Ohio, ca 1815, 1-lb, VG, A **50.00**

Grain Tobacco, pocket tin, front EX, back VG+, D ..**140.00**

Grand Champion Motor Oil, tin, product name lettered above 3 race cars driven by waving drivers, checkered flag, postwar, 1-qt, NM, A **475.00**

Grand Champion Motor Oil, tin, product name lettered above 3 race cars driven by waving drivers, checkered flag, postwar, 2-gal, 12x9", EX, A **175.00**

Grand Council Cigars, box label, inner lid, depicts Spanish American War military leaders, 6x9", VG, D ..**150.00**

Grand Council Cigars, box label, outer, pictures 3 men in front of a staircase smoking cigars, 5x5", M, D **6.00**

Grand Cut Plug Tobacco, trade card, paper litho, pictures woman in green dress, framed, 10x6", VG+, A......**20.00**

Grand Union Tea Co, sign, paper, 'Christmas Morning,' 2 little girls with their dolls, 1894, creases/separation at top metal band, 28x13", A **400.00**

Granger Pipe Tobacco, display sign, cardboard, depicts butler with child & canister of tobacco, 45x29", VG, A.................**100.00**

Granger Pipe Tobacco, tin round, EX, D.................**15.00**

Granite Iron Ware, poster, paper, overall wear, matted & framed, 33x17", G, A **525.00**

Granulated 54 Tobacco, pocket tin, blue & yellow, leaf logo, Made By John Weisert Co, NM, A **100.00**

Grape Kola, dispenser, figure-8, floral decor with gold-leaf lettering & banding on white, rear pump, replaced lid, 19x10", EX, A.................**850.00**

Grape Ola, dispenser, textured glass font on embossed white porcelain base, bakelite spigot, ca 1918, 11x8x8", EX, A **175.00**

Grape Ola, sign, embossed tin, Drink above diagonal Grape Ola with basket of grapes below, It's Real Grape, 14x19", EX, A.................**45.00**

Grape-Crush, dispenser, embossed purple glass, barrel-shaped with pump, rare, 15", VG, A **1,500.00**

Grape-Julep, sign, tin, black with embossed white letters & border, Drink...In Bottles, 1930s, minor scratches/dent, 10x28", EX+, A.................**50.00**

Grape-Nuts, sign, embossed tin, little girl & her dog, To School Well Fed on Grape-Nuts, fading/wear, self-framed, 30x20", G, A **650.00**

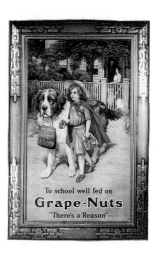

Grape-Nuts, sign, embossed tin, scuffs/fading, self-framed, 30x20", VG, A.................1,050.00

Grapette, sign, porcelain, horizontal, D **165.00**

Gravel Springs Mineral Water, sign, tin, ovaled image of mother giving daughter a drink, product name arched above, minor scratches, 19x13", A **175.00**

Great American Insurance Co, sign, tin, shows bold image of Uncle Sam with lettering above & below, ca 1917, hairline scratches/chips, 23x17", VG, A **450.00**

Great American Tea Co, tin, rectangular canister, pictures a cockatoo & factory scene with fancy graphics, early, minor chips, 10", EX, A.................**500.00**

Great Atlantic & Pacific Tea Co, poster, paper, depicts Uncle Sam, a woman, & a grocer in superb color, matted & framed, 8x10", A.................**250.00**

Great Charter Cigars, box label, inner lid, depicts Jefferson signing the Declaration of Independence, 1907, 6x9", EX, D **35.00**

Great Hartshorn's Root Beer, sign, cowboy on horse with mug & root beer extract, lettering above & below, Clear The Way For The Best..., vertical, A **1,750.00**

Great Northern Railroad, calendar sheet, February 1931, portrait of Indian, Many Mules, matted & framed, 28x15", G, A.................**125.00**

Great Northern Railroad, calendar sheet, July 1931, portrait of Indian, Yellow Head, matted & framed, 28x15", NM, A.................**120.00**

Great Northern Railroad, calendar sheet, 1928, pictures Little Plum, chief of the Blackfoot, matted & framed, 27x15", NM, A.................**135.00**

Great Seal Talcum, tin, shaker top, EX, D.................**35.00**

Great West Cut Plug Tobacco, lunch box, tin, lettered logo, only Canadian-made lunch box, Montreal & Granby Canada, 5x8x5", VG, A 100.00

Great West Tobacco, puzzle pocket mirror, celluloid, mustached man in hat smoking pipe, 10¢ Everywhere, Cut Tobacco, 2" diameter, NM, A 175.00

Greater Columbia Cigars, box label, inner lid, depicts Liberty in front of globe showing American territories, 1899, 6x9", M, D 45.00

Greater Sheesley Shows, poster, paper, depicts a minstrel surrounded by comical scenes, Donaldson litho, has been folded, 42x28", EX, A 350.00

Green Bell Whiskey, shot glass, Green Bell Whiskey, Reinhold Kroll etched in lg letters, EX, D 18.00

Green Giant, doll, cloth, Little Sprout, Chase Bag Co, 12", G, D 10.00

Green Goose Cut Plug Tobacco, tin, lg goose to left of product name, Smoking & Chewing, rectangular, extremely rare, EX, A 400.00

Green Mountain Distillery, shot glass, ...Makers Of The Celebrated...Rye & Bourbon, Kansas City Mo etched in lg letters & script, gold rim, EX, D 28.00

Green Ray Motor Oil, tin, yellow with green graphics, car races upwards from logo at bottom left, lightning bands, 1925-45, 2-gal, 12", EX, A 300.00

Green River Syrup, dispenser, logo on river scene, painted metal base with glass top, originally held a 1-gal bottle, 11x9x8", G, A 45.00

Green River Whiskey, charger, tin, Black man with sad mount, She Was Bred In Old Kentucky, some wear, 24" diameter, G, A 300.00

Green River Whiskey, sign, tin, classic image of Black man & mule, She Was Bred In Old Kentucky, ornate frame, 24x33" without frame, VG, A 300.00

Green Turtle Cigars, lunch box, tin, turtle smoking cigar on inset with decorative border, slip lid, wire handle, some wear, 5x8x5", VG+, A........................275.00

Green Turtle Tobacco, lunch box, tin, turtle logo, decorative border, slip lid & wire handle, some scratches/minor pitting, G-, A 140.00

Greenway's Brewery, sign, embossed cardboard, ca 1910, 20x15", EX, A.............................325.00

Greenway's Brewery, sign, paper, Victorian couple on bench holding Greenway's menu, India Pale Ale, matted & framed, 12x15", EX, A..................................110.00

Greenway's Brewing & Malting Establishment, poster, colorful image of the Syracuse NY brewery, some staining, G+, A 3,200.00

Greenway's India Pale Ale, tray, deep-dish, Greenway's lettered on diagonal with Back Again above, product name below, 12" diameter, EX, A 55.00

Greenway's Present Use XXX & Export Ales, sign, tin litho, logo in center, company name above & product names below, framed, 24x17", G-, A 195.00

Grenadier Cigars, box label, inner lid, depicts 18th century soldier at encampment, 6x9", M, D 75.00

Greyhound, sign, porcelain, red border around white top, blue bottom, 1940-50, 24x40", NM, A 100.00

Greyhound Motor Fuel, sign, Super Greyhound lettered above racing dog, Motor Fuel Below, 1940s, touched up, EX, A 325.00

Griffith & Boyd Fertilizers, poster (may be a calendar top), paper, girl in fur hat & coat, creases/slight wear, matted & framed, 25x20", EX, A..........................250.00

Griffith & Boyd Fertilizers, poster (may be a calendar top), paper, stock image of Asti girl in profile, creasing, matted & framed, 24x20", VG+, A........................150.00

Griffith & Boyd Fertilizers, sign, elegant woman in profile seated in front of a flower garden holding a rose, dog at her feet, ca 1915, 22x16", A 160.00

Grommes & Ullrich's Rye, sign, paper, depicts pilgrims meeting Indians of Illinois, Marquette Pur Rye, original mat & frame, 32x42", VG, A 400.00

Groub's Belle Coffee, tin, woman in flowered hat, press lid, one of rarest coffees, slight dulling of color/overall wear, 1-lb, 6x4", EX, A...........................**1,400.00**

Groves Shoe Co, thimble, aluminum whistle, green band with company name, EX, D................................**30.00**

Guardian Assurance Co, ledger marker, tin, Kellogg & Bulkeley, ca 1890, 12x3", EX, A **175.00**

Guide Output Meter, light tester, chrome sphere with black knobs & meters, 1930-40, 12x12", EX, A **150.00**

Guinea Gold Coffee, grinder, cast iron & tin with wooden back, pictures medallions & lettering, 15x4x6", G, A **140.00**

Gulf, pocket knife, D **35.00**

Gulf Penetrating Oil, tin, cream letters on blue over lg circle with Gulf in 3 colors on orange, text on back, 1936-40, 5-gal, 15x9", VG, A..............................**30.00**

Gulflube Motor Oil, tin, lettered blue band at top, Gulf in 3-color letters on orange circle, 1939-42, no top, 5-qt, 10x7", EX, A..**50.00**

Gulftane, pump sign, porcelain, D **35.00**

Gumbert's Creme Desserts, tin, pictures double desserts, Imitation Butterscotch Flavoring, press lid, 8-lb, round, A..**45.00**

Gussard Corsets, pocket mirror, 3", VG, D **80.00**

Gutmann's Special Cigars, box label, inner lid, depicts 2 gentlemen playing cards with dog watching, product name above & below, 6x9", M, D **50.00**

Gutterman's Sewing Silk, spool cabinet, wood with glass top, hinged lid, 9x14x20", EX, A **425.00**

❧ H ❧

H Wagener Brewing Co, tip tray, labeled bottle in center, Salt Lake City Utah, rare, minor rim chips, 5" diameter, NM, A...**230.00**

H&K's Mighty Good Coffee, can, cardboard, person in nightclothes holding cup, square, NM, A.............**210.00**

H&R Arms Co, sign, embossed tin, pictures rifle & revolver, brown & blue lettering on light blue, surface spotting, 10x14", VG+, A...........................**625.00**

Habana Cigars, box label, inner lid, depicts cherubs & flowers, 6x9", M, D **12.00**

Habana Cigars, box label, inner lid, depicts fan, tulips, & leaves, 6x9", M, D **5.00**

Haberle Brewing Co, calendar poster, 1912, paper, Congress Beer sign above 2 men toasting barmaid, Wolf & Co litho, framed, 17x23", EX, A................**275.00**

Haberle Brewing Co, match striker, stoneware, 5x7", appears EX, A **350.00**

Haberle Brewing Co, sign, oak, company name lettered over cavalier pouring brew, product names at side, Syracuse below, 14x20", VG, A **125.00**

Haberle Brewing Co, tray, tin, eagle logo above globe lettered Premium Stock Lager on yellow ground, Syracuse, ca 1905, 12" diameter, EX, A **150.00**

Haberle Brewing Co, see also Congress Beer

Haberle Lager, sign, etched reverse painting on glass, company name & Lager lettered around eagle logo, framed, 20x16", G, A.....................................**160.00**

Haberle's, tray, deep-dish, eagle logo above lg company name & list of products on green background, ca 1950, 12" diameter, NM, A................................**18.00**

Haberle's Black River Ale, tray, jumping bass, minor scratching/edge wear, rare, 12" diameter, NM, A.**165.00**

Half & Half Burley & Bright Tobacco, pocket tin, appears NM, D..**18.00**

Half & Half Burley & Bright Tobacco, pocket tin, VG+, D **15.00**

Hall Co's Quality Ice Cream, tray, kids surrounding woman with tray of ice cream, decorative border with lettering, minor scratches, 13x11", EX, A.............**375.00**

Hambone Cigars, blackboard, early, 20x13", VG, D ..**50.00**

Hamburger Helper, radio, Helping Hand, D.............**30.00**

Hamilton Watch, sign, tin litho, 13x9", G, A........**250.00**

Hamilton-Brown Shoe Co, sign, paper litho, depicts bare-chested toddler trying on shoe, Baby's First Shoes, St Louis USA, 31x23", G, A...........................**70.00**

Hamm's Beer/United, mug, aluminum, The Only Way To Fly, D..**35.00**

Hampden Brewing Co, sign, tin with hanging chain, unattractive man with tray, Who Wants The Handsome Waiter?, ca 1934, 11" diameter, NM, A **100.00**

Hampden Brewing Co, tray, pictures 'The Handsome Waiter,' ca 1934, chipping/whiting spots to image, 13" diameter, G, A **45.00**

Hancock Mutual Life, thimble, aluminum, company name imprinted on bottom band, EX, D **4.00**

Hand Bag Tobacco, lunch box, modeled as a hand bag, EX, D **75.00**

Handwerger's Liquor House, tray, porcelain, red lettering on white, Compliments Of The Season, Reliable, Fair Treatment..., oval, rim wear, A **90.00**

Handy Dyes, sign, paper, cherubs hanging clothes on line & laying fabric in yard to spell Handy Package Dyes, framed, 12x17", EX, A **50.00**

Hanley Rye, tray, 14x17", EX, A **550.00**

Hanley's Ale, sign, mixed media on paper, pictures a bulldog flanked by stars, product name below, minor flaws, 14x18", EX, A **110.00**

Hanley's Peerless Ale, tray, depicts animated gent lifting glass in toast, The James Hanley Co, Providence RI, minor wear, 12" diameter, NM, A **45.00**

Hannis Distilling Co, poster, factory scene, Hannisville Distillery, Martinsburg W Va, original mat, minor stain on mat, framed, 20x18", EX+, A **450.00**

Happiness Candy Stores, tin, depicts various animals in sporting events on all sides, slip lid & handle, appears EX, A **80.00**

Happy Home Peanut Butter, pail, tin, pictures peanuts with product name above & below, press lid & bail, flaking/chipping on side, rare, A **240.00**

Happy Thought Wave Line Plug Tobacco, sign, paper, colorful image of a sailor, Wilson & McCallay Tobacco Co, framed, rare, 39x28", EX+, A **2,000.00**

Hard A Port Cut Plug Tobacco, tin, sailor at wheel with nautical motif, American Can Co, rounded corners, flakes/chips/dents, rare, 3x6x4", VG, A **475.00**

Hardee's, doll, cloth, Gilbert Giddy-Up, Chase Bag Co, 1971, 14", F, D **7.00**

Hardee's, Pound Puppies, brown, black, or gray, EX, D, each **10.00**

Hargrave Secret Service, pump sign, porcelain, red, black, & yellow, Warning above eagle on globe flanked by Crime Does Not Pay, 1920-30, 4x4", A **15.00**

Harley-Davidson Genuine Motor Cycle Oil, tin, orange & black, Harley-Davidson lettered over Motor Cycles shield, Genuine Oil above & below, 1935-45, 1-qt, NM, A **40.00**

Harper Whiskey, tray, 'Remember the Maine' with border of cannons & flags, chipping to image & rim, 12" diameter, VG, A **95.00**

Harrington & Richardson Arms Co, calendar, 1902, cardboard, November pad, framed, 20x11", VG+, A ..**450.00**

Harris Oils, tin, Sign of Quality over wood barrel with word Oils as bands, America's Leading..., 1935-45, no top, 5-qt, 10x7", VG, A **75.00**

Harrisburg Pilot, calendar, 1928, paper, pictures gypsy girl, Not A Newspaper But A Weekly Group Of Concisely..., framed, 45x22", EX, A **90.00**

Hartford Insurance, ring, Jr Fire Marshall, D **15.00**

Hartman's Family Liquor, display, die-cut cardboard, embossed image of winged cherub & maid in a boat, framed, 16x14", EX, A **155.00**

Hartwell Handles, display, tin box, depicts mule-driven wagon, Genuine Hickory Tool Handles, overall wear, 8x14x6", VG, A **45.00**

Harvard Ale, sign, die-cut tin, figural mug picturing costumed characters enjoying mugs of beer, fading/chips/dents, 13x9", G, A **75.00**

Harvard Brewing Co, art plate, stock girl with calender rim, 1907, overall slight fading to color, 10" diameter, VG, A **80.00**

Harvard Brewing Co, poster, paper, Harvard U regatta seen through portaled stone wall, factory scene below, framed, 32x23" overall, VG, A **700.00**

Harvard Brewing Co, sign, tin, colorful Morrocan interior with woman pouring glass of beer, minor hairlines, 37x28" without frame, EX, A **1,700.00**

Harvard Brewing Co, tray, deep-dish, couple at table with waiter, lettering on rim, rust spots on edge/scratches, 12" diameter, VG, A **175.00**

Harvard Brewing Co, tray, 13" diameter, VG, A **275.00**

Harvard Cigars, cigar cutter, wind-up, depicts Harvard boy on front, lettering on all sides, 7x9", VG, A ..**120.00**

Harvard Cigars, sign, hand-painted Harvard boy with product name over top of his head, company name below, 37x25", EX, A **600.00**

Harvard Jumbo Peanuts, tin, pictures pennant-waving peanut, Prepared by Willard Supply, Chicago, general wear, 10-lb, 10x8", VG, A **60.00**

Harvester Cigars, tin, 5x6", G-, A..........................**450.00**
Hassan Cork Tip Cigarettes, sign, cardboard, depicts uniformed man in fez flanked by lettering & product, lettering above, 30x23", appears EX, D **100.00**
Havoline Motor Oil, tin, cream & blue with red circle at center, cream & blue letters, Insulated in red on blue, 1940s, 5-qt, 10x7", EX, A **25.00**
Havoline Oil, tin, navy blue with product name & cream-bordered red dot, Indian Refining Co Inc, NYC, ca 1915-25, 1-gal, 6", EX, A **170.00**
Havoline Oil, tin, white on blue with red dot, ca 1915-25, half-gal, 6", VG, A **155.00**
HB Gardner Cigars, sign, tin litho, Chief Joseph Bryant among tobacco plants holding box, framed, rare, 10x14" without frame, EX, A **1,100.00**
Heart O' Pennsylvania Motor Oil, tin, red heart on silver, 100% Pure, 2500 Mile Guarantee, ca 1935-45, silver is faded, 1-qt, 6", EX, A..........................**45.00**

Hecker's Buckwheat, sign, Hecker, Jones, & Jewell Milling Co, ca 1893, minor tears, 29x42", G+, A..........**1,100.00**
Heidlemen's Old Style Beer, sign, light on top, 22x15", EX, D..........................**25.00**

Heildeman's Old Style Lager Beer, recipe booklet, 1945, '300 Ways Of Making Delicious Sandwiches,' 96 pages, VG, D..........................**5.00**
Heim Beer, tray, factory scene flanked by logo, decorative rim, oval, 14x17", VG, A **800.00**
Heineken Beer, display, composition, 3-D, colorful Dutch boy & lg bottle, 1950s, 18x14", EX+, D..........................**100.00**
Heineken Beer, windmill, electric, wings need small repair, 18", EX, D **150.00**
Heinz, cookbook, 1925, paperback, 'Heinz Book Of Salads,' 95 pages, D..........................**10.00**
Heinz, cookbook, 1930, paperback, 'Heinz Book Of Meat Cookery,' 54 pages, D..........................**8.00**
Heinz, cookbook, 1939, 210 pages, D **10.00**
Heinz, pin, figural pickle, 1", D..........................**20.00**
Heinz, sign, green die-cut pickle with white lettering, Heinz Est 1877, 38" long, appears EX, A **260.00**
Heinz, toy delivery truck, metal, logo beside door, Rice Flakes, Spaghetti, Tomato Ketchup on side of bed, EX, A..........................**425.00**

Heinz, vinegar barrel, glass, 14", VG, A **550.00**
Heinz Apple Butter, crock, pictorial & information label, slip lid, pictorial label has sm chips/back label is damaged, 8x4" diameter, VG, A **225.00**
Heinz Apple Butter, crock, stoneware with paper label depicting fruit, company name, & product, bail with wood handle, no lid/torn label, A **40.00**
Heinz Ketchup, display, die-cut cardboard stand-up, red & green, folds out to hold bottle, NRA logo, seam separation, 12x15", VG+, D..........................**65.00**
Heinz Pickles, bucket, banded wood with bail handle, fruits & vegetables on paper label, Preserved Sweet Pickles, 13", G, A..........................**90.00**
Heinz Pickles, bucket, wood with decal picturing fruit & beef, handle intact, some letters worn off on decal, round, A **90.00**
Heinz Preserved Strawberries, crock, stoneware with paper label depicting fruit, company name, & product, clamp-on lid & bail, EX, A..........................**290.00**
Heinz Pure Food Products, tin, pictures pickle, no lid, 12x6" diameter, G, D..........................**65.00**
Heinz Vinegars, sign, full-color image of product & plate of food, Four Kinds, Cider, White...Tarradan, ca 1920, horizontal, framed, A **130.00**

Hollandina Cigars, box label, inner lid, depicts a Dutch woman & windmill surrounded by decorative border, 6x9", M, D **11.00**

Hollingshead's Castor Axle Oil, sign, colorful image of the product surrounded by fancy graphics, creases/nail hole, 10x7", G+, A......................................**200.00**

Holsum Bread, match holder, tin litho, pictures loaf of bread on blue background, 5x3", G-, A **100.00**

Home Brewing Co, tray, illustrator image of girl in profile in checked dress & plumed hat, ca 1913, oval, 16x13", G, A......................................**90.00**

Home Insurance Co, ledger marker, tin litho, dark brown with gold lettering, Capitol $1,000,000, ca late 1800s, 12x3", G, A......................................**120.00**

Home Insurance Co, trade card, pictures girl standing by tree, NM, D **4.00**

Home Run Cigarettes, sign, cigarette pack on wood colored background, Quality Not Style, 9" diameter, EX, A......................................**800.00**

Home Run Cigarettes, sign, stone litho on cardboard, baseball scene, 1900, rare, 25x18", EX, D **6,500.00**

Home Run Tabac A Cigarettes, tin, baseball player swinging at lg ball with Home Run on white band above, slip lid, ca 1950, round, M, A **30.00**

Home-Run Stogie, tin, JA Riaby Cigar Co, 6x4" diameter, G, A **1,200.00**

Home-Run Stogie, tin, product name & 3 for 5¢ on lg sign behind batter & catcher on light ground, Riaby Cigar Co, 6x4" diameter, EX, A..........1,400.00

Home-Run Stogie, tin, product name & 3 for 5¢ on lg sign behind batter & catcher on light ground, Riaby Cigar Co, 6x4" diameter, EX+, A......................**1,600.00**

Honest Scrap Tobacco, sign, cardboard, framed, 22x30", G+, A......................................**600.00**

Honest Weight Tobacco, sign, full-color image of a child in a scale, product name above & below, 1887, matted & framed, rectangular, EX, A **150.00**

Honeycomb Cigars, box label, inner lid, depicts the word Class over full-spread tail of peacock, product name above, 6x9", M, D......................................**30.00**

Honeymoon Tobacco, pocket tin, D 550.00

Honeymoon Tobacco, trolley sign, cardboard litho, couple canoeing in moonlight, Penn Tobacco Co, Wilkes-Barre Pa, framed, 11x21", EX, A......................**325.00**

Honeymoon Tobacco, trolley sign, cardboard litho, girl & boy riding sled, Penn Tobacco Co, Wilkes-Barre Pa, framed, 11x21", EX, A......................**425.00**

Honeysuckle Tobacco, tin, picturing bees & honeysuckle blossoms, slip lid, Montreal Canada, denting/chipping, 5x5" diameter, G-, A......................................**110.00**

Honeywell Co Air Cleaner, doll, cloth, Allergic Annie, Chase Bag Co, 15", F, D......................................**14.00**

Hood Tire Dealer, sign, die-cut porcelain man in red jacket, white pants & black boots, 1930-40, touch-up to hat, rare, 36x10", EX, A **2,000.00**

Hood Tires, sign, blackboard-type tin, pictures the Hood Tire man, Ask The Why Of The Extra Ply, dents/scratches, 11x17", G+, A **85.00**

Hood Tires, sign, die-cut tin, tire man holding dealer banner & gesturing for customer to stop, ca 1910-20, framed, 43x18", EX, A......................................**1,100.00**

Hood's Ice Cream, sign, tin, 2-sided flanged circle with cow's head in center, product name lettered above & below, 19x22", VG, A **160.00**

Hood's Sarsaparilla, calendar, 1888, die-cut little girl's face, framed, 18x11", EX, A......................**325.00**

Hood's Sarsaparilla, calendar, 1890-91, cardboard, depicts little girl in profile, incomplete pad, framed, 17x10", VG+, A......................................**350.00**

Hood's Sarsaparilla, calendar, 1892-93, incomplete pad, framed, 14" diameter, VG+, A **350.00**

Hood's Sarsaparilla, calendar, 1896-97, depicts girl with a scarf, framed, 13x9", VG+, A **425.00**

Hood's Sarsaparilla, plate, cardboard, farmer, Black man, & dog in pursuit of a hawk, To Purify the Blood..., ca 1885, 9" diameter, VG, A **300.00**

Hood's Sarsaparilla, plate, cardboard, shows 2 birds on front & testimonials on back, matted, overall wear/discoloration, 9" diameter, EX, A **25.00**

Hood's Sarsaparilla, sign, die-cut cardboard litho, little boy sitting on a box holding the product, framed, minor creasing, 19x11", EX, A......................**1,000.00**

Hood's Sarsaparilla, sign, die-cut paper litho, pictures little girl holding product, framed, 19x9", EX, A **950.00**

Hoody's Famous Peanut Butter Cookies, pail, depicts 2 girls on a seesaw, with logoed peanut as the base, press lid & bail, rare, A..........**480.00**

Hoody's Peanut Butter, pail, depicts boy & girl on seesaw eating 'Hoody's Goodies,' lid & bail, minor chips/dents, 4x4" with bail, VG, A **675.00**

Hoosac Tunnel, sign, paper litho, ca 1875, rare, 28x24", VG, A 6,200.00

Hoosier Boy Coffee, tin, paper label, 1-lb, VG+, A **80.00**

Hoosier Boy Tobacco, tin, pictures little boy holding a bucket of paint, Fishback Co, press lid, EX, A.....**300.00**

Hoosier Brand Pioneer Coffee, tin, state of Indiana in center, 1-lb, EX, A **110.00**

Hoosier Cream, tray, pictures a lady & a tiger, decorative border, heavy wear, round, A **35.00**

Hoover, thimble, aluminum, Hoover, Home, Happiness on worn blue band, D **3.00**

Hoover Vacuums, tape measure, D **28.00**

Hope Chest Cigars, tin, paper label, depicts woman dreaming of hope chest, landscape background, overall wear, 5x6" diameter, G-, A **70.00**

Hope Mills Coffee, store bin, image of girl with lifesaver looking out to sea, rare, lg chips/scratches/minor dents, 21x13" square, G-, A **425.00**

Horlick's Malted Milk, canister, aluminum, product name encircled with scalloped border, slip lid with knob, round, 10", NM, D **70.00**

Horse Shoe Cut Plug Tobacco, sign, embossed tin, minor dents, framed, 24x36", VG+, A 6,500.00

Horseshoe Brand Clothes Wringers, display rack with 1 wringer, wood with easel back, lettering on top, 56x15", EX, A..........**220.00**

Horsford's Acid Phosphate, display case, etched glass in metal frame, lettering on bowed front, ...For Indigestion, Nervousness, 12x21x22", EX, A **300.00**

Horsford's Bread Preparation Baking Powder, sign, paper, girl with arms folded resting chin on hand with product & lettering above & below, framed, 26x18", EX, A..........**100.00**

Hoster Brewing Co, calendar, 1900, pictures a young lass in decorative oval, calendar sheets in each corner, matted & framed, 23x17", EX, A..........**1,050.00**

Hoster Brewing Co, sign, tin, pictures drunken monk against beer barrels, minor overall wear/scratches, oval, 16x20" without frame, G+, A **85.00**

Hostess Bakery, doll, inflatable, Happy Ho Ho, 1970s, 48", EX, D..........**8.00**

Houghton Co Brewers, calendar, 1901, pictures a dog with dead game bird in his mouth, 21x17", A..........**75.00**

Houston Ice & Brewing Co, tip tray, depicts a girl in profile, Magnolia Brewery, lacquer spotting to image/rim wear, 4" diameter, VG, A **200.00**

Howe Scale Co, sign, paper, shows woman standing on platform scale, printed by Donaldson Bros Litho, ca 1889, approx: 29x15", G, A **300.00**

Howe Scale Works, sign, tin Kellogg & Bulkeley Co litho, 20x28", VG+, A **2,200.00**

Howel's Cherry-Julep, dispenser, red potbelly with lettering, replaced pump, minor foot chips/body scratches, 15" diameter, VG, A **850.00**

Howel's Orange-Julep, dispenser, orange potbelly with lettering, original pump, some discoloration/crack on top rim, 15" diameter, EX, A..........**700.00**

Howel's Orange-Julep, syrup bottle, with measuring cap, label under glass, Drink Howel's Orange-Julep, 13", EX, A **400.00**

Hoyt's But-Kiss-Candy, display box, shaped like railroad car, Hoyt's Box Car No 1901, logo on side door, overall wear, 11x19x8", VG, A **550.00**

Hoyt's German Cologne, poster, paper, girl surrounded by flowers for The Most Fragrant perfumes, matted & framed, 28x22", VG, A **400.00**

Hoyt's German Cologne, sign, tin, ca 1880s, framed, 23x15", EX, A..........**500.00**

HP Hood & Sons Milk, sign, porcelain, cow in center bordered by lettering, 28" diameter, EX, A **295.00**

Hubbard's Gloucester Biscuits, box, wood with lift lid, paper label depicting clipper ship on front, 12x22x14", G, A **45.00**

Hubert Fischfer Brewery, tray, porcelain, white with blue lettering & eagle transfer, Lager, Ales, & Porter, wear/rim chips, 12" diameter, VG, A **85.00**

Hudson's Bay Tea, tin, litho panels of Fort Garry 1835-1882, Jack Canuck in North West 'today' & the Golden West, hinged top, 7x4x4", G, A **45.00**

Humane Horse Collars, pocket mirror, tin, EX, D **45.00**

Hummer Cigars, box label, inner lid, depicts humming bird hovering around flower on tobacco plant, product name above, 6x9", M, D..........**8.00**

Humphrey's Veterinary Remedies, cabinet, tin, wood front, refinished, restored, 28x22x9", G, A **1,400.00**

Humphreys' Veterinary Specifics, cabinet, embossed composition with raised horse's head on textured background, overall soiling, 28x21x11", EX, A **2,000.00**

Humphreys' Remedies, sign, tin, blue & white, lists several remedies for humans, minor bends, wood frame, 17x16", EX, A **85.00**

Hunham's Cocoanut, thermometer, brass, 1888, VG, D **250.00**

Hunkel's Seeds, sign, paper, elegant woman with fresh vegetables surrounded by other legumes & flowers, ca 1925, framed, 31x23", EX, A **425.00**

Hunt's Health Pills & Liver Cure, sign, tin, girl in sailor suit flanked by lists of cures, Little Gem, Kellogg & Bulkeley, ca 1880-90, 6x7", EX, A **275.00**

Hunter Baltimore Rye, sign, tin, horse & rider jumping a fence, First Over The Bars, HD Beach Co litho, ca 1910-20, wood frame, 24x18", NM+, A **1,400.00**

Hunter Rye, display, die-cast polychrome figure of hunter on horse waving hat, Hunter Rye lettered on base, 4", EX, A **20.00**

Hunter's, syrup dispenser, hourglass shape with clear glass top on milk glass bottom marked Hunter's, metal lid, appears, EX, A **80.00**

Hunter's Return Cigars, box label, inner lid, 2 hunters holding antlers of enlarged deer, 6x9", VG, D **75.00**

Huntley & Palmer, biscuit tin, cupids at play, appears EX, D **350.00**

Huntley & Palmer, biscuit tin, embossed snakes with floral border, ca 1907, rectangular, appears EX, A **60.00**

Huntley & Palmer, biscuit tin, farmhouse, NM+, A ..**375.00**

Huntley & Palmer, biscuit tin, figural stack of plates, round, appears, EX, A **220.00**

Huntley & Palmer, biscuit tin, Library, figural stack of books, A **155.00**

Huntley & Palmer, biscuit tin, pocket book form with embossed lizard, VG+, A **65.00**

Huntley & Palmer, biscuit tin, square box with oriental motif, lg dragon in center, appears EX, A **150.00**

Huntley & Palmer, biscuit tin, square with oriental-style handles, exotic bird pictured on front, VG, A **90.00**

Huntley & Palmer's Ginger Nuts, sign, tin, John Ginger logo, edge wear, 18x18", A **300.00**

Hupfel Brewing Co, tip tray, factory street scene, Established 1854, minor rim chips, 5" diameter, NM, A **240.00**

Hupfel Brewing Co, tip tray, pictures factory street scene, Established 1854, 5" diameter, NM, A **135.00**

Hurcules Powder Co, sign, paper, whimsical winter scene of boy hunting with muzzleloader & dog, ca 1920, 25x16", EX, A **850.00**

Hurcules Powder Co, sign, paper, winter scene of 2 boys with muzzleloaders, ca 1924, 25x16", VG, A **500.00**

Hussey & Co, match holder, die-cut tin figural, colorful image of nymph holding banner, While Others Think We Work, rare, 7x3", G+, A **1,600.00**

Hustins Beer, sign, tin, interior scene with 2 monks & a drunken man, C Shonk litho, few scratches, matted & framed, oval, A **600.00**

Huston's Biscuits, box, wood with lift lid, paper label on front with lettering & logo, 8x22x14", NM, A **20.00**

Huxley's Plasma, tin, paper label, with floral design, 1912, G, D **10.00**

Huyler Cigars, box label, outer, pictures a musician, 5x5", M, D **4.00**

Huyler's Candy, sign, reverse-painted glass light-up, Victorian couple seated on ground, Now If He Only Had A..., framed, 22x34", EX, A **260.00**

Hy-Quality Coffee, display, hanging, die-cut cardboard, 38x16", EX+, A **775.00**

Hy-Quality Coffee, sign, hanging, die-cut cardboard, woman on a swing with a cup of coffee, framed, 35", G, A **350.00**

Hyroler Whiskey, tip tray, pictures man in a tuxedo, product & company name around rim, Louis J Adler & Co, round, appears EX, A **35.00**

Hyvis Motor Oil, tin, easy pour, red logo & white letters within yellow ring on black ground, 1915-25, 5-gal, 17x14", EX, A **110.00**

∽ I ∼

Ice Cream Dairy Co, pocket mirror, Springfield Ill, appears EX, D **45.00**

Ide Collars, sign, 3 men wearing Ide collars, Thorndike – Kempton, Two Heights..., 1920, matted & framed, 10x18", appears EX, A **110.00**

Ideal Coffee, tin, depicts silver coffee service with product name above & below, slip lid, 1-lb, round, appears EX, A **40.00**

Ideal Leather Polish, match holder, tin litho, colorful image of product, Ask Your Dealer For Ideal Polish, It Saves $, 6x4", VG+, A **325.00**

IGA, doll, cloth, IGA Cowboy, 12", G, D **8.00**

Illinois Watch Co, sign, reverse-painted glass, locomotive & tender in gold & black, 1925, minor lifting, 12x20" without frame, EX, A.............................**175.00**

Illinois Watches, sign, tin litho, railroad engineer with oil can & watch, Springfield, soiling/scratches/wear, self-framed, 13x19", G, A **275.00**

Imperial Club Cigars, sign, embossed tin, shows an open cigar box, The Best For The Money, Sentenne & Green, minor chips, 10x14", VG, A **45.00**

Imperial Copper Polish, can, paper label over cardboard body, pictures policeman & lettering, press lid, some paper loss, 5x3" diameter, G, A.............................**45.00**

Imperial Cough Drops, tin, early Ginna 2-color with topography display, slip lid, overall 8x6x4", G-, A **25.00**

Imperial Cube Cut Tobacco, humidor, glass with embossed logo, 8", M, D **85.00**

Imperial Egg Food, sign, paper litho, pictures men unloading an egg train, logo at bottom left, ca 1900, rare, framed, 28x22", EX, A **2,000.00**

Imperial Monogram Pure Rye Whiskey, shot glass, product name etched on 4 lines in sharp lettering, unmarked Cincinnati brand, some damage, D.......**10.00**

Imperial Peanuts, tin, 10-lb, 10x8", G, A **150.00**

Inca Maiden Coffee, pail, double-sided can with maiden & native scene, slip lid & bail, general wear/minor in-painting, 4-lb, 8x8", G, A **125.00**

Incandescent Light & Stove Co, tip tray, kitchen scene with woman at stove & child sitting on floor, lettering on surface & rim, 4" diameter, EX, A **65.00**

Independant Stove Co, paperweight, cast iron elephant figural, embossed Independant Stove Co, Owosso Mich, EX, A.............................**40.00**

Independent Brewing Co, tray, Liberty Bell in center, Liberty Brews, Private Stock, Auburn NY, 12" diameter, NM, A.............................**300.00**

Independent Lock Co, sign, die-cut tin, double-sided, figural key, Fitchburg Mass, ca 1920-30, 1 side faded, 14x32", G+, A **200.00**

Independent Motor Oil, tin, shield contains marching Colonial Army in sepia on gold-yellow ground, Altoona Pa, 1915-25, 1-gal, 11", EX+, A **220.00**

Independent Telephone Co, hanging shade, milk glass with red, white, & blue emblem, Local & Long Distance, globe: 8", fitter ring: 4", EX, A **950.00**

India Wharf Brewing Co, tumbler, etched factory scene, NM, A.............................**105.00**

Indian Gasoline, sign, porcelain, top half is multicolor mosaic-like symbols on yellow, bottom background is green, 1940, 18x12", NM, A **335.00**

Indian Medicine Co, sign, paper, extremely rare depiction of Indian medicine man, matted & framed, some wear, 24x15" overall, G-, A **100.00**

Indian Motorcycle Oil, tin, New to left of script Indian & round logo, red & white background, ca 1935-45, sm dent, 1-qt, 6", EX+, A **110.00**

Indian Motorcycles, sign, tin over wood frame, Indian head logo in center, Mathews Co, 1920-30, overall rust spots, rare, 14x20", A **550.00**

Indian Oil, tin, ca 1915-30, 1-gal, 11", EX+, A....**1,000.00**

Indian Premium Motorcycle Oil, tin, round Indian logos flank word Indian on top band, Premium on explosion graphic on yellow, 1935-45, 1-qt, EX+, A.............**100.00**

Indianapolis Brewing Co, tip tray, labeled bottle in center, Lieber's Gold Medal Beer, few sm rim chips, 5" diameter, NM, A **25.00**

Indianapolis Brewing Co, tray, depicts bottled beer, glass, & dead birds, Duesseldorfer Beer & other lettering on rim, some wear, 11x13", EX, A **50.00**

Indianapolis Brewing Co, tray, 3 gents by a roaring fire in interior, lettering on rim, scratching/area of color loss, 11x13", G, A.............................**125.00**

Ingersoll Watches, display case, tin & glass, paint loss to lower front/edge chipping, 11x12", G, A.............**50.00**

Ingersoll Watches, sign, 2-sided flanged die-cut tin, Ingersoll across pocket watch, We Have Ingersoll Watches, above, 17"x9", G-, A **120.00**

Inland Pride Beer, tray, labeled bottle & glass of beer, Inland Brewing & Malting Co, Spokane Wash, scratches/crazing, 12" diameter, VG, A **225.00**

Inland Pride Beer, tray, pictures bottle & glass, 12" diameter, VG, D **225.00**

Interlux Paint, thermometer, painter with can of product in center, degree numbers around perimeter, A..**110.00**

International Brewing Co, tray, deep-dish, 3-quarter length portrait of woman in lg hat, overall wear, rare, 12" diameter, G-, A **75.00**

International Harvester Co, match holder, tin, You Can't Beat the Osbourne Line of Harvesting Machines & Farm Implements, 5x3", VG, A **180.00**

International Harvester Co, stickpin, D **15.00**

International Navigation Co, ledger marker, tin, double-sided, steamship scene, list of fleet & officers on reverse, ca 1900, 12x3", NM, A.............................**500.00**

International Poultry Food, sign, paper, children in chicken yard with lettering over border of double rows of chickens, framed, 21x28", EX, A **65.00**

International Stock Food, sign, paper, has been trimmed, chips/creases, framed, 29x23", G, A .100.00

International Stock Food, sign, paper, image of pig, horse, & bull wanting contents of 3 Feeds package, 29x18" without frame, G, A **175.00**

International Stock Food, sign, paper, shows pig with overturned bucket of corn & 3 Feeds Tub, creases/border wear, 28x22" without frame, G, A **130.00**

International Tailoring Co, thermometer, wooden, pictures lion, 7x22", A...**140.00**

Interwoven Men's Hosiery, sign, die-cut cardboard stand-up, Santa holding Interwoven sock, The Santa Claus Favorite, restored, 23", A **225.00**

Invader Motor Oil, tin, armored knight on horse in black semicircle on yellow, Chas Kellom & Co on black bottom band, ca 1950, 1-qt, NM, A **15.00**

Invader Motor Oil, tin, yellow with knight on horse in black semicircle, Chas F Kellom on black band at bottom, 1935-45, 5-qt, 10x7", EX, A............................**75.00**

Invader Oil, tin, knight on horse in red circle at upper right, diagonal yellow stripe, Chas Kellom & Co, 1915-25, 1-gal, 11", EX, A **700.00**

Iron City Beer, can, pictures the 1979 champs, Pittsburg Pirates, EX, D **10.00**

Ironport, dispenser, potbelly, 19x16", VG, A **1,750.00**

Iroquois Beer, tip tray, Iroquois label on turquoise background, edge wear, rare, 4" diameter, NM, A.........**70.00**

Iroquois Brewery, tip tray, 4" diameter, NM, A........**125.00**

Iroquois Brewery, tray, Indian in canoe with 2 bottles of beer, encircled Indian heads on border, surface chips, 12" diameter, G-, A...**375.00**

Iroquois Brewery, tray, 3 labeled bottles grouped together on leafy background, Iroquois & Buffalo on rim, rim chips, 12" diameter, EX, A **150.00**

Iroquois Cigars, sign, paper, depicts Indian logo surrounded by factory scenes, sepia tones, framed, 22x18", NM, A...**625.00**

Iten's Biscuit Co, thimble, aluminum, company name on black band, EX, D **4.00**

Ithica Guns, sign, embossed tin litho, opened double-barreled shotgun surrounded by ornate decor, ca 1895, 7x14", G, A...**450.00**

Iver Johnson Revolver, sign, 2-sided die-cut tin, pictures hands holding revolver & hammer, Hammer The Hammer, oval, 12x16", VG, A **700.00**

Ivorine Cleanser, sign, scene with people & lg elephant, Ivorine on saddle blanket, Wonderful Cleanser, corner worn, A..**375.00**

Ivory Soap, sign, cardboard, interior view of shelves of products & 3 busy clerks, may have been trimmed, paper loss, 28x22", G, A **100.00**

Ivory Soap, sign, cardboard, some wear, framed, 25x17", VG, A..1,050.00

Ivy Parlor Stove, sign, paper litho, lady in black dress by new stove, 1870-90, edge tears/light stain, rare, 24x22", VG, A **200.00**

IW Harper Whiskey, sign, Vitrolite, depicts cabin interior with bearskin on wall, dog stands by guns & hunting equipment, 30x24", M, A **800.00**

∽∞ J ∞∽

J Leisy Brewing Co, tip tray, unusual card hand scene in center, The Scat Players Dream, rare, 5" diameter, EX, A...**200.00**

J Leisy Brewing Co, tray, 14x17", EX+, A...........1,900.00

J Sterling Morton Cigars, box label, inner lid, depicts this famous 1903 Nebraska politician, 6x9", M, D..........**6.00**

J&P Coats Spool Cotton, cabinet, oak with 2 drawers having silvered tin fronts, J&P Coats For Hand & Machine, 7x20x15", VG, A.................................**200.00**

J&P Coats Spool Cotton, poster, pictures Robinson Crusoe, The Best Thing Out, J&P Coats Cotton, some stains, framed, 18x22", G, A **425.00**

J&P Coats Spool Cotton, sign, paper litho, seated woman watching man fishing, J&P Coats Spool Cotton Is Strong!, stained, framed, G-, A **275.00**

J&P Coats Spool Cotton, sign, paper over plaster, Gulliver & the Lilliputians working with the Best Six Cord Spool Cotton, 19x22", G, A **225.00**

J&P Coats Spool Cotton, sign, pictures an elegant woman in a bonnet, Best Six Cord Spool Cotton, matted, decorative frame, 21x16", appears EX, A......................**650.00**

J&P Coats Spool Cotton, spool cabinet, wood, 4-drawer spool-shaped body wrapped in twine to represent product, rests on side, 22x18x19", G-, A........400.00

J&P Coats Spool Cotton, spool cabinet, 6 drawers with lettering on drawers & cabinet back, wear to finish, 26x22x20", G-, A **400.00**

Jack & Jill Peanut Butter, pail, Canadian, product name superimposed over Jack & Jill with lettering below, slip lid & bail, rare, VG, A **110.00**

Jack Daniel's Whiskey, tin, for poker chips, depicts oval portrait of Jack Daniel's, includes chips, some wear, rectangular, A **40.00**

Jack Frost Sugar, doll, 1967, cloth, Chase Bag Co, 18", F, D...**8.00**

Jack Frost Sugar, doll, 1973, cloth, Chase Bag Co, 18", EX, D **11.00**

Jack Sprat Peanut Butter, store container, tin, press lid, extremely rare, 25-lb, 10x10", G+, A **400.00**

Jackie Coogan Peanut Butter, pail, black & red can with illustrated image of Jackie on circular inset, slip lid & bail, dents/scratches, 3x3", VG, A **500.00**

Jackie Coogan Peanut Butter, pail, illustrated image of Jackie on circular inset on black & pale green can, scratching/denting, 7-oz, 3x3", G+, A **425.00**

Jackie Coogan Peanut Butter, pail, multiple photos of Jackie, slip lid & bail, overall wear, rare, 3x3", VG, A **300.00**

Jackie Coogan Peanut Butter, pail, black & white image, 1-lb, 3x4", G, A......................................210.00

Jackie Coogan Peanuts, tin, pictures Jackie Coogan riding an elephant on green background, Salted Nut Meats, press lid, 7x7" diameter, VG, A **125.00**

Jacob Esch Whiskey, shot glass, Jacob Esch, 447 Cedar Street, St Paul Minn etched in lg letters, fancy designs above & below, M, D..**16.00**

Jacob Hoffman Brewing Co, sign, paper, pictures flowers in a vase, glass of wine, & cigar, framed, 31x21", NM, A..**50.00**

Jacob Schmidt Brewing Co, hunt scene on canvas, 3 men enjoying Schmidt's beer among dead game, company name on gilt frame, rare, 20x30", NM, A...........**1,300.00**

Jahn's Ice Cream, lamp shade, colorful leaded glass, NM, A 1,400.00

Jantzens, scale, raised dial, green paint, Art Deco base, child & adult sizes given rather than weight, rare, VG, A..**295.00**

Jap Rose Bath Soap, display, die-cut tin, oriental children with an oversized bar of soap encased in a bubble, ca 1909, rare, 13x19", EX+, A......................................**800.00**

Jap Rose Bath Soap, display with 6 original boxed soaps, die-cut tin, rare, 13x18", NM, A.........................**1,500.00**

Japo Borax Cleanser, tin, paper label picturing Japanese girl on skates, press lid, round, appears EX, A **25.00**

Japp's Hair Rejuvenator, sign, tin, depicts woman & man in oval insets in upper corners with 7 swatches of hair, self-framed, 9x13", D...**95.00**

Jas E Pepper Whiskey, tray, deep-dish, Born With The Republic on banner arched above Yankee Doodle image, 12" diameter, NM, A **95.00**

Jas E Pepper Whiskey, tray, deep-dish, Born With The Republic on banner arched above Yankee Doodle image, 12" diameter, EX, A **60.00**

JB Pace Tobacco, tin, circular logo & company logo on lid, JB Pace Tobacco Co's Scroll Cut Twist, slip lid, pre-1901, rectangular, EX+, A..**45.00**

JE Patzlsperger Shoes, match holder, tin litho, pictures The Popular Shoe Man & a pair of gold shoes, simulated wood background, 5x3", NM, A.................**300.00**

Jell-O, booklet, 1915, 'Jell-O & The Kewpies,' EX, D...**35.00**

Jell-O, booklet, 1931, 'Greater Jell-O Recipe Book,' 47 pages, D **9.00**

Jell-O, dish, 1 side has extension, 1910, light flaking/tiny glaze crack, 4", A 250.00

Jell-O, leaflet, 1916, bride on cover, 'America's Most Famous Dessert,' D **45.00**

Jell-O, leaflet, 1917, recipes, 20 pages, D **9.00**

Jell-O, leaflet, 1932, recipes, D **7.00**

Jell-O, leaflet, 1963, 'Joys of Jell-O,' 95 pages, D...........**2.00**

Jell-O, sign, paper litho, printer's proof, Genesee Pure Food Co, ca 1900, 42x20", NM, A 950.00

Jersey Cigars, box label, inner lid, depicts Latin lady with cow flanked by palm trees, product name above & on side of cow, 6x9", M, A...**35.00**

Jersey-Creme, dispenser, 16x7" diameter, EX, A **700.00**

Jersey-Creme, tray/sign, profile of girl wearing a bonnet, lettered rim, C Shonk litho, overall crazing, 12" diameter, EX, A...**250.00**

Jetter Brewing Co, sign, tin litho, mountainous wooded scene with elk bellowing at bottle of Gold Top brew, self-framed, 32" long, G-, A **175.00**

Jewel Coal, sign, porcelain, white lettering on black with orange border, Ask Your Neighbor!, octagonal, 19x19", M, A..**85.00**

Jewel Tea Co, thimble, aluminum, company name & slogan on worn blue band, D **3.00**

Jewelo Cigars, box label, inner lid, pictures a man & woman surrounded by green border, 6x9", M, D **4.00**

JG Dills Best Cut Plug Tobacco, tin, Victorian lady logo, rectangular with round corners, A **20.00**

JG Hoffman & Sons Co, sign, printer's proof, 2 factory views, oval portrait of JG Hoffman in upper right, ...Harness Leather, horizontal, A **1,900.00**

JI Case Threshing Machine Co, sign, embossed tin, 1 of 3, ca 1880-90, wood frame, 14x20", EX, A 4,600.00

Jim Dandies Peanuts, tin, pictures a baseball scene, At 'Em & Eat 'Em, press lid, 1916, minor scratches, 11", A..**1,500.00**

JM Wyatt's Blacking, box, wood, paper label on inner lid pictures a ship & men attacking a sperm whale, label has sm holes, early, rare, A **210.00**

Joe Lewis Cigars, box label, inner lid, depicts black & white photo of Joe Lewis in bordered rectangle, Eyra Cigar Co Makers, 6x9", M, A....................................**45.00**

John B Busch Brewing Co, sign, paper, Victorian interior with family around table enjoying Busch Beer, matted & framed, 25x19" overall, G+, A **200.00**

John C Roberts Shoes, sharpening stone, D **15.00**

John Deere, ballpoint pen & mechanical pencil set, D ..**15.00**

John Deere, catalog, 1940s, hay tools, some color, D ..**50.00**

John Deere, sign, embossed metal, green & yellow, depicts tractor, Two Cylinder Tractors Sold Here, 11x15", EX, D...**10.00**

John Deere, sign, lighted, Quality Farm Equipment, framed, elongated, appears EX, A **525.00**

John Deere, thimble, plastic, EX, D **3.00**

John Dewar Whiskey, pitcher, appliqued crock, made in England, NM, A **35.00**

John H Lane, shot glass, John H Lane, 91 Broad Street, Pawtucket RI etched on 3 lines in sharp lettering, EX, D..15.00

John H Mann & Co Teas & Coffee, tin, pictorial scenes on 3 sides, yellow & black, slip lid, Isley & Co, flaking on all sides, 11x5x5", G, A 30.00

John H Mann & Co Teas & Coffee, tin, pictorial scenes on 3 sides, yellow & black, slip lid, Isley & Co, flaking on all sides, 12x7x7", VG, A....................................60.00

John Hancock Mutual Life Insurance, calendar, paper litho, Werner, 10x8", M, A 60.00

John Jamison & Son Dublin Whiskey, sign, tin, JJ&S, Established AD 1780, some scratching to lettering/minor chipping, self-framed, 22x28", G, A 75.00

John Morrell Meats, tape measure, celluloid, D 30.00

John P Squire & Co, see Squire's

John Ruskin Cigars, tin, lg picture of man on front, minor flaking, square, EX, A 120.00

John Spengler Wholesale Liquors, shot glass, John Spengler Wholesale Liquors, Kansas City Mo etched in lg letters, vertical ribbing, EX, D.......................................15.00

John W Masury & Son, see also Masury's Paints

John W Masury & Son House Paints, sign, tin litho, ca 1890, 28x20", VG, A 5,500.00

John Walter & Co, tip tray, pictures hunting scene with dog, Opening Souvenir, Eau Claire Wis, 1907, 4" diameter, VG, A..95.00

John Wilkinson Co, catalog for woodworking implements, 56 illustrated pages, 1885-86, edge wear on front cover/discoloration on back, D......................35.00

Johnnie Walker Black Label Scotch, playing cards, yellow logo on black background, 12 Years Old, complete, D 5.00

Johnson & Johnson, sign, paper litho, My Baby Gets The Best flanked by baby & J&J logo, 12x48", NM, A...50.00

Johnson Garage, sign, tin, ca 1920s, bent corners/wrinkling, 14x20", A 350.00

Johnson Motor Oil, tin, winged hourglass logo with Time Tells, black on orange & cream, ca 1935-45, 1-qt, EX, A 120.00

Johnson Outboard Motors, sign, tin, white with green winged horse on red banner, 2-sided, dealer's name on attachment, 1950, 27x39", VG, A..........................550.00

Johnson's Baby Powder, tin, 3x11" square, EX, D 20.00

Johnson's Liniment, display, die-cut cardboard, elderly man & woman holding product, 25x30", G, A.....120.00

Johnson's Log Cabin Coffee, store bin, tin litho cabin figural, Columbia Can Co, St Louis, hinged lid, no chimney/minor scratches, 25x24x18", EX, A 850.00

Johnson's Peacemaker Coffee, sign, die-cut cardboard litho, log cabin figural with lettering on the roof, framed, minor stains, 14x14", VG+, A..................210.00

Johnston Harvester Co, sign, paper, depicts colorful image of Globe mower, printed by Gies & Co, some wear, 18x24" without frame, EX, A 150.00

Johnston Hot Fudge, dispenser, aluminum with pottery insert, Art Deco graphics in red on silver ground, 12x9" diameter, EX, D 125.00

Jolly Monk Cigars, box label, inner lid, depicts portrait of monk with product name above & on banner below, 6x9", VG, D...40.00

Jones Ice Cream, sign, tin, product name in center, Fresh Daily, E Mackey & Co above & below, vertical rectangle, appears EX, A...90.00

Jones Spring & Wire Co, display cabinet, oak, 7 drawers, embossed painted tin fronts, 21" long, G+, A 80.00

Jos Doelger's Sons Beer, sign, die-cut tin, fat brewmeister with a mug of beer, Lager Beer, rust hazing/pitting, 27x20", G-, A 225.00

Jos Doelger's Sons Beer, sign, die-cut tin litho, ca 1890, 28x20", EX, A 1,100.00

Jos Doelger's Sons Lager Beer, tin sign, portly gent in apron holding mug of beer in window-like opening at center, framed, A..160.00

Joseph Burnett & Co Hair Products, sign, canvas roll-down, woman holding a bottle & incense burner, Use Cocoaine For The Hair, 27x14", G-, A 550.00

Joy Detergent, doll, inflatable, Joy, EX, D 20.00

JP Bennett Coffee, tin, detailed image of The Bennett Coffee & Tea House on side of yellow & black can, screw lid, 3-lb, 8x6", G+, A 275.00

JP Hoeltgen Optometrist, clock, wood with reverse-painted glass panel, 33x14", VG+, A.................1,900.00

JS Fry & Sons Candy, tin candy container, pictorial & figural reusable toy bank, Montreal Canada, overall wear, 4x5x3", VG, A 150.00

Ju-Vis Beef Tea, sign, heavy enamel, lg cup on right reads A Breakfast Cup 1¢, Sold In Penny Packets, some chips/pits, rectangular, A **65.00**

Judge Brewer Cigars, box label, inner lid, depicts portrait of judge with name above & below, 6x9", M, D ...**60.00**

Judge Day Cigars, sign, cardboard, depicts US Supreme Court & box of product, minor water stain/some specks, framed, 20x26", VG, A **450.00**

Juicy Fruit, match holder, tin, oval portrait of the founder, The Man Juicy Fruit Made Famous, EX, A............**240.00**

Julius Caesar Cigars, box label, inner lid, depicts Caesar sitting in a chair, 6x9", M, D **18.00**

Jumbo Spark Plugs, display, die-cut tin litho, colorful image of an elephant & Jumbo Molit spark plug, minor scratches, 14x11", VG+, A **1,050.00**

Jung Brewing Co, glass, etched factory scene, NM, A**75.00**

Jung Brewing Co, sign, tin, oval insert, self-framed, 33x23", VG, A...1,700.00

Jung's, seed catalog, 72 illustrated pages of fruits, flowers, & vegetables, 1940, G, D **8.00**

Junius Cigars, box label, outer, pictures a knight in armor, 5x5", M, D **5.00**

Junket, display, die-cut pop-up, lettering on tablecloth, some wear, 9x13x5", G, A **275.00**

Just Suits Cut Plug, sign, porcelain, 4-color, encircled B-L on product tilted to the right, lettering above & below, some wear, 12x8", VG, A......................................**110.00**

❦ K ❧

Kahn Bros Social Club Whiskey, sign, reverse-painted glass, acid-etched letters in gold & silver, oak frame, 19x13", EX, A 1,950.00

Kaier's Beer, tip tray, long-haired girl in profile, product name & Bottled & Pasturized on rim, 4" diameter, NM, A...**75.00**

Kak Kan Koffee, store bin, slip lid, round, EX, A.......**25.00**

Kamargo Coffee, tin, pictures Indian chief & teepees, slip lid, some chipping/minor scratching/overall wear, 1-lb, 6x4", VG, A **500.00**

Kansas City Brewing Co, tip tray, girl holding roses in center, company name & Bohemian Beer on rim, 4" diameter, NM, A **100.00**

Kansas City Brewing Co, tip tray, star-burst logo encircled with 3 bands, company name & Old Fashion Lager Beer on rim, rare, 4" diameter, EX, A **100.00**

Kar-A-Van Coffee, tin, blue camel & desert scene in center oval, 1930-40, 1-lb, 6x4", VG, A **10.00**

Karo, sign, metal, Indian & can of syrup at left of lettering, There's A Wealth Of Health In Karo, 9x18", EX, D..**10.00**

Kasco Feeds, sign, tin, Cow Pass above product name & sun rays, 500 Feet below, EX, A.............................**80.00**

KC Baking Powder, sign, tin, product name in lg letters, For Better Baking below, ca 1940, horizontal, appears EX, A **35.00**

KDX for Dandruff, barber bottle, label under glass, minor edge chipping on label, 1910, 9", NM, A **135.00**

Kearney Brothers Coffee, tin, Coffee on diagonal banner in center, wood knob on lid, 1-lb, EX, A **50.00**

Keebler, doll, elf, vinyl, 1964, 7", EX, D **8.00**

Keeley Brewing Co, sign, tin, hanging, facsimile of the exhibit at the 1911 Brewers International Exposition, 14" diameter, EX, A **650.00**

Keeley Stove Co, match holder, die-cut tin litho, early, rare, NM, A 300.00

Keeley Stove Co, match holder, die-cut tin litho, list of various stove brands surrounded by fancy graphics, 6x4", G+, A **200.00**

Keg Pipe Tobacco, pack (full), pictures keg, EX, D ...**20.00**

Kelley Matches, vendor, 1¢, metal & glass, Box Matches One Cent, Matches in bold letters on both sides, ca 1920-30, 14x11", EX, A...**750.00**

Kellogg's, book, moving picture, 1909, EX, D.............**28.00**

Kellogg's, cookbook, 1978, D **6.00**

Kellogg's, display, cardboard, with doll clothes, cloth patterns, 1 Free with 2 Packages Kellogg's Wheat Krispies, EX, A...**140.00**

Kellogg's, doll, cloth, Crinkle Cat, 1935, 12", F, D.......**30.00**

Kellogg's, doll, cloth, Dandy Duck, 1935, 12", G-, D..**40.00**

Kellogg's, doll, cloth, Dig 'Em, 1973, 17", G, D.............**9.00**

Kellogg's, doll, cloth, Tony Tiger, 1973, 14", G, D **9.00**

Kellogg's, recipe divider folder, pictures Yogi Bear, 1960, EX, D..**10.00**

Kellogg's, salt & pepper shakers, ceramic, Snap & Pop, EX, D..**75.00**

Kellogg's, tin, American Can Co, 4-oz, VG, A.............**60.00**

Kellogg's, toy, wind-up, plastic, Tony Tiger, EX, D **65.00**

Kellogg's Frosties, playing cards, Tony the Tiger eating cereal with lettering above, They're Gr-r-reat!, copyright 1978-80, complete, D **5.00**

Kellogg's Toasted Corn Flakes, sign, die-cut cardboard, girl hugging corn stalk surrounded by cereal boxes, appears EX, A...**875.00**

Kellogg's Toasted Corn Flakes, sign, 2-sided die-cut metal, 1910, rare, 20x13", VG, A 1,200.00

Kelly Springfield Tires, sign, porcelain, 2-sided angle-type, red & white, Gas & Oil lettered vertically at left of lady in tire, 29", VG, A **7,000.00**

Kemp Golden Glow Peanuts, tin, logoed label, slip lid, scratching/denting/overall wear, 10-lb, 10x8" diameter, G, A...**45.00**

Kemply Ice Cream Co, playing cards, stemmed dish of ice cream below Mfgrs Of Quality Ice Cream Endeavor Wis, geometric border, some wear, D **5.00**

Kendall Mfg Co's Soapine, see Soapine

Kendall Motor Oil, tin, easy pour, refinery scene between two lines of product name on red ground, 1915-25, 5-gal, 17x14", EX, A..................................**110.00**

Kendall Motor Oils, sign, porcelain, 2-sided, Service on arrow below circle with hand pointing 2 fingers above product name, 29x36", EX, A **225.00**

Kendall 2000 Mile Oil, sign, 2-sided die-cut metal, can shape with hand pointing 2 fingers above product name, 1930s, 20x12", EX, A **160.00**

Kendall 2000 Mile Oil, sign, 2-sided tin, hand pointing 2 fingers above product name, 1940, scratches/scuffs, 12" diameter, VG, A.......................................**40.00**

Kendall 2000 Mile Oil, tin, hand pointing 2 fingers above product name, 1-qt, EX, A **25.00**

Kendall 2000 Mile Oil, tin, hand pointing 2 fingers above product name in cream oval, 1935-45, no top, 5-qt, VG+, A **40.00**

Kendall's Spavin Cure, poster, paper, woman giving medicine to horse with dogs & people watching, some wear, matted & framed, 33x27", VG, A.................**250.00**

Kennedy's Chimnie Fadden Biscuit, sign, depicts the Bowery boy, framed, approx: 24x18", EX, A 425.00

Kenny's Cheon Tea, tip tray, pictures elegant woman in a green dress, decorative border, rare, appears worn, round, A **65.00**

Kent Cigarettes, playing cards, open box & soft pack of Kents in front of chess set, complete, M, D...........**10.00**

Kentucky Cardinal Cigars, box label, inner lid, cardinal perched on branch flanked by medals with product name above, 6x9", M, D **40.00**

Kentucky Club Tobacco, pocket tin, few sm scratches, G, D..**15.00**

Kentucky Fried Chicken, bank, Colonel Sanders, 13", EX, D..**15.00**

Kentucky Tavern Straight Whiskey, shot glass, ...Jas Thompson & Bro, Louisville Ky etched in lg letters with few fancy scrolls, early, EX, D...............................**16.00**

Kerr Glass, booklet, 1943, 'Home Canning Book,' National Nutrition Edition, 56 pages, D **9.00**

Kerr Glass, recipe booklet, 'Food! Old As The Hills Yet Ever New,' 12 pages, D...**4.00**

Kessler Brewery, sign, tin, pictures the US Gunboat, Helena, decorative border, framed, 18x24", appears EX, A..**975.00**

Keystone Watch Cases, sign, paper, tan & beige colors, early, rare, framed, 20x28", G+, A 1,200.00

Khush-Amadi Talc, tin, fairy standing at edge of lily pond, shaker top, rare, 5x3x2", EX+, A **200.00**

Kickapoo Indian Sagwa, sign, paper, Indian with product, Cures All Diseases...Stomach, Liver..., copyright 1892, oak frame, 42x28", NM, A **50,000.00**

Kik Cola, calendar, 1954, little girl sitting on beach ball with a glass of Kik, full pad, 33x16", NM, D **40.00**

Kik Cola, calendar, 1955, young boy in straw hat holding glass of Kik, full pad, 26x13", NM, D **40.00**

Kikkoman Soy Sauce, fan, bamboo stick, ca 1940s, EX, D **15.00**

Kimball Phonographs, sign, tin, bold lettering with little girl & phonograph at left, WW Kimball Co, 80 Broadway, Detroit..., 1915, 12x36", A **550.00**

Kineo Stoves, trade card, skating scene with boy falling down, D **5.00**

King Alfred Cigars, clipper & clock, heavily embossed cast iron, clipper mechanism missing, 14", VG, A **175.00**

King Arthur Flour, pot scraper, heavy plastic, D **6.00**

King Cole Coffee, tin, original lid, good sheen, 1-lb, 6x4" diameter, EX, A **350.00**

King Cole Coffee, tin, some wear, 8-oz, 3x5" diameter, G+, A...**110.00**

King Cole Tea & Coffee, door plate, rounded corners, 11x3", M, A **140.00**

King Dutch Cigars, tin, comical image of king, Stogies, 3 For 5¢, Made In Pittsburgh, slip lid, overall wear, 6x4" square, G, A...**55.00**

King Edward Tobacco, pocket tin, logo with portrait & royalty seal, Montreal Canada, some wear, 5x3x1", G, A..**300.00**

King Hiram Havana Cigars, sign, curled tin, circular bust portrait of a girl (Griselda) flanked by logo, 1907, minor scratches, 14x14", NM, A **300.00**

King Midas Flour, recipe booklet, 'Bread, Rolls, Biscuits,' 12 pages, VG, D **4.00**

King Roger Cigars, sign, printer's proof, depicts King Roger flanked by logo, High Grade 5¢ Cigar, ca 1900, matted & framed, 26x21", EX, A **180.00**

King Vega Cigars, box label, outer, pictures man on a horse, 5x5", M, D...**4.00**

King's Brewing Co, tip tray, pictures a nurse carrying a tray, Panama Pacific International Exposition, sm rim scratch, oval, 6x5", NM, A.....................................**35.00**

King's Herald Cigars, dispenser, depicts man reading from paper with King's Harold on diagonal, 5¢ Cigars, Cincinnati Ohio, 15x20x11", VG, A **100.00**

King's Puremalt, sign, pictures waitress holding tray & labeled bottle, black background, framed, 19x13", appears EX, A...**425.00**

King's Puremalt, tip tray, labeled bottle in center, Strengthening, Good For Insomnia, Healthful, minor rim chips, oval, 5x6", NM, A **45.00**

King's Puremalt, tip tray, waitress holding tray & bottle, Panama Pacific International Expo Medal below, ca 1915, oval, 6x4", EX+, A...**40.00**

King's Puremalt, tray, Panama Pacific International Expo logo below image, oval, VG+, A **140.00**

Kingan's Reliable Arms, sign, cardboard, sailor navigating in heavy storm within decorative oval border, 1890-1910, original frame, rectangle, A **625.00**

Kinney Brothers Cigarettes, sign, paper, intricate interior scene with costumed people dancing, overall darkening, 26x36" without frame, NM, A.........................**150.00**

Kinsports Cigars, box label, inner lid, depicts bust of a man, ship, & cigar factory, 1913, 6x9", M, D..........**30.00**

Kirk & Co Soap, sign, paper litho, several workers washing up, rare, framed, 41x43", appears EX, A **340.00**

Kirk's Flake Soap, sign, framed, 29x20" without frame, EX, A...**475.00**

Kirkman's Soap, sign, paper litho, lg image of little girl with St Bernard dog, light wear on edges, A **300.00**

Kis-Me Gum, sign, die-cut cardboard litho, brightly colored image of girl in fancy chair, American Chicle Co, framed, 11x10", EX, A **500.00**

Kis-Me Gum, sign, die-cut cardboard litho, 2 girls with fans surrounded by flowers, American Chicle Co, framed, oval, 10x15", EX, A **550.00**

Kis-Me Gum, sign, embossed die-cut tin, woman with red bow in hair in oval bordered with flowers, 18x14" without frame, G, A.................................**200.00**

Kis-Me Gum Co, sign, die-cut, ca 1900, framed, 20x14", EX, A...**170.00**

Kissel's Garage, poster, paper, pictures a tow truck on circular background, product name & lettering above & below, 22x17", EX, A.................................**20.00**

Kist Beverages, door plate with handle, red, white, & black Deco design, Enjoy Kist..., vertical, EX, A ...**20.00**

Kist Beverages, sign, tin, pictures labeled bottle on right side, Get Kist Today, ca 1940, horizontal rectangle, self-framed, EX+, A **70.00**

Kist Orange, sign, die-cut cardboard stand-up, pretty girl displaying product, Get Kist Here, Orange & Other Flavors, 12x14", NM, D **55.00**

Kist Orange Soda, tray, 1930s, VG, D.................................**125.00**

Kleanbore, see Remington

Kleenatub & Wrigley's Scouring Soap, clock, oak with glass front, 34", NM, A **1,500.00**

Kleinert's Dress Shields, poster, paper stone litho, ...These Are The Best, 19x14", EX, A **110.00**

Kling Brewing Co, tip tray, Drink Prost Beer, A Beer For Guest..., fancy rim, 4" diameter, NM, A **170.00**

Kling Brewing Co, tip tray, pictures a well-dressed gentleman pouring a beer, Kling's Prost, rim chips, 5" diameter, EX, A.................................**55.00**

Klondike Gold & Aluminum Paint, sign, embossed tin die-cut, 13x19", VG, A **2,500.00**

Knapsack Rye, sign, reverse-painted glass, soldier looking at sign on a tree, John Ellwanger Co, 1899, marked frame, 25x18", NM, A.................................**9,000.00**

Knickerbocker Beer, tray, pictures 3 scenes with product name above each, round, appears EX, A **15.00**

Knickerbocker Mills Coffee, tin, black & green 4-sided can with different images, sm slip top, overall chipping/general wear, 7x4" square, G, A.................................**90.00**

Knox Gelatine, leaflet, 1915, 'Knox Dainty Desserts For Dainty People,' 41 pages, D **12.00**

Knox Gelatine, leaflet, 1933, 'Knox Gelatine Desserts, Salads, Candies & Frozen Dishes,' 75 pages, D **9.00**

Knox Gelatine, playing cards, box of Knox above Get To Know Knox, The Real Gelatine on white with gold & blue border, complete, D.................................**5.00**

Knox Gelatine, sign, cardboard, lady with box of Knox & display of desserts, Try a...Dainty, Recipe In Each Box, framed, 21x15", EX, A **190.00**

Knox Gelatine, sign, paper, 18x27", VG, A **170.00**

Kobolt's Family Liquor Store, tray, ad text on back, 1904, 16x14", NM, A.................................**425.00**

Kodak Film, frisbee (filmsbee), For The Time Of Your Life, EX, D..............10.00

Kodak Film, sign, porcelain, yellow, red, blue, white, & black, pictures 122-6 film in opened box, Developing & Printing, NM, D 100.00

Kodak Tobacco, tin, factory image on lid, Rock City Tobacco Co, Toronto Canada, chipping on lid/good color sheen, 4x5x2", VG+, A 100.00

Kola-Mint, dispenser, wood, barrel-shape, painted red logo, lift-off top, metal spigot, faded lettering, 19", G+, A...**40.00**

Konjola Medicine, display, cardboard with die-cut letters atop, pictures bottles & cure rate chart, dirt spots/edge damage, 34x47", EX, A **150.00**

Kool Milds, playing cards, graphics depicts pack of Kool Milds, complete, M, D **8.00**

Koppitz-Melchers Pale Select Beer, tray, lettered logo surrounded by images of all 4 seasons, decorative border, 12" diameter, VG+, A..............**280.00**

Koppitz-Melchers Pale Select Beer..., tray, star logo flanked by Pale Select Beer & Extra Dublin Porter, winter scene below, decorative rim, oval, G, A **140.00**

Korbel Sec Champagne, sign, tin litho promoting California winery, colorful image of a woman wrapped in a grapevine, framed, 13x19", VG, A **275.00**

Korn Krisp, sign, paper, Eat Korn Krisp above bay with ship & lg product on shore, First Wireless Telegram..., framed, 20x27", EX, A **200.00**

Kraft Kraylets, sign, die-cut tin, embossed pig figural, NM, D..............**295.00**

Kramer's Beverages, sign, tin, horizontal, D **35.00**

Kruger Brewing Co, tip tray, foaming tankard surrounded by hops & wheat, High Grade Beer & company name on rim, 4" diameter, EX, A **105.00**

Kryptok Eyeglasses, sign, reverse painting on glass, Invisible Bi-Focal Without Seam Or Cement, The Master Lens, framed, 9x12", EX+, A **325.00**

Kuntz Brewery, tip tray, Kaufman & Strauss litho, 13" diameter, EX, A..............400.00

Kyanize Varnish, pocket mirror, black & white, pictures 2-faced man, EX, D **28.00**

L

L Haywood, sign, white lettering on brown flanked by encircled portraits, Ladies & Gents Hairdresser, Waving..., framed, 14x50", A **280.00**

L Hoster Brewing Co, tray, company name over factory scene, Weiner Beer & other lettering on rim, oval, 14x17", G, A **700.00**

La Alegria Cigars, box label, inner lid, depicts 3 happy peasant women, 6x9", EX, D **28.00**

La Carita Cigars, box label, inner lid, pictures woman holding violets, 6x9", M, D **6.00**

La Choy, doll, cloth, La Choy Girl, 15", G, D **6.00**

La Crosse Athletics Canvas Rubber Soled Shoes, sign, die-cut cardboard, lg shoe with boy sliding into home plate & boy ready to catch ball, 20x13", EX, A **100.00**

La Eolia Cigars, box label, inner lid, elegant woman surrounded by decorative border, 6x9", EX, D **12.00**

La Flor De Seward Cigars, box label, inner lid, depicts La Flor De Seward in profile flanked by books & Capitol building, 6x9", EX, D **45.00**

La Gora Cigars, box label, inner lid, depicts Arabian hunter, camel, & elephant, 6x9", VG, D **25.00**

La Korina Talcum, tin, shaker top, EX, D **18.00**

La Muleta Cigars, box label, inner lid, depicts woman on mule, 1900, 6x9", EX, D **30.00**

La Palina Cigars, humidor, brass, D **40.00**

La Reala Habana Cigars, box label, inner lid, depicts Cuban coat of arms & cigars, 1900, 6x9", M, D **18.00**

La Reclama Habana Cigars, box, wood, pictures lady on inside label, 3 sections, lid has metal hinges & clasp, VG, D **20.00**

La Rosa Macaroni, pamphlet, 1929, '101 Ways To Prepare Macaroni,' 31 pages, VG, D **4.00**

La Tour Coffee, store bin, tin, slant front, hinged lid, yellow & red lettering on black, shows coffee sack, WS Quinby Co, 19x18", EX, A **400.00**

La Vera Cigars, box label, outer, pictures a woman in profile, 1921, 5x5", M, D **4.00**

Lacquerwax, sign, embossed tin litho, shows product over 1940s car, Motorists Relax With..., Lasts Twice As Long, 13x20", NM, D **125.00**

Ladies Home Journal Patterns, sign, product name in gold on black, Patterns flanked by red circles with ladies faces in gold, framed, 12x32", NM, A **380.00**

Ladies Short Smokes, sign, cardboard litho, 2 elegantly dressed gentlemen in top hats in front of theater, framed, 36x25", M, A **100.00**

Lady Madison Shops, thimble, plastic, EX, D 3.00

Lafean's Cough Drops, tin, product name in lg letters above & below Strictly Pure, slip lid & wire handle, round, appears EX, A......................................**50.00**

Laflin & Rand Powder Co, poster, paper, pictures an elk startling a sleeping hunter, 1905, horizontal creases, framed, 29x15", G, A......................................**550.00**

Laflin & Rand Powder Co, sign, cardboard, 4 images of men & boys with rifles, some staining/spotting/chipping, matted & framed, 24x45", G, A **250.00**

Lakritsia Licorice, tin, Halva, pictures children on yellow background, slip lid, NM, A **35.00**

Lambertville Rubber Co, calendar, 1912, paper litho, minor wear, framed, 36x21", A......................**400.00**

Lammers Bottling Co, see CA Lammers Bottling Co

Lamp Works, thimble, plastic, company name & address in black on cream background, EX, D......................**3.00**

Land of Sunshine Cigars, box label, inner lid, depicts pretty woman by water, 6x9", EX, D **50.00**

Lang's Red Cross Cough Drops, tin, pictures Red Cross nurse in floral border, product name above & lettering below, slip lid, rectangular, EX, A......................**170.00**

Langenfeld's Ice Cream, tray, depicts lg block of Neapolitan with 2 Kewpies & Kewpie golfer enjoying ice cream, 13" square, EX, D......................................**275.00**

Langsdorf's Quality Cigars, box label, inner lid, depicts lady & 3 gentlemen in formal attire with product name above & below, 6x9", M, D **40.00**

Larinca Cigars, box label, outer, pictures a woman & tobacco fields, 5x5", M, D **10.00**

Lash's Kidney & Liver Bitters, sign, wood, girl with horse, The Perfect Laxative, Meyercord Co, fading/crazing to image, 14x20", G **225.00**

Last Issue Cigars, sign, paper on tin, Smoke The Best above S Levy & Bro's, product name & portrait over Albany NY, EX, A......................................**110.00**

Lauer Brewing Co, sign, paper, classical girl in chariot drawn by goats, lettering above & below, framed, 24x18", VG, A......................................**225.00**

Lautz Bros & Co Marseilles Soap, sign, paper, depicts baby in round tub with sponge, towel, & product, lettering above & below, framed, 36x28", VG, A.....**650.00**

Lavender & Old Lace Cake Makeup, jar, with contents, in original box, M, D **15.00**

Lawrence Barrett Cigars, sign, porcelain, depicts encircled portrait of Lawrence Barrett, curved corners, 32x24", EX, A......................................**1,300.00**

Lawrence Cigars, box label, inner lid, depicts building with product name above, 6x9", M, D..................**85.00**

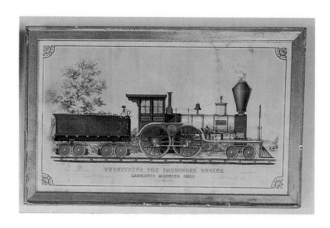

Lawrence Machine Shop, poster, paper litho by Chandler & Co, Boston, rare, approx: 22x38", G, A.......**1,850.00**

Lax-Ets, match holder, tin litho, colorful image of an open tin of Lax-Ets, 5x3", EX, A......................................**50.00**

LC Smith Guns/Hunter Arms Co, litho, depicts dog with duck in its mouth on oval bordered by lettering & trim in embossed diamond-shaped frame, 33x30", EX, A......................................**1,850.00**

Le Roy Little Cigars, sign, tin, Gypsy leaning on package with lettering above & below, Kellogg & Buckeley litho, 1880s, framed, 16x12", NM, D **600.00**

Lea & Perrins, booklet, 1936, 'Success in Seasoning,' 47 pages, D **4.00**

Lee Shirts & Pants, sign, embossed tin, black letters on yellow background, Union Made Guaranteed, 12x23", appears EX, D......................................**30.00**

Lee Work Clothing Dept, sign, tin, Lee logo each end, wood frame, 7x60", VG, A......................................**150.00**

Legends Cigars, box label, inner lid, depicts ancient Romans & woman holding leaf, 6x9", VG, D.........**40.00**

Leidiger Brewing Co, tip tray, girl in duster outfit, Merrill Wis on rim, 7x5", EX, A......................................**160.00**

Leidiger Brewing Co, tip tray, girl in open robe with roses at bottom, Bottled Beer, Merrill Wis on rim, 7x5", EX, A......................................**175.00**

Leisy Brewing Co, see J Leisy Brewing Co

Lembeck & Betz Airship Delivery, tray, few stains, 13x13", VG+, A......................................**1,700.00**

Lemon-Cola, tray, depicts girl pointing out to viewer, Right to the Point, inpainting to rim & image, oval, 16x13", G-, A **65.00**

Lemp Ale, sign, die-cut tin, elegant girl sitting on counter edge holding a lg bottle, may be 1 of a kind, 16", appears EX, A **1,600.00**

Lenhert's Brewing Co, tip tray, pictures a dog smoking a cigar, Drink Lehnert's Beer, Made in Catasauqua Pa, 1910, 4" diameter, NM, A **325.00**

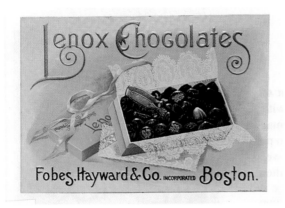

Lenox Chocolates, sign, embossed tin over cardboard, 9x14", EX+, A.....................................600.00

Lenox Tobacco, pocket tin, pictures early automobile, some dents/crazing, rare, G+, A............................**200.00**

Leonard Silks, clock top from spool cabinet, LEONARD SILKS used as numbers on round clock face, domed top, walnut housing, 10x21", A **230.00**

Lesh's Arkoline Products, tin, product name in black-lined red letters, ca 1915-25, half-gal, 6", EX+, A.35.00

Lever's Glycerine, display case, wood frame with milk glass inserts, lettering on marquee top, Pure Double Distilled, 18x15", appears EX, A............................**250.00**

Levi's, display, approx: 31x15x10", G, A **1,050.00**

Leviathan Belting, calendar, 1911-13, metal, EX, D ..**27.00**

Libby's Corned Beef, sample tin, EX+, A **45.00**

Libby's Mince Meat, sign, paper, pictures an old farmer eating pie, tear/paper loss, 30x15", A **475.00**

Liberty Bell Jams & Jellies, display, bell shape with red & gilt lettering, faded, 20", appears EX, A...............**100.00**

Liberty Bell Salted Peanuts, tin, depicts Liberty Bell logo, press lid, scratches/chips/discoloration, 10x8" diameter, G-, A **60.00**

Liberty Bread, display case, wood frame & back panel with logo reverse-painted on glass inserts, ca 1930-40, 31x28x22", NM, A..**425.00**

Liberty Root Beer, barrel dispenser, wood with hand-painted picture of man, Ask One Who's Had One, Your Choice 5¢, rare, EX, A **425.00**

Lieberman's Beer, tray, stock image of Griselda in circular inset, Lager Beer & other lettering on rim, 13" square, VG, A **100.00**

Life Pipe Tobacco, pocket tin, Life lettered above tobacco leaf on red with yellow & white border, Kentucky White Burley below, M, A **775.00**

Life Savers, display box, tin rare, 16x9x5", EX+, A........**1,700.00**

Life Savers, display rack, tin litho, shows 4 flavors, includes 3 original cardboard boxes, minor rust/blemishes, 9x12x4", VG, A **260.00**

Life Savers, doll, with comb, Mike-E-Mint, scented, 1981, EX, D...**15.00**

Life Savers, playing cards, featuring graphics of rows of different flavors of Life Savers, complete, D.............**5.00**

Light House Peanut Butter, pail, depicts rope-bordered logo of boat & lighthouse, slip lid & bail, rust on rim & lid/spots/chips, 4x4", G, A....................................**150.00**

Lilac Talc Powder, tin, lettering & flowers, shaker top, appears EX, A **40.00**

Lilacs & Roses Talc, tin, missing cap, EX, D **10.00**

Lilly White, tin, for motor oil, yellow with black stripes, flower bouquet & Petroleum Products in center, 1915-25, 1-gal, 6", EX, A **100.00**

Lily of the Valley Coffee, tin, lilies in bloom as product logo, 1-lb, 6x4" diameter, EX, A **175.00**

Lima Shovels & Draglines, watch fob, D...................**22.00**

Lime Kiln Club Cigars, box label, inner lid, men at a meeting having a good time, 1883, 6x9", M, D ...**250.00**

Lime Kiln Club Cigars, sign, paper on canvas, 1882, 24x31", NM, A...4,250.00

Lime Kiln Club Tobacco, trade card, paper litho, colorful image with figures, A Bird In The Hand Is Worth Two..., framed, 14x17", EX+, A **525.00**

Lincoln Club Coffee, tin, paper label of Abe Lincoln, Andersen-Ryan Coffee Co, Duluth Minn, slip lid & bail, 5-lb, 9x8" diameter, VG+, A **145.00**

Linindoll's Celebrated Ale Taps & Faucets, paperweight, half-length male figure atop rectangular glass base with lettering, diagonal corners, appears EX, A.............**20.00**

Linser's Brewery, tray, the American Maid serving bottles of beer, Have It At Home! When You Want It!, decorative border, 11x13", EX, A **450.00**

Linser's Brewery, tray, the American Maid with bottles of beer, Have It At Home! When You Want It! on decorative border, 11x13", VG+, A..............**350.00**

Lion Brand Shirts, mirror, cast iron lions at top of frame, 16x13", G, D..............**55.00**

Lion Coffee, store bin, wood, slant top with lion-drawn chariot & lettering, lion's head on front with lettering, 32x22", EX, A..............**350.00**

Lion Head Motor Oil, tin, Monarch of Oil above yellow, red, & black banner with lion's head, red background, ca 1935-45, 1-qt, NM, A **35.00**

Lion Perforated Toilet Paper, roll of product, wrapping pictures recumbent tiger, 1889, 5x5", EX+, A.........**60.00**

Lipton Tea, tin, pictures tea pickers & buffalo, top has been painted with gold paint, 4x5x4", EX, D.........**75.00**

Lipton Tea, tin, workers picking tea in Ceylon, early, 7x9", EX, A **70.00**

Lipton's Instant Cocoa, sign, tin, minor edge wear, self-framed, 13x9", NM, A.............425.00

Lipton's Tea, sign, flanged, red & white lettering on green background, no graphics, 10x19", appears EX, A..**60.00**

Lipton's Tea & Coffee, puzzle, mounted with original shipping envelope, Jig-Saw Puzzle With Each Purchase..., framed, vertical rectangle, EX, A............**150.00**

Lipton's Teas, sign, cardboard, girl with product & tea set, product name above, Will You Have Some below, wood frame, 23x17", NM, A **1,000.00**

Listers Fertilizers, calendar, 1899, woman with sheaves of wheat & farm beyond, full pad, matted & framed, 29x19", EX, A............**125.00**

Little Colonel Play Suits, sign, paper, framed, 9x24", EX, A............**45.00**

Little Lord Cigars, box label, inner lid, depicts young boy holding a whip, 1895, 6x9", EX, D............**25.00**

Little Lulu Kleenex, display, 3-D stand-up with hole in hand for 1 tissue, 1950, 7x10", D **11.00**

Log Cabin Brownies, biscuit box, log cabin-shaped cardboard with Palmer Cox Brownies, rare, minor edge nicks/chips, 3x4x3", VG+, A **50.00**

Log Cabin Coffee, tin, pictures log cabin, key-wind lid, minor chipping, 1-lb, 4x5", VG, A............**250.00**

Log Cabin Smoking Tobacco, display, wooden box with hinged lid, lg interior label with man outside of cabin smoking pipe, 8x15x9", G, A **500.00**

Log Cabin Syrup, bank, glass, cabin figural, EX, D **32.00**

Log Cabin Syrup, container, plastic wigwam, yellow lettering, ca 1950s, rare, 2x2" diameter, D............**6.00**

Log Cabin Syrup, tin, Dr RU Well, cartoon style, rare, EX, D **250.00**

Log Cabin Syrup, tin, Express Office, EX, D............**150.00**

Log Cabin Syrup, tin, Frontier Inn, pictures cowboys & horse, 5-lb, D............**220.00**

Log Cabin Syrup, tin, Home Sweet Home, 12-oz, D **150.00**

Log Cabin Syrup, tin, log cabin figural, EX+, A......55.00

Log Cabin Syrup, tin, boy with lasso, 1-lb, D...........**110.00**

Log Cabin Syrup, tin, pictures children playing, Towel's, 33-oz, NM, D **135.00**

Log Cabin Syrup, tin, pictures pancakes, G, D...........**10.00**

Log Cabin Syrup, tin, red, 5-lb, D............**50.00**

Log Cabin Syrup, tin, Stockade School, EX, D **150.00**

London & Lancashire, sign, reverse-painted glass, oak frame, 27x23", EX, D............**100.00**

London & Lancashire Fire Insurance Co of Liverpool, sign, reverse-painted glass, red beveled shield with lettering, oak frame, 27x23", EX, A **100.00**

London Life Cigarettes, sign, tin, ca 1910-15, self-framed, 39x28", EX, A.....................950.00

London Life Cigarettes, sign, tin, depicts Europeans at a sporting event under a logoed tent, self-framed, 39x28", EX, A **1,200.00**

London Sherbert Tobacco, pocket tin, front VG, back EX, D...**175.00**

London Spires Cigars, box label, inner lid, depicts London's skyline, 6x9", EX, D **8.00**

Long Distance Tobacco, package label, EX, D **10.00**

Long Tom Smoking Tobacco, tin, pictures man in checkered suit, slip lid, chipping/denting/scratches, 2x5x4", G, A **150.00**

Longines-Wittnaur Watches, mechanical display, die-cut, watchmaker behind counter, Let Us Check Your Watch, ca 1920-30, 12x14", EX, A **550.00**

Longley Hats, lamp, milk glass with brass base, colorful decal with logo & eagle atop, 18x15" diameter, EX, A **475.00**

Loose-Wiles Nobility Chocolates, display, die-cut tin litho, 30x18", NM, A...........................8,250.00

Lord Calvert Superb American Whiskey, charger, embossed portrait of Lord Calvert in center, lettering on rim above & below, 23" diameter, appears EX, A..**30.00**

Lord Delaware Cigars, box label, inner lid, depicts portrait of Lord Delaware flanked by harbor & shoreline with name above, 6x9", M, D.........................**40.00**

Lorillard's, see also P Lorillard

Lorillard's Redicut Tobacco, lunch pail, tin, hinged lid with wire handle, A 175.00

Los Angeles Brewing Co, tip tray, factory scene with early motorized wagon, The Home of East Side Beer, 4" diameter, NM, A **300.00**

Los Angeles Brewing Co, tip tray, factory scene with horse-drawn wagon, The Home East Of East Side Beer, 4" diameter, NM, A **300.00**

Lotos Export Beer, tip tray, pictures labeled bottle & glass on a table, Adam Scheidt Brewing Co, Norristown Pa, 4" diameter, G, A **50.00**

Lotus Salted Peanuts, tin, Lotus label on violet & white, press lid, Vollmayer-Kaufmann Co, dents/chips, 11x8", VG, A **110.00**

Louisiana Expo Cigarette, pack (full), 1984 Souvenir, NM, D...**10.00**

Lovell & Covell, pail, tin, depicts scenes of Little Red Riding Hood, slip lid & bail, rare, VG+, A **40.00**

Lowenbrau Beer, coaster, from 1964 World's Fair, EX, D...**3.00**

Lowenbrau Beer, replica wooden wagon pulled by 4 composition draft horses, leather tack, on mahogany board, 60" long, A **850.00**

Lower Canada Maple Syrup, tin, sugaring scene surrounded by leaves & portrait on yellow & black can, press lid, overall wear, 3x3", diameter, G, A........**115.00**

Lower Canada Maple Syrup, tin, sugaring scene with maple leaves & beaver on red & black can, soldered seam, ca 1870, rare, 7x5" diameter, G+, A............**400.00**

Lowney's Chocolates, sign, bellboy carrying lg box of chocolates, Treat With Package Of Medal Of Honor..., 1918, matted, horizontal, EX, A **60.00**

Lowney's Chocolates, sign, paper, red roses & an open box of chocolates, The American Beauties, matted & framed, creases, 23x13", VG, A **110.00**

Lowney's Cocoa, chalkboard, 33x15", EX, A.............**180.00**

Loyl Coffee, tin, eagle on red, blue, white can, Cummings Bros, Portland Me, slip lid, bright color/chips, 1-lb, 6x4" diameter, EX, A **150.00**

Lucky Bill Cigars, box label, outer, pictures a young boy wearing knickers, 5x5", M, D **3.00**

Lucky Curve Plug Cut Tobacco, tin, pictures baseball player on front & lid, company name on sides, slip lid, rare, 4x7x5", VG+, A **750.00**

Lucky Curve Plug Cut Tobacco, tin, slip lid, 4x7x5", G-, A 575.00

Lucky Strike, pocket mirror, depicts a cowboy standing to 1 side of a Lucky Strike window sign, ca 1920, 2" diameter, VG+, D...**22.00**

Lucky Strike, pocket tin, white, upright, D **350.00**

Lucky Strike Cigarettes, sign, cardboard, 29x14", A **210.00**

Lucky Strike Cut Plug Tobacco, tin, 5x3x1", EX, D...**45.00**

Lucky Strike Flat Fifties Cigarettes, sign, minor edge damage, framed, 39x26", EX, A **275.00**

Lucky Strike Tobacco, clock, Roman numerals, RA Patterson Tobacco Co, original working condition, 14" diameter, EX, A **550.00**

Lucky Strike Tobacco, clock, wood with printed dial, reverse-painted glass panel, Harris, Gage, & Tolman, Portland Maine, 24", EX, A **1,100.00**

Lucky Strike Tobacco, sign, cardboard litho, pictures Gracie Allen with a CBS Radio microphone, framed, 21x14", EX, A **120.00**

Lucky Strike Tobacco, sign, cardboard litho, pictures 2 bathing beauties frolicking at pool side, framed, 21x10", EX, A **120.00**

Lucy Gray Cigars, box label, inner lid, depicts girl in kilt with name above, 6x9", M, D **65.00**

Luden's Cough Drops, sign, cardboard litho, pictures girl in bed beside a list of uses & open box of cough drops below, framed, 10x7", EX, A **500.00**

Luden's Cough Drops, sign, die-cut tin, pictures open box of cough drops, heavily worn, 7x8", A.................**250.00**

Luden's Menthol Cough Drops, sign, 2-sided die-cut tin wall-mounted holder for 12" round tray, rare, 13x19", EX, A..**12,000.00**

Luden's Menthol Cough Drops, tin, lettering on 1 side, Menthol Cough Drops Give Instant Relief, early, slip lid, 8x6x4", VG+, A...**50.00**

Lutted's Cough Drops, store container, glass, log cabin figural with lettering on roof, ca 1895-1905, 7x8x6", EX, A **350.00**

Lutted's Cough Drops, store container, glass, log cabin figural with lettering on roof, ca 1895-1905, chips under lid, 7x8x6", VG, A......................................**200.00**

Luxite Hosiery, sign, WWI era, framed, 11x21", appears EX, A **110.00**

Lydia E Pinkham's Vegetable Compound, display, die-cut, Lydia Pinkham looking at seated mother & child promoting Vegetable Compound For Women, 30x22", VG, A **230.00**

Lyon Diamonds & Watches, sign, reverse-painted glass, gold with black lettering, damage along lower edge, 60" long, A...**170.00**

Lyra Cigars, box label, inner lid, pictures woman playing harp, 6x9", M, D **3.00**

≈∾ **M** ∾≈

M&W Gas & Oil Co Better Oil, tin, text on side, Indiana Pa on back, ca 1915-25, 1-gal, 11", EX, A.....**2,200.00**

Ma's Root Beer, sign, cardboard, Drink Old Fashion Ma's Root Beer, 1940s, 12x10", EX, D **5.00**

MAC Cigars, sign, tin, product name above & below sm diamond logo, Manufactured by Celesting Fernandez Co, horizontal rectangle, A **10.00**

MacLaren's Peanut Butter, pail, tin, children playing tea party, original slip lid & bail, MacLaren Wright Ltd, Canada, 4x4" diameter, VG, A.............................**125.00**

Macwhyte Wire Rope, sign, glass, gold & black lettering, We Sell Macwhyte..., 10x18", appears EX, A.........**90.00**

Macy's Coffee, tin, pictures Macy's in inset with decorative border, slip lid, slight denting/scratching/chipping, 1-lb, 6x4", VG, A **425.00**

Madame Butterfly Cigars, tin, shows pictures of butterfly & oriental woman surveying naval ship, scratches/edge wear/chips, 5x6" diameter, G+, A **70.00**

Madie Cigars, box label, inner lid, depicts peasant girl, 6x9", M, D **12.00**

Madison Cigars, poster, paper, image of Indian princess in profile, 1906, matted & framed, 34x19", EX, A.....**300.00**

Maerzen-Senate Beer, tray, picturing the Chr Heurich Brewing Co, decorative rim, 13x16", VG, A 1,150.00

Magic Yeast, calendar, 1915, paper litho, barefoot boy carrying yeast & a stick, by Ketterlinus, Philadelphia, 18x10", VG, A **225.00**

Magic Yeast, sign, paper litho, ca 1890-1910, 2 sm tears near bottom, 15x10", EX, A.....................100.00

Magnolia Petroleum Co, sign, porcelain, 2-sided, flower &...Gasoline For Sale Here circled by letters, 1920, 29" diameter, G+, A.....................**425.00**

Magnolia Pipe Line Co, sign, porcelain, white with red text, Danger High Pressure..., horse in top corners, 1930, flaking at holes, 8x15", A.....................**150.00**

Mahoney Whiskey, tip tray, depicts possibly the Jefferson Memorial, chipping/spotting, 4" diameter, G+, A...**45.00**

Maier Brewing Co, tray, shows colorful factory scene, Kaufmann & Strauss, ca 1906, bright colors/rim chips/scratches, 13" diameter, EX, A **850.00**

Maier Brewing Co, tray, young woman flanked by lettered logo, Standard of Perfection, Los Angeles USA, ca 1909, 13" diameter, EX, A **275.00**

Mail Pouch, sign, counter-top, cardboard, depicts harpooner & 2 ladies, Real Man's Choice, 1920-30, 21x14", G, A.....................**55.00**

Mail Pouch Tobacco, pouch (full), pictures Mail Pouch, EX, D.....................**25.00**

Mail Pouch Tobacco, thermometer sign, porcelain, yellow & white on blue, dated Yourself To The Best, dated 1915, rare, 27x7", EX, A **325.00**

Maillard Chocolates, box, cardboard with cloth & linen appliques of romantic scenes, square, A **65.00**

Majestic Ranges, sign, Majestic Malleable Iron & Steel Ranges, St Louis, USA, framed, 22x46", EX, A......**150.00**

Malachrino Cigarettes, display, tin, 4-fold, pictures Arabs, 13x20", EX, D **325.00**

Malayan Cigars, box label, inner lid, depicts Malaysian dancer, 6x9", M, D.....................**28.00**

Maltby's Cocoanut, store bin, gold, black, & silver stenciled graphics, Highest Centennial Award, some paint loss/scratches/dents, VG, A **145.00**

Maltby's Cocoanut, tin, depicts tropical scene with coconut in circular inset, Maltby's Patent Prepared Cocoanut, vertical, EX, A **50.00**

Maltex Cereal, sign, paper, pictures kids at table, 1950s, 16x21", EX, D.....................**20.00**

Maltosia Beer, see German American Brewing Co

Mammoth Salted Nuts, tin, picturing an elephant, black & white, press lid, Kelly Co, paint loss/scratches on side, 10-lb, 11x8", G, A **125.00**

Mammy Beverage Co, soda bottle, glass with embossed mammy, 1910, 14", EX, A **30.00**

Mammy Salted Peanuts, tin, press lid, extremely rare, 10-lb, NM, A 21,000.00

Mangus Beck Brewing Co, see Beck's Bottled Beer

Manhattan Automobile Cylinder Oil, tin, Old Manhattan map center right, list of products at left, 1910-20, paint loss at bottom, 1910-20, 1-gal, 10", EX, A.............**400.00**

Manhattan Sugar Cones, tin, pictures a cone & product name in lg letters, slip lid & bail, round, 20-lb, appears worn, A **65.00**

Manitou Table Water, sign, paper litho, Indian labeled bottle surrounded by vignettes of people using product, All Use It, 29x22", VG, A **500.00**

Manitowoc Speed Shovel, watch fob, nickel & enamel, D.................**28.00**

Manson Campbell Co, sign, tin, images of founder & products including carts, mill, brooder, chicks, gold & gray embossed edges, 23x33", G, A.................**350.00**

Many Miles Motor Oil, tin, orange racer with driver, 3-color prize ribbon to left, For Economy & Satisfaction..., 1925-45, 2-gal, 12x9", VG, A **200.00**

Marathon Motor Oil, tin, easy pour, green with runner to left of 3-line product name, Transcontinental Oil Co, 1915-25, 5-gal, 17x14", VG, A **325.00**

Marathon Motor Oil, tin, marathon runner in lower left, Best In The Long Run, Transcontinental Oil Co, ca 1924-30, 1-gal, 6", VG, A **100.00**

Marathon VEP Motor Oil, tin, marathon runner in blue & red-bordered circle on white, blue & white lettered bottom band, ca 1932-40, 1-qt, EX+, A **75.00**

Marble Arms Co, compass, brass, D.................**30.00**

Maremont Turn-Plate Mufflers, sign, paper, salesman explains to couple the dangers of carbon monoxide, lettering above & below, 34x21", EX, A **10.00**

Marine Tobacco, tin, marine pictured on tortise shell background, Canada, chipping/scratches to lid/wear on sides, 3x4x1", G+, A.................**150.00**

Mark Twain Cigars, box label, inner lid, depicts bust portrait of Mark Twain superimposed over fishing scene, 6x9", M, D **5.00**

Marksman Cigars, cigar box, cardboard, depicts 2 men shooting guns, 5¢, 3x5x1", G, A **25.00**

Marlboro Cigarettes, playing cards, Marlboro logo right side up & upside down in black, red, & white, complete, M, D **9.00**

Marlin Firearms Co, sign, paper litho, pictures cowboy approaching an elk, Forbes, 1905, horizontal creases, framed, 24x14", VG, A **525.00**

Marquette Club Cigars, box label, inner lid, depicts man entering billiards club, 6x9", M, D.................**125.00**

Marriott's Great America, doll, Bugs Bunny, D **10.00**

Mart Hayes Wines & Liquors, shot glass, Mart Hayes Wines & Liquors, 101 S Division St, Grand Rapids Mich etched on 5 lines in sharp lettering, M, D **16.00**

Martin's VVO Whiskey, sign, circle inset of fighter on the ropes with Radio Returns Of Louis Schmeling Fight above, 22x14", appears EX, A **10.00**

Marx Brewing Co's Banner Beer, tip tray, pictures girl with carnations, lettering on rim, background/rim chips, 4" diameter, EX, A **60.00**

Mary Garden Talc, tin, EX **15.00**

Maryland Club Mixture Tobacco, store bin, shows the Maryland Club & hunting dogs on sides, lid missing, chips/overlaquer/soiled/dents, 15x10x8", G-, A .**125.00**

Mascot Crushed Cut Tobacco, pocket mirror, celluloid, dog in center with lettering around border, 2" diameter, NM, A.................**30.00**

Mason & Hamlin Pianos, sign, tin litho, depicts piano in center, Grand & Upright, Boston, New York, Chicago, scratches, framed, 32" long, VG, A **1,400.00**

Mason Campbell Co Limited, sign, tin, Mason Campbell centered in oval bordered farm incubators, brooders..., rare, self-framed, 23x33", EX+, D **750.00**

Mason Mints, sign, product name superimposed over triangular logo on blue, lettering & product on yellow, 1920s, framed, 11x22", A **180.00**

Mason's Root Beer, sign, Mason's over lg M, Drink above, Root Beer, Ice Cold below, 9" diameter, M, D **30.00**

Massachusettes Bonding & Insurance Co, sign, wood, logo of Massociate Indian, Surety Bonds of All Kinds, 31x17" without frame, VG, A.................**250.00**

Massasoit Coffee, presentation sign made by workers for president, cut-out linen logo on art board, hand-lettered, framed, 39x34", EX, A.................**325.00**

Massatta Talcum, tin, shaker top, EX, D **18.00**

Master Guard Cigars, pail, tin, shows dog with pail in mouth, Stogies 3 For 5¢, slip lid & bail, overall wear, 6x6" diameter, G-, A.................**325.00**

Master Mason Smoking Tobacco, pocket tin, rare, 4x3", G+, A.................**600.00**

Master Mason Tobacco, poster, Smoke Master Mason Tobacco above man smoking pipe & squaring 5 packages of product, framed, rare, 22x15", EX, A **900.00**

Mastiff Tobacco, sign, paper litho, portrait of a dog & box of cigars, framed, 14x10", EX, A **225.00**

Masury's Paints, see also John W Masury & Son

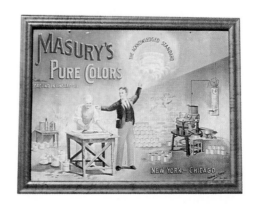

Masury's Pure Colors, sign, tin, muted colors with matte finish, Sentenne & Green litho, 2 sm nail holes in top edge, framed, 18x24", EX, A....**2,000.00**

Mathie Brewing Co, tray, pictures hula girl with ukelele, Los Angeles, 13" diameter, EX, A **250.00**

Mathieu Syrup for Coughs & Colds, thermometer, wood, shows product, printed in English & French, Canada, some chipping/darkening, 24x4", G, A **175.00**

Matoaka Tobacco, pocket tin, pictures Pocahontas, EX, D **1,500.00**

Maull's Barbecue Sauce, playing cards, bottle of Maull's in red on white with red & gold decorative border, complete, D **8.00**

Maumee Brewing Co, tip tray, Let Your Ashes Repose Here & Drink Bull Frog arched above & below frog on lily pad, 4" diameter, G, A **350.00**

Mauser Mill Co, clock, painted tin, 6x5", EX, D **48.00**

Mavis Chocolate Drink, sign, tin, 2-sided, flanged, Real Chocolate Flavor, bottle in lower right corner, 1920-30, 12x10", EX, A **45.00**

Max Factor, display, 4 sections featuring Ellen Drew & Patricia Morison, edge wear, 44" long, G **45.00**

Maxoil, tin, Maxoil in red across early car graphic, script Special, Cylinder Lubricant, white background, ca 1940, 1-qt, NM, A **55.00**

Maxwell House Coffee, bear, 1971, EX, D.................**25.00**

Maxwell House Coffee, cookbook, 1927, 22 pages, D **7.00**

Maxwell House Coffee, cookbook, 1965, D **5.00**

Maxwell House Coffee, mug, EX, D.............................**5.00**

May Co Department Store, tip tray, pictures young girl with flower in her hair, Ohio's Largest Department Store, ca 1910, 4" diameter, NM, A.....................**95.00**

May Queen Tobacco, pocket tin, flat, rare, EX, A **975.00**

Mayer's Boots & Shoes, sign, product name & circular logo, For Sale By QB Scott, ca 1910, horizontal, appears EX, A **30.00**

Mayo's Plug, banner, cloth, blue product name atop a crowing rooster standing on product, yellow background, framed, 29x17", EX, A..............................**180.00**

Mayo's Plug, sign, porcelain, rooster on plug of tobacco, Smoking Cock O' The Walk, Light & Dark, discoloration/chips, 13x7", VG, A....................................**80.00**

Mayo's Tobacco, creamer pail with handle, logoed paper label, label has fading & pieces missing at edges, 10", VG, A **125.00**

Mayo's Tobacco, lunch pail, tin, collapsible, Cut Plug, original bail with wood handle, 4x8x5", EX, A **250.00**

Mayo's Tobacco, roly poly, Dutchman, slight overall fading/denting/chipping, 7x6" diameter, G, A **425.00**

Mayo's Tobacco, roly poly, Mammy, slight overall darkening/denting/chipping, 7x6" diameter, G+, A **475.00**

Mayo's Tobacco, roly poly, Man From Scotland Yard, overall soiling/minor chipping/spotting/slight dents, 7x6" diameter, G+, A..........................**1,050.00**

Mayo's Tobacco, roly poly, Satisfied Customer, overall darkening/denting/wear to image/scratching/chipping, 7x6" diameter, G+, A...**425.00**

Mayo's Tobacco, roly poly, Singing Waiter, overall soiling/minor denting/chips, 7x6" diameter, G+, A ...**425.00**

Mayo's Tobacco, roly poly, Store Keeper, overall darkening/denting/chipping, 7x6" diameter, G+, A **400.00**

Mayo's Tobacco, sign, cardboard, colorful image of men smoking pipes in touring car, Off For The Day With..., ca 1915, 12x19", NM, A..**275.00**

Mayo's Tobacco, sign, paper roll-down, pretty girl in evening gown, framed, 28x13", NM, A.................**125.00**

Maytag, tin, Maytag crest above Maytag Co, Newton Iowa USA, handle & long pour spout, EX, A **30.00**

McAlpin Virgin Leaf Fine Cut Chewing Tobacco, store card, 3-quarter view of woman in landscape holding tobacco pail, minor wear, 10x6", EX, A **45.00**

McAvoy's Malt Marrow, tip tray, boy with pipe & bottle of malt, dog at his feet, 'Not' Made in Germany, copyright 1899, 12" diameter, VG+, A **500.00**

McAvoy's Malt Marrow, tray, boy with pipe & bottle of malt, dog at his feet, Beats Em All, copyright 1899, chips/fading, 12" diameter, G, A **150.00**

McCallum Silk Hosiery, sign, Art Deco lady by Mary MacKinnon, 7x9" without frame, A.......................**175.00**

McCormic Deering Farmall, instruction book for tractor, D **25.00**

McCormick Harvesting Machine Co, sign, paper, 'Battle Of Atlanta, July 22nd, 1864,' machinery vignettes in top corners, decorative frame, 30x40", EX, A.............**500.00**

McCormick Harvesting Machine Co, sign, paper, 'Battle Of Gettysburg, July 3rd, 1863,' surrounding a harvesting machine, framed, 24x35", G, A **275.00**

McCormick-Deering Cream Separator Oil, tin, yellow with white-banded red square, superimposed black open-book shape with letters, 1915-25, half-gal, 7", EX, A **20.00**

McCormick's Jersey Cream Sodas, toy drum, cardboard with tin top & bottom, depicts product advertising on side, overall wear, 6x9" diameter, G-, A **90.00**

McCray Refrigerators, thermometer, Mobile, AL, D .**25.00**

McCullough's Leap Rye Whiskey, tray, pictures frontiersman with Indians in background, Krauss & Co, ca 1890-1900, rare, 12" diameter, EX, A **250.00**

McDonald Sap Spout, tray, shows winter scene with insert of sugaring implements, Granby Quebec Canada, some wear, oval, 16x19", G+, A **300.00**

McDonald's, book, 1965, 'Let's Eat Out,' family parked at early McDonald's, rare, 30 pages, D **75.00**

McDonald's, doll, cloth, Hamburglar with cape, Chase Bag Co, 17", F, D **8.00**

McDonald's, doll, cloth, Ronald McDonald, Chase Bag Co, 13", VG, D...**12.00**

McDonald's, doll, cloth, Ronald McDonald, 4", G, D....**6.00**

McDonald's, doll, 1981, Professor Gadget, EX, D **15.00**

McDonald's, glass, Muppet Caper, 1981, EX, D **7.00**

McKesson & Robbins, sign, full-color image picturing 4 medicinal products with logo in center, ca 1920, matted, horizontal, appears EX, A..............................**160.00**

McKesson's Aspirin, thermometer, product name at top, bottle & box below, long vertical form, NM, D ...**250.00**

McKesson's Baby Powder, tin, 2 nude children warming in front of fire in inset with decorative border, minor chipping, 6x3x2", VG+, A **250.00**

McLaughlin's Coffee, trade card, depicts girl playing teacher, D **5.00**

McNess Breakfast Cocoa, see FW McNess Breakfast Cocoa

Mecca Cigarettes, sign, cardboard, woman viewed from behind looking over her shoulder, 1912, original frame, 40x22", VG, A **250.00**

Mecca Cigarettes, sign, paper, woman viewed from behind looking over her shoulder, gold lettering, 1912, original frame, 20x11", VG, A **350.00**

Medaglia D'Oro Coffee, tray, lady with cup superimposed over scenic background, New York World's Fair 1939, appears EX, A **60.00**

Meek Co Manufacturing & Printing, tip tray, stock image of girl in profile, lettering on bottom rim, white specks/slight wear, unusual, 4" diameter, EX, A..**225.00**

Meg's Macaroni Co, pamphlet, 1960s, 'Delicious Ways To Make Pennsylvania Dutch Bott Boi,' Pot Pie, 40 pages, EX, D **4.00**

Melachrino Cigarettes, sign, tin quadruple fold, product name above Arabian scene flanked by boxes of product, 20x13", EX, A...**325.00**

Mellwood Whiskey, tip tray, bottle flanked by Bottled In Bond, appears worn, round, A................................**30.00**

Melotte Cream Separators, calendar, 1903, framed, 18x23", D **65.00**

Melrose Gasoline, pump sign, porcelain, D **295.00**

Mennen, sign, die-cut tin, flanged, scrollwork bracket supporting flat pan behind waist-length depiction of child, rare, EX, A **7,750.00**

Mennen's Borated Talcum Powder, sign, 2-sided die-cut tin wall-mounted holder for 12" round tray, rare, 15x20", EX, A...**8,500.00**

Mennen's Sen-Yang Talcum, trolley sign, cardboard litho, pictures a can of talc & oval portrait of a man in lower left, framed, 11x21", G+, A **90.00**

Mennen's Talcum, tin, pictures baby, shaker top, 1950s, EX, D...**25.00**

Mennen's Toilet Powder, poster, little girl upper left, man with mustache in bottom right, product pictured in center, framed, 9x13", EX, A **255.00**

Mentholatum, sign, die-cut tin, pictures girl with injured boy, 19x15", EX, D...**185.00**

Merchant's Gargling Oil, broadside, paper, framed, 27x12", EX+, A...**1,500.00**

Merchant's Savings Bank, tape measure, Holyoke Mass, D...**15.00**

Merchants Queen Cigars, box label, inner lid, pictures a woman with fields in the background, 6x9", M, D ..**5.00**

Meredith's Diamond Club Pure Rye, china jug, 6", G, D **15.00**

Meriden Brewing Co, sign, wood litho, 19th-century man & woman sitting at a table drinking Nutmeg Beer, Sentenne & Green, 14x20", G-, A.................................**25.00**

Merit Separator Co, tip tray, embossed, pictures cream separator & lettering, fluted edges, minor wear/overall soiling, EX, A...**175.00**

Merkle's Blu-J Brooms, display rack, metal frame, tin litho end panels, holds 12 brooms, 35", EX, A **150.00**

Merrick's Spool Cotton, clock, schoolhouse octagonal, Roman numerals, glass replaced with plastic/retouched dial/reworked bezel, 25x17x5", A **450.00**

Merrick's Spool Cotton, spool cabinet, cylindrical oak case with curved glass, lettering on glass, 22x18" diameter, EX, A..**650.00**

Merry War Lye, match holder, tin litho, colorful wash tub figural with washer woman, 6x4", VG, A **210.00**

Metro, gas globe, milk glass, red with cream band with red & green letters, round, 1930-40, 17", M, A...........**350.00**

Metropolitan Life Insurance, calendar, 1899, pictures 8 children, framed, 12x20", M, D...................**85.00**

Metropolitan Life Insurance, cookbook, 1934, 'The Family Food Supply,' depicts assorted vegetables, 23 pages, VG, D **5.00**

Metz Beer, bank, ceramic, embossed letters, barrel shape, EX, D **22.00**

Mexican Tiger Cigars, tin, pictures tiger mauling a man, Bruno Stogie Co, Cleveland Ohio, rare (may be one of a kind), 7x6" diameter, G, A.....................**750.00**

Meyer's Ice Cream, tray, stock image, EX, A **775.00**

Meyer's Velvet Ice Cream, tray, children surround mother holding tray of ice cream, decorative rim with lettering, vertical rectangle, EX, D **550.00**

Michelin, display, plastic figural, Michelin man holding up steel-belted tire, 60", appears EX, A **800.00**

Michelin, figure, cast iron Mr Bibendum trademark, hose opening in mouth, original worn painted finish, 14", A.....................**1,050.00**

Michelin, patch box, tin sign with Michelin man patching second man's hand over compartments, wall hanging, 1920-30, 9x16", VG, A **250.00**

Michelin, sign, porcelain, square with V bottom, Michelin in yellow over navy, lg Michelin man & tire, France, 1950, 18x15", EX, A.....................**220.00**

Michelob Beer, sign, light-up, 12x14", NM, D.............**25.00**

Michigan Central & Great Western Railroad, trade card, pictures Niagara Falls, D **10.00**

Mil-Kay Vitamin Drink, sign, depicts waiter serving product on tray, decorative border with banner atop, horizontal rectangle, VG, A.....................**95.00**

Milburn Wagon Co, sign, embossed tin, classic Western scene, Toledo Ohio, discoloration/rust spots/ scratches, rare, framed, 20x28", G-, A **1,700.00**

Milburn Wagon Co, sign, paper litho, colorful image of older couple in wagon watching lady on bicycle, Toledo Ohio, framed, 21x27", EX, A **2,600.00**

Milky Way, sign, die-cut cardboard, Off For The Milky Way, planets, row of milk glasses, boy astronaut, 1950, 33x20", M, A **80.00**

Mill-Town Cigars, tin, image of Pittsburgh's factories, Stogies, overall wear/chipping/staining/dents, 4x6" square, G-, A.....................**75.00**

Milla Egyptian Cigarettes, pack (full), depicts exotic woman, EX, D **15.00**

Miller & Rittenhouse Licorice Lozenges, tin, glass front flanked by Licorice Lozenges, Mellor & Rittenhouse arched above, slip lid, rectangular, worn, A...........**65.00**

Miller Beer, sign, neon letters, Miller High Life, original packing crate, 16x22" including crate, G, A...........**80.00**

Miller Bicycle Lamps, sign, celluloid, cardboard, Miller in blazing elongated diamond with lamp above & couple on bikes, framed, 19x15", EX, A.....................**70.00**

Miller Furniture, sign, die-cut tin, man holding a sign, Miller Has It, Furniture, 1900s, very rare, A **2,100.00**

Miller High Life, sign, pink, white, & green neon logo, no transformer, A **80.00**

Miller High Life, tray, deep-dish, 1940s, 13" diameter, NM, A **140.00**

Miller High Life, tray, 25" diameter, NM, A **1,350.00**

Miller High Life, tumbler, glass, Miller label, 6", D.....**16.00**

Miller Lite, mirror sign, 12x12", NM, D **18.00**

Miller's Pretzels, tin, little baker standing each side of lg pretzel, Perfect Health Food, A **20.00**

Milo Egyptian Cigars, sign, embossed statue of Venus, 31x23", A.....................**65.00**

Milward's Helix Needles, cabinet, walnut, 2 drawers have glass inserts with reverse-painted lettering, 13" long, NM, A.....................**300.00**

Milwaukee Binders & Mowers, match holder, tin, brown with gold lettering, Always Reliable, C Shonk litho, 5x3", VG+, A.....................**100.00**

Milwaukee Harvesting Machines, match holder, tin litho, cowboy holding figural basket, Always Reliable, Light Draft, 5x4", EX, A **375.00**

Minard's Liniment, display, die-cut cardboard, costumed girl holding package of product, horizontal creasing, edge damage, 21x9", VG+, A.....................**160.00**

Minard's Liniment, sign, die-cut cardboard trifold stand-up, depicts devilish figures above copy, Relieves Backache..., 28x38", VG, A **60.00**

Miners & Puddlers Smoking Tobacco, pail, tin, pictures workmen in trademark inset, B Leidersdorf Co, slip lid & bail, chipping/paper residue, 7x6", VG, A........**100.00**

Minneapolis Underwear For Children, sign, die-cut cardboard, Diaper Supporting Bands, A Mother's Idea flanked by happy & sad toddlers, crease, EX, A **90.00**

Minute Maid, clown mask, original envelope, D ...**15.00**
Minute Maid, monkey mask, original envelope, D **15.00**
Miracle Whip Salad Dressing, radio, jar figural, D....**40.00**
Miracle-Aid Soft Drink, display, colorful box including 24 packs of Miracle-Aid in 3 flavors, several bends/tears, G, D **20.00**
Mirelle Talcum, tin, pictures lady, Deco styling, shaker top, EX, D **29.00**
Mirro Aluminum, recipe booklet, 'Food Surprises From The Mirro Test Kitchen,' 16 pages, D.........**8.00**
Miss Revlon, doll, bride, Ideal, rewigged, 18", EX, D .**35.00**

Mission Orange, sign, porcelain bottle cap, flanged, 18x19", EX, A **50.00**
Mission Orange, sign, tin litho, product name in lg white letters on dark blue background, rust spots on edges, 15x28", A.........**10.00**
Mission Orange, syrup dispenser, embossed barrel-shaped pink glass container on black glass base, metal lid with knob, EX, A **150.00**
Mission Orange, thermometer, tin, soda bottle on blue ground, Real Fruit Juice & bottle cap above, Naturally Good below, 5x17", G, A.........**35.00**
Mission Orange Drink, sign, tin with wood frame, orange tree, bottle & Ice Cold on left, 5¢ in bottom right corner, 1930-40, 12x29", EX, A **40.00**
Missouri Pacific Railway, poster, has photo of US Grant's cabin on advertising mat, color distortion to sepia photo, 20x26" without frame, G, A **50.00**

MJ Theisen, pocket mirror, red & white on black, 3" diameter, D **14.00**
Mobil, sign, die-cut porcelain winged horse, red, white, & black, touched up/2 sm chips, ca 1920-30, rare size, 36", A **600.00**

Mobil, sign, die-cut porcelain winged horse, red, white, & blue, 1920s, touched up, rare size, 24", A..1,450.00
Mobil, sign, die-cut porcelain winged horse, red & white, 1930-40, 28x37", EX, A.........**750.00**
Mobil, sign, die-cut porcelain winged horse, red & white, 1930s, areas touched up, 48", A.........**475.00**
Mobil, sign, die-cut porcelain 3-D horse, red & white, 1950s, 3 repaired areas, 17x92", A **700.00**
Mobil Regular, sign, Mobil in blue & red horse within shaped reserve above Regular, 1962-66, some touch-up/minor scratches, 12x14", A.........**25.00**
Mobilgas, gas globe, milk glass with winged horse in red with blue outlines, dark blue Mobilgas, 1936-47, 16x15" diameter, EX, A **310.00**
Mobilgas, pump sign, die-cut porcelain, red horse & blue letters on white shield, red wing mounts, 1948-62. 10x24", NM, A.........**300.00**
Mobilgas, thermometer sign, porcelain, red horse at top, Friendly Service in square at bottom, 1920-30, flaking/fading, 35x4", A.........**300.00**
Mobiloil, bank, glass baseball form, winged horse emblem, A.........**30.00**
Mobiloil, curb sign, red winged horse in white circle over lettered navy rectangle, navy stand, 1940s, 89x36", EX, A.........**250.00**

Mobiloil, gas globe, milk glass with relief maroon & black Gargoyle, 1930-38, some repaint, 12x16", A 1,500.00
Mobiloil, oil bottle, has flat sides & spill-proof top, Arctic grade, 1-qt, D **75.00**
Mobiloil, oil bottle rack, holds 8 diamond-shaped bottles, D..**85.00**
Mobiloil, pump sign, die-cut porcelain, white shield with winged horse logo & black letters, Socony-Vacuum, 1946-50, 8x8", NM, A...**450.00**
Mobiloil, sign, tin, red with Gargoyle logo & letters arranged vertically, self frame, 1920s, 56x14", NM, A **600.00**
Mobiloil, sign, porcelain, red, black on white, Ask Here For & Gargoyle logo over striped band, 1920-30, flaked edges, 33x29", A...**325.00**

Mobiloil, sign, porcelain, 1920s, 24x20", NM, A ..255.00
Mobiloil, tin, cream with red letters & red & black Gargoyle, red bottom band with logo, ca 1939-42, 5-qt, 10x7" diameter, NM, A **90.00**
Mobiloil, tin, Gargoyle logo over Mobiloil A (Heavy Medium) & lines of text, red & black on cream, 1915-25, 5-gal, 15x9", VG, A..**65.00**
Mobiloil Arctic, sign, tin, red with black-lined white letters, SAE Body No 20, panel from a wire oil carrier, 1915, scarce, 7x18", VG, A **60.00**
Mobiloil BB, tin, Gargoyle & logo in red & black on cream, Socony-Vacuum Product, ca 1933-38, no top, 1-qt, 6", EX+, A...**80.00**
Mobiloil Quality Motor Oil, display rack with 6 qt cans, metal frame with white-painted tin, coiled wire handle at top, 1930s, 29x26", EX+, A **700.00**

Mobiloil Socony-Vacuum, curb sign, porcelain, blue & red letters on white with logo, red stand, 1930s, scratches, 63x30", EX, A **275.00**
MobiLubrication, sign, porcelain, white & orange with red horse logo & blue letters, shaped top corners, 1950s, appears NM, 11x26", A...**250.00**
Model Smoking Tobacco, pocket tin, red & silver, G, D **20.00**
Model Smoking Tobacco, sign, tin, caricature of mustached man with smoking pipe, Yes, I Said 10¢, Model Smoking Tobacco, 11x34", VG, A **50.00**
Model Smoking Tobacco, sign, tin, depicts caricature of Indian smoking a pipe & displaying product, Did You Say 10¢, 15x6", NM, A..**65.00**
Model Smoking Tobacco, sign, tin, smiling bald man with pipe, Did You Pay 10¢, 12x35", EX, D **95.00**
Modox, soda glass, embossed letters & Indian head, Drink Modox, 5x5x3", NM, A..**55.00**
Modox, tip tray, pictures Indian's face with die-cut feathers, Made From Indian Herb, scratches, 4x5", G, A......**325.00**

Moerlein Beer, tip tray, various gold medals on rim, 12" diameter, EX+, A..**165.00**
Mogul Egyptian Cigarettes, sign, pictures an Arab & product in lower left, framed, 17x13", EX, A........**100.00**
Mogul Timing Gears, sign, die-cut cardboard, genie on pillow holding logo, Green Gear, 16x11", M, A **20.00**
Mohawk Carpets, doll, cloth, Tommy, Chase Bag Co, early 70s, 15", VG, D **10.00**

Mohawk Chief, tin, slip lid, 5x6x4", EX, A 1,700.00

Mohawk Chieftan Motor Oil, tin, white lettered band at top, rest is royal blue with Indian in red circle, ca 1935-45, 1-qt, 6", NM, A..............................**100.00**

Mohican Coffee, tin, slip lid, minor chips/scratches/ overall wear, 1-lb, 6x4", VG, A.....................................**200.00**

Mohican Pure Cream Cheese, tin, Indian logo superimposed over cattle scene, original bail, lid missing, 30-lb, A..**80.00**

Mohican Pure Cream Cheese, tin, Indian logo superimposed over cattle scene, original press lid & bail, 30-lb, VG, A..**130.00**

Moline Wagon Co, sign, paper, double-sided, angel with scythe sitting in a tree, Moline wagons & buggies on reverse, ca 1890, 10x7", A.......................................**70.00**

Molsen's Ale, table, blue & white porcelain top with painted wood base, 26" diameter, G, A................**45.00**

Mona Motor E-Medium Oil, tin, light blue with touring car, motorcycle, tractor & other vehicles in operation, 1915-25, 1-gal, 11", EX+, A.......................................**750.00**

Mona Motor Oil, tin, light blue, ca 1915, half-gal, 6x8x4", NM, A...250.00

Mona Motor Separation Oil, tin, light blue with touring car, motorcycle, tractor & other vehicles in operation, ca 1920, half-gal, 6x8x4", EX+, A.........................**135.00**

Monadnock Coffee, tin, pictures New Hampshire mountain scene, Holbrook Grocery Co, NH, slip lid, scratches/chips, 1-lb, 6x4", VG, A.........................**120.00**

Monamobile Oil, pour can, touring car & bicycle passing a house on painted label (85% remains), Monarch Mfg Co, 1946-60, rare, 8", EX, A.................................**180.00**

Monarch Cocoa, tin, sample, EX, D..........................**65.00**

Monarch Peanut Butter, drum, tin, double-sided, 'Teenie Weenie' (monkey) making sandwiches on reverse, 55-lb, 13" diameter, VG, A.................300.00

Monarch Peanut Butter, pail, shows 'Teenie Weenie' (monkey) logo & lettering, lid & bail, overall wear, smaller version, 3x3" diameter, G, A...................**150.00**

Monarch Peanut Butter, pail, shows 'Teenie Weenie' (monkey) logos & lettering, lid & bail, 4x4" diameter, G+, A **150.00**

Monarch Popcorn, pail, rare version of 'Teenie Weenie' (monkey) image on blue background with shooting popcorn, lid & bail, 4x4", VG, A.........................**250.00**

Monarch Toffies, store bin, 'Teenie Weenie,' overall wear, 15x12", VG, A 205.00

Monkey Brand Cigars, box label, inner lid, depicts 2 monkeys in jungle setting, 6x9", EX, D.........................**32.00**

Monkey Brand Soap, sign, tin, monkey with soap, The Missing Link Of All Cleaning, black & cream, Standard Adv Co, rare, 28x20", VG, A.................................**400.00**

Monroe Beer, tip tray, depicts North & South American continents encircled with stars, Rochester NY, 4" diameter, NM, A...**55.00**

Monroe Brewing Co, tip tray, king holding forth a frothy tankard, lettered rim, 4" diameter, NM, A.............**100.00**

Monroe Brewing Co, tray, king holding forth a frothy tankard, lettered rim, 12" diameter, EX, A.............**150.00**

Montauk Beach, poster, paper on canvas, vacationers at various activities, 1925, 26x22", A **1,100.00**

Monte Cristo Cigars, tin, oval portrait inset of Count Edmund Dante (1 in the Liberty historical series), slip lid, 6x6" diameter, EX, A **305.00**

Monte Cristo Tobacco, tin, logo on the diagonal, ca 1890, heavy wear, elongated, A **20.00**

Montgomery Ward, calendar, 1900, paper litho, colorful image of Montgomery Ward building in Chicago, framed, rare, 23x16", EX+, A...............................**325.00**

Montgomery Ward Tea, box, cardboard with tin lid, 5-lb, 1913, EX, D...**40.00**

Monticello Distilling Co, sign, embossed tin, pictures The Home of Thomas Jefferson, minor fading/overall chips, self-framed, 28x39", G, A.......................................**375.00**

Montreal Malt Rye, shot glass, product name etched in lg letters, bright gold rim, EX, D.................................**17.00**

Monumental Beer, tip tray, deep-dish, labeled bottle in center, Perfect Brew, The World's Best Bottle Beer, 4" diameter, EX, A **200.00**

Moonlight Mellos Candy, tin, depicts angel on stringed decoration, Patterson Candy Co, Toronto Canada, some wear, 5x11" diameter, EX, A **35.00**

Moore & Quinn Ale & Porter, tray, deep-dish, top green with red company name & Est 1881, bottom red with green Ale & Porter, 12" diameter, EX, A **13.00**

Moore & Quinn's Diamond Ale, tray, deep-dish, 13" diameter, NM, A **18.00**

Moore's C-75 Motor Oil, tin, yellow top with winged logo over oval with C-75, lettered black bottom band, ca 1935-45, 1-qt, VG, A...**15.00**

Moore's Cough Drops, tin, pictures a bird on the bottom, slip lid, rare, rectangular, A **45.00**

Morning Glory Coffee, pail, black, red, & green with store & street scene, slip lid & bail, some chips, 1-lb, 6x4", G, A...**210.00**

Morning Glow Coffee, tin, 3-masted ship on background of sun's rays in center, RL Gerhart & Co, NM, A..**110.00**

Morris Supreme Peanut Butter, pail, press lid & bail, minor fading/overall wear, 4x4", VG, A.........500.00

Morrison's English Remedies, cabinet, chestnut with glass door & 2 shelves, lettering on decorative top, 28x17x9", M, A **800.00**

Morton Salt, pencil clip, celluloid, EX, D......................**5.00**

Morton Salt, thimble, porcelain, blue Morton logo, gold band top & bottom, Franklin USA, EX, D...............**15.00**

Morton's Iodized Salt, display, die-cut cardboard, Morton girl & lg box, some damage, 22", A **60.00**

Morton's Salt, pocket mirror, 4" diameter, D.........25.00

Mosco Corns & Callouses Cream, sign, die-cut cardboard, seated girl on right, 30¢ & 50¢ prices by jar on left, 1940s, M, A **40.00**

Mosemann's Peanut Butter, pail, tin, yellow with product name on front, animals on sides, press lid & bail, NM, A **150.00**

Moses Cough Drops, tin, depicts portrait of Dr Moses on front & back, slip lid, rectangular with rounded corners, 2x3", NM, A...**200.00**

Moses Orange Cough Drops, tin, depicts Dr Moses flanked by Cough Drops, lettering above & below, sm slip lid, 5-lb, vertical, 8", EX, A............................**160.00**

Mother Penn Motor Oil, tin, white with picture of Mother Penn in circle above product name, 1879 each side, 1950s, 1-qt, 6", NM, A **55.00**

Mother's Oats, sign, paper, child with pipe wearing dad's clothing, bright colors, American Lithographic Co, 1902, 24x17", VG, A **145.00**

Mother's Oats, sign, paper, nude boy wrapped in animal skin, tramp art frame, 23x16", VG, A **85.00**

Mother's Oats, sign, paper, small child in a blue suit, from the Great Western Cereal Co, overall creases, framed, 24x17", VG, A **45.00**

Mother's Worm Syrup, match holder, die-cut tin litho, rare, 7x2", VG+, A **1,100.00**

Motley's Best Tobacco, tin, lettering on lid with man's portrait on inset in lower left corner, square corners, minor chipping, 2x5x3", VG, A **100.00**

Motor Stogies, tin, for cigars, auto scene in yellow & blue, 6", EX, A **425.00**

Motorist Cigars, box label, outer, depicts Mercury driving through flames, 5x5", M, D **6.00**

Moxie, display, ca 1898, embossed cardboard stand-up, shows boy & girl with parasol, minor soil/minimal edge wear, 9x7", NM, A **600.00**

Moxie, display, ca 1908-11, embossed die-cut tin, head of Moxie boy in round hat, 7x5", EX, A....................**290.00**

Moxie, display, die-cut cardboard, girl offering product from behind glass bowl holding bottles on wooden case, 43x21", G, A **600.00**

Moxie, display, die-cut cardboard with 3-D cut-away bottle, 30x12x5", VG, A **110.00**

Moxie, display, die-cut cardboard, water stains/minor edge chips, 42x18", G, A 170.00

Moxie, display, die-cut wood, bottle holder reglued/minor paint chips, G, A.....................225.00

Moxie, display, die-cut wood, some repaint/paint loss to head, rare, 35x10x10", G, A 200.00

Moxie, fan, cardboard, pictures Frances Pritchard holding glass of Moxie, 10x8", EX, A **55.00**

Moxie, fan, cardboard, girl & Moxie boy, sm, D.........**37.00**

Moxie, fan, die-cut portrait of a girl in a bonnet, Drink Moxie, appears EX, A **20.00**

Moxie, gravy boat & saucer, china, Drink Moxie, girl transfer, bird pattern border, hairlines, VG, A.............**125.00**

Moxie, jacket, soda fountain coat with yellow & green Moxie images, rare, approx: medium size, EX, A ..**90.00**

Moxie, match holder, die-cut tin figural of labeled bottle, Learn To Drink Moxie, Very Healthful, edge damage, 7x3", VG+, A...**450.00**

Moxie, mug, china, girl transfer in center, flare-footed, 3" diameter, VG, A..**105.00**

Moxie, parasol, yellow & green Moxie images, original condition with minor soiling/age staining, VG, A **175.00**

Moxie, photo, 4 early Moxie delivery trucks, appears to be a reprint, framed, 11x14", NM, A...........................**30.00**

Moxie, poster, cardboard, father & son picnicking after the hunt, Enjoy A Lift The Healthful Way, Drink Moxie, 31x40", G, A **105.00**

Moxie, sign, die-cut cardboard, Moxie boy pointing his finger behind sign, Drink Moxie in white on red ground, 17x17", EX, A..**180.00**

Moxie, sign, embossed tin, people running to bottle of Moxie in the Hall of Fame, dents/scratches, self-framed, 54x19", VG, A **275.00**

Moxie, sign, 1940, paper litho in oak frame, I've Got Moxie in lg letters, black & red on orange & yellow stripes, 4x15", EX, A..**45.00**

Moxie, sign, 1960s, flanged, Drink Moxie in oval, 36" long, D..**250.00**

Moxie, sign, 2-sided die-cut tin, Moxie man pointing over Drink Moxie lettering, 6x6", NM, A.....................**550.00**

Moxie, syrup bottle, glass with orange label, tin top, EX, A..**200.00**

Moxie, thermometer, tin, Drink Moxie above pointing Moxie man, Always A Pleasure..., vertical, rounded corners, appears EX, A...**100.00**

Moxie, thermometer, We've Got Moxie, A Great New Taste, 16x6", G, A..**50.00**

Moxie, tip tray, ca 1907, blond Moxie girl's head (face forward) with glass, I Like It, 6" diameter, NM, A ...**275.00**

Moxie, tip tray, gold & maroon on cream, rare double-tailed Moxie logo, National Health Beverage on rim, 4" diameter, M, A **450.00**

Moxie, tip tray, label on green simulated wood, Moxie Makes You Eat, Sleep..., some fading/scratching, 6" diameter, G, A..**140.00**

Moxie, tip tray, 1900-10, Moxie girl tipping glass, green background, I Just Love Moxie..., HD Beach litho, 6" diameter, NM, A **225.00**

Moxie, tip tray, 1900-10, Moxie girl tipping glass on floral background, I Just Love..., 6" diameter, EX, A **200.00**

Moxie, sign, embossed tin, 28x20", EX, A 13,000.00

Moxie, sign, tin, Drink Moxie, Very Healthful, To Eat Better, Sleep..., NY Metal Ceiling Co, self-framed, 22" diameter, EX, A **650.00**

Moxie, sign, tin, girl on horse in a speeding car, Drink Moxie, Distinctively Different, image corrosion, 13x19", G, A **145.00**

Moxie, sign, tin, Moxie girl leaning on back of chair enjoying product, Kaufmann & Strauss litho, wood frame, 31" high, G, A...**4,200.00**

Moxie, sign, tin flange, double-sided, Drink Moxie, overall dirt/scratches, oval, 9x18", G+, A **100.00**

Moxie, sign, 1900, cardboard easel-back, depicts 1700s girl, 6x5", NM, D **400.00**

Moxie, tip tray, 1905, close-up of girl's face & hand holding glass, I Just Love..., simulated wood rim, 6" diameter, EX, A..200.00

Moxie, tip tray, 1905, simulated wood rim, 6" diameter, G, A..**125.00**

Moxie, tray, 1910, metal with handles, image of a woman drinking Moxie applied under glass, I Like It, 10" diameter, EX, A **300.00**

Moxie, tray, 1910, metal with handles, Moxie boy image applied under glass, flaking under glass, 10" diameter, G+, A **250.00**

Moxie, tumbler, glass, Licensed Only For Serving, 4", NM, D..**40.00**

Mozart Cigars, tin, portrait label on wood-grained background, slip lid, minor chipping/denting, 6x6" diameter, EX, A **245.00**

Mr Barny Clockmaker, sign, porcelain on tin in cast iron frame embossed Watches, Clocks etc, 2-sided pocket watch, 1900-20, 17x20", EX+, A...........................**450.00**

Mr Big Toilet Tissue, kitten, plush, EX, D.................**18.00**

Mrs Butterworth's Syrup, doll, cloth, Mrs Butterworth, 11", G, D **5.00**

Mrs Dinsmore's Cough Drops, tin, encircled portrait depicts Mrs Dinsmore with product name above & below, screw top, 8x5" square, G, A **140.00**

Mt Lassen Siphon Water, siphon bottle, glass with tube, nozzle, & valve, red label, Susanville Ca, D.........**128.00**

Mt Pleasant Peanut Butter, pail, lettering over graphic of mountain, slip lid & bail, 1-lb, NM, A **70.00**

Mt Vernon Brewing Co, poster, paper, mounted patriots toasting Washington at Mt Vernon, Lager Beer, matted & framed, 35x27", VG, A **200.00**

Muehlebagh's Pilsener Beer, match holder, bottle-shaped die-cut tin, soiling/paint loss/irregular hole at top, 7x2x1", G, A **255.00**

Muehlebagh's Pilsener Beer, tip tray, labeled bottle in center, Pilsener Beer, Purest & Best, 5" diameter, NM, A...**35.00**

Mueller Brewing Co, tip tray, girl flanked by Art Nouveau border, Two Rivers Wis, background scratches/minor rim chips, 4" diameter, EX, A..................................**95.00**

Mumm's Extra Rye, sign, cardboard, fox hunting scene with dogs, horses, & hunters, original mat & frame, 20x24", EX, A **40.00**

Munsing Union Suits, display, die-cut tin & wood, figure taking off coat mounted on a box, minor surface wear/nail hole in neck, 14", VG, A **375.00**

Munsing Wear, book dispenser, tin, pictures mother fixing daughter's hair, Fashion Books Take One, ca 1905-10, 15x12x15", EX, A....................................**1,400.00**

Munsing Wear, sign, paper litho, pictures 1920s lady in bra & bloomers holding mirror, Underlying Loveliness, verticle, appears EX, A **120.00**

Munsingwear, penguin, vinyl, EX, D...........................**20.00**

Munsingwear, sign, litho on canvas, 2 red-haired girls showing grandma their Munsingwear, brass tag on wood frame, 28x36", EX, A **700.00**

Munyon's Homoeopathic Home Remedies, cabinet, wood, tin front with product name above price list of cures, several drawers in back, 20x14", EX, A **450.00**

Munyon's Homoepathic Home Remedies, display, tin, slant front picturing Mr Munyon with lettering on all sides, multiple-drawered backing, 12x14x14", G+, A **450.00**

Murad Cigarettes, sign, paper litho roll-down, gypsy woman & camel carrying cigarettes, ca late 1890s, minor creasing, 21x14", VG, A **280.00**

Murad Cigarettes, sign, Turkish woman holding tray flanked by lettering & surrounded by cigarette packages, horizontal rectangle, EX, A **600.00**

Murine, poster, cardboard, 28x18", VG+, A............**2,300.00**

Murray Soda Water Flavors, tray, deep-dish, 2 colonial gents facing each other trying different flavors, scuffs/rim chips, 12" diameter, EX, A **100.00**

Myers Pumps, sign, enamel, flanged, woman squirting man with water pump, Look For the Name...On Pumps & Hay Tools, 14x18", G-, A **90.00**

Myrtle Grove Cigarettes, sign, framed, 24x12", A .**180.00**

Myrtle Grove Cigarettes, sign, product name above & below 20 sports players cards, In Tins & Packets Only, framed, 24x12", A...**110.00**

N

Nabisco, container, brass & cardboard, open front with rounded corners, Baked By Nabisco, National Biscuit Co above, 11x11", M, A...**60.00**

Nabisco's Mr Salty Pretzels, doll, cloth, Mr Salty, 11", G, D..**10.00**

Nabob Baking Powder, tin, a cake with product name above & below, press lid, 12-oz, appears worn, A ..**10.00**

Naco Cork Gaskets, display, tin litho with cork gaskets, For Ford, 20x34", VG, A.......................................**140.00**

Nadruco Royal Rose Talcum Powder, tin, lettering & roses, shaker top, rare, NM, A **120.00**

Napoleon Cigars, sign, tin, depicts portrait of Napoleon on red ground, Powell & Goldstein, Oneida NY, self-framed, 19x16", appears EX, A..............................**475.00**

Napoleon Flour, sign, cardboard, double-sided, back-ground touch-ups, 16" diameter, VG, A............**95.00**

Narragansett Ale, tray, Narragansett on the diagonal with The Famous Old lettered above & Ale below, decorative rim, 13" diameter, EX, A **20.00**

Narragansett Brewing Co, tip tray, Narragansett on diagonal with Made Of Honor circular logo below, company name on rim, 4" diameter, EX, A............................**55.00**

Narragansett Famous Ale & Lager, tray, Narragansett on diagonal with Ale above & Lager below, Malt Extract, oval, 14x17", G, A.....................................**80.00**

Narragansett Ginger Ale, sign, die-cut wood, Narragansett on diagonal with Ginger Ale above & below, slightly arched, 10x41", EX, A **130.00**

Nash, desk ornament, white metal, commemorates the company's 50th anniversary, 1952, 6" long, EX, A.**50.00**

Nash, salesroom poster for the Nash car, depicts various models, 18 Beautiful Models..., late 1940s, 52x39", appears EX, A...**50.00**

Nash's Coffee, tin, 2 trumpeters herald Fathers of Confederation, Jubilee Coffee, original slip lid & bail, 5-lb, 9x8" diameter, VG, A **250.00**

Nathan's, sign, silkscreen, Famous Frankfurter & Soft Drink Stand in black & white on colorful wavy background, framed, 44x83", A...**900.00**

National Beauty Cigars, sign, tin, girl surrounded by banners of nations with lettering above & below, wear, 14x20" without frame, G, A **200.00**

National Biscuit Co, biscuit box, polished brass front with tin logoed insert, NM, D **95.00**

National Biscuit Co, display rack, oak, 3 shelves, lettering on top & bottom, 57x25x10", EX, A......................**700.00**

National Biscuit Co, sign, 1920, framed, 11x21", A.160.00

National Bohemian/National Beer, globe, 2-sided reverse-painted glass, metal rim, animated 1-eyed mustached face, Oh Boy What A Beer, 16" diameter, VG, A **350.00**

National Brewery Co, tray, 1890-1900, 10x14", EX, A...400.00

National Brewery Co, tray, factory image with product, St Louis Mo, lettering on decorative border, image hazing/hole in rim, 10x14", VG, A......................**250.00**

National Brewing Co, sign, paper, pictures elegant woman in plumed hat holding flowers, Syracuse NY, ca 1911, framed, 23x18", VG, A **875.00**

National Brewing Co, sign, reverse-painted glass, company name over patriotic logo, Ales, Porter, & Stock... below, paint wear, 24x34", A **105.00**

National Brewing Co, sign, tin, black & gold factory scene, original frame, 34x24", G, A **750.00**

National Brewing Co, sign, tin, 2 musical maidens in flower garden, Syracuse NY, Kaufmann & Strauss litho, self-framed, 22x17", VG, A......................**405.00**

National Brewing Co, tip tray, animated golf scene, Steelton Pa, rare, 4" diameter, NM, A **275.00**

National Brewing Co, tip tray, deep-dish, cowboy with bottle riding horse, The Best in the West, San Francisco, rim chips, 4" diameter, NM, A......................**650.00**

National Brewing Co, tip tray, portrait of a pretty girl, National Beer, San Francisco Cal on rim, 4" diameter, EX, A......................**150.00**

National Brewing Co, tray, deep-dish, National on diagonal above Brilliant Ale, Porter, & India Pale Ale on green ground, 12" diameter, G-, A......................**10.00**

National Brewing Co, tray, deep-dish, pictures 2 horse's heads, Derby Cream Ale, Kaufmann & Strauss, Syracuse NY, 12" diameter, NM, A **225.00**

National Brewing Co, tray, girl with bow & flowers in her hair facing right, company name & products on rim, oval, 17x13", EX, A **175.00**

National Brewing Co, tray, monk with missing teeth, India Pale Ale, Brilliant Ales, Syracuse NY, oval, 17x14", VG, A **100.00**

National Brewing Co, tray, pictures flamingos on black background, Brilliant & India Pale Ale, Syracuse NY, letters touched up, 12x17", G, A **95.00**

National Brewing Co, tray, rolled rim, gent in hat & apron contemplating a brew, Brilliant & India Ale on rim, oval, 14x17", VG, A......................**125.00**

National Brewing Co, tray, tin litho, logoed star on gold, Brilliant Ale, India Pale, & Porter, C Shonk litho, 12" diameter, EX, A......................**50.00**

National Cigar Stand, lantern, mica with fringed bottom, rare, EX, A.....................................4,000.00

National Cigar Stand, shade, glass dome on each side, etched glass panels, Lord Carver 10¢, 3 For 25¢, repaint/touch-ups/missing fringe, 21x23x11", VG, A **1,700.00**

National Coffee, tin, paper label with patriotic symbols, Roasted Coffee, slip lid, paper loss/stains/rust, 1-lb, 6x4" diameter, F, A......................**15.00**

National Commerce Cigars, box label, outer, pictures a train & ship, 5x5", M, D **5.00**

National Dry Hop Yeast, sign, paper, pictures girl with fan & product, 19x12", EX, A......................**20.00**

National EN-AR-CO Motor Oil, tin, product name on cream, turquoise band with boy & chalkboard, red bottom with company name, 1935-45, 1-qt, NM, A ...**35.00**

National Fire Insurance Co, ledger marker, tin, 1890, 13x3", EX+, A **135.00**

National Fire Insurance Co, sign, reverse-painted glass, National above Lady Liberty with flag, shield, & eagle, text below, framed, 29x20", NM, A **350.00**

National Lead Co, paperweight mirror, colorful image picturing Dutch boy, stains, 4" diameter, VG, A **100.00**

National Licorice Co Lozenges, tin, glass front, lettering & fancy graphics on reverse, decorative hinged lid, rectangular, A.................**30.00**

National Life Insurance Co, calendar, 1958, pictures bears, EX, D.................**10.00**

National Life Insurance Co, ledger marker, tin litho, gold lettering on black, Kellogg & Bulkeley, ca late 1800s, 12x3", G, A.................**130.00**

National Macaroni Mfg Ass'n, pamphlet, 1931, 'Thrift Recipes' by Patricia Powell, 16 pages, VG+, D........**6.00**

National Mazda Electric Lamps, display, electrified tin litho & cardboard, pictures product surrounded by fancy graphics, 13x28", VG+, A.................**425.00**

National White Rose Gasoline, thimble, aluminum whistle, red band with company name, EX, D **30.00**

National Yeast Co, cookbook, 1886, paperback, 47 pages, D.................**5.00**

Nature's Remedy, display box, etched reverse-painted glass in copper framed light box, Better Than Pills, For Liver Ills, 25¢, 20x27x6", EX, A.................**400.00**

Nature's Remedy, sign, 2-sided mirror-backed glass with reverse painting in lighted hanging wooden frame, wear, 24x17x12", G+, A **800.00**

Nature's Remedy, thermometer, porcelain, chips around hanging holder, D **95.00**

Navarre Steel Cut Golden Sun Coffee, spoon, tin, 4", G, D.................**60.00**

Navy Motor Oil, tin, Navy lettered diagonally over red anchor on navy ground, Motor Oil below, 1917, half-gal, NM, A.................**90.00**

Navy Motor Oil, tin, Navy lettered diagonally over red anchor on navy ground, Motor Oil below, 1917, 1-gal, 11", VG, A.................**60.00**

NCS Cigars, tin, pictures Capitol building, Hand Made, Long Filler, slip lid, scratches/chips/overall wear, 6x4" square, G, A.................**105.00**

Ne-Gro Cleanser, tin, back view of a man seated on a ledge, from Montreal Canada, press lid, round, appears EX, A.................**140.00**

Nebraska Girl Cigars, box label, inner lid, depicts lady in riding habit on strutting horse with product name above, 1902, 6x9", M, D **22.00**

Necco Wafers, dispenser, 5¢, tin, 18", VG, A **100.00**

Nehi, calendar, 1936, paper, portrait of woman, calendar includes historical events, matted & framed, 29x17", VG, A **180.00**

Nehi, sign, paper litho on artist board, Genuine Nehi In This Bottle Only flanked by bottle & woman's legs, 19x40", EX, A **130.00**

Nesbitt's Orange, thermometer, bottle cap logo above scholar saying 'Don't Say Orange Say Nesbitt's,' rounded corners, vertical, A **35.00**

Nestle, doll, cloth, Little Hans The Chocolate Maker, Chase Bag Co, 1970s, 13", G, D **58.00**

Nestle's Chocolate Blocks, display case, glass with metal frame, More For Your Money, 2¢ Milk or Almond, ca 1910-20, 5x11x7", NM, A.................**350.00**

Nestle's Iced Tea, cooler, green stoneware, M, D ...**250.00**

Nestle's Original Toll House Cookies, cookie jar, ceramic, lettering in oval with eagle atop, row of stars on rim, cookie on reverse, gold trim, M, D **110.00**

Nestle's Quik, bunny, 1985, new, EX, D **15.00**

New Day Cigars, box label, inner lid, depicts lg sun rising above tobacco field with product name above, 1935, 6x9", M, D **4.00**

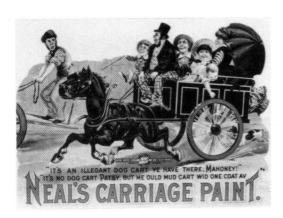

Neal's Carriage Paint, display, die-cut cardboard, some wear, 14x20", VG, A **350.00**

Neal's Carriage Paints, sign, embossed tin litho on wood lath, pictures carriage & figures flanked by product, nail holes, G+, A.................**450.00**

New Home, sign, paper, framed, 20x15", EX, A...**150.00**

New Home Sewing Machine, sign, paper with wooden rollers at each end, depicts dead game, sm machine at bottom right, Forbes litho, 26x20", NM, A **150.00**

New Home Sewing Machine Co, sign, paper, colorful image of girl with machine, Orange Mass USA, 1910, framed, minor creasing, 20x16", VG, A.................**195.00**

New Home Sewing Machine Co, sign, paper, family at sewing machine with dog at their feet, framed, minor color loss at center, 18x24", VG, A **125.00**

New Home Sewing Machine Co, sign, paper over cardboard, view of factory buildings in Orange Mass, stains, 20x24" without frame, G, A **45.00**

New Home Sewing Machine Co, tip tray, whimsical picture of Granny fixing grandson's pants while he's wearing them, ca 1900-10, 4" diameter, EX+, A............**155.00**

New King Snuff, pocket mirror, patriotic eagle logo with encircled portrait & lettering atop, EX, A **45.00**

New Lebanon Brewing Co, tip tray, colorful lettered logo in center, Lebanon Pa, 4" diameter, NM, A............**85.00**

New Life Beer, tray, deep-dish, girl in gown seated on crescent moon holding beer, touch-up to background/rim chips, 12" diameter, G, A **150.00**

New Process Gas Range, calendar sign, 1898, cook holding loaf of bread baked in New Process Range, full pad, matted & framed, 28x20", EX, A **200.00**

New Process Gas Range, match holder, silver image on red, 3x2", EX, A **125.00**

New Process Gas Ranges, match holder, tin litho, 3x2", EX, D...**100.00**

New York & Kentucky Co OFC Rye, tray, lg elk & mountain scene in center, Sold Only In Glass, 1900, light wear/scratches, 13" diameter, A **65.00**

New York Daily News, sign, paper litho, pictures running newsboy with busy street scene beyond, matted & framed, vertical rectangle, EX, A **280.00**

New York Enamel Paint Co, sign, cardboard, before & after houses promoting company's product, very rare, 21x26" without frame, G-, A **450.00**

Newbro's Herpicide, sign, 2-sided die-cut paper litho with hanging cord, 9x18", EX+, A **800.00**

Newcomer Cigars, box label, outer, 5x5", M, D **2.00**

Newsboy Plug Tobacco, sign, paper on cardboard, 32x24", VG, A **13,000.00**

Newton's Heave, Cough, Distemper, Indigestion Cure, tin, driver & sulky with lettering above, screw lid, vertical square with rounded corners, 8", NM, A........**110.00**

Newtone Handphones, tip tray, elegant woman surrounded by flowers, ca 1910, 4" diameter, NM, A.**170.00**

Newville Pure Rye Whiskey, shot glass, etched, ...CB Wagner, Carlisle Pa, entwined CBW in circle above Pure Rye, fancy scrollwork, gold rim, D................**22.00**

Niagara Shoes, sign, tin, lg oval with falls on dark green above (product) For Youthful Feet..., 1920-30, 19x9", EX+, A **150.00**

Niagara Starch, trade card, pictures boy holding swing with 2 girls on it, D **4.00**

Niagara Pepsin Gum, vendor, glass cylinder with metal lid on square glass & metal base, 1¢, clockwork mechanism, rare, NM, A...**7,000.00**

Nichol Kola, sign, tin, ca 1930s, 36x12", A **60.00**

Nine O'Clock Washing-Tea, sign, embossed tin, rare, 27x90", EX, A **13,000.00**

Nine O'Clock Washing-Tea, sign, embossed tin, smaller version of sign with woman holding package..., wear, 13x14" without frame, G-, A **275.00**

NOCO Motor Oil, tin, Viking with Norse on shield in center, cream letters on blue background, postwar (WWII), 1-qt, 6", NM, A **10.00**

None Such Condensed Mince Meat, sign, tin litho, pictures Indian chief referred to as Old Sleepy Eye, framed, 28x20", EX+, A................................**4,700.00**

Noonan's Cleansing Cream, sample tin, pictures lady with mirror, 1930s, 2" diameter, EX, D **25.00**

Normodust, tin, with partial contents, depicts the Normodust girl, Dustbane Mfg Co, round, 10", A **15.00**

Norseman Snuff, sign, tin, product superimposed over elderly man & little girl, Pals in upper right, self-framed, 18x14", A **75.00**

North American Van Lines, doll, vinyl, 11", EX, D ..**18.00**

North Pole Cut Plug Tobacco, tin, black & white, polar bears, slip lid, fading/scratches, 4x6", VG, A..........**75.00**

North Pole Cut Plug Tobacco, tin, US seal on red, white, & blue can, North Pole Cut Plug, minor fading to lid/slight denting, 3x6x4", G, A **75.00**

North Pole Cut Plug Tobacco, tin, white lettering on blue & red shield logo, The United States Tobacco Company, minor flaking, rare, 3x6", A **75.00**

North Pole Smoking Tobacco, lunch pail, tin, 6x6x4", G, A..........................**150.00**

North Star Tobacco, pocket tin, flat, extremely rare, EX, A **925.00**

North West Paper Co, playing cards, Canadian Mountie standing beside horse with mountains beyond, lettering below on yellow, complete, D **5.00**

Northampton Brewing Co, tip tray, hand grabbing 3 labeled bottles, Lager Beer, 4" diameter, NM, A ..**105.00**

Northern Brewing Co, tip tray, lettered logo in center, Wachter Bros Beer, rare, 4" diameter, EX, A........**190.00**

Norumbega Park, sign, paper, colorful vignetted display of park attractions, ca 1910, 28x22", EX, A ..1,300.00

Nourse Heavy Duty Oil, tin, white, orange, & black, Viking with Nourse Shield stands on hill, Kansas City Mo, postwar (WWII), 6", EX, A **35.00**

Nourse Motor Oil, tin, easy pour, Viking with Nourse shield on light blue above lettering, Kansas City Mo, 1915-25, 5-gal, 17x14", EX, A....................**300.00**

Nourse Motor Oil, tin, Viking with Nourse shield on cream ground, Jack Nourse Oil Co, Kansas City, Omaha, 1917, 1-gal, 11", VG+, A **650.00**

Nourse Motor Oil, tin, Viking with Nourse shield stands on hill, ship & Vikings in background, postwar (WWII), sm dent, 1-qt, EX+, A **20.00**

NuGrape, menu board, tin, NuGrape & bottle above board, rounded corners, vertical, EX, D **40.00**

NuGrape, sign, cardboard, pictures bottle in center, A Flavor You Can't Forget, Had Yours To-day?, appears EX, A **30.00**

NuGrape, sign, tin, red, yellow, & black on white, Drink NuGrape, Contains Pure Grape Juice, rounded corners, 19x27", EX, D....................**40.00**

Number Five Cigars, mirror, beveled glass with reverse-painted letters, framed, on bias: 27x27", G-, A........**75.00**

Nut House Brand Nuts of Quality, tin, 20-lb, A........**50.00**

Nut House Salted Nuts, tin, 2-line product name over drawing of house on pink background, press lid, 30-lb, A..........................**50.00**

Nye's National Hay Rake, sign, paper, bold graphic of hay rake machine, Self-Dumping, Milton Bradley Co litho, matted & framed, 17x21", VG, A **125.00**

Nysis Talcum Powder, tin, stylized Egyptian motif, Air Float Talc For Men, overall wear/slight nicking, triangular, 6x2", G, A **25.00**

⚬ O ⚬

O'Keefe Brewery Co, sign, factory scene with horse-drawn carriages & figures, Toronto Ltd, rare, framed, 41x55", appears EX, A....................**1,800.00**

O'San Cigars, box label, inner lid, colorful Egyptian scenes, 6x9", M, D **5.00**

O'Sullivan's Heels, sign, full-color image of a car & horse-drawn wagon above lettering, Leather Heels Are..., ca 1920, matted, EX, A....................**45.00**

O'Sullivan's Heels, sign, man's foot on blue background & lettering on yellow, 8000 Times A Day, Your Heels Strike..., framed, 11x20", EX, A....................**120.00**

Oak Hill Coffee, tin, Oak Hill over cup of coffee in lg oval, 1-lb, EX, A....................**40.00**

Oak Motor Oil, sign, porcelain, wood-grained Oak & Motor Oil on lg tree, Summer & Winter, 1 Grade..., 1930-40, 15x26", EX+, A **1,000.00**

Occident, display piece, celluloid, shows various components of wheat flour, M, A **200.00**

Ocean Liner Motor Oil, tin, orange with blue band outlined in cream-colored waves, pictures ship, Traymore...NY, 1925-45, 2-gal, 12x9", VG+, A **110.00**

Oceanic Cut Plug Tobacco, tin, pictures a ship, slip lid, Scotten & Dillon Co, 5x6x5", EX, D **110.00**

Oceanic Tobacco, package label, EX, D....................**10.00**

Oconto Brewing Co, tip tray, pictures pretty girl in profile, Compliments of The Occonto Brewing Co, 4" diameter, NM, A....................**90.00**

Oertel Brewing Co, tip tray, pictures girl holding a dove, in subtle colors, Cream & Lager Beer, rim/background chips, 4" diameter, EX, A **45.00**

Oh Boy Gum, sign, tin, 16x8", NM, A **120.00**
Ohio Blue Tip Matches, paperweight mirror, factory scene & box of matches, 4" diameter, VG+, A **70.00**
Ohio Boys Cigars, tin, 3 oval portraits of Hayes, McKinley, & Garfield, denting/rust spotting/darkening/scratches, 6x4" diameter, G-, A...**175.00**
Ohio Farmers Insurance Co, sign, embossed tin with copper wash, depicts farmer sitting on fence with raised letters above & below, 24x18", EX, A **225.00**
Ohio Rake Co, sign, paper litho, pictures Statue of Liberty surrounded by farm implements, Krebs Co, framed, 22x28", VG, A **275.00**
Oilzum Motor Oil, sign, tin litho, black & white letters on orange background, If Motors Could Speak..., 18x60", appears EX, D...**180.00**
Oilzum Motor Oil, tin, Oilzum lettered on hat of man in goggles on half orange & half white ground, Motor Oil below, 1950-60, 1-qt, VG, A **90.00**
Oilzum Motor Oils & Lubricants, tin, Oilzum... lettered on hat of man in goggles in lg white O, America's Finest Oil below, 1935-45, no top, 5-qt, EX, A.....**135.00**

Oilzwel Motor Oil, tin, red circle on blue with red & yellow lettering, 1950, 2-gal, 12x8", NM, A 35.00

Ojibwa Fine Cut Chewing Tobacco, pail, tin, yellow can shows Indian with tobacco leaves standing at water's edge, slip lid & bail, 6x6" diameter, G, A.............**120.00**
Ojibwa Fine Cut Chewing Tobacco, store container, cardboard, paper label with Indian holding tobacco leaves at water's edge, water stain, 11x8x7", G, A.........**175.00**
Ojibwa Fine Cut Chewing Tobacco, tin, Indian with tobacco leaves standing at water's edge in filigree inset, slip lid, some wear, 2x7" diameter, VG, A............**130.00**
OK Stock Food, sign, paper, pastoral scene with animals, Food For All Farm Stock, sm tear at bottom, 28x21" without frame, EX+, A **100.00**
Old Abe Chewing Tobacco, tin, orange with black, Abraham Lincoln on lid with eagle above & flanked by plantation scenes, 2x3" diameter, EX, A **550.00**
Old Abe Chewing Tobacco, tray, Abraham Lincoln flanked by plantation scenes, logoed eagle atop, Bright on rim, appears worn, 8" diameter, A..............................**450.00**
Old Abe Chewing Tobacco, tray, Abraham Lincoln flanked by plantation scenes, logoed eagle atop, Dark on rim, appears worn, 8" diameter, A..............................**450.00**
Old Abe Cigars, tin, paper label with image of Lincoln, some loss to label, 6x6" diameter, F, A...................**25.00**
Old Bagby, shot glass, Old Bagby etched on 1 line in lg letters, M, D **15.00**
Old Boone Distillery, sign, tin, log cabin distillery in backwoods of Kentucky, Thixton Millett Distillers, 1904, self-framed, 15x23", VG, A...................................**550.00**

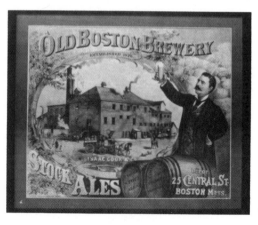

Old Boston Brewery, sign, paper, matted & framed, 18x22", A...1,050.00
Old CC Whiskey, shot glass, Old CC Whiskey etched on 3 lines in thick letters, EX, D **16.00**
Old Chum Tobacco, thermometer, porcelain, Smoke Old Chum, The Tobacco of Quality, Sherbrooke Quebec Canada, some wear, 39x8", EX, A........................**175.00**
Old City Peanut Butter, pail, tin, shows boy fishing, horse-drawn sled scene opposite, original sip lid & bail, very rare, 15-oz, 4x4", EX, A **2,300.00**
Old Colony Brewing Co, poster, photo of brewery, some restoration to sky/minor chipping, matted & framed, 29x35", G, A **75.00**
Old Colony Mixture Tobacco, see Bagley's Old Colony Tobacco, tin, pilgrim scene on silver can, embossed ash tray slip lid, flared bottom, 6x6" diameter, VG, A...**100.00**

Old Crow Cigars, box label, inner lid, depicts lg black crow perched on log by tobacco field with product name above, 6x9", M, D **45.00**

Old Crow Distillery, sign, paper, factory scene surrounded by an etched & reverse-painted glass border, framed, 27x35", VG+, A **1,400.00**

Old Dan Cigars, box label, inner lid, depicts head portrait of white horse flanked by horseshoes, Old Dan above & below, 6x9", M, D.........................**50.00**

Old Darling Bourbon & Rye, sign, reverse-painted glass, 24x34", G, A.........................**425.00**

Old Dutch Beer, figure, plaster, animated German man with bottle of Old Dutch, The World Knows No Finer Beer on base, 14", VG+, A.........................**112.00**

Old Dutch Cleanser, stickpin, enameled, D **35.00**

Old Dutch Cleanser, watch fob, enameled, D............**65.00**

Old English Tobacco, sign, paperboard, depicts 18th century men at fireplace with lettering atop, Curve Cut Pipe Tobacco, framed, 31x24", A.........................**175.00**

Old Fire Side Tea, tin, depicts couple by the hearth in circular inset, slip lid, 5x5x3", G, A **10.00**

Old Forester Whiskey, ink blotter, green & blue lettering on bright pink, Old Forester, $29.50 Delivered...Brown-Forman Distillery, 7x4", M, D **3.00**

Old Glory Cigars, tin, depicts eagle, 3 for 5 cents, humidor lid, slight fading/minor denting/chipping, G, A...**115.00**

Old Gold Cigarettes, pocket tin, short, EX, D............**20.00**

Old Grand-Dad Whiskey, ink blotter, product name at top center flanked by whiskey bottles, Bottled In Bond..., 6x3", M, D **10.00**

Old Grand-Dad Whiskey, shot glass, Old Grand-Dad Whiskey etched on 3 lines in thick letters, cut panels around side at base, EX, D **18.00**

Old Grand-Dad Whiskey, sign, tin, oxen leading wagon with whiskey barrels down road, Direct From The Hills Of Kentucky, framed, 28" long, F, A.........................**240.00**

Old Grist Mill Dog Bread, display, mechanical cardboard, approx: 26x36x4", G-, A **275.00**

Old Guckenheimer Rye Whiskey, sign, cardboard litho, farmer in field of rye pointing to oversize bottle, Best Rye in the Field, framed, 11x15", G+, A **250.00**

Old Harvest Corn Whiskey, sign, tin, elderly couple with baby & lg whiskey bottle, He's Gittin Mo Like His Dad..., worn, rectangular, A **675.00**

Old Hickory Wagons, match holder, tin, product name above green & red wagon, 5x3", G, A **175.00**

Old Hickory Wagons, match holder back plate, tin, product name above red & green wagon, bend at corners/chips/wear, 5x4", VG, A **100.00**

Old Homestead Coffee, tin, pictures homestead, International Coffee Co, New York, slip lid, general wear/scratches/chips, 1-lb, 6x4", G+, A.........................**50.00**

Old Honesty Tobacco, sign, blue lettering on yellow, encircled dog's head in left corner, Chew Old Honesty Plug Tobacco, framed, 19x49", A.........................**170.00**

Old Joel Whiskey, shot glass, Drink Old Joel Whiskey, D Feltenstein Distributor, St Joseph Mo etched in lg letters on 5 lines, EX, D **20.00**

Old Judge Orange Pecoe Tea, tin, bright red paper label picturing an owl, square, 3", EX, D.........................**35.00**

Old Judson Whiskey, match holder, tin, child offering glass to rain-soaked father while mother helps with coat, 7x2x1", G, A **125.00**

Old King Cole Tobacco, tin, paper label of Maxfield Parrish painting 'Old King Cole,' slip lid, minor scuffs/chipping/soiling, 5x4x2", VG, A...........**150.00**

Old King Cole Tobacco, tin, paper label of Maxfield Parrish painting 'Old King Cole,' press lid, creases/scuffing/soiling, 4x4" diameter, EX, A **300.00**

Old King Cole Tobacco, tin, paper label of Maxfield Parrish painting 'Old King Cole,' slip lid, rust/scratches, 4x4" diameter, G, A.................**150.00**

Old Manion Coffee, tin, pictures mansion in oval, Steel Cut, CW Antrim & Sons, NM+, A.........................**110.00**

Old Master Coffee, poster, bust portrait of a bearded man, product name above & lettering below, 20x14" without frame, EX, A **260.00**

Old Master Coffee, tin, B on shield trademark, B-B Co, press lid, chips/wear, 1-lb, 6x4", VG, A.................**55.00**

Old Master Coffee, tin, portrait of gentleman in floral-framed oval above product name, EX+, A **75.00**

Old McGregor Bourbon, sign, tin litho, pictures whiskey barrel with encircled images below, Hulman & Fairbanks, early, framed, 12x16", VG, A **750.00**

Old Ox Cart Beer, opener, D..............**10.00**

Old Reliable Butts, sign, cardboard, depicts 2 men & woman in formal wear, Man's Best Friend, matted & framed, overall wear, 19x15", VG, A..............**175.00**

Old Reliable Coffee, pocket mirror, dock worker resting by crate of coffee, 2" diameter, NM, A..............**40.00**

Old Rip Long Cut Tobacco, tin, Old Rip on diagonal band, red slip lid, 7x4x3", VG, A..............**150.00**

Old Roman Whiskey, shot glass, product name etched on 2 lines in lg letters, M, D..............**18.00**

Old Rose Bud, sign, tin, Old Rose Bud with jockey astride, original frame, slight wear/retouched frame, 22x30" overall, EX, A **250.00**

Old Seneca Cigars, tin, Indian chief with Old Seneca superimposed on headdress, Stogies 3 for 5¢, slip lid, wear, 6x4" diameter, G+, ...**225.00**

Old Shay Beer, tray, horse-drawn carriage with product name above, round, appears EX, A **15.00**

Old Soldier Smoke Or Chew, pail, tin with paper label picturing a soldier, A Goodrich Co, slip lid & bail, rare, EX, A **75.00**

Old Squire Pipe Tobacco, pocket tin, squire in circular inset with lettering above & below, EX+, D..............**250.00**

Old Topper Ale, cash register sign, reverse-painted glass, lighted, man in top hat logo on right, 1920-40, minor paint loss, 7x12", A..............**40.00**

Old Topper Talc For Men, tin, gentleman in top hat on both sides, rare, EX, A **220.00**

Old Tucker Rye, sign, tin litho, 'Suspects His Master,' bulldog peaking into a jug, Brown Forman Co Distillers, self-framed, 9x13", A..............**180.00**

Old Virginia Cheroots Tobacco, cigar box, pictures Black gentleman on labels, 5x13x8", VG, A..............**25.00**

Old Virginia Cheroots Tobacco, sign, cardboard, depicts cowboy smoking cigar on blue background, 23x15", appears EX, A **300.00**

Old Virginia Cheroots Tobacco, sign, cardboard, depicts Uncle Sam smoking cigar on yellow background, 23x15", appears EX, A..............**450.00**

Old Virginia Cheroots Tobacco, sign, paper, shows woman graduate surrounded with lettering, matted & framed, 25x20", VG+, A **275.00**

Olgilive Flour Co, sign, paper, Canadian Victory surmounting globe & flanked by product, original frame, wear, 35x28", G+, A **250.00**

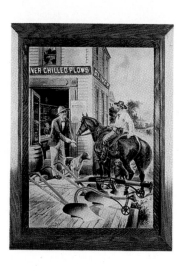

Oliver Chilled Plows, sign, embossed tin litho, a South Bend Ind Co, ca 1890s, 33x24", EX, A..........9,500.00

Oliver Chilled Plows, sign, embossed tin litho, man on horse & salesman in front of store, a South Bend Ind Co, 1890s, framed, 33x24", VG, A..............**6,000.00**

Oliver Plows, mirror, celluloid, James Oliver with name above & lettering below, oval, 3", NM, A..............**70.00**

Oliver Plows & Implements, sign, embossed tin, plow in upper left corner, Jarrett's Hdw Store, Emmaus Pa, overall wear, 10x20" without frame, VG, A..............**200.00**

Ology Cigars, display, die-cut easel-back, depicts man with golf club beside product name in lg yellow letters, 25x37", appears EX, A **160.00**

Olympia Beer, bank, can shape, horseshoe, EX, D....**10.00**

Omar Cigarettes, sign, cardboard, 2 men smoking cigarettes, black background, Omar Turkish Blend, original frame, 22x15", EX, A..............**250.00**

Omar Cigarettes, sign, cardboard, 2 men smoking cigarettes, black background, The Joy Of Life, 20 for 15¢, framed, 30x22", G-, A **20.00**

Oneida Brewing Co, tray, porcelain, pictures Shenandoah, chief of the Oneidas, Ales & Porter, minor edge chipping, 12" diameter, VG, A..............**95.00**

Oneida Motor Oil, tin, yellow with blue bands, circle with Indian at river in center, West Penn Oil Co, 1925-45, 2-gal, 12x9", VG, A..............**80.00**

Ontario Brand Peanut Butter, pail, depicts lake with lettering & checkered border above & below, press lid & bail, appears EX, A..............**65.00**

Opaline Motor Oil, tin, speeding roadster above product name, ca 1916-18, 1-gal, 11", EX+, A..............**1,400.00**

Opera Beauties Cigars, tin, opera lady in center of lid, rounded corners, 4x5", EX, A **150.00**

Opia Cigars, sign, tin, woman's image in crescent moon with poppies & stars, 5 cents, The Smoker's Dream, oval, 17x20", EX, A **3,500.00**

Orange Flower Cigars, tin, pictures white flower of the orange fruit, 5¢, slip lid, chips/scratches/dents, 5x6" diameter, VG, A.........................**125.00**

Orange Nip, dispenser, footed orange potbelly with spigot on side, lettering transfers, chipping/crazing, 22x20" diameter, G+, A...........................**350.00**

Orange-Crush, bottle opener, D **25.00**

Orange-Crush, clock, regulator, wood & glass, round numbered dial with reverse-painted glass below advertising products, 36x19", G, A **175.00**

Orange-Crush, drink rack sign, 2-sided, orange, blue, & white, Enjoy Orange-Crush, Naturally It Tastes Better, 10x15", EX, D.........................**34.00**

Orange-Crush, paperweight, glass, depicts bottle at left, Orange-Crush, Lemon-Crush, Lime-Crush, Augusta Ga, approx: 3x4", NM, D **145.00**

Orange-Crush, patch, cloth, Little Giants, M, D **5.00**

Orange-Crush, soda jerk hat, paper, orange, blue on white, 14" long, NM, D....................**8.00**

Orange-Crush, syrup dispenser, figural glass with embossed orange top on black glass Deco base, overall wear, 16x12" diameter, G, A....................**150.00**

Orange-Crush, thermometer, metal, depicts brown bottle of Crush on white, Get The Happy Habit, rounded ends, 19x6", EX+, D **165.00**

Orange-Crush, thermometer, tin bottle figural, 29", EX, D **45.00**

Orange-Crush, thermometer, Orange-Crush bordered by numbers, glass face, 12" diameter, EX+, D............**55.00**

Orange-Crush, thimble, aluminum whistle, orange band with Drink Orange-Crush For Health, EX, D.........**30.00**

Orange-Crush, see also Crush

Orange-Crush Bottling Co, paperweight, glass, shows bottle at left of lettering, Orange, Lemon, Lime-Crush, rounded corners, 3x4", NM, D.................**150.00**

Orange-Julep, tray, depicts seated sunbather holding parasol & glass, Drink Orange-Julep on dark rim, rectangular, 13", VG, A **45.00**

Orcico Cigars, tin, slip lid, minor scratches/edge chips/dents, 5x6x4", VG, A....................**250.00**

Orletta Cigars, box label, outer, pictures an elegant woman surrounded by medallions, 5x5", M, D......**12.00**

Ormont Violet Talcum, tin, pictures Deco lady on violets on both sides, slip lid, rare, rectangular, EX, A....**260.00**

Orphan Boy Smoking Tobacco, carton label with product packet, depicts donkey with lettering above & below, framed, vertical, EX, A **25.00**

Ortlieb's Lager Beer & Ale, tray, product name in center, logo above & lettering below, Wells Brewed, Full Bodied, Aged, round, appears EX, A...........................**35.00**

Oscar Mayer, doll, inflatable, Little Oscar, lg, EX, D...**15.00**

Oscar Mayer, Weinermobile, 10", D **35.00**

Oswego Bridge Co, sign, tin litho, sepia-toned image of the bridge over Delaware River at Port Jervis NY, self-framed, 14x19", EX, A **375.00**

Otasco, radio, miniature car battery figural, in original box, M, D **50.00**

Othello Ranges, match holder, tin litho, stove on white background, wear on striker box, 5x3", VG, A **100.00**

Otto Huber Beer, tray, depicts 2 women & a man seated at a table watching little boy with empty beer mug, oval, appears EX, A...........................**350.00**

Our Chief, cigar snipper, key-wind, D **185.00**

Our Jewel Coffee, tin, decorative can with portrait of child in diamond inset, original slip lid with knob, 6x4" diameter, VG, A.....................**110.00**

Our Kitties Cigars, box label, inner lid, pictures a black & white cat in front of a curtain, 6x9", M, D **6.00**

Owl Chop Teas, tin, ornate owl logo, hinged lid, Montreal Canada, overall fading/wear, 9x7x5", G, A............**85.00**

Oxford Chocolate, mirror, round with handle depicting female scholar, 4" diameter, EX, A **45.00**

Ozark Air Lines, playing cards, sun rising over shoulder of the Statue of Liberty, Ozark Flies Your Way, complete, M, D **10.00**

Ozark Air Lines, playing cards, white Ozark logo on forest green with white border, ...Up There With The Biggest, complete, M, D **5.00**

P

P Lorillard & Co, cabinet, extremely rare, EX, A .**2,000.00**

P Lorillard & Co's '49' Cut Plug Smoking Tobacco, sign, paper litho, colorful image of a man leaning on log cabin, framed, 12x9", VG+, A **1,100.00**

P Lorillard & Co's Honey-Comb Cut Plug Tobacco, sign, paper, costumed woman by stone wall promoting product, framed, 25x18", EX, A........................**1,350.00**

P Lorillard & Co's Maccoboy Snuff, store bin, tin, hinged lid, some wear, very rare Ginna litho, octagonal, 6x8x5", G, A...**700.00**

P Lorillard Co's Captive Smoking Tobacco, crate label, paper, depicts woman being tugged on by cherubs, lettering above & below, ca 1874, matted & framed, 22x19", EX, A **200.00**

P&H Service, sign, cast iron oval, Founded In 1884 by Pawling & Harnechfeger, ca 1900, rare, EX, A.......**25.00**

Pabst Blue Ribbon Beer, clock, metal figural, electric, bartender & beer bottle flank round clock face, logo on front of bar, 11x12", EX, A **80.00**

Pabst Blue Ribbon Beer, display, metal, waiter's arm holds beer sign, EX, D **95.00**

Pabst Blue Ribbon Beer, miniature can, full, VG, D **6.00**

Pabst Blue Ribbon Beer, sign, tin, depicts Pabst bottle, glass, & mail, The Brew Of Quality, self-framed, 10x13", EX, A **220.00**

Pabst Blue Ribbon Beer, sign, white Blue Ribbon lettered on blue wavy band, blue Pabst & Beer on white above & below, blue edge, 30x42", NM, A.....................**110.00**

Pabst Brewing Co, puzzle, 33 to 1, 2-sided, depicts beer cans on geometric background, 9 pieces, each 2" square, 6" square total, D......................................**30.00**

Pabst Brewing Co, sign, cardboard, colonial gentlemen in library drinking steins of Pabst beer, 1936, framed, 34x46", VG, A **50.00**

Pabst Brewing Co, sign, paper, minor stains along lower edge, 34x45", A **1,800.00**

Pabst Brewing Co, sign, paper, 2 bottles & glass of beer with oysters, factory framed, 27x30", G+, A.........**540.00**

Pabst Brewing Co, sign, paper litho, view of brewery, lady & logo on left, Capitol Ten Million Dollars, ca 1910, framed, EX, A **2,300.00**

Pabst Malt Extract, poster, paper, illustrated image of knight astride swan in water, The Best Tonic, tears/chips/wrinkles, 22x14", EX, A **95.00**

Packard, ad, full page featuring the 1928 convertible coupe, D **5.00**

Packard, sign, porcelain steel figural, Authorized Service Station, possibly contemporary, 29", NM, A.........**450.00**

Packard, sign, tin, Packard in script over round logo, blue & red on white, 1930s, 20x20", EX+, A.................**425.00**

Packard's Black '0' Shoe Polish, sign, cardboard, boy in center oval pointing at product, lettering above & below, Toronto litho, 11x7", VG, A......................**95.00**

Packer's Tar Soap, tin, D..**10.00**

Packers' Union Animal Matter Fertilizers, calendar, 1915, depicts 2 Indians seated on mountain top, January pad, center crease, framed, vertical rectangle, A **25.00**

Page's Ice Cream, tray, Brownies with dish of ice cream, logo above, HD Beach litho, 13x11", EX, A.........**225.00**

Palmer's Lotion & Talc For Men, tin, embossed, appears EX, D...**35.00**

Pan American, playing cards, white Pan American logo on light blue background with white border, complete, M, D...**6.00**

Pan-Am Gasoline & Motor Oil, sign, 2-sided porcelain, Pan-Am on horizontal band with Gasoline lettered above & Motor Oils below, 48" diameter, A **170.00**

Pan-Dandy Bread, paperweight, 2x4", D...................**20.00**

Pan-Handle Scrap Tobacco, sign, cardboard, Currier & Ives, 1890, framed, 16x22", G-, A **250.00**

Pan-Handle Scrap Tobacco, sign, paper litho, 'The Darktown Fire Brigade To The Rescue,' product & lettering atop, ca 1900, horizontal rectangle, A......**425.00**

Panama Ribbon Cigars, box label, inner lid, depicts Panama Ribbon on diagonal fringed band with canal scene below, 5¢, 6x9", M, D **15.00**

Pankey Motor Oil, tin, cream with red border & letters, Finest Quality Pankey Oil Co, Brookfield Mo below, ca 1915-25, half-gal, EX, A......**55.00**

Pansies Salted Peanuts, tin, logoed label, Whole Blanched Jumbo, Chicago United Fig & Date Co, press lid, 10-lb, 11x8", VG, A......**110.00**

Pansy Chocolates, tray, pretty girl with roses, lettering on rim, rectangular with rounded corners, scratching/rust spots, 18x12", G, A......**80.00**

Para-Field Motor Oil, tin, depicts early oil well on yellow background, Definitely Superior Lubrication, ca 1935-45, 1-qt, VG, A......**110.00**

Paraland Gas, globe, plastic frame, oval, EX, D......**185.00**

ParaPride Motor Oil, tin, red with plane & 2 speeding cars, Canfield Oil Co on blue band below, ca 1935-45, 1-qt, EX, A......**50.00**

Pard Dog Food, clock, electric, Swift's dog with bobbing head, working condition, 16" square, VG+, ...**425.00**

Paris Garters, sign, cardboard, 6 legs in 1 garter in a circle above lettering, Happy Legs Are Here Again!, 44x29", VG, A......**45.00**

Park-Davis Vitamin Products, display cabinet, tin litho with curved glass, a variety of products displayed, lettering on top piece, vertical, EX, A......**190.00**

Parke's Newport Coffee, pail, tin, slip lid & bail, 5-lb, appears EX, A......**50.00**

Parke's Newport Coffee, store bin, tin, graphics with lettering, slip lid, 3-lb, round, appears EX, A......**75.00**

Parker Dufold Pens, clock, electric, square wood case with round glass front, figural pen second hand, lettered center, 19x19", NM, A......**330.00**

Parrot Peanut Butter, pail, tin, shows parrot on circle, original press lid & bail, Westport Co Ltd, Canada, scratching/chipping, 4x4", G+, A......**2,300.00**

Parrot Peanut Butter, tin, shows parrot on circular background, press lid, Westport Co Ltd, Canada, 13-oz, 4x3" diameter, G+, A......**425.00**

Pat Hand Tobacco, pocket tin, few nicks on & near lid, EX, D......**175.00**

Pat Hand Tobacco, tin, depicts hand & lettering, slip lid, lid dented/side scratched, round, F, A......**25.00**

Patriot Tobacco, tin, lettered black & yellow upright can, original slip lid, Quebec, Canada, rare, 7x5" diameter, G-, A......**125.00**

Patterson Hammock Couches, mirror, lady lounging on hammock on a porch surrounded by lettering, rectangular with rounded corners, 3", EX, A......**425.00**

Patterson Tobacco Co, sign, hanging, 2-sided die-cut tin, pipe figural, Lucky Strike on 1 side, Tuxedo Tobacco on reverse, 9x19", VG+, A......**1,500.00**

Pattons Auto Gloss Finish, sign, paper litho, shadow box with samples of various colors, minor restoration, 21x15", G, A......**750.00**

Paul Jones Pure Gin, sign, die-cut tin, little boy on wood pile with another getting splinter out of his foot, some restoration, 20x14", A......**450.00**

Paul Jones Rye, sign, tin, Comrades For 81 Years, Beach Co litho, faded/pitted, self-framed, 28", F, A......**75.00**

Paul Jones Tobacco, pocket tin, blue, 7", NM, D **950.00**

Paul Jones Whiskey, sign, tin, original frame & display case, 45x32", EX, A......**500.00**

Paycar Scrap Tobacco, sign, depicts a hand pointing to the product, Here's The Tobacco You'll Like, ca 1910, framed, 14x11", appears EX, A......**45.00**

PC Winged Radiator Cap, sign, cardboard, radiator cap above ad copy in rectangular inset bordered by arrows pointing inward, 14x12", G, A......**8.00**

PCW Cough Drops, tin, brown, product name & fancy graphics, slip lid, heavily worn, rectangular, A......**45.00**

PCW Cough Drops, tin, green, product name & fancy graphics, slip lid, heavily worn, rectangular, A......**30.00**

PCW Cough Drops, tin, product name in lg letters over fancy graphics, slip lid, round, appears worn, A ...**40.00**

PCW Cough Drops, tin, red, product name & fancy graphics, slip lid, heavily worn, rectangular, A **35.00**

PCW Cough Drops, tin, yellow, product name & fancy graphics, slip lid, heavily worn, rectangular, A......**30.00**

Peachy Chewing Tobacco, pack (empty), paper, appears G, D......**10.00**

Peacock Ink, ink bottle with octagonal tin case, peacock motif, removable shoulder cap, minor chips/rubs, 3x2", EX, A......**95.00**

Pearl Lustre Dyes, cabinet, wood with tin front depicting sunburst with Dyes lettered in center, lettering above & below, 22x17x7", VG, A...**850.00**

Pears Soap, sign, die-cut paper, elderly woman scrubbing little boy's ears, cardboard frame, 13x5", appears EX, A...**150.00**

Pears Soap, sign, from the original painting by Miss Mary Grove, 'Impudent Hussies,' 1902, 20x25", A...........**70.00**

Pears Soap, sign, paper, children being bathed, possibly trimmed at top, framed, 10x8", EX, A **55.00**

Pears Soap, statue, porcelain, elderly woman scrubbing little boy's ears, several repairs, rare, A **280.00**

Peerless Dyes, cabinet, wood, tin front, ca 1890, rare, 31x23x11", VG, A..7,950.00

Peerless Dyes, cabinet, wood, tin front, product name on diagonal band divides train & camel caravan, ca 1890, rare, 31x23x11", G-, A.......................................**1,600.00**

Peerless Dyes, cabinet, wood, tin front, woman, peacock, & butterflies, 40 Colors, 10¢ A Package, missing rear doors, 26x18x10", G-, A **650.00**

Peerless Dyes, cabinet, wood with tin front, colorful image of a gypsy woman with camel caravan below, ca 1888, rare, 26x19x10", VG, A **2,300.00**

Peerless Fixtures Co, catalog, 16 pages of bean counters, Peerless Counters, The Peerless Fixtures Co, Marshall Michigan, 11x9", NM, A...**80.00**

Peggy O'Moore Cigars, box label, outer, pictures little girl & her father flanked by logo, 3x5", M, D **2.00**

Penereco Motor Oil, tin, Wm Penn dressed in silver above black banner, 100% Pure... below, ca 1935-45, scratches/no top, 1-qt, VG, A **25.00**

Penguin Motor Oil, tin, dark blue with red & white oval picturing penguin, Traymore Lubricants NY, ca 1925-45, 2-gal, 11x9", EX+, A **120.00**

Penn Airliner Motor Oil, tin, white with green bottom, plane flying through ring with product name at top, 1925-45, 2-gal, 12x9", VG, A..................................**130.00**

Penn Champ Motor Oil, tin, gold with dark & light diamond shapes as background, 10w-20w-30w- on black at center, ca 1960s, 1-qt, VG, A **10.00**

Penn Drake Ethyl, gas globe, milk glass, product name & oil well logo encircle Ethyl logo, 1930-40, 16x15" diameter, EX, A...**500.00**

Penn Drake HD Motor Oil, tin, logo over HD in large red letters on white, yellow band at bottom, 1965-70, 1-qt, 6", NM, A...**30.00**

Penn Empire Motor Oil, sign, cardboard, round logo in center, More Miles, Less Cost lettered in top corners, 1932, very rare, 20x21", VG, A **250.00**

Penn Star Motor Oil, tin, red, white, & blue stripes with lettering on each, DOC symbol on white, Derby Oil Co, 1920-30, half-gal, EX, A **25.00**

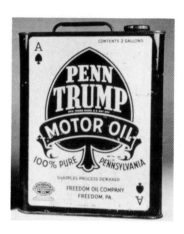

Penn Trump Motor Oil, tin, ca 1925-45, 2-gal, 12x9", VG, A 150.00

Penn-Bee Motor Oil, tin, 2 lg black & yellow bees in red circle over product name, priced at 35¢, ca 1935-45, 1-qt, 6", EX, A...**140.00**

Penn-Drake Motor Oil, sign, embossed tin, orange & black oil well logo far left, Use Penn-Drake Motor Oil, 1925-35, 10x28", EX, A **175.00**

Penn-Drake Motor Oil, sign, porcelain, black & white oil well over 3-line product name, ca 1930-40, 27x21", NM, A...**1,200.00**

Penn-Drake Motor Oil, tin, red with oil well graphic, Original Drake Well, 1859 across top, white letters, postwar, 1-qt, 6", EX, A.......................................**35.00**

Penn-Drake Motor Oil, tin, top is yellow & white striped with logo, 10w-40 on white stripe, Hi-Compression on red below, 1968-70, 1-qt, NM, A **35.00**

Penn-Drake Racing Motor Oil, tin, checkered flags on yellow background, black lettering on white band below, 1965-70, 1-qt, 6", NM, A.............................**40.00**

Penn-Wave Motor Oil, tin, blue & red letters on banner over logo on yellow background, Motor Oil in blue at bottom, ca 1935-45, 1-qt, EX+, A **65.00**

Penn-Wave Motor Oil, tin, yellow with red bands, ca 1940-50, 2-gal, 11x8", NM, A **30.00**

Penn's Fountain Pens, tin, pictures fountain pen on lid, Penn's Natural Leaf Thin, rectangular, VG+, A.......**20.00**

Penna Bottling & Supply Co, mug, ceramic, tan & brown, birds on branch above Dove Brand on banner, Ginger Ale, 1900, 5", EX, A **65.00**

Pennant Double Chocolate Chips, store bin on wheels, tin, circus scene surrounds outer sides, hinged lid opens to ad, 10 Cookies 10¢, 7x14x10", EX, A **110.00**

Pennant Motor Oil, tin, pennant over black circle, Wonder Lubricant For Fords, Pierce Petroleum Corp, 1915-25, half-gal, 6", NM, A **70.00**

Pennelene Auto Oil, tin, green with black-shadowed gold letters, Penn Soo Oil Co, Sioux Falls SD at bottom, ca 1950s, half-gal, 6", EX, A **60.00**

Pennfield Motor Oil, sign, curb-type, porcelain, yellow & black logo left of oil derrick, red stand, 1930s, touched up, 50x31", EX, A **950.00**

Pennsylvania Motor Oil, tin, map of 5 states & oil fields on yellow background, 2 logos below, ca 1935-45, 1-qt, EX, A **150.00**

Pennsylvania Motor Oil, tin, scene titled 'Pennsylvania Scenery Along The Bucktail Creek' under product name, 1925-45, 2-gal, 12x9", VG+, A **95.00**

Pennsylvania Motor Oil, tin, yellow with blue border, map of 5 states & oil fields, Superior-Penn, 1925-45, 2-gal, 12x9", EX, A **80.00**

Pennsylvania Oil, sign, die-cut porcelain, text each side, black & yellow, 1920s, faded/flaking, 9x12", A 160.00

Pennsylvania Rubber Co, ash tray, figural glass tire, 4" diameter, EX, A...**60.00**

Penntroleum Motor Oil, tin, motor boat under bridge with touring cars & people, airplanes overhead, 2 logos below, ca 1935-45, 1-qt, EX, A **150.00**

Pennzoil, sign, porcelain, black with yellow sunburst behind logo with red bell, 1920s, 15x13", NM, A ..**325.00**

Pennzoil, sign, porcelain, sunburst effect around lg logo with red bell & black letters, 1920s, holes flaked, 15x27", VG, A **195.00**

Pennzoil, sign, porcelain, Supreme PA Quality over logo with brown & tan bell, 1920s, round, M, A..........**750.00**

Pennzoil, sign, porcelain, yellow with black Pennzoil across red bell, Property of Pennzoil..., 1910-20, flaking/rust, 3x9", VG, A **165.00**

Pennzoil, sign, porcelain each side, red arrow & Expert Lubrication on white, 1930-40, 9x30", EX, A **160.00**

Pennzoil, sign, tin, Supreme Pennsylvania Quality upper left, Pennzoil over black bell on orange, 1940-50, 12x36", NM, A...**100.00**

Pennzoil, sign, tin, yellow with black bands each end, Sound Your & lg Z in red & black, 1945-48, self-framed, 60x12", NM, A...**275.00**

Pennzoil, sign, tin, 2-sided, Bonded Pennzoil Dealer as arched support for lg logo with red bell, 1920-30, faded/scuffs, 12x16", A **255.00**

Pennzoil, tin, depicts lg airplane over oval with product name & red bell, 3 owls at left, ca 1935-45, 1-qt, 6", EX+, A **60.00**

Pennzoil, tin, easy pour, yellow with product name over black & silver bell, ca 1915-25, 5-gal, 17x14" diameter, VG, A 130.00

Pennzoil, tin, for motor oil, Be Oil Wise to left of 3 owls perched on oval with red bell, ca 1935-45, no top, 5-qt, 10x7", VG+, A...**90.00**

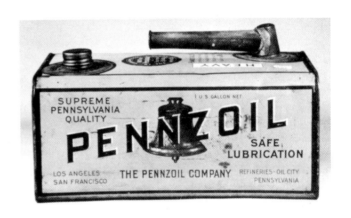

Pennzoil, tin, for motor oil, yellow with black & silver letters & bronze bell, 1915-25, 1-gal, 6", EX, A .300.00

Pennzoil, tin, logo on lg red, yellow & black graphic design, Executive Offices Oil City/Los Angeles, 1915-25, 5-gal, 15x9", EX, A...**20.00**

Pennzoil, tin, Pennzoil in black superimposed on red bell in yellow oval with black & yellow border, 1925-30, 1-gal, 11", VG+, A...**50.00**

Pennzoil, tin, United Air Lines Uses...Exclusively over lg plane, 3 owls left of logo on yellow, 1935-45, no top, 5-qt, VG, A **85.00**

Pennzoil, tin, yellow with black & silver letters superimposed on silver bell, Safe Lubrication, ca 1915-25, 1-gal, 11", VG+, A...**170.00**

Pennzoil, tin, yellow with 3 owls over oval with black letters & red bell, ca 1935-45, 1-qt, VG, A **55.00**

Pennzoil Gasoline, gas globe, milk glass with product name encircling lg Ethyl logo with text, New York NY, 1926-30, worn, round, 17", A...**450.00**

Pennzoil Motor Grease, tin, yellow with blue bell, blue & white product name, 1935-45, handles each side, 25-lb, 10x11", VG, A **45.00**

Penreco Motor Oil, tin, white with Penreco on black banner below colonial man, 100%...Motor Oil, 1920-30, 2-gal, 12x9", G+, A **25.00**

Pep Boys Motor Oils, tin, shows Pep Boys over 600 Transmission diamond logo, 1929, 1-gal, 10", G, A **250.00**

Pep Boys Western Motor Oil, tin, pictures Pep Boys on bucking horse, vivid colors, ca 1925-45, 2-gal, 12x9", EX, A **210.00**

Pepperidge Farm, cookbook, 1963, hard-bound, M Rudkin, 440 pages, D **14.00**

Pepperidge Farm, gingerbread boy, EX, D **20.00**

Pepsi-Cola, bottle, 1930s, clear with paper label, 12-oz, M, D.......................................**32.00**

Pepsi-Cola, bottle, 1930s, green with paper label, 12-oz, M, D.......................................**55.00**

Pepsi-Cola, calendar, 1944, pictures lady in rocker & 2 men, EX, D **60.00**

Pepsi-Cola, card hanger, 1940s, bottle hanging from Pepsi sign, never used, 16x6", NM, D.......................................**215.00**

Pepsi-Cola, clock, plastic & metal light-up, 16" diameter, EX, D **160.00**

Pepsi-Cola, coaster, 1940s, Pour Your Own...The Perfect Mixer, 4" diameter, EX, D **6.00**

Pepsi-Cola, cookbook, 1940, paperback, D.............**14.00**

Pepsi-Cola, display, 1930s, die-cut counter-top, Pepsi-Cola 5¢ over Bigger Better on scroll wrapped around 6 bottles, 15x17", NM, A **230.00**

Pepsi-Cola, display, 1960s, die-cut cardboard stand-up, EX, A **45.00**

Pepsi-Cola, display, 1960s, die-cut cardboard stand-up, Santa standing sideways with Pepsi, bottle cap logo at hip, 20", NM, A **65.00**

Pepsi-Cola, glass, bulbous stem, EX, D **5.00**

Pepsi-Cola, glass, embossed, flared, EX, D **7.00**

Pepsi-Cola, glass, stained-glass effect, EX, D **5.00**

Pepsi-Cola, glass, 1966 Collector Series, Batman, DC Comics, EX, D.......................................**15.00**

Pepsi-Cola, glass, 1971 Collector Series, Flash, DC Comics, EX, D **15.00**

Pepsi-Cola, glass, 1973 Collector Series, Tweety Bird, EX, D.......................................**10.00**

Pepsi-Cola, glass, 1976 Collector Series, Roadrunner & Wile E Coyote, Warner Brothers, EX, D **10.00**

Pepsi-Cola, glass, 1976 Collector Series, Shazam, DC Comics, EX, D.......................................**15.00**

Pepsi-Cola, glass, 1976 Collector Series, Sylvester & Friends, EX, D.......................................**10.00**

Pepsi-Cola, glass, 1976 Super Series, Aqua Man, EX, D ..**15.00**

Pepsi-Cola, glass, 1978, 101 Dalmatians, Disney, EX, D..**20.00**

Pepsi-Cola, glass, 1978 Collector Series, Goofy, Happy Birthday Mickey, EX, D.......................................**20.00**

Pepsi-Cola, glass, 1978 Collector Series, Lady & Tramp, Disney, EX, D **15.00**

Pepsi-Cola, glass, 1978 Collector Series, Mickey & Minnie, Happy Birthday Mickey, EX, D **15.00**

Pepsi-Cola, glass, 1978 Collector Series, Pluto, Happy Birthday Mickey, EX, D.......................................**15.00**

Pepsi-Cola, glass, 1978 Collector Series, Porky & Petunia Pig, Warner Brothers, EX, D **15.00**

Pepsi-Cola, glass, 1978 Collector Series, Robin, DC Comics, EX, D.......................................**15.00**

Pepsi-Cola, glass, 1978 Collectors Series, Horace & Clarabell, Happy Birthday Mickey, EX, D **20.00**

Pepsi-Cola, miniature bottle, 4", D **14.00**

Pepsi-Cola, pencil, 1950s, mechanical, EX, D.............**30.00**

Pepsi-Cola, pin, 1939, Drink Pepsi-Cola, Delicious, Healthful, marked Pepsi-Cola Co, New York, D...............**13.00**

Pepsi-Cola, push bar, 1930s, porcelain, ...On Lips of Millions, 10x3", NM, D **100.00**

Pepsi-Cola, push bar, 1950s, porcelain, French, Pepsi-Cola flanked by Buvez Glace, 3x30", EX, D **60.00**

Pepsi-Cola, push bar, 1950s, porcelain, Have A Pepsi flanked by bottle cap logos, 3x30", EX, D.............**75.00**

Pepsi-Cola, push bar, 1950s, porcelain, Pepsi-Cola flanked by Enjoy & Iced lettered on vertical stripe background, 3x30", NM, D **100.00**

Pepsi-Cola, radio, 1950s, tuner is bottle cap, rare, 24x8", EX, A.......................................500.00

Pepsi-Cola, salt & pepper shakers with box, bottle-shaped with blue & yellow dome tops, 5", D **30.00**

Pepsi-Cola, sign, 1920s, embossed tin, Drink Pepsi-Cola, 5¢, Refreshing & Healthful, red on white, creasing, framed, 6x17", G, A **155.00**

Pepsi-Cola, sign, 1920s, embossed tin, red & blue on white, framed, 6x17", EX+, A 250.00

Pepsi-Cola, sign, 1930s, tin, depicts 5¢ bottle, More Bounce To The Ounce, 26x10", EX, D 18.00

Pepsi-Cola, sign, 1930s, tin, EX, A 75.00

Pepsi-Cola, sign, 1940s, tin, Tops, pictures streaming caps, 12x36", NM, D 120.00

Pepsi-Cola, sign, 1950s, cardboard, 11x27" without frame, A 110.00

Pepsi-Cola, sign, 1950s, tin, pictures a bottle of Pepsi & card with ribbon, More Bounce To The Ounce on card, 48x17", A...220.00

Pepsi-Cola, sign, 1950s, 2-sided flourescent, bottle cap beside lettering over vertical stripes, Take Home..., 17x27x5", EX, D.................................200.00

Pepsi-Cola, sign, 1960s, celluloid & tin, pictures Black girl with bottle, oval, 8x12", EX, D 55.00

Pepsi-Cola, sign, 1960s, tin litho, 31" long, VG, A 40.00

Pepsi-Cola, thermometer, 1950s, Pepsi cap atop, Any Weather's Pepsi weather on card with ribbon below, rounded corners, 27x7", NM, A 90.00

Pepsi-Cola, thermometer, 1950s, tin, pictures a bottle cap above, The Light Refreshment lettered below, some rust, 27x7", A 25.00

Pepsi-Cola, thermometer, ca 1960s, tin, yellow, 27x7", M, D..23.00

Pepsi-Cola, tip tray, 1908, decorative border, C Shonk litho, 6x4", VG+, A.............................325.00

Pepsi-Cola, tip tray, 1908, decorative border, rare, 6x4", VG, A.......................................575.00

Pepsi-Cola, tip tray, 1908, 6x4", EX, A 500.00

Pepsi-Cola, tray, 1940s, Enjoy atop Pepsi-Cola on white banner, Hits The Spot flanked by music notes below, 11x14", EX+, D 100.00

Pepsi-Cola, trolley sign, 1941, cartoon by Whitney Darrow, D..65.00

Pepsin Mansfield Gum, display, 16x7x7", EX, A ..1,600.00

Pepsodent, display, floor, die-cut cardboard, Black man smoking cigar, Oh! Sho-Sho Pepsodent! copyright 1930, 61", VG, A 550.00

Pepsodent, display, floor, die-cut cardboard, Black man with product, Um! Um! Ain't Dis Something!, copyright 1880, 54", VG, A 300.00

Pepsodent, premium, ...Moving Picture Machine With 2 Sets Of Pictures Featuring Disney's Snow White..., original carton, M, A 150.00

Pequea Snelled Hooks, sign, celluloid over metal, depicts jumping fish with lettering above & below, various hooks at the sides, 14x11", EX, A.................30.00

Perfect Circle Piston Rings, sign, tin litho, with comic image of oil hog, Don't Drive An Oil Hog, bends/surface loss, 36x29", VG, A 1,000.00

Perfect Coffee, tin, red, blue, & gold background, slip lid, AH Perfect & Co, 1-lb, EX, D...................42.00

Perfection Cigarettes, sign, printer's proof, pictures woman in red hat & product on dark blue, light blue border, 1900s, framed, 29x23", EX, A 375.00

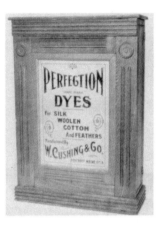

Perfection Dyes, cabinet, wood, lettering on tin front insert, 24", EX, A 250.00

Perfection Dyes, sign, tin, For Silk, Woolen, Cotton, & Feathers, Manufactured By W Gushing & Co, ca 1885, framed, 14x10", NM, A 500.00

Permanere Finishes, sign, tin, minor overall wear, rare, 13x20" without frame, EX, A..............8,000.00

Perry Davis' Pain Killer, sign, tin, pictures horse-drawn wagon carrying product, logoed fence, rust spots/fading, rare, horizontal rectangle, A..................250.00

Pet Milk, can opener, D..................................10.00

Pet Milk, sign, metal, depicts 2 cans of milk with display of foods, Bake Them In Pet Milk, 9x20", EX, D...........7.00

Peter Cooper Rye, tip tray, bust-length portrait of pretty girl, The Peer Of Ryes, 4" diameter, G+, A 120.00

Peter Doelger Bottled Beer, tip tray, eagle logo in center with company & product name lettered on rim, rare, 6x5", NM, A..150.00

Peter Doelger Bottled Beer, tip tray, eagle logo in center with company & product name lettered on rim, 4" diameter, NM, A 120.00

Peter Doelger Bottled Beer, tip tray, factory scene in center, First Prize flanked by product name, New York lettered on rim, 6" diameter, EX, A **350.00**

Peter Doelger Bottled Beer, tray, decorative rim, rare, EX, A...**475.00**
Peter Doelger Bottled Beer, tray, factory scene flanked by bottles with early airplanes overhead, decorative border, some wear, oval, 14x17", G, A.......................**600.00**
Peter Hand Brewing Co, tray, deep-dish, woman with flowers & circular logo surrounded by company brands & ornate graphics, oval, 15x19", NM, A **1,500.00**
Peter Krantz Brewery, tray, bulldog on red background, Lager Beer & Porter lettered on rim, minor overall spotting, 13x11", EX, A **325.00**
Peter Rabbit Baby Powder, tin, storybook scene, shaker top, wide, NM, A..**180.00**
Peter Rabbit Peanut Butter, pail, tin, shows Peter & his pals, logo atop, press lid & bail, Newton Tea & Spice Co, EX, A **675.00**
Peter Rabbit Peanut Butter, pail, tin, shows Peter & his pals, original slip lid & bail, Kelly Confection Co, Canada, some wear, rare, 4x4", G-, A....................**430.00**
Peter Schuttler Wagons, sign, paper litho, horse-drawn wagons coming down mountain trail, water damage/sm tears, 18x24" without frame, A **450.00**
Peters Cartridge Co, calendar, 1908, boy carrying rifle & Canadian geese, full calendar, 27x14", EX, A.......**900.00**
Peters Cartridge Co, calendar, 1925, pictures flying mallards, September pad, framed, 33x18", EX, A.......**350.00**

Peters' Weatherbird Shoes, sign, paper litho, original decorative frame, rare, 22x30", EX, A **1,500.00**

Petrol, sign, figures looking at an early automobile with logo atop & corner vignettes, framed, 20x15", appears EX, A **250.00**
Peugeot, sign, depicts an early red convertible, bicyclers, smokestacks, & lion, Peugeot in yellow below, framed, 64x49", EX, A...**950.00**
Pfaff's Lager, thermometer, wooden, appears working, wear to background color/lettering, 21x5", G-, A ..**25.00**
PH Mayo & Brother Tobacco, sign, cardboard litho, double-sided, factory scene with horse-drawn wagons, Richmond Virginia, 13x20", NM, A.......................**650.00**
Pheasant Pure Lard, tin, paper label with 2 pheasants & lettering, slip lid, round, 13", G, A **140.00**

Philgas, salt & pepper shakers, light green plastic, in original box, 2", M, D..**20.00**
Phillip Morris Cigarettes, sign, tin litho with raised rim, lion logo with decorative border, tiny rust spots on edge, 16" diameter, G, A....................................**425.00**

Phillips Trop-Artic Motor Oil, tin, ca 1935-39, minor paint loss at top, 1-qt, EX, A **110.00**
Phillips Trop-Artic Motor Oil, tin, white pinstripes on blue with lg orange & blue shield in white circle, ca 1940-43, 1-qt, 6", NM, A **170.00**
Phillips 66, sign, embossed die-cut porcelain, orange & black lettering, 1956, 48x48", EX+, A **230.00**
Phillips 66 Aviation Engine Oil, tin, silver stripes on light blue with lg winged shield logo, airplanes around top, ca 1950-59, 1-qt, 6", EX+, A **40.00**

Phillips 66 Premium Motor Oil, tin, cream pinstripes on maroon, red & black shield logo in cream circle above product name, 1946-53, 1-qt, NM, A **30.00**

Phoenix Beer, window, stained glass, very colorful, 31x69", NM, A **800.00**

Phoenix Brewery, tip tray, phoenix rising from log fire, Buffalo NY, 4" diameter, NM, A **125.00**

Phoenix Brewery, tray, phoenix rising from log fire, decorative rim, Buffalo NY, chipping to image/rim, 12" diameter, VG, A **75.00**

Phoenix Brewery, tray, 15x18", EX, A **230.00**

Phoenix Insurance Co, sign, tin, light & dark blue early-style lettering on white, Hartford Conn, 12x20", NM, A **220.00**

Phoenix Insurance Co, sign, tin, phoenix rising from crown of flames above banner, Wells & Hope litho, 20x14" without frame, VG, A **900.00**

Phoenix Violet Talcum Powder, tin, lettering & violets, shaker top, EX, A **40.00**

Pickanny Brand Jumbo Salted Peanuts, tin, depicts girl holding product with doll at feet, lettering above & below, press lid, good color, 10-lb, EX, A..........**280.00**

Pickwick Ale, sign, tin, depicts horse-drawn cart with 3 barrels of ale, Ale That Is Ale, sm scratch, wood frame, 25" long, G+, ...**100.00**

Pickwick Ale, sign, tin litho, 3 gents toasting with mugs of ale, Harvard Brewing Co label at bottom, 28x22", VG+, A **675.00**

Pickwick Club Tobacco, tin, figures around table in circular inset on lid, Pickwick Club Mixture, square corners, 2x4x3", EX, A **400.00**

Picobac Tobacco, pocket tin, depicts hand holding leaf, The Pick of Tobacco, ca 1930, EX, A.......................**40.00**

Picobac Tobacco, sign, tin, lettered store sign with image of pocket tin, Pick of Tobacco, wear, framed, 37x73", G, A **75.00**

Picobac Tobacco, sign, tin, pictures upright pocket tin, wear/denting/staining, framed, 37x73", F, A **30.00**

Piedmont Airlines, playing cards, Piedmont in red printed vertically on white with light blue logo above, light blue border, complete, M, D **7.00**

Piedmont Cigarettes, chair, wood with 2-sided porcelain insert advertising product, slat seat, stenciling on 2 sides, 31x16x18", EX, A.......................**90.00**

Piedmont Cigarettes, chair insert, white on blue porcelain, diagonal Piedmont with Smoke above, The Cigarette Of Quality below, 12x12", EX, A.............**35.00**

Piedmont Cigarettes, sign, porcelain, some inpainting, general wear, 46x30", G, A.......................**100.00**

Piedmont Cigarettes, sign, porcelain with curved corners, pictures open pack of cigarettes, Virginia Cigarettes, rubs/edge wear, 14x16", EX, A.......................**375.00**

Piedmont Cigarettes, sign, tin, depicts Washington's return to Mt Vernon, ca 1900, framed, 24x31", EX, A **425.00**

Piedmont Cigarettes, sign, tin, depicts Washington's return to Mt Vernon, some paint loss/overall spotting, framed, 17x27", F, A **50.00**

Piel Bros East New York Brewery, sign, tin, depicts 2 elves with beer bottles, America's Finest Pure Malt Beer, very unusual & rare, 13" diameter, EX+, A.**425.00**

Pierce Oil Corporation, tin, blue & cream pennant centered on checkered stripe, red background, Superior Quality, 1915-25, half-gal, VG+, A **100.00**

Pierce's Fine Paints, sign, tin, flanged, pictures a paint can, Pierce's Fine Paints For Sale Here, horizontal rectangle, EX, A **150.00**

Pillsbury, chef, 1971, 16", EX, D.......................**15.00**

Pillsbury, cookbook, 1911, paperback, 'The Pillsbury Cook Book,' 125 pages, D **20.00**

Pillsbury, cookbook, 1951, paperback, 2nd Bake-Off, '100 Prize-Winning Recipes,' D **18.00**

Pillsbury, cookbook, 1960, paperback, 'Best Cakes,' 65 pages, D **7.00**

Pillsbury, cookbook, 1974, paperback, 'Pillsbury Silver Anniversary Bake-Off,' 92 pages, D **7.00**

Pillsbury & Co (Chas A), sign, paper, eagle on barrel, New York & Liverpool harbors, factory inset, very rare, 30x24", VG, A **1,700.00**

Pillsbury Co, doll, cloth, Poppin' Fresh with cloth chef's hat, 13", F, D **10.00**

Pillsbury Co, mug, Poppin' Fresh, 1979, 5", VG, D ...**10.00**

Pillsbury Co, salt & pepper shakers, Dough Boys, sm chip, D...**15.00**

Pillsbury Flour, bin, tin, Dough Boy, 1960s, G, D **10.00**

Pillsbury Flour, sign, paper litho, colorful image, creases/edge loss, framed, 30x15", G+, A 425.00

Pilot Chewing Tobacco, tin, airplane skywriting Pilot, 10¢ Plug, Montreal Canada, scratches/minor dents, 4x5" diameter, VG, A **65.00**

Pilot Chewing Tobacco, tin, pictures unusual aircraft CF-ARO, 10¢ Plug, Montreal Canada, overall chips/dents, 4x5" diameter, G, A.......................................**65.00**

Pilot-Knob Coffee, tin, pictures Pilot Mountain of North Carolina, Bowers Brothers Inc, original lid & bail, 5-lb, 9x8" diameter, VG, A **300.00**

Pilsener Brewing Co, tip tray, pictures labeled bottle & glass, Cleveland Ohio, minor rim chips, 4" diameter, NM, A **45.00**

Pin Head Cigarettes, sign, paper litho, alluring girl wearing a low cut gown, rich muted colors, ca 1900, edge tears, 25x16", VG, A **300.00**

Piper Heidsieck Plug Tobacco, poster, paper, half-length portrait of a woman, National Tobacco Works, Louisville Ky, matted & framed, 33x23", G, A......**350.00**

Piper Heidsieck Plug Tobacco, sign, tin, champagne bottle popping plug & package of tobacco, rubbing/crazing of color/minor rust, 18x15", G+, A **450.00**

Pippins Cigar, sign, embossed tin, lettering & apple on blue background, H Traiser & Co Inc, Boston, 10x20", F, A...**30.00**

Pippins Cigar, sign, embossed tin, lettering & apple on blue background, H Traiser & Co Inc, Boston, 10x20", G, A...**85.00**

Pittsburgh Brewing Co, tip tray, pictures 3 men with bottles & glasses, None Better, Teck Beer, oval, 6x5", NM, A...**125.00**

Pizza Hut, doll, Pizza Pete, D **30.00**

Pizza Time, doll, dog, Duke La Rue, D **10.00**

Plain Monarch Cigars, box label, inner lid, depicts cowboy with lasso on galloping horse, product name above, 1904, 6x9", M, D.................................**75.00**

Plano Harvesting Machinery, calendar, 1904, pictures little girl with hat full of cherries & machinery vignettes below, July pad, framed, 21x15", A **340.00**

Planters, 'Paint Book No 2,' 1929, NM, D.................**120.00**

Planters, Bic lighter, blue with yellow Mr Peanut logo, M, D...**10.00**

Planters, bowl, plastic, EX, A.................................20.00

Planters, buckle, gold-tone metal figural of Mr. Peanut, M, D...**10.00**

Planters, charm bracelet, D...**25.00**

Planters, chopper tin, grinder attachment for top of salted pecans can with removable Mr Peanut top, overall wear, 4x4", EX, A.................................**225.00**

Planters, cuff links, gold-tone metal, Mr Peanut, D **75.00**

Planters, display, cardboard, Mr Peanut in nut-shell canoe & girl with parasol, ca 1920s, fading/creases, rare, 6x9x1", G, A **450.00**

Planters, display, die-cut stand-up figural of Mr Peanut, 48", D...**18.00**

Planters, display, die-cut tin, Mr Peanut on top of dispenser which would hold 5¢ Jumbo Peanut Block, overall wear, 12x5x5", VG, A **1,300.00**

Planters, display stand, papier mache, Mr Peanut standing beside mottled embossed display tray, overall wear, 14x11x11", G+, A **1,550.00**

Planters, doll, cloth, Mr Peanut, EX, D **15.00**

Planters, Mr Peanut, metal figural in classic pose on base, 8", EX, A...**250.00**

Planters, Mr Peanut, papier mache, mouth lights up, very early, 24", VG+, A **2,800.00**

Planters, paint book, 1949, EX, D **30.00**

Planters, parade costume, Mr Peanut, A...................**400.00**

Planters, peanut butter maker, Mr Peanut, in original box, M, D...**25.00**

Planters, pen & pencil set, in original box, M, A **25.00**

Planters, pencil, mechanical, Mr Peanut floating in oil, EX, A...**45.00**

Planters, pencil, mechanical, Mr Peanut form, in wrapper, M, D...**22.00**

Planters, plate, pewter, Super Bowl XIII, lg, D...........**75.00**

Planters, radio, Mr Peanut figural, original box, M, D **75.00**

Planters, refrigerator magnet, Mr Peanut, D **12.00**

Planters, salt & pepper shakers, Mr Peanut form, plastic, in original box, M, D **25.00**

Planters, salt & pepper shakers, plastic, Mr Peanut, green, 3", D...**8.00**

Planters, sign, cardboard die-cut, 1939 World's Fair, 7", VG, D...**15.00**

Planters, sign, tin, pictures Mr Peanut flanked by 5¢ Bag, Planters Peanuts Sold Here lettered above & below, vertical, A **110.00**

Planters, spoon, gold-tone metal with enamel Mr Peanut, demitasse, D **22.00**

Planters, store container, glass jar, embossed image, peanut finial lid, 12x8" diameter, EX, A.........275.00

Planters, store container, glass jar, embossed peanut at each corner, peanut finial, 1920s, 14x8", NM, A ..**250.00**

Planters, store container, glass jar, painted-on Mr Peanut on 2 sides, tin lid, Canadian, 64-oz, A **100.00**

Planters, store container, glass jar, round with red-printed label, knob on lid, rare, A **160.00**

Planters, store container, glass jar, square with peanut finial, Planters at shoulder, A.................................**50.00**

Planters, store container, glass jar, 4-sided, painted-on Mr Peanut on 2 sides, tin lid, Canadian, 128-oz, A....**110.00**

Planters, store container, glass jar, 7 embossed sides & 1 with paper label, peanut finial lid, rim chips, octagon, 13x8", EX, A...**175.00**

Planters, store container, glass jar with embossed peanuts, figural lid, rim chips, 14x9", EX, A **200.00**

Planters, store container, glass jar with 7 embossed sides, knob on lid, minor chips, octagon, 13x8", NM, A**125.00**

Planters, tin, Mr Peanut & Pennant on pennant over Salted Peanuts, A...**55.00**

Planters House Coffee, tin, pictures factory with product name above & below, slip lid, round, VG, A.......**140.00**

Planters Peanut Butter, pail, press lid & bail, very elusive, 4x4", VG, A..**1,250.00**

Planters Salted Peanuts, sign, embossed tin, shows Mr Peanut with fingers made of peanuts, minor edge loss/dents/chips, rare, 10x24", G-, A....................**250.00**

Planters Salted Peanuts, tin, 2 red elongated diamonds lettered Clean & Crisp, Delicious, Golden-Meated, press lid, good color, 10-lb, VG, A **395.00**

Player's Cigarettes, sign, pictures 26 fish in rectangular insets on green background, John Player & Sons, framed, 24x12", EX, A **160.00**

Player's Navy Cut Tobacco, ash tray, ceramic, sailor encircled with lettering & rope border, ca 1940, 6" diameter, EX, D **23.00**

Pleasing Brooms, rack, tin sign on front, EX, D.......**195.00**

Plenamins Vitamins, sign, lighted, Plenamins lettered over Tops In Vitamins, Benjamin Moore & Co Paints & Varnishes below, EX, A.......................................**60.00**

Plexo Suspenders, trolley sign, cardboard, depicts 'Man of Action' bowling, Fifty Cents Everywhere, 21x11" without frame, VG+, A **100.00**

Plow Boy Tobacco, lunch pail, product name above & Smoking below, wire & wood bail, heavy wear, rare, rectangular, G, A **55.00**

Plow Boy Tobacco, pack, plow boy, VG, D **20.00**

Plow Boy Tobacco, pail, tin with paper label depicting plowboy by field, slip lid & bail, 5-lb, EX, A..........**30.00**

Plow Boy Tobacco, store bin, shows packaged product on 4 sides, bow front & hinged lid, 11x8x11", G, A..**1,350.00**

Plymouth Cigars, tip tray, bust-length portrait of pretty girl, lettered on rim, scratches/rust, 4" diameter, G-, A...**40.00**

Poker Tobacco, tin, embossed, chipping/dents, rare, 2x4x3", G+, A...**325.00**

Polarine, tin, For Motor Lubrication, Will Flow at Zero, touring car by lake, text on back, 1911-13, 1-gal, 11", G, A **425.00**

Polarine, tin, For Motor Lubrication, Will Flow at Zero, touring car by lake, text on back, 1911-13, 1-gal, 11", EX+, A..**2,000.00**

Polarine Friction Reducing Motor Oil, tin, touring car & thermometer centers winter & tropical scenes on cream, text on back, 1911-23, 5-gal, 15x9", VG, A...**475.00**

Polarine Motor Oil, tin, yellow with inset of early touring car on road, Standard Oil Co at bottom, ca 1898, half-gal, 6", EX+, A...**425.00**

Polarine Motor Oil, tin, 2-tone blue letters on yellow over scene with car, Standard Oil Co Ind, text on back, 1911-13, 5-gal, 15x9", G+, A **450.00**

Polarine Perfect Motor Oil, pump sign, porcelain, lettering on lg triangle, text on both sides, 1926-50, flaking, 7" diameter, A...**350.00**

Police Foot Powder, tin, pictures a police officer, ca 1910, rare, EX, A...**180.00**

Poll-Parrot Shoes, sign, die-cut cardboard with fabric, Poll-Parrot Shoes For Children flanked by parrot & children, framed, 13x20" EX, A **450.00**

Poll-Parrot Shoes, sign, little boy in checked outfit holding a parrot, Happy Shoes For Happy Feet lettered below, 21x13", EX, A...**45.00**

Poll-Parrot Solid Leather Shoes, watch fob, metal, celluloid center pictures a parrot, Star Brand Shoes Are Better in relief on reverse, 1920s, VG, D.....................**26.00**

Pollack's Crown Stogies, sign, cardboard, depicts canister full of cigars on its side, A Man's Smoke, framed, 25x16", EX, A...**30.00**

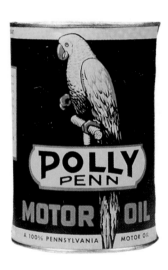

Polly Penn Motor Oil, tin, ca 1935-45, 1-qt, NM, A.**900.00**

Pont Brand Marshmallow Candy, tin, duel horse logo on blue background on original slip lid, Quebec Canada, some wear, 5x12" diameter, VG, A.....................**175.00**

Pontiac Authorized Service, sign, porcelain, 2-sided, silhouetted Indian logo in red, white, & blue, overall wear, 42" diameter, G-, A **115.00**

Pony Brand Sugar Butter, pail, depicts 2 ponies on hind legs, company name below, Canadian, press lid & bail, EX+, A...**360.00**

Pony Post Cigars, box label, inner lid, pony express rider with product name above, 6x9", M, D..................**18.00**

Pony Post Cigars, box label, inner lid, pictures horse & rider with stagecoach in background, 6x9", EX, D **16.00**

Popel-Giller Co, tip tray, pictures girl holding roses & sipping a beer, High Grade Bottle Beer, rim chips, 4" diameter, NM, A **125.00**

Popeye Bubble 'N Clean, box of powder bath bubbles, with contents, A..**15.00**

Poplar Bear Chewing & Smoking Tobacco, fan hanger, die-cut cardboard, 2-sided bear holding project lettering on chest, legs, feet, 14x12", EX, A **1,150.00**

Popper's Ace Cigars, tin, shows airborne biplane, 10¢, Made By E Popper & Co Inc NY, slip lid, good sheen, overall wear, 6x5" square, EX, A..........................**325.00**

Portage Cord Tires, sign, tin litho, for Portage Rubber Co of Akron Ohio, self-framed, 38x26", VG, A **550.00**

Portage Rubber Co, sign, tin, shows white Portage Cord tire rolling down country lane, ca early 1900s, framed, 26x38", EX, A...**750.00**

Portner's Brewing Co, tip tray, labeled bottle in center, Portner's Hofbrau, 5" diameter, NM, A **175.00**

Possom Cigars, tin, pictures an opossum flanked by logo, slip lid, some paint missing on lid, round, A **65.00**

Post Sugar Crisp, bear, original package, M, D **18.00**

Post Toasties, sign, cardboard, Post Toasties arched above sleeping girl & dog, Sweet Memories, 24x17", EX, A ..**200.00**

Post Toasties, sign, cardboard, product name in yellow on red atop little girl, cat, & product in front of fireplace, 41x31", EX, A..**1,500.00**

Post Toasties, sign, paper litho, pictures little girl & boy hugging, product name below, white background, framed, rectangular, EX, A **25.00**

Potosi Brewing Co, sign, tin, ca 1905-10, self-framed, 23x33", EX, A...**2,400.00**

Power-Lube Motor Oil, tin, ca 1915-25, 1-gal, 11", appears NM, A...**1,300.00**

Powow Brand Salted Peanuts, tin, headdressed Indian on bright green background, lettering above & below, press lid, overall wear, 10-lb, 10x8", G, A **500.00**

Powow Brand Salted Peanuts, tin, headdressed Indian on bright green background, lettering above & below, press lid, 10-lb, 10x8", EX, A **650.00**

Pozzoni's Medicated Complexion, sign, cardboard litho, lettering surrounded by encircled portraits & product, some dust staining, framed, 16x16", VG, A **175.00**

Prairie Flower Tobacco, pocket tin, flat, extremely rare, EX, A **1,000.00**

Prairie Queen Flour, thimble, aluminum, product name on worn blue band, D **3.00**

Pratts Poultry, sign, paper, rooster pulling a cart laden with hen & eggs, water stain on left side, framed, 16x20", VG, A **450.00**

Pratts Veterinary Remedies, cabinet, wood with embossed tin front picturing a horse & list of products, rubs/chips, 33x17", G-, A....................................**650.00**

Pratts Veterinary Remedies, cabinet, wood with embossed tin front picturing a horse & list of products, 33x17", EX, A...**950.00**

Pratts Veterinary Remedies, calendar, 1911, lady feeding apple to horse, full pad, matted, 16x10", NM, A ..**225.00**

Premier Beer, tray, still life with lobster & beer, overall wear to image/chipping/some overpaint drips, 10x13", G-, A **25.00**

Prestone Anti-Freeze, thermometer, porcelain, You're Safe...& You Know It in oval at bottom, 4-color, 1940s, 36x9", EX+, A **85.00**

Prichard's Health Salt, sign, embossed tin, For Headache Drink..., pictures man pointing upwards over illustration of product, 12x4", D **850.00**

Primley's California Fruit & Pepsin Chewing Gum, display case, wood & glass, gold lettering on curved glass front, 9x17", EX, A **700.00**

Primley's California Fruit Chewing Gum, sign, cardboard, bear holding gum pack while ogling beehive, Sweeter Than Honey, 1 of 2 known, framed, 27x19", VG, A **3,000.00**

Primley's Pepsin Sticks Chewing Gum, sign, embossed tin, ca 1890, 19x13", EX, A..........................**17,000.00**

Primus Motor Oil, tin, Primus above racetrack with 4 racers on black device over striped backdrop, 1925-45, 2-gal, 12x9", EX, A **900.00**

Prince Albert & Camel Cigarettes, sign, double-sided, flanged, Prince Albert pocket tin on 1 side, pack of Camels on the other, wear, 18x11", G-, A **225.00**

Prince Albert Tobacco, sign, pictures Indian referred to as Chief Joseph, framed, 31x25", NM, A 2,300.00

Prince Albert Tobacco, sign, tin, depicts 10¢ tin & 5¢ pouch with lettering, self-framed, 13x39", NM, A .**250.00**

Prince Maurice Cigars, box label, outer, pictures a man in royal attire, 5x5", M, D **6.00**

Prior Beer, button, celluloid, beer can flanked by Liquid Luxury, product name above & below, 9" diameter, EX, A **30.00**

Pro-phy-lac-tic Combs, display, tall slant-front with display of combs, EX, A **90.00**

Proctor & Gamble, alligator, Uncle Albert, EX, D **15.00**

Providence Salad Oil, tin, depicts various scenes with product name above, vertical with rounded corners & sm screw top, 10", EX, A **70.00**

Providence Washington Insurance Co, sign, framed, 27x21", EX, A 850.00

Prudential Life Insurance, needle threader, tin, 2x1", EX, D **15.00**

Prudential Life Insurance Co, thimble, plated brass, company name embossed on band, EX, D **8.00**

Prudential Life Insurance Co, trade card, pictures salesman at door, NM, D **8.00**

Prune Nugget Tobacco, sign, paper roll-down, girl surrounded by colorful fruit vines & flowers, Shrober Carqueville litho, 30x15", NM, A **425.00**

Puck Tobacco, tin, unusual hockey player motif, 25¢, original slip lid, slight fading/chips/dents, 4x3" diameter, G, A **125.00**

Pug 5¢ Cigar, figure, plaster, Attenberg & Bros on base, some paint chips, 16", A 700.00

Pulver Gum, vending machine, porcelain, white lettering on red, 20x9x5", G, A **450.00**

Pulver's Cocoa, tip tray, pictures product package with girl's portrait, lettering on rim, rust/chips, 4" diameter, VG, A **300.00**

Punch Cigars, tin, Punch medallion on front & back, round, 6", EX, A **80.00**

Punxy Special Beer, tray, shows swashbucklers in tavern scene at play & at sport, discoloration/whiting to image/rim chips, 12x17", G, A **25.00**

Pure As Gold Cup Grease, tin, product name in square & band on top half, Pep Boys shown at bottom, with contents, 1930-40, 5-lb, 5x7", VG+, A **60.00**

Pure As Gold Motor Oil, tin, white letters on red square at top, Pep Boys in lower right, back is dented, 1925-45, 2-gal, 11x9", EX+, A **200.00**

Pure Oils, tin, arrows flank round logo, cream letters on blue, ink stamp: Tiolene Heavy Motor Oil, ca 1920, 1-qt, 4", EX, A **450.00**

Pure Spices, cabinet, tin, 6 drawers with white porcelain knobs & gold lettering, ca 1890, 13x24x12", A...1,100.00

Pureoxia Ginger Ale, display, die-cut cardboard, elephant riding in a Rolls Royce, Frank Archer Invites You...Moxie-Land, rare, 28x38", VG, A **100.00**

Purex Bleach, monkey, white plush, original package, M, D **20.00**

Purina Rat Killer No 19, display, counter-top, dark blue cardboard, inset with 12 orange paper-covered tins, 16x12", G **25.00**

Puritan Cut Plug Tobacco, tin, pictures a sailboat, ca 1920, rectangular with rounded corners, EX, A......**80.00**

Puritan Motor Oil, sign, tin, policeman (hand is Stop sign) left of product name, Pure PA, yellow & black, 1930, minor edge wear, 11x35", A **325.00**

Purity Bread, display case, wood with etched glass front, Ask For Purity Bread & Rolls above, Goudy & Kent below, 35x28", EX, A **425.00**

Purity Ice Cream, tray, depicts a pair of kewpies & dish of ice cream, logo in upper left corner, minor flaking, square, EX, A..**130.00**

Purity Ice Cream, tray, depicts kewpie in blue hat straddling a ball bat enjoying ice cream, lettered rim, chips/scratches, 13x10", D **300.00**

Purple Ribbon Cigars, box label, inner lid, pictures a purple ribbon on yellow background & a plantation scene, 6x9", M, D **5.00**

Putnam Dyes, box, wood, depicts General Putnam on a horse, 10x21", VG, A 310.00

Putnam Dyes, cabinet, tin, pictures soldier on a horse, Each Package Dyes or Tints..., interior contains product, 15x19x8", G-, A **95.00**

Putnam Dyes, cabinet front, tin, pictures soldier on a horse, Each Package Dyes or Tints, Wool, Silk, Cotton..., 15x19", G, A **25.00**

Putnam Dyes, fan, cardboard litho, Gen Putnam & British Dragoons, corner crease, D **20.00**

Putnam Horse Shoe Nails, sign, paper, image of horse-drawn carriage, The Only Safe Nail To Drive, ca 1888, matted & framed, 26x33", G-, A **200.00**

Pyramid Automobile Brushes, display case, wood & glass pyramid shape with back door, sides & front decorated, 31x23x8", EX, A **375.00**

Pyrex, cookbook, 1953, 'Pyrex Prize Recipes,' 128 pages, D .**5.00**

❧ Q ❧

Q&Q Perfectos, calendar, 1910, elegant red-haired woman in a sheer blouse, Quinn Bros Makers, Troy NY, framed, 30x20", EX, A......................................**2,200.00**

Quadrigua Cloth/Ely Walker, thimble, plastic, red logo on cream background, EX, D **3.00**

Quaker Alcohol, tin, Rust-Proof Anti-Freeze in red letters partially contained in large Q, Completely Denatured, 1930, 1-gal, 9", VG+, A.......................................**50.00**

Quaker Bitters, sign, paper, early image of Quakers with product, heavily worn, rare, framed, 27x12", A **45.00**

Quaker Bread, trade card, pictures Santa in window & 2 children reading, NM, D **10.00**

Quaker City Motor Oil, tin, city skyline in navy on cream, 100% Pure PA lettered on orange, ca 1946-50, minor scratches/no top, 1-qt, VG+, A **70.00**

Quaker Maid Golden Table Syrup, tin, pictures maid in between 2-line product name, A............................**60.00**

Quaker Motor Oil, tin, large orange-banded green circle with Quaker man's portrait, ca 1915-25, 1-gal, 10", NM, A **475.00**

Quaker Oats, display, die-cut tin, classic Quaker Oats man in the form of a counter display, ca 1920-30, 25x20", EX, A **950.00**

Quaker Oats, doll, cloth, Crackels Boy, ca 1924-30, 17", G, D **190.00**

Quaker Oats, doll, cloth, Puffy, 1930, 16", G, D **190.00**

Quaker Quality Cigars, box label, inner lid, pictures a Quaker smoking a cigar, 6x9", M, D **7.00**

Quaker State Insured Lubrication, tray, porcelain, presented to HS Morris (company official) & so inscribed, 1920s, minor rim flaking, 12x14", A **55.00**

Quaker State Medium Heavy Oil, tin, black & cream Quaker State arched over oil can on green background, Certified & Guaranteed, 1915-25, 11x7", G+, A......**50.00**

Quaker State Medium Oil, tin, black & cream Quaker State arched over logo, black band top & bottom, ca 1915-25, 1-gal, 11x7", VG+, A 85.00

Quaker State Motor Oil, sign, 2-sided porcelain, 2 logos with Certified Guaranteed below, rounded top with square bottom, 1930s, 29x27", NM, A **220.00**

Quaker State Motor Oil, sign, 2-sided porcelain, 2 logos with Certified Guaranteed below, rounded top with square bottom, 1930s, 29x27", G, A **120.00**

Quaker State Racing Oil, sign, tin, white with green letters, checkered flag with logo on far left, 1967, spotting/edge wear, 5x26", VG, A **135.00**

Quandt's Beer & Ale, coaster, depicts Mercury on top of the world, Famous Beer & Ales lettered below, minor edge chips, 4" diameter, NM, A.................**25.00**

Queen Bee Chop Tea, store bin, tin, roll top with knob, shows bee with lettering above & below on front side, Thos Wood & Co, 21x20", F, A **185.00**

Queen Insurance Co, ledger marker, tin, Kellogg & Bulkeley litho, 12x3", EX, A..**150.00**

Queen of Virginia Tobacco, sign, paper litho, woman on a bench at the shore, WW Russell Mfg, Richmond Va, framed, 10x7", VG+, A **45.00**

Queen Quality Nuts, tin, round, A..........................**5.00**

Queen Quality Salted Peanuts, tin, logoed label with lettering, press lid, some scratching/wear, 10-lb, 10x8" diameter, VG, A **170.00**

Queen Quality Shoe Dressing, sign, embossed tin on cardboard, pictures product & red lettering on yellow background, creasing/edge wear, 9x13", VG, A **165.00**

Queen Quality Shoes, sign, reverse-painted glass, depicts queen in center oval flanked by Queen Quality, The Famous Shoe, 15x42", EX, A **150.00**

Queen-Cola, sign, embossed tin, Drink Queen-Cola at left of bottle (resembles Coca-Cola graphics), 10x25", appears VG, A **40.00**

Queen-Cola, sign, tin litho, bottle in center, Ask For Queen Cola, It's Different & Better, border stains, framed, 21", VG, A **100.00**

Quick Meal Steel Ranges, match holder, tin litho, pictures fowl on water within an oval, wear on match container, 5x3", G+, A **150.00**

Quincy Cigars, tin, shows view of Boston's Fauneuil Hall & Quincy Market, slip lid, slight lid wear/chips/spots, 5x5" diameter, EX, A **125.00**

～ R ～

R&G Licorice Lozenges, tin, glass front, patriotic logo above American Licorice Co on reverse, logo on decorative lid, rare, rectangular, A..............................**130.00**

R&T Whalen Tobacco, sign, tin litho, logoed tobacco leaf flanked with portraits of 2 gentlemen, Rochester NY, ca 1878-85, 20x14", F, A **275.00**

R-Pep, sign, die-cut tin, bottle figural, logo on red & yellow striped bands, ingredients on yellow band, ca 1930, 47", EX, A...**100.00**

Radio Coffee, tin, early radio with lg speaker horn, sm round lid, extremely rare, 3-lb, rectangular, approx: 9", G-, A..**175.00**

Railway Express Agency, sign, embossed tin, depicts train with figures loading rail car, For Fast Dependable Service, self-framed, 10x15", EX, A **250.00**

Rainier Beer, sign, tin, colorful image of girl resting head on growling bear, Seattle Brewing Co, rolled edge, ca 1913, 15x15", EX, A..........................**300.00**

Rainier Beer, tray, pictures Evelyn Nesbitt, decorative rim, 13" diameter, EX, A...............................**450.00**

Raleigh Cigarettes, holder, clear, EX, A **90.00**

Ralston Purina Co, ash tray, ceramic, shaped like dog's feeding bowl with the Ralston wagon graphic on white background, 6" diameter, D...................................**35.00**

Ralston Purina Co, doll, cloth body with vinyl head, Scarecrow, 23", G-, D **25.00**

Ramer's Chocolates, sign, tin, depicts several boxes of chocolates, A Package For Every Taste, strong colors, self-framed, 13x19", G, A **60.00**

Ramsay's Limited, tin, pictures a little Dutch girl with a box of chocolates, A **95.00**

Randolph Macon Cigars, sign, tin, woman offering cigar to man on red velvet-like background, brown border, EX, A.............................1,000.00

Rapid-Kool Milk Conditioner, sign, tin, product name in center, lettering above & below, 10x28", M, D **35.00**

Raser's Root Beer, sign, paper, girl on floor writing on slate, minor stains, ornate frame, on the bias: 25x25", EX, A **600.00**

Raspberry Charms, trolley sign, product & spilling basket of raspberries, Specially Tasty...Fruit Tablets, 1920, horizontal, EX, A...**180.00**

Ravenswood Table Water, tray, red & green, pictures a tree in center, Backed By The Red Raven People lettered on rim, round, A **10.00**

Rawleigh's Cold Tablets, tin, D **15.00**

RC Allen, cash drawer, salesman's sample, cast aluminum, D...**50.00**

RCA, bank, red plastic with embossed RCA tube logo on top, We Use RCA Tubes...in white, 4x5", M, D **40.00**

RCA, cast magnesium logo removed from the RCA building in Charlotte NC, depicts Little Nipper 40" tall, Victrola 40" long, A **3,000.00**

RCA, doll, Radiotrons wooden mascot, M, A.............**550.00**

RCA Television Tubes, sign, embossed tin, depicts round RCA logo with RCA Television Tubes lettered below, wood frame, 15x17", NM, D **60.00**

RCA Victor, figure, papier-mache, Nipper, 41", D..**1,350.00**

RCA Victor, post card, hold-to-light, 1907, D.............**10.00**

RCA Victor, puzzle, opera scene, record shape, dated 1908, D..**75.00**

RCA Victor Records, sign, composition board, 78 rpm record form with RCA label, 47" diameter, G, A .**110.00**

Reading Brewing Co, sign, tin litho, striking image of a turn-of-the-century factory in Reading Pa, framed, 28x40", EX, A..**3,500.00**

Real Silk Hosiery Mills, thimble, aluminum, company name & address on worn blue band, D.................**3.00**

Record Bond Cigars, box label, inner lid, pictures a hand full of currency, 6x9", M, D...................................**4.00**

Recruit Little Cigars, sign, cardboard litho, depicts young man in uniform holding box of cigars, framed, 15x20", EX, A **275.00**

Red Bell Fine Cut Tobacco, pail, depicts bell in circular inset with lettering above & below, slip lid, A **10.00**

Red Bloomers Cigars, box label, outer, pictures a red rose on wood grain background, 5x5", M, D **4.00**

Red Cap Cigars, box label, outer, depicts lady in red, 5x5", VG, D **12.00**

Red Cough Drops, tin, pictures eagle atop product name, Bone Eagle & Co below, sm wire handle on screw lid, rectangular, EX, A **150.00**

Red Crest Tobacco, lunch box, fiberboard, pictures a rooster & silver lettering, 4x8x5", EX, A **35.00**

Red Cross Cigars, sign, reverse-painted glass, restored, framed, 22x28", A **200.00**

Red Cross Coffee, tin, Red Cross arched above circular cross logo, 1-lb, vertical rectangle, EX, A **100.00**

Red Cross Stoves & Ranges, trade card, depicts cavalry at battle, J Ottmann litho, 7x6", EX, A **10.00**

Red Dot Cigars, tin, shows woman's face on red dot with product name above, slip lid, slight scratches/edge wear, 6x5" square, VG, A **50.00**

Red Feather Coffee, tin, product name, lg feather in center, NM, A...**65.00**

Red Feather Peanut Butter, pail, tin, logo over Red Feather image, original slip lid & bail, Imperial Cocoa & Spice Co, Canada, 1-lb, 4x4", VG, A **500.00**

Red Goose Shoes, bank, tin, green with paper label, old, round, EX, D...**125.00**

Red Goose Shoes, clicker, yellow with Red Goose logo, 1950s, M, D...**12.00**

Red Goose Shoes, display, goose figural, lg, NM, A .**290.00**

Red Goose Shoes, helmet, child's, cloth hat with straps, D...**45.00**

Red Goose Shoes, pencil box, wood with sliding top, old, 2x9", EX, D **85.00**

Red Goose Shoes, shoe horn, metal, D **12.00**

Red Goose Shoes, sign, die-cut, boy holding goose by the neck, ca 1910, EX, D...**275.00**

Red Goose Shoes, string holder, hanging, die-cut tin, product name in white on goose figural, 29" including old string ball, A...**1,050.00**

Red Goose Shoes, thimble, aluminum, product name on worn red band, D **3.00**

Red Goose Shoes, thimble, plastic, red logo on cream, EX, D...**3.00**

Red Hat Motor Oil, tin, 1926-30, 1-gal, 11", NM, A **1,200.00**

Red Hawk Cigars, box label, inner lid, depicts Indian in headdress with weapon & shield, product name above, 1902, 6x9", M, D **60.00**

Red Horse Powder, ledger marker, tin litho, red & brown with gray lettering, Cyrus Brown, Druggist, Milton Pa, ca 1800s, 12x3", G, A **160.00**

Red Indian Cut Plug Tobacco, display box, cardboard, Indian logo with product name above & below, minor cracks/chips, rare, 5-lb, 14x8x6", VG+, A **550.00**

Red Indian Cut Plug Tobacco, lunch box, tin, wire handle & latch, rare, 5x8x5", VG+, A **1,400.00**

Red Indian Cut Plug Tobacco, poster, paper, Indian pointing bow & arrow at tobacco tin, 5 cts, Must Have It lettered below, framed, 28x22", EX, A **900.00**

Red Indian Cut Plug Tobacco, tin, black & gold Indian logo on blue background, American Tobacco Co, embossed slip lid, 7x5" diameter, EX, A.................**425.00**

Red Indian Cut Plug Tobacco, tin, black & gold Indian logo on blue background, American Tobacco Co below, embossed slip lid, 7x5" diameter, G, A ...**300.00**

Red Jacket Mild Smoking Tobacco, sign, depicts baseball scene, It's A Hit... lettered above, Tin 10¢ below, 31x24", EX, A...**70.00**

Red Keg, dispenser, red barrel with green bands & red lettering, slight discoloration/minor scratches, 15x8", VG, A...**2,000.00**

Red Man Chewing Tobacco, sign, tin, head of Indian at left of Red Man Chewing Tobacco, America's Best Chew above, horizontal rectangle, EX, A **100.00**

Red Man Cigars, sign, paper litho, woman in white, framed, 10x6", VG+, A **40.00**

Red Man Cigars, sign, paper litho, woman in yellow, framed, 10x6", VG+, A **40.00**

Red Man Tobacco, store display, cardboard, pictures Indian in headdress, Made From Good Cigar Leaf, holds 36 packages, EX, A **185.00**

Red Raven, tip tray, red bird with glass & labeled bottle, white background, vertical rectangle, EX, A..........**80.00**

Red Raven, tray, rolled rim, depicts raven next to glass & bottle of tonic, For Headache, For Indigestion, square, NM, D..................................**275.00**

Red Raven Aperients, tray, pictures nude little girl with product & raven, logo & lettering on border, Ask The Man, round, EX, A **130.00**

Red Ribbon Beer, tray, pictures lake & woods with bear getting into a case of Red Ribbon, rounded corners, scratches, 13x13", G, A **300.00**

Red Rock Cola, thermometer, metal with 3-color paint, 1939, edge chips, 27x7", A...............................50.00

Red Rose Coffee, sign, tin, pictures a tin labeled Esterbrook's Red Rose Coffee with a rose in center, 16x18", M, D **160.00**

Red Rose Feeds, pocket knife, 3 blades (pen, clip, & spray), 3" long, VG, D 23.00

Red Rose Tea, door plate, It's Good Tea on the diagonal, Red Rose Tea above, decorative die-cut ends, 9x3", NM, A **165.00**

Red Seal Brand Peanut Butter, pail, black & silver lettering & graphics on yellow background, press lid & bail, 1-lb, EX, A...............................**10.00**

Red Seal Dry Battery, sign, tin, automobile driver in goggles holding 2 batteries, The Guarantee Protects You, self-framed, 19x27", G, A.....................**160.00**

Red Seal Lye, pocket mirror, tin litho, EX, D **45.00**

Red Seal Peanut Butter, pail, tin, depicts children's nursery rhymes, slip lid & bail, G, A **50.00**

Red Top Motor Oil, tin, Take A Spin With lettered above a red top & touring car, Topp Oil & Supply Co below, 1917, half-gal, 6", VG+, A **300.00**

Red Turkey Brand Coffee, tin, press lid, 1-lb, EX, A **65.00**

Red Wolf Coffee, tin, namesake on label, Ridenour-Baker Grocery Co, Kansas City Mo, slip lid & bail, rare, 6-lb, 9x8" diameter, G, A **500.00**

Reddy Kilowatt, display figure, wood kilowatt man in red & white with light-up nose & ears, stands on gray box, 1940s, 25x10", EX, A 450.00

Reddy Kilowatt, stickpin, D **15.00**

Reddy Kilowatt, tie clasp, red enamel on metal, D **25.00**

Redford's Navy Cut Tobacco, sign, paper, sailor climbing flag pole in red, white, & blue, paper chipping to edge/overall wear, 30x20", G, A..............................**75.00**

Redicut Tobacco, lunch box, tin, shows hands holding product, Just Break Off A Piece To Fit, flat lid, wire handle, 7x8x4", G+, A **125.00**

Reed & Finberg Clothing, sign, painted wood, bowed boards above & below, straight board across middle, lettering on all 3 boards, 94" long, G, A **525.00**

Reed's Tonic, clock, wood with reverse-painted glass, pendulum & key, 24x10", EX, A **850.00**

Reed's Tonic, clock, wood with reverse-painted glass, Reeds Tonic Cures Malaria..., ornate grahics, pendulum & key, 24x10", NM, A **1,300.00**

Reel Man Talcum Powder, tin, depicts trout fisherman in stream, minor chipping mostly on raised rim & top, 5x3x1", EX+, A..................................**175.00**

Regal Cube Cut Smoking Tobacco, pocket tin, red, white, & blue logo, worn, A...............................**160.00**

Regal Cube Cut Smoking Tobacco, pocket tin, unique rolled cover & image of 2 lions, minor chipping/wear, rare, 4x4", VG, A **125.00**

Rehetti Tabs, sign, 1920, framed, 11x21", EX, A ..200.00

Reinken's Havana Cigars, sign, tin, profile of girl with roses in her hair, repainted border/rust hazing/general wear, 14" diameter, G-, A 40.00

Reis Union Suits, sign, depicts tiny man shouting 'Passengers On This Car Will Please Change To...,' logo below, framed, 12x21", EX, A 80.00

Remington, calendar top, 2 hunters with dogs on town street, Fire Arms, Loaded Shells...below, edge tears/creases, 22x15", A 220.00

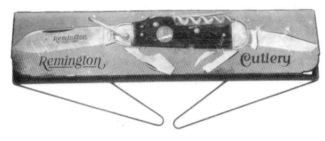

Remington Cutlery, display, tin stand-up, scuffing/paint loss, 8x32", G, A 350.00

Remington Kleanbore, banner, canvas, big game hunter shooting attacking lion flanked by lettering, Come On In & Shoot above, 50x56", G, A 70.00

Remington Kleanbore, sign, die-cut, comical image of game animals with product, Horrible News! lettered below, 17x30", NM, A 375.00

Remington Kleanbore, sign, die-cut cardboard, pictures boy aiming rifle, 32x25", EX, A 120.00

Remington Kleanbore, sign, die-cut cardboard, pictures 3 boys with rifle & target, product & game below, 20x13", EX, A 80.00

Remington Typewriters, mirror, pictures typewriter, To Save Time Is To Lengthen Life, Parisian Novelty Co, Chicago, 4" diameter, D 65.00

Remington-UMC, guide, Recommended Game & Trap Loads, pictures various fowl with formula amounts for correct shot, framed, 26x20", VG, A..........................100.00

Remington-UMC, poster, depicts pointer on blue snow with a case of Remington Nitro Club Shells, black oak frame, 24x30", NM, D 225.00

Remington-UMC, poster, paper, 'In A Tight Place,' pictures kneeling hunter aiming at bear, bottom metal strip missing, 24x16", EX, A 250.00

Remington-UMC, poster, paper with metal bands, shows man being greeted by his dogs, ...Metallic Cartridge Co below, creases, 25x17", A 350.00

Remington-UMC, sign, depicts father & son rabbit hunting, Arrow, Nitro Club, & Wetproof Shot Shells lettered below, 23x15", VG, A..........................250.00

Remington-UMC, sign, die-cut cardboard stand-up, framed, 20x14", EX, A 375.00

Remington-UMC, sign, paper, old hunter seated on stoop cleaning shot gun with products & decoys around him, framed, 24x18", VG, A..........................65.00

Remington-UMC, sign, paper roll-down, dog with hunter aiming rifle at birds in flight, 26x18", NM, A 500.00

Remington-UMC, sign, paper roll-down, 2 dogs with hunter carrying a rifle, 26x18", NM, A 450.00

Remington-UMC, sign, paper roll-down, 2 hunters on a mountain top, 26x18", NM, A 550.00

Renown Motor Oil, tin, cream with Renown lettered diagonally in green & blue, Standard Oil Co, 1925-45, 2-gal, 11x7", VG+, A 75.00

REO Tobacco, tin, lettered logo encircled by belt, Best Virginia Leaf Smoking Mixture, overall wear, 5x4x2", G+, A..........................60.00

Repeater Fine Cut Tobacco, pocket tin, pictures man on a horse, Mild Smoking Tobacco, rounded corners, 3x4", EX, A 35.00

Revelation Smoking Mixture, tin, D 10.00

Rex Flintkote Roofing, match holder, tin litho, colorful barn, lettering on box, faded, 5x3", VG+, A.........350.00

Reynolds Wrap, pamphlet, 'Casual Cooking,' blue cover, 15 pages, 1954, G, D 5.00

Reynolds Wrap, pamphlet, 'New Holiday Know-How For Use With Reynolds Wrap,' 16 pages, Ackme Markets, 1957, EX, D 6.00

Reynolds Wrap, pamphlet, 'Preparing Foods With Reynolds Wrap Pure Aluminum Foil,' peach & blue cover, 34 pages, 1950s, G+, D 5.00

Reynolds Wrap, pamphlet, 'The Way Mama Cooked It,' all black, 31 pages, 1981, VG, D 4.00

Reynolds Wrap, pamphlet, 'Vacation How-to With America's No 1 Traveler' (no cooking), 16 pages, 1955, EX, D..........................3.00

RG Sullivan's 7-20-4 Cigars, sign, porcelain, red, white, & yellow on black, RG Sullivan's on curved banner over lg 7-20-4, Cigar below, 11x23", M, A..........................70.00

Rheingold Beer, tray, 2 German gents toasting, Prosit, oval inset with decorative border, ca 1912, overall wear, 13x11", G, A...**40.00**

Rheingold Extra Dry, Shea stadium seating plan, Sponsor Of The World Champions, featuring Mets World Champions, self-standing, EX, A...........................**140.00**

Rheingold Extra Dry, sign, red & blue neon logo, no transformer, A...**100.00**

Rice Seed Co, calendar, 1906, cardboard litho, pictures little girl with orchid border, December pad, framed, 18x12", VG, A..**40.00**

Rice's Pan-Dandy Bread, box, wood with tin sign on front & lid, G, A..**250.00**

Richardson Root Beer, dispenser, wood barrel with chrome straps & legs, metal lined, logoed, knob on lid, 1940-60, 20x13" diameter, EX, A...................**150.00**

Richardson's Wash Silks, spool cabinet, wood with glass front, 36x24x12", EX, A................................**650.00**

Richlube Motor Oil, tin, yellow & cream product name on dark blue, early racing car with 2 passengers over logo, 1915-25, half-gal, NM, A...............................**850.00**

Richmond Straight Cut Cigarettes, charger, tin, pictures man lighting cigarette, spotting/scratches/edge wear, 19" diameter, G, A.....................................**170.00**

Richmond Straight Cut Cigarettes, sign, pictures an elegant woman & an open package of cigarettes, ca 1910, rectangular, EX, A.......................................**270.00**

Ricksecker's Sweet Clover Cologne, dispenser, end-of-the-day glass bottle with 2 applied handles, original stopper, 9", EX, D...**110.00**

Ridlingtons Black Pear Scotch Whiskey, match holder & ash tray, porcelain, pictures a pear & blue lettering on both sides, 4x5", EX+, A...............................**120.00**

Right-Cut Chewing Tobacco, dispenser, tin, pictures man in oval at top, The Good Judge Recommends... lettered below, scratches/rust, 11", G, A.......................**50.00**

Rigor & Gretz Brewing Co, calender top, paper, lady in plumed hat, stole, & muff, company seal in upper left corner, wear, approx: 23x17", G-, A.................**100.00**

Riley's Bunny-Bons, tin, depicts rabbit scenes on all sides, slip lid, some wear, rectangular, A.................**130.00**

Ringer & Co Brewery, see Geo Ringer & Co

Rip Van Winkle Cigars, box label, outer, man with trees & mountains in the background, 5x5", M, D.........**10.00**

Rising Sun Brewing Co, tray, deep-dish, girl in gown seated on crescent moon holding a Seeber Special beer, 12" diameter, VG, A....................................**200.00**

Rising Sun Stove Polish, sign, paper litho, colorful image of a woman atop factory view, For Brilliancy, Durability..., framed, 28x18", EX, A........................**1,200.00**

Rising Sun Stove Polish, sign, paper roll-down, elegant woman leaning on banister, A Thing Of Beauty Is A Joy Forever above, 1880s, 29x13", EX, A..................**650.00**

Ritz Crackers, sign, cardboard, red logo atop yellow Ritz in blue circle, Baked By National Biscuit..., red lettering, 1940, 26x13", A...............................**60.00**

Ritz Crackers, sign, die-cut, full-color image, framed, EX, A...**55.00**

Rival, cookbook, 1975, 'Rival Crock-Pot Cooking,' 208 pages, D...**7.00**

Rival Dog Food, clock, wood frame, red, blue, & black on white, Time To Buy Rival Dog Food encircled by numbers, square, EX, A......................................**90.00**

Rival Twist Chewing Tobacco, tin, red & black on yellow background, The Best Chew, square with rounded corners & slip lid, EX, A..................................**35.00**

Road Boss Motor Oil, tin, pictures tractor in field, truck, & car in shades of green on cream, 1925-45, 2-gal, 12x9", EX, A...**100.00**

Road Runner Motor Oil, can, waxed cardboard, road runner in white circle on yellow, 100% Virgin..., Arnold Distributing, 1975-85, 1-qt, NM, A...................**25.00**

Robert Burns Cigars, charger, tin, Robert Burns & cigar box on plaid background, Beach Art Display, scuffing to letters, 24" diameter, G, A.........................**275.00**

Robert Burns Cigars, sign, pictures man in yellow vest & blue jacket on plaid background, 1905, crazed/sm holes, rare, 24" diameter, A.........................**375.00**

Robert Fulton Cigars, tin, depicts circular portrait surrounded by flowers, slip lid, good sheen, overall wear, 6x6x4", VG, A..**155.00**

Robert H Graupner's Brewery, tray, deep-dish, factory & street scene, Export, Elfenweiss, Porter, & Ale, rust spots/chipping, 12" diameter, VG, A.................**400.00**

Robert Smith's Misty Ale, cup, ceramic, 4", EX, D ...**25.00**

Robin Hood Flour, statue, 1930s, M, D **20.00**

Robinson Crusoe Glue, trolley sign, cardboard litho, pictures man getting ready to make glue, Gloucester Mass, framed, 11x21", VG+, A.................................**155.00**

Robinson Crusoe Peanuts, tin, depicts Crusoe on the beach, minor denting/scratches/chipping, press lid, 10-lb, 10x8" diameter, VG, A..........................**400.00**

Robinson Crusoe Peanuts, tin, depicts Crusoe with a dog surrounded by peanuts, HA Robinson Co Inc, general wear, 10-lb, 10x8" diameter, G, A **400.00**

Robinson's Sons, see E Robinson's Sons

Rocco Bros & Co, trade card, pictures 2 robins in winter scene, Genuine California Wines..., advertising & price list on reverse, 4x6", D......................................**8.00**

Rochelle Club Beverages, sign, embossed tin, depicts soda bottle, Decidedly Better, Westchester Bottling Works..., 12x24", EX, A **80.00**

Rochester Brewery, sign, paper, depicts 2 classical women with beer hall scene below, ca 1890, framed, 32x22", NM, A **1,500.00**

Rock Spring Brewery, calendar, 1898, girl standing on chair talking on 3-box wall phone, full pad, matted & framed, 14x20", VG, A **900.00**

Rocket Motor Oil, tin, Rocket lettered over red & blue rocket, red background, Motor Oil on blue palette, 1925-45, 2-gal, 12x9", EX+, A..........................**65.00**

Rockford Oats, bowl, ironstone, Staffordshire, 6" diameter, VG, D **50.00**

Rockford Watches, match holder, tin litho, colorful image of hand holding stop watch, The Standard of Time, rare, 5x3", G+, A **525.00**

Rockford Watches, tip tray, die-cut, pictures girl sitting in front of a tree, product name above, decorative border, rectangular, EX, A......................................**40.00**

Rocky Fork Whiskey, sign, reverse-painted glass, lettered, flaking/fading, wood frame, 28" long, A **175.00**

Roderick Lean Mfg Co Farm Implements, poster, paper, horse & oxen-drawn harrows working in the blazing sun, holes/wrinkles, framed, 32x27", G, A **300.00**

Roessle Brewery, sign, 3 vignettes of factory views surrounded by hops motif, Brewers & Bottlers Of Premium Lager Beer..., 20x28", EX, A **700.00**

Roly Poly, see Mayo's Tobacco

Romance Chocolates, sign, paper on linen, Norman Rockwell, 40x20", EX, A 1,400.00

Root Bros, catalog, '7th Edition Price List Of Tools & Material...,' 24 pages illustrated in black & white, Ohio, 1893, VG, D **25.00**

Rose Leaf Tobacco, dispenser, tin litho with glass top, lettering on side, 9" diameter, EX, D......................**30.00**

Rose Valley Whiskey, glass, highball, product name etched on 2 lines in lg letters over Highball & Is Good, Louisville Ky brand, 4", EX, D......................**15.00**

Rosebud Tobacco, sign, cardboard, men on dock watching sailing schooners, package of tobacco in foreground, framed, 21x35", VG+, A......................**60.00**

Round Oak Stoves, Ranges & Furnaces, sign, die-cut Indian (Doe-Wah-Jack), rare, framed, NM, A.......**275.00**

Round Trip Smoking Tobacco, lunch pail, encircled cruise ship flanked by Cut Plug, product name above & below, no handle, worn, rectangular, A..............**240.00**

Round Up Cigars, box label, inner lid, pictures a cowboy at campfire, watermark in corner, 6x9", EX, D.........**5.00**

Royal Baking Powder, sign & display book, paper on posterboard, shows product, book, & gingerbread man, Beautiful Fairy Book..., 30x20", M, A **30.00**

Royal Crown Cola, sign, tin, depicts bottle, D............**75.00**

Royal Crown Cola, thermometer, tin, thermometer bulb on arrow pointing up, product name above, Best By Taste Test below, 26x10", EX+, D **60.00**

Royal Crown Pomade, tin, D..................................**13.00**

Royal Dutch Coffee, tin, logoed, slip lid, circular, appears EX, A **40.00**

Royal Lancer Cigars, playing cards, ads on aces, pinochle, 48 cards, original box, VG, D **25.00**

Royal Navy Tobacco, tin, pictures smiling pipe-smoking sailor, Cut Plug Smoking Tobacco, Canada, general wear, 5x4x3", VG+, A..........................**45.00**

Royal Palm Selyzer, siphon bottle, glass with tube, nozzle, & valve, trademark label with palm tree, marked top, Terre Haute Ind, D **130.00**

Royal Purple Grape Juice, tray, pretty lady facing right, Nature's Best Drink in gold around perimeter, American Art Works, 1890-1920, 13", VG **80.00**

Royal Stoves, tip tray, picturing Royal kitchen range, embossed bent rim, Westman Bros, Canada, unusual piece, 4x3", G, A **75.00**

Royal Violet Borated Talcum Powder, tin, pictures pretty lady flanked by floral decor, ca 1925, EX+, A......**110.00**

Royce's Improved Talcum Powder, tin, yellow, pictures a baby with product name above & below, slip lid, round, EX, A..**150.00**

Rubsam & Horrmann Bottled Beers, tray, pictures a semi-nude woman in floral scene, rare, EX, A..................**550.00**

Rubsam & Horrmann Brewing Co, tip tray, pictures girl in center, product name above, Stapleton, SI, NY below, edge chips, rare, 4" diameter, EX, A.........**125.00**

Rubsam & Horrmann Brewing Co, tip tray, semi-nude woman, Bottled At The Brewery, A Temperate Drink above & below, 4" diameter, NM, A **400.00**

Ruckles Cocoa, sign, tin, girl with tray standing on right, cocoa can in corner, For Over 30 Yrs..., vertical rectangle, EX, A **525.00**

Rudolph Valentino Cigars, box label, outer, pictures actor beside product name & signature, 3x5", M, D.**3.00**

Ruhstaller Lager Beer, tip tray, serving girl with steins of Gilt Edge beer, Best Beer Brewed... lettered above & below, 4" diameter, NM, A **175.00**

Rumford Baking Powder, spatula, D..........................**10.00**

Rumsey's & Co Ltd, sign, paper, 18x25", VG+, A .**1,400.00**

Runkel Brothers Breakfast Cocoa, sign, paper, family seated in a landscape having cocoa, New York & Chicago lettered above, framed, 24x18", EX, A **1,300.00**

Runkel Brothers Breakfast Cocoa, sign, tin, 19x14", NM, A...**3,100.00**

Runkel Brothers Chocolate, tin, Essence Of lettered above soda locker, product name above & below, screw top, 5-lb, 10", VG, A **125.00**

Runkel Brothers Cocoa & Chocolate, sign, tin, titled 'Drinking Cocoa At The Court Of Louis XV,' ca 1904, self-framed, 29x22", EX, A **950.00**

Ruppert Beer & Ale, sign, reverse-painted glass, product name in silver on black, beaded trim, 1920s, oval, framed, NM, A **125.00**

Ruppert Beer & Ale, sign, reverse-painted glass, product name in silver on black, beaded trim, 1920s, oval, framed, VG, A...**40.00**

Ruscher & Co Lager Beer, calendar, 1899, striking girl with flowers, incomplete pad, framed with metal strips, NM, A **950.00**

Russ Bros Velvet Ice Cream, tray, mother & son having dish of ice cream, decorative rim, round, EX, A ..**400.00**

Russell & Clark Spool Cotton, spool cabinet, wood, 3 lg drawers over 6 side by side sm labeled drawers, original condition, 19x22", EX, A **1,000.00**

Russell Emulsion, sign, ca 1920, framed, 12x22", appears EX, A **55.00**

Russell's Exquisite Mixture Tobacco, tin, girl pictured in inset on lid, lettering, square edges, early Hasker & Marcuse tin, chips/denting, 2x5x3", G-, A.........**1,000.00**

Russels' Ales, sign, tin, 2 men unloading barrels, The Beer From The Country, yellow background, overall wear, self-framed, 29x21", A **70.00**

Russolene Brand Motor Oil, tin, red-banded cream background, Russolene Brand superimposed on red diamond, ca 1915-25, 1-gal, EX+, A **110.00**

Rutland Roof Coating, pail, tin, 2 encircled images of men using product, press lid & bail, ca 1940, EX, A **70.00**

Ryan's, see also Thomas Ryan

Ryan's Ale & Lager, tray, pictures a standing bulldog, product name above, Our Products Guaranteed below, 13" square, EX, A **300.00**

Ryan's Lager & Sparkling Ales, tray, pictures bouquet of daisies, A Liquid Bread lettered above, product name on decorative rim, 13" diameter, NM, A **350.00**

Ryan's Lager & Sparkling Ales, tray, 13" diameter, appears EX, A **500.00**

Ryan's Pure Beers, sign, paper, circular Indian logo above hand pouring glass of beer, lettering below, matted & framed, 11x8", EX, A **65.00**

Ryan's Pure Beers, tip tray, pictures a long-haired girl, lettering on rim above & below, ca 1907, 4" diameter, NM, A **100.00**

S

S&H Green Stamps, tip tray, blonde-haired girl in profile with 8 stamps & lettering on rim, crazed/stains, 4" diameter, G, A **30.00**

S&H Green Stamps, tip tray, dark-haired girl in profile with 4 stamps & lettering on rim, crazing to colors, 4" diameter, EX, A......................................**75.00**

Safe Hit, fruit crate label, framed, A.......................**15.00**

Sailor's Pride Cut Plug Tobacco, tin, encircled stalk of tobacco leaves & Sailor's Pride trademark, slip lid on bottle-shaped neck, 6x5" diameter, G-, A **350.00**

Saiz De Carlos Elixir, sign, tin, shows mustached man at table drinking Elixir, decorative border, thin frame & hanger, 20", VG, A **300.00**

Salada Tea, door push, porcelain, D **250.00**

Salada Tea, sign, die-cut porcelain, bright red lettering, 5x12", M, A **130.00**

Salmon's Tea, tin, pictures a fish, 1x3", G, A.............**95.00**

Sambo Axle Grease, tin, child in center circle on checkered background, Nourse Oil Co, 1930s, 3-lb, 5x5", EX, A......................................**135.00**

Sambo Axle Grease, tin, child in center circle on checkered background, Nourse Oil Co, ca 1930s, 3-lb, 5x5", G, A **55.00**

Sambo's Restaurant, coaster, Bicentennial, EX, D **3.00**

Sambo's Restaurant, doll, cloth, Dakin, EX, D...........**15.00**

Samoset Chocolate, plaster relief, Samoset Indian in a canoe in 3-D, Boston Sculpture Co, 26x19", G, A **70.00**

Samsonite Finishes, demonstrator case, stripes of the colors that could be ordered including New Alligator Finish, some wear, rectangular, A **175.00**

San Felice Cigars, sign, tin, depicts man at desk enjoying cigar, The Cigar Of Unchanging Quality, scratches, self-framed, 13" long, G, A **160.00**

San Marco Selected Long Filler Tobacco, tin, EX, D ..**18.00**

San Miguel Beer, miniature can, empty, missing label, D **2.00**

San Miguel Beer, miniature can, full, label torn, D.......**5.00**

Sanders & Co, sign, paper, for Glycerin & Rice for Complexion, bust portrait of a young girl, water stains, framed, 18x24", G-, A **45.00**

Sandwich Mfg Co, poster, paper, various equipment in 3 registers, lettering above & below, matted & framed, 35x30", G-, A **95.00**

Sandwich Mfg Co, sign, paper, features the Hay Press, & the New Way Large Bail, lettering above & below, matted & framed, 23x29", G, A **125.00**

Sanford's Inks & Adhesives, display, 3-piece die-cut tin litho, center: 20x13", hands: 8x4", EX, A ..12,000.00

Sanford's Inks & Mucilage, sign, hanging, embossed tin litho, pictures an assortment of products, creases/surface loss on edges/face, 14x20", G-, A **950.00**

Sanford's Inks & Mucilage, sign, hanging, embossed tin litho, pictures an assortment of products, light rust on edges/inks, 14x20", G, A **1,075.00**

Sanilac Cattle Spray, thermometer, wood, black & white cows in pasture, 1930s, minor scuffs, 19x9", A **400.00**

Sanitol Talc, tin, G, D......................................**12.00**

Sapolin Aluminum Enamel, sign, tin litho with hanging chain, pictures woman ready to use product beside lettering, early, rare, 10x13", G+, A......................................**325.00**

Sapolin Enamels, Guildings & Stains, shadow box sign, wood & glass, gnomes painting a rainbow from biplane, ca 1911, rare, 19x20", EX, A................**1,025.00**

Sapolin Stove Pipe Enamel, sign, tin, product & stove images with 3-dimensional additions to stove top & furnace boiler, some wear, 25x18", G, A...................**325.00**

Sarony Cigarettes, roulette game, tin, portrait of handsome man, spinner missing, A................................**20.00**

Satin Cigarettes, charger, tin, shows girl in wide-brimmed hat with cigarette pack, 20 For 15 cts, lettering on border, 19" diameter, G, A **350.00**

Sauer's Flavoring Extracts, clock, red, green, & black reverse-painted tablet in gilt, round clock face, 43x15", EX, A **700.00**

Sauer's Flavoring Extracts, display cabinet, oak with glass front, lettering etched in gold, green, & red, eagle atop, 20x15x10", EX, A **1,000.00**

Savage Arms, poster, 'First in the Field,' Hy Hintermeister, EX, A **90.00**

Savoy Coffee, tin, cream background with red & royal coat-of-arms label, press lid, square, 9", VG, D **42.00**

Sayman Salve, sample tin, 1" diameter, NM, D **12.00**

Scandinavian American Line, sign, tin litho, pictures a steamship at full sail, self-framed, EX, A **800.00**

Scarless Gall Remedy, tin, pictures team of horses pulling a plow, D..**10.00**

Schepp's Coconut, tin, red, depicts monkey with lettering, sm slip lid, vertical rectangle graduates to larger top, 6", F, A...**70.00**

Schlitz Beer, blotter, pictures woman holding Pilsener glass, G, D...**4.00**

Schlitz Beer, poster, colorful image of the brewery, framed, 24x36", VG+, A **1,300.00**

Schlitz Beer, poster, paper litho, EX, A **1,175.00**

Schlitz Beer, sign, glass in brass back-lit frame, 15x22", EX, A...**150.00**

Schlitz Beer, sign, yellow & white neon logo, no transformer, A..**15.00**

Schlitz Beer, tip tray, Drink Schlitz Beer, Jos Gahm & Son in center, The Beer That Made Milwaukee... on rim, 4" diameter, EX, A...**55.00**

Schlitz Beer, tip tray, logo & lettering in center, Jacob Schreiber & Son... on rim above & below, chips, 4" diameter, EX, A...**55.00**

Schlitz Beer, tray, 5 images surrounding logo, logoed rim, round, EX, A...**10.00**

Schmidt's Meats, ash tray, oval, D **7.00**

Schober's Beer, tip tray, girl with dove in subtle colors, Export Beer In Bottles, San Antonio..., decorative rim, 5" diameter, NM, A..**200.00**

Schrade Cutlery Companies, display case, oak with slanted etched glass front, Warrented Pocket Knives..., 11x23", VG, A..**160.00**

Schrader Balloon Tire Gauge, can, red with black top, Test Your Tires Every Friday..., hinged door opens for gauge storage, 1920-30, 20x7", VG, A..............**160.00**

Schrader Tire Guages, display cabinet, tin litho, figural, original paper inserts, catalog & valve parts, 15", EX, A..**425.00**

Schrafft's Chocolate, candy dish, wheel-cut floral, product name etched in base, 4x7" diameter, M, A............**60.00**

Schrafft's Chocolate, pail, depicts 'The Old Woman Who Lived in the Shoe' nursery rhyme, press lid & bail, 4x4", container EX, lid G-, A..**320.00**

Schrafft's Chocolate, sign, canvas, depicts bust portrait of the Chocolate Girl, puncture in lower left/chips, framed, 29x23", G-, A..**115.00**

Schrafft's Chocolate, sign, cardboard, little girl eating chocolate while little boy & puppy watch, lettering below, arched top, 19x12", EX, A **60.00**

Schrafft's Chocolate, sign, paper, pictures Schrafft's Chocolate girl seated in a landscape, tears/creases/soiling, framed, 32x23", G-, A...................................**50.00**

Schultz Beer & Ale, tip tray, lettered logo in center, Union City NJ, rare, minor chips, 4" diameter, EX, A........**60.00**

Schuster Stores, toy, wooden car cut-out with Merry Christmas on side, ca 1940, EX, A.....................**20.00**

Schweppes Ginger Ale, push bar, porcelain, black, gold, & white on green, Ask For Schweppes Dry Ginger Ale, 3x30", EX+, D **55.00**

Scissors Cut Plug Mild Tobacco, tin, NM, A **2,550.00**

Score Card Tobacco, tin, depicts score card including Ty Cobb, Honus Wagner, & others, A Big Hit below, slip lid, rare, 5x4" diameter, G, A...............................**425.00**

Scottie Cigars, tin, pictures Scottie dog, humidor lid, some scratches/chips/dents/darkening of lid, 5x5" square, G, A..**75.00**

Scotts Emulsion, sign, tri-fold, mother & baby in oval center with lettering above & below flanked by products & features, 25x48", EX, A **30.00**

Scotts Tablets, tin, portrait of a lady logo & company name, rectangular with rounded corners, M, A......**80.00**

Seagram Distillery Co, post card, linen, shows factory buildings, Seagram Distillery Company, Louisville Ky on blue sky, probably 1940s, M, D **2.00**

Seagram's, sign, plastic, electric, 3-D, #7 with crown on top stands on the word Sure, Seagram's printed on #7, 11", G+, A...**5.00**

Seagram's Whiskey, poster, paper, lg horse & jockey parade after the Ontario Jockey Club race, 1905, matted & framed, 38x52", EX, A **800.00**

Seal of North Carolina Plug Cut Tobacco, box, wood with paper labels, some staining on labels/minor chipping/wear, 2x5x4", VG, A **55.00**

Seal of North Carolina Plug Cut Tobacco, folding chair, wood, Eastlake impressed decor on wood stiles surrounding label, scarce, 33x17x20", G-, A..............**125.00**

Seal of North Carolina Plug Cut Tobacco, sign, die-cut cardboard litho, colorful image of 3 men holding product, early, framed, 14x9", EX, A **350.00**

Seal of North Carolina Plug Cut Tobacco, tin, depicts 2 ladies in classical setting with cornucopia, slip lid on bottle neck, overall wear, 6x5" square, G, A........**175.00**

Seal Rock Cut Plug Tobacco, tin, pictures sea-washed rocks, square corners, some scratches/minor chips/lid distortion due to denting, 2x5x3", G+, A **125.00**

Seal Skin Cigars, box label, inner lid, depicts a seal on floating ice, product name above, Dearstyne Bros Tobacco Co, 1880, 6x9", M, D................................**45.00**

Sealect Brand Milk, sign, shows faces of 2 red-haired girls, A Growing Child Should Have..., Sheffield Farms Co, ca 1920, framed, 11x21", A **65.00**

Sealtest Ice Cream, sidewalk sign, tin, Insist on Sealtest Ice Cream on rectangular blocks of color, logo at bottom, metal frame, 32", EX, A **35.00**

Sears, Roebuck & Co, catalog, 1930-40, 'Modern Homes,' shows house plants & prices, minor tears, G, A **30.00**

Sears, Roebuck & Co, catalog, 1932, Norman Rockwell illustration, D **65.00**

Sears, Roebuck & Co, toy, 1950s, van trailer & hauler, in original box, M, A **450.00**

Seaside Honey, pail, tin, pictures kids on the beach, slip lid & bail, EX+, A...**75.00**

Seattle Brewing & Malting Co, tip tray, mountains & Ranier Beer logo in center, Alaska-Yukon Pacific Exposition 1909... on rim, 4" diameter, NM, A..............**400.00**

Seattle Brewing & Malting Co, tray, decorative rim, some wear, 12" diameter, G+, A.......................525.00

Seattle Brewing & Malting Co, tray, pictures woman with black hair & Ranier Beer logo in center, lettering on decorative rim, 12" diameter, VG+, A **400.00**

Sebasticook, ice pick, D **15.00**

Seeandbee, tip tray, pictures lg ship, Cleveland & Buffalo, Great Ship Seeandbee around rim, oval, EX, A ...**250.00**

Seiberling Tires, ash tray, tire, D **12.00**

Seitz Beer, tip tray, deep-dish, eagle logo, Brewers Since 1821 lettered above, background crazing/wear, 4" diameter, EX, A **55.00**

Seitz Brewing Co, tip tray, brown & gold with eagle logo on wide center band, lettered rim, staining/rim chips, rare, 4" diameter, VG, A..**175.00**

Selick's Violet Talcum, tin, oval portrait of a Victorian woman on front & back, Borated & Perfumed, CH Selick Perfumer New York, rare, VG, A.................**25.00**

Seminola Cigars, box label, inner lid, pictures an Indian princess in native dress, 6x9", M, D **8.00**

Sen-Sen Breath Mints, display, die-cut tin with attached wooden shelf, pictures Sen-Sen sweetheart, 5¢, minor overall wear, 7x6x3", EX, A **145.00**

Senate Coffee, tin, capitol building logo on vertical striped background, slip lid, fading/overall wear, 1-lb, 6x4" diameter, G, A **120.00**

Seneca Cameras & Roll Film, sign, 2-sided die-cut tin with flange, 14x14", EX, A............................2,000.00

Senora Cubana Cigars, box label, outer, pictures a Spanish woman, 5x5", D, M...**2.00**

Sensation Cigars, tin, Sensation 5¢, Creates a Desire, embossed rim, good sheen, minor chipping, uncirculated, 5x6" diameter, VG+, A **350.00**

Seven-Up, see 7-Up on page 168

Shamokin Pure Lard, pail, tin, pictures Indian in headdress in profile, Shamokin Packing Co, slip lid & bail, 9x8" diameter, VG, A...**60.00**

Sharp's Toffee, tin, embossed barrel shape, trademarked image of monocled maven & leering parrot, slip lid & & bail, 9x7" diameter, G, A...................................**105.00**

Sharples Tubular Cream Separators, calendar, 1922, depicts 3-quarter side view of woman in hat, January pad at right of ad copy, vertical, EX, A.................**110.00**

Sharples Tubular Cream Separators, match holder, die-cut tin litho, mother, daughter, & product with cows atop, lettering on holder, 7x2", EX, A...................**450.00**

Sharples Tubular Cream Separators, match holder, die-cut tin litho, woman using separator with cows above, lettering on holder, 7x2", EX, A............................**350.00**

Sharples Tubular Cream Separators, poster, paper, comical scene of farmer & his wife using separator, water stain at bottom, 29x42", VG, A **300.00**

Sharples Tubular Cream Separators, sign, embossed tin, separator in lower right corner with lettering above & at left, The World's Best, 14x10", G, A...................**55.00**

Sharples Tubular Cream Separators, sign, paper, girl in bonnet using product, ornate graphics, The Right Now Separator..., 27x18" without frame, A **1,100.00**

Sharples Tubular Cream Separators, sign, tin, pictures mother & daughter using separator, border has minor rubs/scrapes, self-framed, 28x22", EX, A **4,200.00**

Shaw & Goding & Co Stylish Shoes, sign, tin, 3-color graphics on diamond shape, horizontal oval over band flanked by Stylish Shoes, 19th C, 12x14", VG, A ...**60.00**

Shaw's Pure Malt, sign, tin, Victorian scene of robed woman in chair with maid offering spirits, child playing, framed, 22x16", G, A **1,300.00**

Sheboygan Mineral Water & Ginger Ale, tray, deep-dish, seated Indian with 2 Black waiters ready to serve him, product name on rim, rare, round, EX, A **325.00**

Shell, globe, 1-piece embossed figural with red lettering, 18", EX, A **325.00**

Shell, radio, miniature gas pump figural, D **40.00**

Shell, sign, die-cut porcelain-on-tin 3-D shell, yellow with embossed red letters, 1945-48, minor flaking, 48" wide, NM+, A **275.00**

Shell, sign, paper, Cars Love Shell over shell logo & cartoon car whose trail forms a heart, 1959, 48x33", M, A **50.00**

Shell Motor Oil, tin, embossed seashell in center, Shell lettered above & Motor Oil below, swivel spout, ca 1915-25, 1-gal, 11", VG, A...**200.00**

Shell Motor Oil, see also Golden Shell Motor Oil/Auto Oil

Shell Motor Oil, see also Silver Shell Motor Oil

Sherwin-Williams Paints, puzzle, cardboard, house exterior & 4 vignettes of railroad car, coach, cans, & interior, 16x11" without frame, EX, A.............................**70.00**

Sherwin-Williams Paints, sign, die-cut metal, paint pouring from can over globe, Cover The Earth, 30x20", EX, A...**325.00**

Sherwin-Williams Paints, sign, man in top hat at table with poker chips, logo on table top, Don't Gamble... above, framed, 30x20", A **260.00**

Shinola Shoe Polish, shoehorn, Shinola on diagonal band above shoe brushes, The Wonderful Shoe Polish, 5", NM, A **35.00**

Shipley's Sof-Twist Bread, sign, tin, baby, D **150.00**

Shippensburg Working Garmets, match holder, tin, Wear Shippensburg Working Garmets, Made By Rummel, Himes & Co, Shippensburg Pa, appears EX, A **150.00**

Shmidt's Beer, tray, Mayflower passengers & soldiers on land in shades of blue, oval, 16x13", EX, A............**25.00**

Shredded Wheat, post card, Series 412, pictures factory & Niagara Falls, NM, D................................**5.00**

Shredded Whole Wheat, crate, wood with cardboard inserts, 21x33x17", EX, D...**25.00**

Shubs Pipe Tobacco, pocket tin, product name & Richly Blended at top, Finer Mild Blend Of Quality Pipe Tobacco at bottom, EX, A **775.00**

Sickle Plug Smoking Tobacco, crate label, hand holding sickle, with lettering, framed, square, EX, A **55.00**

Signal Gasoline, globe, 3-piece, restored metal frame with some damage on reverse, 19", VG, A **400.00**

Silberman Furs, watch fob, D..................................**150.00**

Silver Bell Tobacco, tin, sides & top picture bannered bell, Rock City Tobacco Co, Toronto Canada, minor edge chipping, 3x3", VG, A **95.00**

Silver Fox Beer, sign, tin, Nation's Premium Beer below product name, 24x35", EX, D **80.00**

Silver Hill Rye, shot glass, Silver Hill Rye, T Hoffer & Co, New Albany Ind etched on 4 lines in block letters & script, EX, D...**18.00**

Silver Moon Brand Coffee, tin, lady in crescent moon, paper label, 1-lb, EX, A **60.00**

Silver Prince Cigars, box label, inner lid, pictures a scholarly man with a beard, 6x9", M, D **3.00**

Silver Sea Coffee, tin, circular logo with product name above & below, slip lid, 1-lb, round, EX, A...........**30.00**

Silver Shell Motor Oil, tin, red with Silver Shell lettered in yellow at top, logo at bottom, ca 1965-70, 2-gal, 12x9", EX+, A **25.00**

Silver Spring Ale, sign, tin, 17x12", EX, A 90.00

Silver Spring Brewery, barrel label, paper litho, portly man with glass of brew bordered by lettering, Victoria BC, 6 Doz Quarts, round, EX, A **30.00**

Sinclair Aircraft, sign, porcelain, 2-sided, white, red, & green, single engine plane bordered by lettering, 1920-30, 48" diameter, EX, A.....................................**1,800.00**

Sinclair Diesel, gas globe, milk glass with plastic casing, white letters on green, ca 1959-70, 17" diameter, M, A **180.00**

Sinclair Dino Gasoline, globe, 3-piece with milk glass frame & 2 identical glass faces, 16", EX, A 525.00

Sinclair Gasoline, bank, tin, pump figural, 4", D **35.00**

Sinclair Gasoline, sign, porcelain, dinosaur logo, red lettering, 1961, 14x12", NM, A **60.00**

Sinclair Oils, Dino Soap, in box, 5" long, M, D 15.00

Sinclair Oils, Dino the Dinosaur, inflatable, 1978, original package, EX, D..**10.00**

Sinclair Oils, pump sign, porcelain, product name around striped logo, 1920-30, flaking at mounting hole, 12" diameter, NM, A **325.00**

Sinclair Oils, thimble, plastic, black dinosaurs & stars on butterscotch swirl background, EX, D......................**3.00**

Sinclair Opaline, pump sign, porcelain, red with product name around green & white striped logo, 1918-30, overall fading, 12x12", VG, A **400.00**

Sinclair Opaline Motor Oil, pump sign, porcelain, green & white letters above dinosaur, Mellowed 80 Million... below, 1936-42, 16" diameter, EX, A....................**650.00**

Sinclair Opaline Motor Oil, sign, porcelain, Authorized Dealer... lettered above & below product name, oil can at rignt, 1918-30, flaking, 20x48", A **325.00**

Sinclair Opaline Motor Oil, tin, green with lg red dinosaur below lettered cream circle, ca 1936-45, no top, 5-qt, 10x7", VG, A **60.00**

Sinclair Opaline Motor Oil, tin, product name in black on cream, green & cream pinstripe background, ca 1918-30, half-gal, NM, A...................................120.00

Sinclair Pennsylvania Motor Oil, pump sign, dinosaur with sign in mouth, Mellowed a Hundred Million Years below, 1932-36, 16" diameter, M, A **1,200.00**

Singer Sewing Machines, calendar, paper, depicts Indian on die-cut animal skin surrounded by calendar sheets, some wear, framed, 26x22", G, A.........................**75.00**

Singer Sewing Machines, salesman's sample, with company name & logo, original case, EX, D...............**150.00**

Singer Sewing Machines, sign, paper, elderly woman & child at sewing machine, circular insets at each corner, matted & framed, 21x20", G, A **375.00**

Singer Sewing Machines, sign, paper litho, vignettes of people from all nations using product, early, oak frame, vertical rectangle, A...........................**160.00**

Singer Sewing Machines, thimble, aluminum, product name on red band, EX, D **6.00**

Singer Sewing Machines, thimble, plastic, Sew & Save The Singer Way in red on cream background, EX, D **3.00**

Sir Haig Cigars, tin, portrait of a soldier on a silhouetted background, Ontario Canada, minor scuffing/rim chips, 5x6" diameter, G+, A..............................**125.00**

Sir Loraine Cigars, box label, inner lid, pictures a knight in armor, bright colors, 1911, 6x9", EX, D **14.00**

Sky-High Motor Oil, tin, product name above red airplane, cream & blue with cream & red striped sides, 1925-45, 2-gal, 11x9", VG, A **150.00**

Skyway Motor Oil, tin, pictures an airplane, 100% Paraffine Base, Airline Oil & Grease Co, Lubbock... below, 1935-45, 1-qt, 6", NM, A **250.00**

Slade's Mustard, box, wood, blue, red, & white paper labels on front & inside lid, stamped lettering on sides & outer lid, 2x20", EX, A **55.00**

Slater's Footwear For Men, Women & Children, catalog, cover depicts ladies' high-lace shoes for $5.95, 8 page black & white illustrations, Boston, 13x10", G, D ..**18.00**

Sleepy Eye Flour & Cereals, sign, die-cut tin, Indian with lettering on his chest, If Not The Best, Ask The Man, few letters worn, rare, 14x10", A...................**2,750.00**

Sleepy Eye Mills, barrel-end label, paper on cardboard, Indian logo, 1910, minor wear 16" diameter, A...**300.00**

Slias King Dry Goods, broadside, paper, black & white with insert of horse-drawn express wagon, Welchville Maine, 14x12" without frame, G, A **20.00**

Slidetite Garage Door, sign, tin litho on cardboard, for Richards-Wilcox Mfg Co, Last Word in Door Hardware, 13x19", EX+, A **1,200.00**

Slidewell's Collars, display case, oak with glass front & sides, contains 14 assorted Arrow display collars, 47", EX, A **675.00**

Slippery Elm Lozenges, tin, glass front insert flanked by list of cures, product name in fancy lettering above, slip lid, 8x7", EX, A **110.00**

Slippery Elm Lozenges, tin, glass front insert flanked by list of cures, product name in fancy lettering above, age discoloration, 8x7", G, A **60.00**

Slippery Elm Lozenges, tin, logoed center, company name above & below, 3x5", VG, A **110.00**

Smile Soda, display, die-cut tin soda jerk with orange head, slight overall wear, 43x27x15", G, A **475.00**

Smith Brothers Cough Drops, dispenser, tin, louvered vertical hinged-top picturing packages of product, general wear, 11x4x4", VG, A.....................................**155.00**

Smith Brothers Cough Drops, display, 2 die-cut cardboard figures of the Smith Brothers, some chipping/creasing, approx: 34x12" each, EX, A ...**150.00**

Smith Brothers Cough Drops, display box, tin litho, 3 images of various box labels, 11x3", plus 2 boxes of cough drops & 2 advertising flyers, NM, A...........**450.00**

Smith Brothers Cough Drops, pocket tin, flat, logo flanked by oval portraits of the Smith Brothers, decorative graphics, early, rare, NM, A **325.00**

Smith Brothers Cough Drops, sign, cartoon image of Smith Brothers, It's Just As..., product name flanked by product below, 1920s, rare, framed, A...................**20.00**

Smith Junior Root Beer, sign, for root beer barrel, tin litho, white & black on orange, Rochester New York, M, A...**30.00**

Smith Wallace Shoe Co, match holder, tin, blue with red & black lettering, Best of Everything in Shoes, 5x3", VG, A..**90.00**

Smith-O-Lene Aviation Brand Gasoline, pump sign, porcelain, lg red & blue plane on light blue center, red letters, 1946-50, 10" diameter, NM, A...................**700.00**

Smith's Ale, sign, etched & reverse-painted glass, Smith's Ale & hops motif, minor color lifting, oval, framed, 10x16", VG, A **65.00**

Smith's Dyspepsia Tablets, pocket tin, portrait of the founder surrounded by fancy graphics beside lettering & company name, flat, EX, A **65.00**

Smith's Ice Cream, sign, tin with mounting flange, product name across top, Smith & Clark Co below, horizontal rectangle, EX, A **140.00**

Smoky City Laundry Flakes, display, cardboard, contains 24 boxes, 1930, 1 tear, NM, A...............................**55.00**

Smucker's Jam, Yogi bear, EX, D 25.00

Snider's Catsup, sign, die-cut tin, 7x10", EX, A ...575.00
Snow Crop Orange Juice, sign, tin, blue with orange border, snow-capped letters over lg juice glass & fruit, 1930-40, sm chips, 20x17", EX+, A 30.00
Snow Shoe Tobacco, package label, EX, D 10.00
Snow's American Made Shoes, sign, cardboard, pictures a shoe & 2 flags, ...For Men, All Styles & Widths, For Sale Here, framed, 21x14", VG, A 45.00
Snuggle Softener, bear, sm, EX, D 9.00
Snyder's Beverages, sign, paper, girl seated in an oval, They Are the Best Beverages, Battle Creek Mich, matted & framed, 23x18", G, A 85.00

Snyder's Ice Cream, tray, stock image of mother & son having dish of ice cream, decorative rim, EX, A ..400.00
Snyder's 200 Oak Cigars, box label, outer, pictures an oak tree flanked by 200 Oak with Snyder's above, 3x5", M, D..1.00
Soapine, sign, beached whale under Soapine, Dirt Killer For Easy Washing in white letters, mounted with border trimmed, A 500.00
Soapine, sign, paper, framed, 26x34", NM, A 16,500.00
Soapine, trade card, die-cut, whale & sailor, 5", NM, D 6.00
Society King Shoes, sign, tin, man in knee-length coat holding top hat flanked by shoes with lettering, self-framed, some wear, 13x9", VG, A 200.00
Socony Special Gasoline, sign, red & blue lettering on milk glass globe, 16" diameter, EX, A 110.00

Soilax Cleaner, box, with contents, EX, D............**1,250.00**
Solarine Metal Polish, match holder, tin litho, pictures the product, Wise Wives Work Wonders With..., heavy fading to match box, A **100.00**
Songster Phonograph Needles, tin, picturing a songbird, M, D **15.00**
Sonn Bro's Whiskies, sign, reverse-painted glass, silver & gilt lettering on black, Fine Old Whiskies, Buckingham Rye, framed, 21x29", NM, A **300.00**
Sonny Boy Cigars, box label, inner lid, pictures a little boy on his father's lap, 6x9", M, D **5.00**
South Bend & Oreno Fishing Tackle, sign, counter top, cardboard, man with arms outstretched flanked by jumping fish, Fish & Feel Fit!, 30x50", NM, A.......**525.00**
South Bend Watch Co, sign, tin litho, pocket watch in ice cube on wood grain background, self-framed, 13x19", EX, A **275.00**
Southern Comfort, bank, mechanical, kneeling rifleman aims at bottle, EX, A..**65.00**
Southern Comfort, sign, neon with 3-D riverboat scene in chrome & black metal frame, 21" long, EX, A......**180.00**
Southern Girl Shoes, sign, embossed tin with hanging cord, elegant woman draped with flowers, Craddock Terry Co, self-framed, 19x13", VG+, A **1,100.00**
Southern Pacific RR, stirrer, plastic, EX, D **5.00**
Southern Rose Hair Dressing & Wave Oil, bottle, with contents, MIB, D..**25.00**
Souvain Tablets, tin, pocket size, M, D **5.00**
Sovereign Cigarettes, sign, paper, girl wearing a crown, appears to be a printer's proof with registration marks intact, framed, 17x11", NM, A............................**30.00**
Spaghetti O's, doll, Wizard, D **20.00**
Spalding Deep-Tilling Machine, sign, paper, farmer on horse-drawn machine flanked by cornfields, Gale Mfg Co, Albion Mich, framed, 18x30", G, A..................**30.00**
Spanish Knight Cigars, box label, inner lid, depicts knight above tobacco field, product name above, 6x9", M, D...**7.00**
Spanish Segaros, sign, paper litho, colorful image of an open box of cigars, Collins Cigar Co, framed, 22x17", VG+, A **110.00**
Sparrow's Chocolate, tip tray, girl standing on chair at table with box of candy, Sparrow Chocolate on decorative border, 8x6", EX, A **290.00**
Spaulding, baseball guide, leather bound, 1932, very rare, EX, A **40.00**
Speed-EE Motor Oil, tin, green with speeding race car in oval over geometric device at center of back side, 1940s, 2-gal, 11x9", VG, A......................................**80.00**
Spencer Matheson Sewing Machine, sign, paper, old lady sewing boy's pants while he's in them, The World's Greatest..., framed, 45x31", EX, A **625.00**
Spencer-Tracy Co, poster, colorful image of man in brown suit, Three Button Novelty Sack, Fall & Winter 1911, framed, 48", EX, A..**675.00**
Spilter's Buttermilk Talcum Powder, tin, very detailed graphics with baby on stork's back, embossed rim, some chipping at rim, rare, 4x3x2", EX, A...........**200.00**
Sprenger Brewing Co, tray, factory image in filigree inset, rim chips, 14x17", NM, A **2,800.00**

Springfield Breweries Co, calendar, ca 1900, coated stock paper litho, young girl in ornate oval frame surrounded by calendar months, 29x21", G, A..........................**225.00**

Springfield Breweries Co, sign, tin litho, 2 couples arriving in an early convertible at a pub, 1910, rare, self-framed, 23x30", EX, D **7,500.00**

Squeeze, sign, tin, back view of girl & boy looking at moon beside lg bottle, That Distinctive Orange Drink, 1920s, 20x27", A..........................**90.00**

Squire's, sign, tin, depicts frontal view of sitting pig with John P Squire's eyes, ca 1906, self-framed, wear, 25x20", VG+, A..........................**2,050.00**

Squire's, sign, tin, frontal view of pig with John Squire's eyes, self-framed, oval, 19x15", EX, A **425.00**

Squirrel Brand Salted Peanuts, pail, tin, depicts squirrel eating nut, press lid & bail, denting/chipping/general wear, 10-lb, 9x8" diameter, G, A **150.00**

Squirrel Brand Salted Peanuts, store container, embossed glass jar, nut figural, knob on lid, minor chips, 15x9", EX, A **150.00**

Squirrel Peanut Butter, pail, tin, pictures squirrel on gold background, Canada Nut Co, minor wear, 34-oz, 5x5" diameter, VG+, A..........................**185.00**

Squirrel Peanut Butter, pail, tin, pictures squirrel on gold background, original slip lid & bail, Canada Nut Co, 4x4" diameter, VG+, A **300.00**

Squirrel Peanut Butter, pail, tin, pictures squirrel on gold background, original press lid & bail, Canada Nut Co, 15-lb, 8x8", VG, A..........................**225.00**

Squirrel Peanut Butter, tin, squirrel logo flanked by ornate graphics, Canada Nut Co above, product name below, press lid, 4x4" diameter, VG, A **100.00**

Squirrel Peanut Butter, tin, squirrel logo flanked by ornate graphics, Canada Nut Co above, product name below, press lid, 7x5", VG, A **125.00**

Squirt, chalkboard, painted tin, embossed letters, boy & bottle at top, 1959, minor scratch on chalkboard, 28x20", A..........................**20.00**

Squirt, cooler, tin litho, rope handle, lg dent on side/some wear, A..........................**25.00**

SS Pierce Co, tip tray, with Spin To Win game incorporated into graphics, EX, A..........................**40.00**

SSS Blood Purifier, display, die-cut cardboard, colorful display of product flanked by satisfied customers, 32x45", EX, A..........................**170.00**

St Charles Evaporated Cream, clock frame, cast iron, cow figural with hole in center for clock, ca 1890, 9x15", EX, A..........................**300.00**

St Lawrence Tobacco, tin, overall scratches/chips, 4x6x3", G+, A **200.00**

St Louis ABC Beers, tray, pictures eagle atop the world with banner & US Flag, decorative border, American Brewing Co, 12" diameter, G+, A..........................**325.00**

Stag Brewing Co, stencil, brass with block letters, 12x17", G, A **20.00**

Stallmans Cigars, tin, slip lid, some wear, oval, 5x5x6", G+, A..........................**85.00**

Standard Beer, sign, light-up with hanging chain, white lettering on red background, 10x26", EX, A..........................**70.00**

Standard Bottling & Extract Co, sign, celluloid litho, woman with flowing hair wearing a red gown, ca 1900, rolled metal frame, 6" diameter, NM, A **95.00**

Standard Brewing Co, sign, tin, execution of Sioux Indians at Mankato & the commanding officers, ca 1910-15, self-framed, 18x26", EX, A..........................**1,800.00**

Standard Brewing Co, tray, depicts execution of Sioux Indians at Mankato & the commanding officers, some crazing, 12" diameter, VG+, A..........................**350.00**

Standard Ice Cream, tray, 4 kewpies play on lg strawberry, Goodness How You Like It, mfg by Parker-Brawner Co, ca 1920, 13" square, EX, D..........................**300.00**

Standard Oil, toy truck, tin, green, red, & yellow, ca 1930s, minor pitting, rare, A.................................**325.00**
Standard Oil Co, checkers, 1938, M.....................**60.00**
Standard Sewing Machines, sign, tin, flag in circle at left of Standard arched over pictured rotary shuttle with other lettering, 10x14", G, A.................................**105.00**
Standard Sewing Machines, sign, tin, flag in circle at left of Standard arched over pictured rotary shuttle with other lettering, 10x14", EX+, A.............................**250.00**
Standard Tobacco, sign, paper, soldier on a charging horse, 5¢ The Standard Since 1847, matted & framed, 20x15", NM, A...**375.00**
Stapels Prepared Wax, tin, pictures a beehive, 3" diameter, EX, D **8.00**
Star & Crescent Cigars, tin, shows crescent & star encircled by flowers & leaves, purchased from lithographer, uncirculated, 5x6" diameter, A **200.00**
Star Biscuits, paperweight, metal, figural mouse & biscuit, D..**85.00**
Star Brand Eggs, crate, salesman's sample with wooden eggs, lettering & logo on lid, 2x4x5", EX, A.........**160.00**
Star Brand Shoes, calendar, 1929, paper, pictures woman at stained glass window, framed, 26x11", EX, A..**140.00**
Star Brand Shoes, clock, 8-sided metal frame with round face on rectangular base, Time To Wear Star Brand Shoes, ca 1920, 4", G, A.......................................**40.00**
Star Brand Shoes, thimble, aluminum, product name on worn blue band, D...**3.00**
Star Brewery Co, poster, paper, factory scene with 6-point star on building top, water stains, matted & framed, 31x43", A..**500.00**
Star Cars, sign, porcelain, 2-sided, Low-Cost Transportation, Authorized Service, 36x24", EX, A...............**450.00**
Star Cord, sign, tin, dealer's name & address over lg tire, Star of Akron logo at bottom, wood frame, 1925, 49x29", G, A..**190.00**
Star Play, cigar label, depicts early baseball scene, ca 1911, may be 1 of a kind, framed, rectangular, EX, A...**300.00**

Star Plug Tobacco, sign, die-cut cardboard litho with double glass, rare, framed, 20" diameter, EX, A....1,600.00
Star Soap, sign, little girl hugging dog, tree in background, For Family Use, Schultz & Co, ca 1890, minor pitting, horizontal, A...**225.00**
Starkist Tuna, camera, Charlie Tuna, D **85.00**
Starkist Tuna, doll, vinyl, Charlie Tuna, 8", VG, D.....**16.00**

Starkist Tuna, pillow, Charlie Tuna, talks, 1970, 15", M, D...**30.00**
Starkist Tuna, radio, Charlie Tuna, D **35.00**
Starkist Tuna, wristwatch, Charlie Tuna, 1971, M, D**125.00**
Starrett Tools, lapel button, D **12.00**

Staver Carriage Co, sign, embossed tin, some discoloration, framed, 20x28", G, A 2,000.00
Stearns Cough Drops, sign, pictures a lg box of menthol cough drops, For Tight Cough, 5¢, ca 1910, framed, rectangular, EX, A...**75.00**
Stegmaier Beer, tip tray, factory scene in center, Wilkes Barre, The Home of Stegmaier Beer on rim, oval, 4x6", A...**35.00**
Stegmaier Brewing Co, sign, tin, Victorian parlor scene depicts mother with infant & maid serving father, self-framed, 22x28", G, A...**1,050.00**
Stegmaier Brewing Co, tip tray, factory, company name & Wilkes Barre Pa on rim, 4" diameter, EX, A **85.00**
Stegmaier Brewing Co, tip tray, pictures a hand grasping 4 labeled bottles, Wilkes Barre Pa & company name on rim, 4" diameter, NM, A **45.00**
Stegmaier Brewing Co, tray, deep-dish, bust-length portrait of girl with long wavy hair, ca 1904, minor soil/residue, 13" diameter, EX+, A **175.00**
Stegmaier Brewing Co, tray, depicts view of factory & trains with Drink Stegmaier's Gold Medal Beer above, lettered rim, 12" diameter, EX, A............................**45.00**
Stegmaier Brewing Co, tray, rolled edge, bust-length portrait of girl with long wavy hair, fade/ring to image/rim chips, 14" diameter, G, A **40.00**
Steko-O Paste, sign, reverse-painted glass, Highest Quality With Economy, The Great... in oval, 1920, minor flaking, 17x23", A **50.00**
Stella-Mae Cigars, box label, outer, pictures a woman in profile on green background, 5x5", M, D.................**5.00**
Stephenson Union Suits, thermometer, porcelain, man in long underwear above & man holding shirt below, For All Seasons, More Wool, More Wear, A **120.00**
Sterling Beer, sign, tin litho, colorful circus scene, Sterling Super-Dry Tops Them All, rust damage in corner, framed, 27x21", EX+, A **450.00**
Sterling Brand Linen Collars & Cuffs, sign, reverse-painted glass, gold letters on black ground with green & white lily & logo, gesso frame, 13x23", F, A ...**200.00**
Sterling Breweries, sign, tin litho, Madison Square Garden scene, Tops Them All, Robert E Weaver artist, 1938, vertical rectangle, EX, A.......................................**850.00**

Sterling Dark Fine Cut Tobacco, store container, tin, pack of product with filigree border, square slip lid on round can, dents/scratches, 12x8", G, A **65.00**

Sterling Gasoline, gas globe, Sterling Gasoline bordering centered logo, Ethyl...Brand Of Anti-Knock Compound, 3 sections, round, EX, A **400.00**

Sterling Gasoline, pump sign, porcelain, oval with product name around Ethyl logo over sunburst effect, 1946-50, 9x11", EX, A **325.00**

Sterling Light Tobacco, store container, tin, logoed L in filigree, square slip lid on round can, overall wear/scratches, 12x8", G, A **60.00**

Sterling Motor Oil, tin, green & black with product name in lg letters over logo, Sterling Oil Co, Oil City PA, 1935-45, 1-qt, NM, A **35.00**

Sterling Oils, sign, tin with Ask For over lettered round yellow logo, 100% Pure logo at bottom, 1930s, corner bent/wear, 20x13", VG, A **120.00**

Sterling Pepsin Gum, sign, cardboard, depicting girl's face & gum package, overall wear, rare, original frame, 35x25", G+, A **160.00**

Sterling Tea, store bin, offset photos of Quebec landmarks inset on 4 sides, hinged lid partially lifting, overall wear, 12x9x9", G, A **300.00**

Stetson Hats, sign, porcelain, product name lettered in black on yellow with geometric border, rounded corners, 8x30", EX, A **255.00**

Stillboma Oriental Polish, tin, picturing a deer, 6x2" square, G, D **10.00**

Stillwell Meat Co, see AJ Stillwell

Stoeckle Brewing Co, tray, depicts satisfied patron with foaming glass & expectant dog, decorative rim, rust spots, 13" diameter, G-, A **55.00**

Stokley Foods, cookbook, 1935, 'Sally Stokley's Prize Recipes,' D **5.00**

Stoll Brewing Co, tray, porcelain, rim chip, 12" diameter, VG, A...**150.00**

Stollwerck Chocolate, vendor, wood, metal, & glass, 1¢ or 5¢, marquee top shows cherubs, Schilling, Stollwerck & Co, ca 1900, 17x9", EX, A **600.00**

Stollwerck Victoria Chocolate, vendor, tin with 2 glass windows, bank figural picturing cherubs dancing & playing, ca 1890-1900, 11x4", EX, A **375.00**

Stonewall Jackson Cigars, display, embossed tin die-cut of open cigar box, McDonald Mfg Co, Toronto, surface loss/rust on edges, 10x11x3", G-, A **275.00**

Stoneware Food Container, sign, tin, colorful image of boy & dog getting donut from crock, We Sell All Sizes, self-framed, 19x13", VG, A **80.00**

Strata Motor Oil, tin, brick red with yellow plane & letters, Tiona Petroleum Co Phila Pa USA on yellow stripe, 1925-45, 2-gal, 12", EX, A **100.00**

Strathmore Hotel & Resort, sign, paper, shows hotel with band playing under cupola, ocean scene in foreground, fading/wear, framed, 24x30", VG, A **250.00**

Stroh's Beer, stein, with lid, Stroh's logo with Alps scene in relief, 9", EX, A **5.00**

Stroh's Bohemian Beer, tray, gentleman serving lager beer, Detroit Mich, Served Wherever Quality Counts, ca 1910-15, 12" diameter, EX, A **450.00**

Stroh's Malt Extract, tip tray, bottle in center, For Weak People & Nursing Mothers, Detroit, overall crazing, 4" diameter, NM, A **250.00**

Stromeyer's Grape Punch, syrup bottle, red, white, & blue label under glass, 12", EX, A **210.00**

Studebaker, sign, reverse-painted glass, Welcome, from dealership ca 1920, emblems each end, original frame, 11x51", VG, A **1,400.00**

Studebaker Service, sign, porcelain-on-metal, yellow with black & white tire behind Studebaker, 1920s, touched up, 24x18", EX, A **725.00**

Studebaker Wagon, sign, embossed tin, pictures the 20th Century Studebaker wagon, South Bend Ind, rust spots/fading, framed, 23x29", G-, A **1,000.00**

Sturdy Motor Oil, tin, cream square with letters superimposed on green tree, Stands Heat, Withstands Cold, 1925-45, 2-gal, 12x9", VG, A **20.00**

Sturdy Motor Oil, tin, letters on white at top, green with tree in circle & It Stands Heat... on banner at bottom, 1925-35, 2-gal, VG, A **45.00**

Success Horse Collar, calendar, 1889, paper, some wear, framed, 26x21", VG, A **375.00**

Success Manure Spreader, sign, tin, horse-drawn manure spreader surrounded by embossed images of lion trademark, Mayer & Lavenson, 20x27", G, A **500.00**

Suchard Cocoa & Chocolate, toy truck, tin litho, double-sided, pictures boy holding can with S wrapped around him, ca 1915, 8x4x3", EX, A **750.00**

Sultana Peanut Butter, pail, press lid & bail, 1-lb, appears EX, A **10.00**

Sultana Spice, tin, black lettering on yellow, black slip lid, round, 4", NM, A **20.00**

Sumatra Seed Leaf Tobacco, sign, paper, pictures little girl in red, Philadelphia, rubs/fading to over-printed letters, 20x15" without frame, EX, A **1,350.00**

Sun Crest, sign for drink rack, blue, orange, & white, Drink Sun Crest It's Best, EX, D **28.00**

Sun Crest Soda, sign, tin, labeled bottle, edge rusting/minor scuffing/bends, 21x7", A **18.00**

Sun Garters, display case for men's sock garters, curved glass & oak, original garter displayed, ca 1902, 11x5x7", VG, A **150.00**

Sun Proof Paints, match striker, tin, pictures a hefty man from behind with logo on his rear, Please Scratch My Back, rare, EX, A **425.00**

Sunbeam Bread, doll, plastic, Little Miss Sunbeam, M, D **125.00**

Sunbeam White Bread, push bar, die-cut polychrome tin, depicts rounded loaf of bread picturing Little Miss Sunbeam, 5x31", G, A **40.00**

Sunkist, crate label, lemons, depicts Santa with full sack, Santa printed in upper right corner, 1928, 9x12", D **7.00**

Sunkist, leaflet, 1916, 'Sunkist Recipes, Oranges-Lemons,' 64 pages, D **4.00**

Sunkist, leaflet, 1933, 'Sunkist Recipes For Everyday,' 35 pages, D **3.00**

Sunny Brook Pure Rye & Sour Mash Whiskey, sign, tin, colorful image, framed, 27x48", VG+, A 2,500.00

Sunny Brook Whiskey, match holder, tin litho, product surrounded by fancy graphics, rust on matchbox, 5x3", G+, A **110.00**

Sunoco Winter Oil & Grease, sign, canvas litho, shows Mickey in Pilgrim's garb shooting at turkey, For Trigger-Quick Starting, fading, 36x35", EX, A **90.00**

Sunray D-X Petroleum Products, pump sign, porcelain, hexagon with sunburst on orange above red & yellow diamond on green, 1955-59, 9x9", EX, A **650.00**

Sunray D-X Petroleum Products, sign, porcelain, 2-sided, hexagon with yellow sunrays on orange, lettered red & yellow diamond, 25", VG, A **425.00**

Sunset Trail Cigars, tin, 2 horseback riders on oval inset on dark blue background, lettering above, slip lid, general wear, 5x6x4", G, A **175.00**

Sunshine Dairy, toy truck, tin, smiling sun logo on back sides, Drink More Milk, ca 1930s, EX+, A **230.00**

Sunshine Soda Crackers, sign, tin, Takhoma Biscuit box with hands breaking crackers apart, 5¢, Loose-Wiles Biscuit Co, 10x28", NM, A **375.00**

Superlative Cigarettes, sign, cardboard litho, elegant woman holding grapes, WS Kimball & Co, Rochester NY, framed, 17x12", EX, A **275.00**

Superol Motor Oil, tin, product name on black over red aircraft flying upward, Rugged Quality to left, ca 1935-45, 1-qt, 6", EX, A **20.00**

Supreme Auto Oil, tin, yellow with silver border, product name in silver, Mfg by Gulf Refining Co, 1915-25, worn, half-gal, 6", VG, A **45.00**

Supreme Dental Powder, tin, D **13.00**

Supreme Peanut Butter, pail, children play with a lobster on the beach, press lid & bail, rare, 9", EX, A **150.00**

Supreme Peanut Butter, pail, tin, shows children at the beach using empty tin to carry sand, original top & bail, overall wear, 4x4", G-, A **165.00**

Sure Shot Chewing Tobacco, store container, cardboard, Indian drawing bow toward sky over product name, lettering on sides, holds 48, EX, A **205.00**

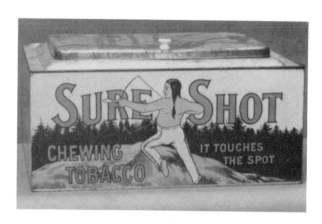

Sure Shot Chewing Tobacco, store container, 7x15x11", EX, A..495.00

Surfolets, sign, tin, Here's The Newest Idea In Surface Wiring Devices, shows various outlets, NM, A.....**110.00**

Susquehanna Cigars, box label, inner lid, pictures 3 Indian women, 6x9", EX, D **10.00**

SW Venable & Co Tobacco, sign, heralding angels leaning on gold seal of St George slaying dragon, framed, 32x26", EX, A......................................650.00

Swallow Coffee, tin, swallow in flight & coffee carrying natives, slip lid, overall wear, 1-lb, 6x4", G, A **300.00**

Swans Down Shortening, leaflet, 1945, 'New Swans Down Desserts & Hot Breads,' D **2.00**

Swansdown Coffee, tin, shows white swan on oval inset, press lid, light wear/minor scratches/chipping/denting, 1-lb, 6x4", diameter, VG, A **265.00**

Sweet, Orr & Co, sign, tin, workmen in tug-of-war, C Shonk litho, rare, framed, 24x32", EX+, A **14,000.00**

Sweet Caporal Cigarettes, die-cut figure of soldier, Kenney Bros litho, framed, 13", EX, A.........................**95.00**

Sweet Caporal Cigarettes, sign, depicts elegant couple gazing at each other while playing cards, red lettering, framed, 21x27", EX, A **1,400.00**

Sweet Caporal Cigarettes, sign, framed, 61x19", A ..**330.00**

Sweet Caporal Cigarettes, sign, tin, girl holds product above head on dark ground, lettered smooth-surface self-frame, round corners, dents, A....................**1,600.00**

Sweet Caporal Cigarettes, sign, tin, girl holds product above head on green ground with trees, lettered hobnail-type gold frame, 31x28", EX, A **725.00**

Sweet Chocolate, vendor, Sweet Chocolate lettered diagonally on decorative front, 1¢, rounded top, ca 1917, 17x2", NM, A **350.00**

Sweet Cuba Fine Cut Chewing Tobacco, pail, wooden tub with bail handle, early tobacco labels with bearded man, paper loss/stains/wrinkling, 11x13", G-, A..**150.00**

Sweet Cuba Fine Cut Chewing Tobacco, sign, paper, framed, rare, VG+, A **650.00**

Sweet Cuba Fine Cut Chewing Tobacco, store bin, slanted hinged lid, chips/dents, 8x8x11", G+, A **125.00**

Sweet Cuba Fine Cut Chewing Tobacco, store bin, tin, profiled lady in oval on bowed front, product pictured on sides, lettered slant top, 8x8x11", F, A...............**40.00**

Sweet Cuba Fine Cut Chewing Tobacco, store bin, yellow with red & black lettering, Genuine...Always Fresh, lettered slant top, 12x18x14", G, A.........................**175.00**

Sweet Cuba Fine Cut Chewing Tobacco, store container, cardboard, Cuban fort in oval inset, slip lid, chips/dents, 12x8x6", G, A **175.00**

Sweet Girl Peanut Butter, tin, 4x4", NM, A **2,300.00**

Sweet Girl Peanut Butter, tin, shoulder-length portrait of curly-haired girl, bail handle, 4x4", VG, A............**900.00**

Sweet Heart Products, door plate, porcelain, heart-shaped with lettering, Hard Wheat Flour, White Corn Flour, White Corn Meal, 5x5", NM, A **80.00**

Sweet Heart Soap, display, baby in wood basket with paper marquee, legs & arms move, electrical, overall wear, approx: 20x33x16", G, A **400.00**

Sweet Mist Chewing Tobacco, pail, tin, shows children at fountain on yellow ground, slip lid & bail, Scotten & Dillon Co, 7x6" diameter, G, A............................**100.00**

Sweet Mist Chewing Tobacco, store container, cardboard, red on yellow, shows children at fountain, Scotten & Dillon Co, slip lid, square, VG, A **140.00**

Sweet Mist Chewing Tobacco, store container, tin, pictures children playing in fountain, yellow & red, slip lid, Scotten & Dillon Co, 11x8", VG, A **125.00**

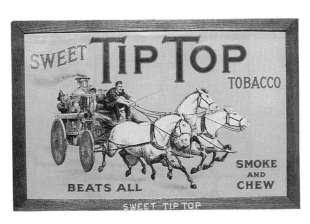

Sweet Tip Top Tobacco, sign, cardboard litho, rare, framed, 23x36", EX, A **1,600.00**

Sweet-Orr, sign, porcelain, blue product name above red & white Union Made logo, Pants, Overalls, Shirts, some wear, 28x72", A **65.00**

Sweetheart Soap, mechanical baby, electrified movable crying baby in basket, Soap That Agrees With Your Skin, chips/wear, 22x31", VG, A **300.00**

Swift & Co, recipe booklet, 1950, 77 recipes using Swiftining shortening, 35 pages, VG, D **5.00**

Swift's Dressed Beef, sign, reversed-painted glass, black lettering on gilt surrounds brown cow against blue sky, framed, 18x32", EX, A **700.00**

Swift's Washing Powder, sign, paper on canvas, wooden hangers, 42x28", G, A **2,250.00**

Sykes Comfort Powder, tin, depicts 2 girls on front & nurse on back, minor chipping/slight color change between can & lid, 5x2x2", VG+, A **150.00**

Sylvania Light Bulbs, talking Bug's Bunny, 1974, 12", G-, D...**20.00**

T&B Tobacco, tin, fancy graphics & logo in silver & black on red, ground, One Pound Myrtle Cut..., slip lid, rectangular, A...15.00

Taft Bros Hay & Grain, sign, brass, Uxbridge Mass, some corrosion/discoloration, 28x28", A 150.00

Taka-Kola, sign, tin, classical woman holding bottle on head in front of clock, Take No Other, wear, self-framed, 13x9", VG, A 650.00

Talisman Cigars, box label, inner lid, depicts Indian maiden, 1898, 6x9", EX, D 24.00

Tam O' Shanter Ales, sign, neon in shadow box-type frame, 30" long, EX, A..230.00

Tankar Special Motor Oil, tin, red with tank car at top, product name in beige circled with black band, 1933-39, 2-gal, 12x9", VG, A.......................................45.00

Tanlac Medicine, display, 3-piece cardboard, bold images from around the world, a factory, & a girl, muted colors, 34x52", VG, A 300.00

Tanlac Medicine, sign, die-cut cardboard, Uncle Sam holding package with world in background, The Master Medicine, wear, 30x20", G+, A............115.00

Taylor's Homemade Peanut Butter, pail, tin, shows Taylor's Homestead in white & blue, original slip lid & bail, AE Taylor, Canada, 1-lb, 4x4", G+, A 400.00

Tech Beer, sign, tin, hunter & pointing dog, Too Good To Forget, Pittsburgh Brewing Co, edge chips, self-framed, 19x27", VG, A 175.00

Ted's Delicious Creamy Root Beer, bottle, 4-color painted-on baseball player, 1950s, light wear/scratches, 8", EX, A..35.00

Ted's Root Beer, pocket mirror, pictures baseball player & labeled bottle, EX, A 15.00

Teddie Brand Jumbo Whole Salted Peanuts, tin, Teddie on lg peanut over peanut fields with river, lettering above & below, press lid, 10-lb, F, A 90.00

Teddie Peanut Butter, pail, depicts logoed peanut seal, press lid & bail, slight scratching/chipping/slight dent, 4x4", VG, A 250.00

Teddy Bear Peanut Butter, pail, tin, shows toy teddy bear, press lid & bail, dents/chips/background paint loss, rare, 4x4", G, A 1,100.00

Telegram Rye, shot glass, Telegram Rye, David Netter & Co... etched in lg letters with image of 2 men at table in center, EX, D 30.00

Temple Table Water, tray, deep-dish, ruined Grecian temple with Temple lettered above & Table Water below, 12" diameter, VG, A...10.00

Temple Table Water, tray, deep-dish, ruined Grecian temple with Temple lettered above & Table Water below, 12" diameter, EX, A...40.00

Tennessee Wagons, match holder, tin litho, picturing the product, rust spots, A.....................................160.00

Tenor Whiskey, tray, depicts a long-haired girl in a bonnet, Ellicott Importation Co, 1908, oval, NM, A....450.00

Terre Haute Brewing Co, tip tray, deep-dish, cherubs above colonial gathering pouring beer into lifted glasses, 4" diameter, EX, A 150.00

Terre Haute Brewing Co, tray, deep-dish, cherubs above colonial gathering pouring beer into lifted glasses, oval, 15x13", G, A..75.00

Tetlows Face Powder, sign, die-cut cardboard, little girl trying to powder face of Union officer, minor paper loss/wear, 19x14", G, A.....................................250.00

Teutonia Insurance Co, sign, paper, Teutonian hoards crushing Roman warriors flanked by directors names, ornate border, ca 1872, 24x19", VG, A 350.00

Texaco, sign, porcelain, star logo each side of No Smoking, black letters on white, ca 1940, 4x23", EX, A**110.00**

Texaco, sign, Texaco etched into red, white, & green leaded glass, circular frame, 30" diameter, VG, A.**550.00**

Texaco Diesel Chief, sign, porcelain, top has lines radiating from center behind star logo, Diesel Fuel, 1962, dent/flaking, 18x12", VG, A 85.00

Texaco Fire-Chief Gasoline, sign, porcelain, product name above star logo & lg fireman's hat, 1940, minor flaking at 1 mounting hole, 12x8", A 115.00

Texaco Fire-Chief Gasoline, sign, porcelain, star logo left of lg fireman's hat, red & black on white, 1952, 18x12", NM, A...25.00

Texaco Marine White Gasoline, pump sign, porcelain, star logo encircled with boat's helm, Marine White in rope letters below, 1947, 18x13", EX, A 1,420.00

Texaco Motor Oil, sign, porcelain, 2-sided with flange, Texaco star logo with lettered border, 24x18", NM/VG, A 155.00

Texaco Motor Oil, sign, tin, product name top left & bottom right, logos in other corners, Insulated, text each side, 1947, 11x21", NM, A **75.00**

Texaco Motor Oil, tin, easy pour spout, Extra Heavy, star logo over 7 lines of text, Texas Co, 1923, 15x4" diameter, VG, A............................**400.00**

Texaco Motor Oil, tin, Handy-Grip Can on right, black-bordered cream square with stream of pouring gas, name, & E, 1927, half-gal, NM+, A **400.00**

Texaco North Shore Petroleum Inc Consignee, sign, die-cut porcelain, lg round star logo above rectangle with 3-line text, 4 colors, 1956, 12x11", VG, A.....**160.00**

Texaco Oil, doll, cheerleader, plus extra outfit, original box, 12", M, D **25.00**

Texaco Sky Chief, calendar, 1940, paper litho, vertical, EX, A............................**50.00**

Texaco Sky Chief Gasoline, sign, porcelain, Sky Chief on band above star logo, Super-Charged With Petrox lettered below, 1957, 22x12", EX, A......60.00

Texaco Sky Chief Gasoline, sign, porcelain, Sky Chief on band above star logo, winged device in background, 1947, 18x12", EX, A............................**45.00**

Texaco Thuban Compound, tin, product name in square on green ground, star logo in center, reverse side identical, 1930s, 5-lb, 10x5", EX, A **150.00**

Texas Brewing Co, sign, paper, factory scene, Milwaukee Engraving & Litho Co, several paper repairs, 27x40", EX, A............................**2,600.00**

Texas Dairy Queen Ass'n, doll, Sweet Nell, EX, D ...**15.00**

Theo Geir Co Vineyards, sign, tin, family toasting with vineyards in the background, Napa & Livermore, Oakland Cal, ca 1895, 14" diameter, EX, A **1,300.00**

Thixton Millett & Co Distillers, sign, depicts log cabin distillery with 3 men & oxen, company name lettered on rock, framed, 20x28", EX, A............................**300.00**

Thomas (Thos) Ryan's Consumers Brewing Co, tray, deep-dish, script lettering on blue background, Indian in headdress, background/rim wear, 12" diameter, VG, A **100.00**

Thomas Ryan, see also Ryan's

Thomas Ryan Sparkling Ale, sign, wood, interior scene of men toasting beer, F Tuchfarber litho, ca 1896, restored, 20x28", G............................**300.00**

Thomas Ryan's Ales & Lager, tray, porcelain, pictures Indian in headdress, curved lettering above & below, gold banded, oval, 16x13", NM, A **235.00**

Thomas Ryan's Consumers Brewing Co, tray, men playing cards with dog asleep on floor, Syracuse NY, image/rim restoration, oval, 17x14", G, A............**130.00**

Thomas' Inks & Mucilage, sign, embossed tin, playful cat spilling bottle of ink among other product bottles, 14x20" without frame, VG+, A **12,250.00**

Thomas' Inks & Mucilage, sign, tin litho, colorful image of product, cat, & puppy on desk top, damage in lower left, rare, framed, 18x11", G+, A 5,000.00

Thompson Products Aerotype Break-In Motor Oil, tin, yellow with black pinstripes, lettered black circle with prop airplane at right, ca 1935-45, 1-qt, NM, A......**80.00**

Thorobred Motor Oil, tin, horse in shades of blue on red circle, cream background, red & cream lettering, ca 1925-45, 2-gal, 9x8", VG, A **55.00**

Three Bee Blacking, sign, embossed tin, depicts turn-of-the-century man having his shoes shined, nail holes/blemishes, framed, 19x14", VG, A.....4,000.00

Three Crow Brand Cream Tarter & Soda, thermometer, yellow with crow logo above & lettering below, arched top, squared bottom, 35x7", EX, A......................**100.00**

Three Twins Cigars, box label, outer, pictures 3 children in a basket, 5x5", D **3.00**

Throat Ease Cough Drops, tin, product name arched above lettering, Nelson, Baker & Co below, slip lid, rectangular, EX, A..**60.00**

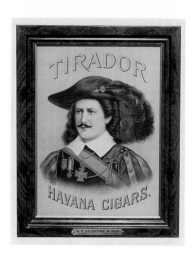

Tiger Chewing Tobacco, lunch pail, tin, depicts red & black tiger over wicker design, minor chipping/denting, 6x8x7", G, A **40.00**

Tiger Chewing Tobacco, sign, cardboard, product name above tiger peering through tall grass with product, 5¢, 1890-1900, framed, 31x25", EX, A **350.00**

Tiger Chewing Tobacco, tin, depicts tiger's head & lettering, rectangular with rounded corners, worn, A ...**10.00**

Times Square Smoking Mixture, pocket tin, pictures Times Square, NM, A **230.00**

Tirador Havana Cigars, sign, tin, AS Valentine & Sons litho, self-framed, 28x23", EX+, A................**1,250.00**

Tivoli Hofbrau Beer, match holder, die-cut tin litho, beer bottle figural, Robert Portner Brewing Co, rare, 7x3", G+, A...**450.00**

Tivoli Select Lager Beer, tip tray, girl holding a glass of Tivoli, A Select Lager, 4" diameter, NM, A...........**550.00**

Tiz Cigars, tin, oval portrait inset over plantation scene, slip lid, dents/spots/chips, 6x6" diameter, G, A ...**215.00**

TJ H's English Horse & Cattle Powder, sign, bull & horse with lettering above & below, Strobridge black & white litho, 1800s, rare, framed, 24x34", NM, D **225.00**

TM Nicholson Co, sign, paper, well-dressed couple in open buggy, Compliments of this Bucksport Maine Co, 22x15" without frame, VG, A **100.00**

Tintex Dyes, display rack, metal with sign attached to top depicting woman displaying dyed cloth, Don't Throw It Away..., EX, A......................................**15.00**

Tiny Tot Toilet Powder, tin, pictures baby, shaker top, NM, A **25.00**

Tiolene Motor Oil, oil bottle rack, holds 16 bottles, solid-hinged cover, 18", D **75.00**

Tiolene Motor Oil, tin, yellow with script in black over bull's-eye, Medium, Pure Oil Co, 1914-17, 1-gal, 11x8", VG+, A..**170.00**

Tiopet Motor Oil, tin, Indian in headdress points finger on red & blue ground, 100% Pure Penn..., no top, very rare, 1946-50, 1-qt, EX, A **350.00**

Tip Top Bread, fan, 1950, D **5.00**

Tobacco Girl Cigars, tin, pictures girl peering through tobacco leaf, 5¢ Straight, slip lid, good sheen, minor wear, 5x6x4", EX, A............................**1,750.00**

Toiletine, sign, die-cut cardboard, smiling man in lettered top hat, Don't Forget Toiletine, Unequalled For Sunburn..., 9x6", EX, A..**15.00**

Tolstoi Russian Cigarettes, sign, cardboard, pictures Tolstoi & pack of cigarettes, 20x15", EX, A................**225.00**

Tom Moore Tobacco, tin, pictures Tom Moore with vignettes in the background, 4x5", NM, A..............**30.00**

Tom Sawyer Apparel for Real Boys, sign, counter top, embossed, Tom painting the fence, 7x22", A.........**15.00**

Tomahawk Motor Oil, tin, dark green & yellow with tomahawk pictured on explosion of light, Hi-Speed, 1925-45, 2-gal, 12x9", VG+, A...**55.00**

Tomahawk Plug Tobacco, sign, die-cut cardboard, moon-lit scene picturing Indian with a tomahawk, decorative frame, vertical rectangle, EX, A **230.00**

Tonka Tobacco, tin, pictures soldiers in the field on lid & flowered urn on side, McAlpin Tobacco Co, Canada, 5x7x4", G+, A 425.00

Tony's Pizza, chef, Mr Tony, EX, D.............**10.00**

Tootsie Roll, vending bank, dispenses Famous Tootsie Roll Candy, A Tootsie A Day Puts A Penny Away, works, in original box, D **60.00**

Tops-All Coffee, tin, pictures logoed woman on top of globe, slip lid, minor dents/rust spots/scratches, 1-lb, 6x4", G+, A **125.00**

Topsy Hosiery, match holder, tin litho, colorful image of young girl lying on the beach, JH Read, Aberdeen Wash, rare, 5x3", EX, A **1,800.00**

Topsy Hosiery, match holder back plate, bathing beauty with logo, match box missing, 5x4", G, A.............**250.00**

Topsy Hosiery, thimble, aluminum, Wear Topsy Hosiery imprinted on band, EX, D............................**4.00**

Torch Light Chewing Tobacco, pack (full), pictures torch, EX, D...**25.00**

Torpedo Tobacco, tin, pictures Arnold Boxinger, Duisberg Germany, ca 1930s, some flaking, scarce, A...........**35.00**

Tortoise Shell Smoking Tobacco, pocket tin, flat, turtle logo, A...**30.00**

Tortoise Shell Smoking Tobacco, tin, embossed turtle with lettering above & below on tortoise-shell ground, rectangular with rounded corners, VG, A **45.00**

Tosetti Beer, tray, stock image of Bertha holding a glass of beer, Majestic Saazer printed on rim, image/rim chips, 13" square, EX, A **100.00**

Tourist Coffee, can, cardboard, pictures lg ocean liner on 1 side, locomotive on other side, EX+, A **170.00**

Town Crier Flour, sign, embossed tin litho, orange lettering on gray faded/creases, 19" long, F, A...............**30.00**

Town Talk Flour, sign, cardboard, depicts Victorian lady slicing bread at right of lettering, Leads The World, 12x15", NM, A **60.00**

Toyland Peanut Butter, pail, depicts toy soldiers on parade, HC Derby Co, New York, press lid & bail, scratches/chips, 1-lb, 4x4", VG, A **200.00**

Toys R Us, giraffe, Geoffrey, D **10.00**

Traffic Motor Oil, tin, blue & white with traffic light over product name, Gulf Oil Corp...Refining Co, 1939-52, 2-gal, 12x9", EX, A **30.00**

Traveler's Insurance Co, ledger marker, tin litho, yellow with ornate lettering, interest table on reverse, late 1800s, 12x3", VG, A **175.00**

Treadwell Whiskey, sign, tin litho, colorful image depicts Custer's last stand, wood-colored border, pinholes, framed, 13x19", VG+, A **1,800.00**

Treasure Line Stoves & Ranges, shovel, tin, promotional item with litho image of woman at range, Home Treasure, Art Treasure, 9x4", EX, A **525.00**

Treasure Line Stoves & Ranges, tip tray, cooking range & base burner flanking factory, D Moore Co, some rust on background/overall wear, 7x4", VG, A.............**75.00**

Treasure Line Stoves & Ranges, tip tray, dual image of woman at fancy cookstove in kitchen & heat stove in parlor, D Moore Co, Canada, 4x8", VG+, A............**85.00**

Trommer's Brewery, tray, pictures 4 labeled bottles, lettering on red & gold border, oval, EX, A **240.00**

Trop-Artic Auto Oil, tin, Satisfied From Pole To Pole, ice scene at top, tropic scene in center, very colorful, 1910-20, 1-gal, 11", NM, A.....................2,700.00

Trop-Artic Auto Oil, tin, touring car in snow, a 2nd on tropical beach, Manhattan Oil Co at bottom, ca 1915-25, half-gal, 6", NM+, A **800.00**

Trop-Artic Motor Oils, tin, cone top, red & black with globe encircled by lettered black border, 1900-1910, very rare, 1-qt, 9", EX+, A **475.00**

Trost Bros, shot glass, Trost Bros, Good Cheer, Louisville Ky etched in lg letters with fancy scrollwork, gold rim, M, D **24.00**

Trout-Line Smoking Tobacco, pocket tin, pictures fisherman netting fish with fly equipment, High Grade Burley Cut, minor chips, 4x3x1", G, A........................**275.00**

Trowbridges Chocolate Chip Cookies, bowl, gold decor & lettering, some brown marks inside, no chips or cracks, 14" diameter, A..**90.00**

Tru-Penn Motor Oil, tin, green with black & white letters, Supreme Quality, Penn, American Lubricants, 1935-45, no top, 5-qt, 10x7", VG, A **130.00**

Truth Bread, box, tin, George Washington scenes on all sides, hinged door, EX, D **225.00**

Tuck's Valentines, sign, die-cut cardboard litho, colorful image of children holding sign, Welcomed Everywhere!, rare, framed, 10x15, EX, A **800.00**

Tucketts Abbey Rough Cut Pipe Tobacco, pocket tin, Gothic cathedral on both sides, 10¢, pinpoint spots & scratches, 4x3x1", VG+, A **160.00**

Tucketts Marquerite Cigars, sign, tin, signed A Asti, 1905-10, simulated wood frame, 29x23", EX+, A......................................2,900.00

Tucketts Orinoco Cut Coarse Tobacco, tin, depicts fisherman sitting down leaning against a tree, A Mild & Cool Smoke, slip lid, Canadian, rectangular, EX, A **45.00**

Tucketts Orinoco Cut Coarse Tobacco, tin, depicts fisherman sitting down leaning against a tree, A Mild & Cool Smoke, slip lid, Canadian, round, EX, A.................**65.00**

Tulane Motor Oil, tin, red with green & white letters extending down highway with early vehicles, 1925-45, 2-gal, 12x9", EX, A....................................**110.00**

Tulip Soap, trade card, pictures 2 girls playing in the sand, NM, D **5.00**

Tums, foldout, 4-part (1 for each letter), cardboard, 5-color, Tums for Acid Indigestion, 1920s, 6x19", NM.........**45.00**

Tung-Sol Auto Bulbs, cabinet, tin, double bulb logo on front, Fixed-Focus Auto Bulbs, Longer Life, Uniform Quality, vertical rectangle, A....................................**85.00**

Tung-Sol Auto Bulbs, cabinet, tin, single bulb logo, Let Tung-Sol Light The Way, 9x20x19", VG, A...........**125.00**

Turkey Brand Coffee, tin, pictures turkey in center, 1-lb, EX, A **255.00**

Turkish Cross-Cut Cigarettes, sign, cardboard litho, head portrait of woman in plumed hat, leaf background, W Duke & Sons Co, framed, 21x9", VG+, A **700.00**

Turkish Cross-Cut Cigarettes, sign, paper, full-length portrait of a woman, W Duke & Sons Co, framed, 41x14", EX+, A..**1,600.00**

Turkish Trophies Cigarettes, sign, product name above woman in profile wearing headband & necklace, green textured background, framed, 31x25", EX, A **575.00**

Turnwrights Toffee De-Light, tin, pictures mother giving her daughter a piggy-back ride, press lid, rare, A .**180.00**

Tuxedo Tobacco, jar, glass, green & black labels on 3 sides shows man smoking pipe, tax stamp on 4th, ca 1900, octagonal, 7x5", VG, A **60.00**

Tuxedo Tobacco, pocket tin, brand name above man in circle at center, NM, G **30.00**

Tuxedo Tobacco, pocket tin, pictures a pipe, A.........**25.00**

Tuxedo Tobacco, trolley sign, cardboard litho, pictures tobacco tin & portrait of the artist, Harrison Fisher, framed, 11x21", EX, A....................................**325.00**

Tuxedo Tobacco, trolley sign, cardboard litho, pictures tobacco tin & portrait of entertainer George M Cohan, framed, 11x21", NM, A **700.00**

Tuxedo Tobacco, trolley sign, cardboard litho, portrait of Tad Dorgan, originator of 'Daffydils,' framed, 11x21", EX, A **125.00**

Tuxedo Tobacco, trolley sign, cardboard litho, portrait of the author George Randolph Chester, framed, 11x21", NM, A **130.00**

TW Donahue Wines, Lager, Ales & Liquors, trade sign, glass of beer surrounded by product name in lg letters, scalloped corners, fading, 29x51", VG, A **425.00**

Twenty Grand Smoother Shaves, sign, die-cut tin, blue & white with bold lettering, scratches, 15x30", EX, A**60.00**

Twin Oaks Tobacco, tin, embossed coffin-shaped can with humidor lid, dents/overall wear, 5x8x4", VG, A......**75.00**

Twin Ports Coffee, tin, pictures colorful freighter, Steel Cut, Eimon Mercantile Co, slip lid, overall wear, 1-lb, 6x4", G, A **225.00**

Two Orphans Cigars, cigar box, shows 2 girls embracing on front & inside lid, 6x5", EX, A.....................**10.00**

Two Orphans Cigars, tin, shows 2 girls embracing, humidor lid, overall scratches/chips/wear to edges, 5x5" diameter, G, A **50.00**

Two Queens Cigars, box label, inner lid, depicts Indian maiden & Miss Liberty, 1894, 6x9", M, D................**45.00**

Two Star Radiators, clock, oak, logo on face & bottom glass, fancy dental molding, 38x16", EX, A **425.00**

Two Wheelers Cigars, box label, inner lid, pictures a young girl with 2 mules, 6x9", EX, D.....................**18.00**

Tydol, sign, 2-sided porcelain, shows Tydol above inverted triangle with Ethyl & other lettering, 1920-40, 30" diameter, VG, A **210.00**

❧ U ❧

Uhl's Vienna Special Beer, tray, gentleman pouring a shot of beer in circular inset, Bethleham Pa, touched up, 13" square, G+, A..**175.00**

Ulmer Installment Co, calendar for Round Oak Stoves & Ranges, 1922, embossed, depicts Indian calling moose, full pad, 21x11", M, A **160.00**

Ulmer Installment Co, calendar for Round Oak Stoves & Ranges, 1923, embossed, depicts Indian couple, full pad, 21x11", M, A **130.00**

Uncle Daniel Fine Cut Dark Tobacco, tin, depicts Uncle Daniel, The Scotten-Dillon Co, Detroit Mich, slip lid, 9" diameter, EX, A...**60.00**

Uncle Green Cigars, tin, depicts portrait inset over field of tobacco, lettering above & below, slip lid, chips/dents, 5x6" diameter, EX, A **115.00**

Uneeda Bakers, poster, paper, fruit cake, National Biscuit Co, 42x28", EX, A **120.00**

Uneek Oil Co, bottle, embossed logo & ribbon design, 1-qt, D **35.00**

Uniform Cut Plug Tobacco, tin, Reliable sailor in wreath inset, slip lid, bright colors, 3x6x4", VG, A...........**125.00**

Uniform Cut Plug Tobacco, tin, slip lid on bottle-shaped neck, inpainting/wear, 6x5" diameter, G, A **225.00**

Union Beer, tray, colorful Heine Dutch boy serving beer & sausage, Beer Drivers' Union 132, some chipping, 13x11", G+, A..**35.00**

Union Blend Tobacco, lunch box, leaf inset on green background, decorative edges, slip lid with wire handle, overall wear, 4x7x5", G-, A **150.00**

Union Brewing & Malting Co, see Cascade Beer

Union Brewing Co, tip tray, labeled bottle in center, Bohemian Export Bottled Beer, Peoria Ill, rim chips, 4" diameter, EX, A **70.00**

Union Commander Cut Plug Tobacco, lunch box, tin, red, gold, & black with image of George Washington, missing clasp, 4x7x5", G-, A **95.00**

Union Jack Cigars, sign, tin over cardboard, man holding cigar, elements of image in color float on black background, 19x13", G-, A **200.00**

Union Leader Cut Plug, sign, paper, ca 1899, minor wear, rare, framed, 30x22", EX, A................4,900.00

Union Leader Cut Plug, tin, shaped like a cream can depicts an eagle on cut plug, minor denting, 9x5" diameter, VG, A...**235.00**

Union Leader Ready Cut Plug, tin, pictures Uncle Sam smoking his pipe, slip lid, 6x5" diameter, EX, A....**70.00**

Union Leader Ready Cut Tobacco, pocket tin, circle inset of Uncle Sam on red, white, & blue background with lettering above, VG, A..**30.00**

Union Leader Tobacco, trolley sign, lettering to the right of slanted tin featuring Uncle Sam, The Best Tobacco Value, 10x25", EX, A **95.00**

Union Mills Flour, sign, full-color image of a little girl lying in a wicker basket with flowers, ca 1905, 14x19", EX, A **140.00**

Union Pacific Tea Co, tray, children & animals in snow around rim, girl with bow in hair in center, ad text on back, 1907, 8" diameter, EX, A **100.00**

Union Razors, sign, embossed tin, depicts North America & a razor strop, overall wear, 14x10", F, A.............**35.00**

Union Sport Cigars, box label, outer, pictures a man in formal attire with yacht & horse race scene in background, 5x5", M, D **6.00**

Union 76 Certified Car Care, sign, porcelain, D **350.00**

United Brand Robes & Pajamas, sign, embossed tin, rare, 18x12", NM, A 4,500.00

United Cigars, sign, double-sided, applied gilt letters on red background, rope background with decorative corners, 12x43", NM, A..**500.00**

United Motors, sign, porcelain on steel, pictures car, ceramic inserts for neon tubing (missing), oval, 36" wide, EX+, A..**550.00**

United States Fidelity & Guaranty Co, calendar, 1900, patriotic image with Naval officers surrounding 2 little boy officers, full pad, framed, 20x14", EX, A **400.00**

United States Sanitary Mfg Co, sign for porcelain enameled bathtubs, pictures topless girl with long brown hair, decorative gold frame, 24x16", EX, A **475.00**

United States 5¢ Cigars, sign, embossed tin, framed, 13x9", G, A..625.00

Universal Boys Pajamas, sign, celluloid, 10x12", M, A **80.00**

Universal Stoves & Ranges, match holder, tin litho, lettering on globe, Made by Ribben & Sexton, 5x3", VG+, A **220.00**

Upholstery Supply Co Milwaukee, catalog, ca 1920, 171 pages of supplies, 11x8", VG, A **5.00**

Upper Ten, sign, embossed tin, product name flanked by tipped bottle & Up! Up! Up!, ...For A Bigger, Better Lift!, 12x29", M, D **65.00**

Uptown Soda, sign, tin, bottle with Drink Uptown on striped background, rounded corners, EX, A.........**25.00**

US Ammunition, calendar, 1917, depicts slain ducks, May pad, framed, 28x18", A **260.00**

US Ammunition, sign, mountain lion & goat, 1920s, decorative frame, vertical rectangle, EX, A.................**380.00**

US Ammunition, sign, tin, pictures military meeting 'At Bisley, England,' bullets on border, fading, lettered self-frame, 22x29", G+, A.................**500.00**

US Cartridge Co, sign, cardboard, pictures hunter with shotgun promoting The Black Shells, background holes/edge chips, 12x8", A.................**125.00**

US Cartridge Co, sign, paper with metal bands top & bottom, flying hawk attacking 2 ducks, The Black Shells, 30x20", G-, A.................**1,800.00**

US Fire Extinguisher, extinguisher, advertising & functional, orange & red with gold eagle, black letters, 1910-20, 22x2" diameter, EX, A.................**20.00**

US Hame Co, string holder, tin, buffalo logo in center with product on either side, US H Co Hames Sold Here, 19" long, G, A.................**270.00**

US Harness Oil, clock, wood with glass face, product name & other lettering encircled by Roman numerals, round, EX, A.................**525.00**

US Marine Cut Plug Tobacco, lunch box, tin, sailor with product leaning from porthole, product name on hinged lid with wire handle, 5x8x5", G, A.................**200.00**

US Tire Co, clock, wood with brass hands, rare, 18" diameter, EX, A.................**4,000.00**

USG Harness Oil, clock, oak & brass, dropped regulator, reverse-stenciled glass pendulum window, ca 1890, octagonal, 25x18x5", EX, A.................**700.00**

Ushers Ales, ash tray, glass, diamond logo, square, EX, A.................**15.00**

Ushers Beer, tray, pictures a farm scene & lg mug of beer, rectangular, EX, A.................**30.00**

Utah-Brau, tray, pictures eagle atop world, America's Finest Beer, Phone West 650, stains/surface loss, 12" diameter, VG, A.................**225.00**

Utica Club Beer, tray, factory image, West End Brewing Co, overall dirt/soiling/scratching to image, 12" diameter, VG, A.................**45.00**

Utica Club Beverages, sign, couple being served by Black boy, flavors listed, West End Brewing Co, ca 1910, celluloid frame, 10x14", EX+, A.................**350.00**

Utica Club West End Brewing Co, tray, depicts view of factory, 12" diameter, VG, D.................28.00

❧ **V** ❧

Valley City Coffee & Spice Mills Coffee, bin, tin, company & product names within scrollwork reserve, 1930, 19x19x13", EX, A.................**750.00**

Valley City Flour, pocket mirror, EX, D.................**85.00**

Valley Forge Beer, display, plastic die-cut, depicts boxers, EX, A.................**50.00**

Valley Forge Special Beer, tray, shows waitress with tray of beer, overall dirt haze, hairline scratch through waitress, 13x11", EX, A.................**80.00**

Valley Forge Special Beer, tray, shows view of Washington's Headquarters, Scheidt's Ale & Porter, 11x13", VG+, A.................**50.00**

Value Cigarros, sign, paper litho, 2 thieves stealing money & cigars from safe, muted colors, ca 1900, matted & framed, 25x16", G, A.................**200.00**

Valvoline Oil Co, tin, trademark in center, black letters on green, pour spout, ca 1873-1881, rectangular, 1-qt, 4", EX, A.................**275.00**

Van Camp's Soup, sign, embossed die-cut tin, Dutch girl & boy holding lg can of soup & dish, product name below, rare, 32x21", NM, A.................**13,000.00**

Van Houten's Cocoa, box, wood, paper label on inner lid, stamped lettering on sides, 5x14x10", VG, A.................**75.00**

Van Houten's Cocoa, sign, stone litho on cardboard, pictures a little girl with a cup of cocoa, 1890, original gesso frame, 32x20", EX, D.................**1,250.00**

Van Houten's Pure Soluble Cocoa, sign, paper litho, depicts eagle above lettering, ...Best & Goes Farthest, original oak frame, 28x36", VG, A.................**45.00**

Vanko Cigars, tin, Vanko on diagonal curved scroll, horse's head in circle inset above left, full view lower right, rectangular, VG, A **30.00**

Varsity Athletic Underwear, sign, embossed, colorful image of a rowing crew in their underwear, framed, hole in center/surface wear, 10x14", G-, A............**525.00**

Vaseline, display box, tin & wood litho, colorful image of Vaseline tubes, hinged opening on reverse, 16x7x7", G+, A...**240.00**

Vaseline, ledger marker, tin litho, shows ruler with large lettering, product info on reverse, ca late 1800s, 12x3", G, A **200.00**

Vaseline, trolley sign, 1920, EX, A...........................**250.00**
Vat 69 Whiskey, pitcher, ceramic, EX, D **10.00**

Veedol, tin, for motor oil, yellow lettering on black background, ca 1915-25, 1-gal, 10", EX+, A 115.00

Velvet Beer, charger, tin, cherubs above colonial gathering pouring beer into lifted glasses, wear, 24" diameter, G-, A...**150.00**

Velvet Coffee, tin, WH Malkin storefront, cup of coffee on reverse, original slip lid, wood-handled bail, 5-lb, 9x8" diameter, G+, A **210.00**

Velvet Night Talcum, tin, shaker top, EX, D.............**38.00**

Velvet Pipe & Cigarette Tobacco, tin, pictures a pipe & burning cigarette with product name above & below, slip lid, round, EX, A..**5.00**

Velvet Tobacco, sign, tin litho, 2 men, little boy, & dog, product in lower left, flaking/paint loss on border, vertical rectangle, A...**225.00**

Velvet Tobacco/Piedmont Cigarettes, sign, 2-sided, flanged, Cigarette of Quality, 10 for 5¢, NM, D....**775.00**

Venus Pencils, tin, flat, picturing Venus & pencil, 7x2x1", G, D...**10.00**

Vernor's Ginger Ale, sign, tin, Drink Vernor's Ginger Ale, oval, 36" wide, EX+, A **60.00**

Vesper Coffee, tin, paper label, slip lid, 1-lb, 6x4" diameter, EX, D 75.00

Veteran Brand Coffee, tin, logoed portrait of a man in profile, minor wear/lid discoloration/bottom fade/scratches, 1-lb, 6x4" diameter, G, A **105.00**

Vico Oils & Greases, sign, porcelain, red & black letters on white, We Sell U, Paraffin Base, 1930-40, edges rough/paint loss, A **50.00**

Victor & Berliner, tip tray, pictures trademarked image of dog & gramophone, crazing/rim chips, 4" diameter, G-, A **55.00**

Victor Adding Machines, sign, cardboard tri-fold, $75 adding machine with features being pointed out through use of strings, 25x48", EX, A....................**30.00**

Victory Candies, bucket, wood, paper label with Statue of Liberty, 7x7" diameter, G, A.................................**15.00**

Victory Tobacco, sign, paper litho, colorful image of 4 women attending Victory, some spotting, framed, 14x19", VG+, A...**350.00**

Victory-V Lozenges, tin, gazebo with flowers & birds surrounding V windows, hinged roof opens, rare & unusual, slight wear, 10x9x8", G+, A....................**400.00**

Victory-V Lozenges, tin, shows kids on sled racing down snowy slopes, slight scratches/rim chips, 1x5x3", VG+, A **45.00**

Village Inn Pancake House, bear, plush, Bucky, appears EX, D **30.00**

Virgin Leaf Tobacco, sign, young girl in a silk bonnet surrounded by greenery, product & company name above & below, 26x14" without frame, A **750.00**

Virgin Smoking Tobacco, pail, patterned tin with paper label, slip lid & bail, creases/chips, 4x4", VG, A...**850.00**

Virginia Cigars, box label, inner lid, depicts woman with long dark hair, 6x9", M, D **26.00**

Virginia Dare Wines, sign, tin, man & woman frolicking through the woods, Garrett & Co Wine Growers, ca 1910-20, wood frame, 46x36", EX, A **1,100.00**

Virginity Smoking Tobacco, see Gail & Ax

W&S Cough Drops, store container, glass with embossed design & letters on lid with knob lid, round, M, A ..**160.00**

Wadhams Tempered Motor Oil, tin, black with white letters, various oil containers in yellow & black, Wadhams Oil Co, ca 1915-25, 5-gal, 15x9", G, A **150.00**

Wagon Wheel Tobacco, pocket tin, pictures a lg wagon wheel on striped background, rare, NM, A **385.00**

Wagoner Beer, thimble, aluminum whistle, blue band with company name, EX, D **30.00**

Wake-Em Up Coffee, tin, product name over Indian in headdress at center, bail handle, NM, A..............**325.00**

Wales-Goodyear Rubbers, calendar, 1906-07, die-cut cardboard litho, double-sided, elegant women prancing in the snow, framed, 10x11", EX, A **150.00**

Walk-Over Shoes, sign, paper, factory view with 2 insets of product, The World's Greatest Fine Shoe Plant, 20x26" without frame, G, A **55.00**

Walk-Over Shoes, sign, product name in lg letters with circular logo on left, Abram R Gerber... below, ca 1910, framed, horizontal, EX, A.......................................**20.00**

Walk-Over Shoes, sign, tin, double-sided, man & woman, C Shonk litho, oval, 28x17", EX, A................**1,700.00**

Walk-Over Shoes, sign, tin, man & lady in ovals flank Walk-Over Shoes, proprietor's name & address below, 12x24", M, A...**80.00**

Walko Poultry Remedies, display, counter top, die-cut cardboard trifold, 34x45", EX, A **70.00**

Walla-Walla Gum, store container, 4-sided glass jar for Pepsin gum, label with Indian, Knoxville Tenn, replaced lid, 11x5", EX, A **400.00**

Walter A Wood Mowing & Reaping Machinery, sign, stone litho, pictures machinery vignettes with Statue of Liberty & NY Skyline beyond, tiger maple frame, 36x46", EX, A **4,200.00**

Walter A Wood Rakes, sign, paper, lettering top right corner, framed, EX, A **1,000.00**

Walter Baker & Co, art plate, tin, depicts logoed portrait of Chocolate Girl, jeweled border, 2 holes in border/wear, 10" diameter, G+, A..........................**85.00**

Walter Baker & Co, cookbook, 1914, depicts Chocolate Girl on cover, 'Choice Recipes,' 64 pages, D............**8.00**

Walter Baker & Co, cookbook, 1928, 'Baker's Famous Chocolate Recipes,' 63 pages, D **6.00**

Walter Baker & Co, cookbook, 1950, 'Baker's Favorite Chocolate Recipes,' 112 pages, D............................**7.00**

Walter Baker & Co, display, die-cut tin, urn shaped with oval tray picturing company products, portrait trademark on urn, 24x17x14", VG, A **1,700.00**

Walter Baker & Co, leaflet, 1932, 'Baker's Best Chocolate Recipes,' D **8.00**

Walter Baker & Co Breakfast Cocoa, sign, tin, Chocolate Girl on silver background, 20x14", G+, A **1,100.00**

Walter Baker & Co Cocoa, tin, depicts Chocolate girl on black background on 2 sides with ornate pattern, screw lid, wear, 6x3" square, G, A......................................**65.00**

Walter Baker & Co Cocoa, tin, depicts Chocolate Girl on light background on 2 sides with ornate pattern, screw lid, 6x3" square, EX, A **75.00**

Walter Baker & Co's Chocolate, Broma & Cocoa, sign, cardboard, interior with colonial people savoring cocoa, water stain wear, 24x27" without frame, G- A **200.00**

Walter Baker & Co's Chocolate & Cocoa Preparations, sign, paper, 1870s factory & street scene of US cocoa company, wear/inpainting, original frame, 27x35", G+, A..**2,500.00**

Waltham Watches, sign, reverse-painted glass, eagle over watch above top section of globe, needs background repair, 16x23", A..**125.00**

Wanamaker's Grand Depot, sign, paper, lettering arched above colonial family on porch accepting fruit from man, 18x24" without frame, EX, A.....................**1,000.00**

War Chest Cigars, box label, inner lid, pictures coins in a treasure chest, 6x9", M, D.......................................**20.00**

Ward's Cake, display case, tin panels & frame with top glass inserts, 21x17x13", EX+, A..................**2,500.00**

Ward's Lemon-Crush, syrup dispenser, lemon figural with original lettering on pump, color chips at foot/light soiling, rare, 12x10", EX+, A **850.00**

Ward's Lime-Crush, dispenser, lime-shaped porcelain, original pump, chip on foot/minor overpainting, rarest of 3, 13x9x7", G+, A...**1,300.00**

Ward's Stationery, sign, etched & reverse-painted glass, Boston Fine Papers & Envelopes, framed, 10x16", EX, A **75.00**

Ward's Vitovim Bread, thermometer, enamel, 1915, 21x9", A **150.00**

Waring Aluron Irons, trade card, hand using product, product name & lettering upper left, horizontal, D **17.00**

Warren Paints & Varnishes, sign, tin, Agency For over lg lettered can, Right Paint To Paint Right, 1930-40, paint loss at edges, 20x13", VG+, A...............................**20.00**

Washburn Cigars, playing cards, colorful aces & jokers, 52 cards with 1 joker & 1 extra, original box, VG, D .**50.00**

Washington Crisps Toasted Corn Flakes, cereal box, Washington in patriotic oval, white lettering on blue above & below, red & white striped ground, 9x6", NM, A **100.00**

Washington's Coffee, display case, wood & glass, Better Coffee That Will Never Disturb You, ca 1920-30, 15x15", NM, A...**300.00**

Water Brothers Brewing Co, glass, etched factory scene, NM, A **30.00**

Waterbury Watches, sign, glass, ruby cut to clear, drilled to hang in store window, 6x15", EX, A.................**130.00**

Waterman Yarn, letter opener, propeller shape, D...**25.00**

Waterman's Fountain Pens, poster, paper, shows Uncle Sam at the signing of the Treaty Of Portsmouth..., ca early 1900s, 26x49" overall, EX, A...2,300.00

Waterman's Fountain Pens, sign, cardboard, Christmas-wrapped packages of Ideal fountain pens, overall wear, 11x21" without frame, G-, A...................................**60.00**

Waterman's Fountain Pens, thermometer, die-cut tin litho, pen figural, Ideal Fountain Pen, black with white & gold, creases, 20x4", VG, A **900.00**

Watertown Consumers Brewing Co, calendar poster, woman holding up bottle & glass of beer, good color, matted & framed, 27x20", VG, A **600.00**

Watney's Ale, sign, elk pictured on reverse milk glass with metal-cased frame, 30x12", NM, A **100.00**

Watson's Imperial Cough Drops, store tin, product name & fancy graphics, slip lid, rare, rectangular, EX, A..**80.00**

WB Cyclist Corsets, sign, paper, images of women at sports, Athletic Purposes..., ca 1895, JP Ottman Litho, matted, 26x20", G-, A...**600.00**

WDC Pipes, display with 4 pipes, tin, easel-back, man smoking pipe, 16x10", EX, A **350.00**

Weaver Hardware, pocket mirror, early store interior, EX, D..**65.00**

Wedding Bell Coffee, display, die-cut cardboard, cabin frames product with seasonal depictions on either side (hot & cold), 17x28", G, A **200.00**

Wedding Veil Cigars, box label, outer, pictures a bride, 5x5", M, D **4.00**

Weed Tire Chains, calendar, 1916, paper, colorful image of 4 women wearing hats within ovals, framed, edge damage, 30x10", VG+, A **250.00**

Weed Tire Chains, sign, mechanical, pictures tire with chain on brick road, adjustable dial to note gasoline price, 23x17", VG+, A...**475.00**

Weekend Special Cigars, tin, paper label with women riding in open touring car & train background, overall wear, 5x4" diameter, G-, A **450.00**

Weideman Boy Brand Coffee, tin, pickers in field & logo of serving boy, slip lid, bright colors, slight denting/scratches, 1-lb, 6x4", VG+, A **750.00**

Weilands Extra Pale Lager, tray, pictures Indian girl in center, decorative border, Kaufmann & Strauss litho, round, NM, A...**575.00**

Weir Plow Co, sign, tin litho, factory surrounded by 6 images of its products, Monmouth Ill, minor fading, framed, 20x28", VG+, A **9,000.00**

Welch Guaranteed Motor Oil, sign, tin, oil can & 31¢ Per Quart on left, Illinois Oil Products Inc, Rock Island, 1930-40, minor scuffing, 9x24", NM, A **245.00**

Welch Motor oil, can, waxed cardboard, Welch Guaranteed on yellow over speeding car, Illinois Oil Products, ca 1962-65, 1-qt, EX, A..**45.00**

Welch's, decal, grape wreath, 12", VG, D **10.00**

Welcome Soap, sign, group of people in center, Curtis Davis & Co, several holes on border, VG, A........**760.00**

Welcome Soap, sign, mixed media, 2 girls in appliqued cloth dresses in a landscape, Curtis Davis & Co, shadow box frame, 28x13", NM, A **850.00**

Welcome Soap, sign, paper, lettering at right of product over coastal scene, Always The Same, Welcome Quality, framed, 17x26", NM, A..................**150.00**

Weld's Ice Cream, tray, depicts a drummer boy surrounded by flags of different nations, logo below, 13" diameter, appears EX, A..................**50.00**

Welm Fabric Center, clock, round dial flanked by CBS 1400, ABC 1400 with Welm above & Fabric Center below, not working, 20" diameter, A..................**40.00**

Welsbach Lighting, tip tray, Victorian household scene with mother & daughter enjoying Welsbach lighting, ca 1910-20, 4" diameter, NM, A..................**120.00**

Welz & Zerweck Brewery, tray, hops motif on rim, rare, EX, A..................**375.00**

Wesson, booklet, 1958, 'Skillet Cookbook,' 64 pages, D..**3.00**

West Electric Hair Curlers, display, tin with hinged slant lid showing product, 9x5x10", G+, A..................**50.00**

West End Brewing Co, calendar, 1907, paper, colorful image of young girl in fancy Victorian setting, full pad, 21x26" without frame, EX, A..................**425.00**

West End Brewing Co, calendar poster, paper, Victorian girl at table, for Pilsener beer, full pad attached, framed, 28x21", VG, A..................**350.00**

West End Brewing Co, tip tray, pretty girl in center, Old Home Week, Aug 3rd to 10th 1914, Utica NY, 4" diameter, NM, A..................**305.00**

West End Brewing Co, tray, liberty lady, eagle, & barrel surrounded by lettering, Utica NY, minor fading/rim chips, 13" diameter, A..................**325.00**

West Hair Nets, display, revolving tin, woman with car & women washing their hair with nymphs in background, ca 1921, 20x12", G, A..................**250.00**

Westclox, display, die-cut cardboard, father & son arriving at work, 3 original working pocket watches, 24x29" flat, VG, A..................**75.00**

Western Airlines, playing cards, boxed, EX, D..........**10.00**

Western Ammunition, sign, embossed tin, depicts product below product name, vertical sides banded in different color, 13x19", EX, A..................**155.00**

Western Assurance Co, ledger marker, tin, logoed lion & unicorn, Kellogg & Bulkeley, 1890, 12x3", EX, A...**95.00**

Western Gun Works, flyer, 2-sided, handguns, pistols, etc, black & white broadside-type print, ca 1876, 22x32" fully opened, G, A..................**45.00**

Western Union Telegrams, sign, 2-sided porcelain, flanged, pictures candlestick telephone, Telephone Your Telegrams From Here, 20x18", G, A..........**200.00**

Western Union Telegraph, sign, 2-sided porcelain, flanged, Telegraph Here, Western Union, 17x25", EX, A..................**140.00**

Western Union Telegraph Office, sign, bold white letters on blue background, heavy wear, horizontal rectangle, A..................**320.00**

Westinghouse Electric Iron, trade card, 2-sided, woman with iron that connects to ceiling fixture, back shows iron with porcelain screw-in cord, D..................**15.00**

Westinghouse Lamp Co, sign, metal, flanged, 2-sided, circular logo with Authorized Agents... over lg W flanked by light bulbs, 13x18", EX, A..................**95.00**

Westinghouse Television, clock, product name in center, round, EX, A..................**55.00**

Weyman's Cutty-Pipe Chewing & Smoking Tobacco, store tin, red & yellow lettering on green, shows pack of product, 5¢, ...New Foil Package, 1920, rare, 13x10x9", EX+, A..................**450.00**

WGY Coffee, tin, depicts coffee server with product name above & below, slip lid, 1-lb, round, EX, A..........**50.00**

Wheat Sheaf Coffee, tin, product name over sheaf of wheat, 1-lb, EX, A..................**105.00**

Wheatlet Cereal, thermometer & barometer, tin with wood frame, Wheatlet Is Eaten & Enjoyed In All Kinds Of Weather, D..................**85.00**

Whip Tobacco, tin, embossed octagon, encircled rider & horse with decorative border, Ready Rolled, overall wear, 6x6", VG, A..................**300.00**

Whistle, sign, pictures hand holding product, Thirsty? Just Whistle in bold letters, Demand The Genuine, 21x28", EX, A..................**280.00**

Whistle, sign, tin, Thirsty? Just- by bottle of product, Certified Pure, Whistle in lg letters, ca 1920s, 12x12", EX, A..................**85.00**

White Cat Cigars, box label, outer, pictures a white cat lying on a cigar, 3x5", M, D..................**2.00**

White Goose Coffee, pail, pictures goose, Shuster-Gormly Co, Jeannette Pa, bail handle, general wear, 5-lb, 8x8", G+, A..................**550.00**

White Goose Coffee, tin, pictures goose, Shuster-Gormly Co, 1-lb, NM, A 725.00

White House Coffee, sign, cardboard, elderly man in patriotic oval at right of coffee can depicting White House, fading, 11x20", G, A 65.00

White King Soap, thimble, aluminum, product name on worn blue band, D 3.00

White King Washing Machine Soap, sign, tin, box of product with soap pouring from it, Granulated printed in upper right corner, vertical, EX, A 80.00

White Label Cigars, sign, embossed tin, shows an open box of cigars, The Favorite Everywhere, Sentenne & Green, 10x14", VG, A 65.00

White Label Coffee, tin, depicts coffeecup with product name above & below, slip lid, 1-lb, round, EX, A .40.00

White Loaf Baking Powder, sign, tin, Wise Women Use over product name, It's Absolutely Pure, 12x15", M, D 600.00

White Mountain Junior, ice cream maker, salesman's sample, wood with old varnish, diamond-shape paper label, worn, 6", A 250.00

White Orchid Cigars, box label, inner lid, pictures a cigar with a white orchid above, 6x9", M, D 6.00

White Rock Beer, tray, girl rests arm on tiger's head, Kaufmann & Strauss, ca 1900s, 13" diameter, VG, A ...250.00

White Rock Table Water, sign, 18x18" with frame, EX, A 350.00

White Rock Table Water, tip tray, girl, 4", VG, D 100.00

White Seal Pure Rye, sign, paper, colorful image of barebreasted women bathing beside Bedouin barge, discoloration, framed, 38x50", G, A 4,750.00

White Sewing Machines, puzzle, paper & wood block puzzle showing interior with lettering, US map on reverse, wear/paper loss, 16x11", G, A 120.00

White Sewing Machines, thimble, aluminum, company name & product imprinted on band, EX, D 4.00

White Swan Coffee, carton, cardboard with paper label of swan on pond, Toronto Canada, overall wear, very rare, 25-lb, 17x11x11", F, A 20.00

White Swan Peanut Butter, pail, tin, red, white, & blue swan, slip lid & bail, White Swan Spices & Cereals Ltd, Canada, 13-oz, 4x4", G, A 180.00

Whitman Candies Peanut Crunch, tin, pictures baseball scenes, EX, A 20.00

Whitman's Chocolates, sign, die-cut metal, circular cutout with delivery man in center, Whitman's at top, Chocolate at bottom, 9", G+, A 50.00

Whitman's Chocolates, sign, porcelain, green with white letters, minor dings, 14x40", A 80.00

Whiz Auto Top Dressing, tin, lettering above & below early touring car on cream with blue border & yellow accents, 1910, 1-pt, 5", EX, A 60.00

Whiz Cup Grease, tin, lettering above early touring car on cream with blue border, wire handle, 1910, faded, 5-lb, 5x7" diameter, VG+, A 160.00

Whiz Gear-Life, tin, yellow with engine flanked by 2 jokers in center, RM Hollingshead Co, Camben NJ, 1910-20, 10-lb, 8x8", VG, A 80.00

Whiz Metal Polish, tin, red with early touring car on yellow, RM Hollingshead Co, Camden NJ, 1910, 1-pt, 6", VG, A 45.00

Wieland's Beer, tray, Indian princess in center, A Western Product, Adloff & Hauerwass, Los Angeles Cal, some wear, 13" diameter, G+, A 300.00

Wieland's Beer, tray, seated girl holding letter, San Francisco, USA, ca 1909, touch-up to background/rim chips, 14x11", VG+, A 200.00

Wielands Extra Pale Lager, tray, Kaufmann & Strauss litho, ca 1902, 13" diameter, NM, A 850.00

Wigwam Coffee, tin, depicts silhouette of Indian rider & teepees at bottom, Indian logo in center, Patent Cut, 1-lb, EX, A **160.00**

Wil-Flo Motor Oil, tin, snow scene with pine trees, At 30 Below written in snow, dark blue background, ca 1935-45, light rust, 1-qt, VG, A **65.00**

Wilbur's Stock Tonic, sign, paper, beer wagon pulled by 6 dappled horses accompanied by running dog, overall wear, 15x32", G-, A **60.00**

Wilcox & White Organ Co, poster, paper, 3-quarter view of woman holding perforated organ roll, matted & framed, 27x23", EX, A **150.00**

Wild Honey Tobacco, pack (full), pictures bees & farm scene, EX, D **20.00**

Wild Root, shaving cup, ironstone, 2 joined cups, green lettering, Buffalo China, 1930s, 3x7", M, A **60.00**

Wild West Bath Soap, display box, interior paper label depicts cowboys lassoing steers, exterior product label, overall wear, 4x16x13", G, A **1,250.00**

Will's Capstan Cigarettes, sign, porcelain, light blue with blue & white lettering, rectangular, 70" long, G-, A ..**25.00**

Will's Woodbines, sign, porcelain, green with white & black lettering, rectangular, 70" long, G-, A **25.00**

William Clarke & Sons Needles, case, oak, with original handles, 2 drawers, A **130.00**

William S Scull & Co Dry Roasted Coffee, store bin, Strong Blend in center oval with product name above & below, worn, A **200.00**

William Tell Cigars, box label, outer, product name over man aiming crossbow at an apple on a boys head, 5x5", M, D **10.00**

Williamatic Spool Cotton, spool cabinet, oak, 4 drawers with original advertising pulls, side decals & Eastlake decoration, 14x24x15", VG, A **450.00**

Williamatic Thread, sign, paper, 'The Great Williamatic Bridge' with ships below & hot air ballon, general wear, 24x31" without frame, G, A **175.00**

Williams & Clark Bone Fertilizer, sign, tin, pictures bull in center surrounded by lettering, High Grade, Quick Acting..., chips/scratches, 20x14", G, A **150.00**

Williams Russin Cough Drops, store tin, slip lid, heavily worn, rectangular, A **60.00**

Williams Shaving Soap, scuttle, porcelain, 2-sided with lettering on 1 side & crossed flags on the other, ca 1908-12, EX, D **225.00**

Williams Toilet Luxuries, paperweight mirror, colorful image of shaving sticks with list of other toiletries around border, 5" diameter, VG+, A **270.00**

Willing Brand Pants & Overalls, sign, decal on wood, train scene with men attired in Willing Brand clothing, Union Made, Detroit, 21x15", EX, A **1,000.00**

Willow Spring Brewing Co, tip tray, deep-dish with unusual graphics, Stars & Stripes with eagle in center, rare, 4" diameter, EX, A **150.00**

Wilson-Murray Co Cocoa Syrup, jug with handle, white with brown top, paper label with logo & 1 Gal Cocoa Syrup lettered above, Shake Well, 12", EX, A **65.00**

Wilson's Corned Beef, trade card, pictures 2 sailors on a ship, NM, D **6.00**

Winchester, calendar, 1898, paper, 2 hunters with downed buck, Ammunition, framed, 26x14", VG+, A **750.00**

Winchester, calendar, 1914, paper, hunter with dogs in a cornfield, paper loss/creasing, 30x15", G-, A **100.00**

Winchester, catalog, 1950, 'Arms & Accessories,' color illustrations, 60 pages, VG, D **60.00**

Winchester, catalog, 1968, color illustrations, 48 pages, in original cover, M, D **16.00**

Winchester, potato sack, burlap, 3-color overprint of Conestoga wagon with Winchester rifle, Jones Produce Co, 100-lb, 36x22", VG, A **10.00**

Winchester, saleman's handbook, 1956, black & white & color illustrations, 84 pages, NM, D **80.00**

Winchester, sign, paper, pictures 2 dogs, logo & shells around border, Rifles & Shotguns For Sale Here..., HR Poore, 32x42", G, A..**650.00**

Winchester After Shave Talc, tin, shaker top, hunter & dog, 5", EX, A **75.00**

Winchester Big Game Rifles & Ammunition, poster, ca 1904, hunter & dead mountain goat in filigree inset, lettering above & below, framed, 26x15", EX, A......**600.00**

Winchester Cartridges & Guns, sign, brass, embossed lettering & border, guns & dead birds hanging from moose antlers, We Recommend..., sm, EX, A **150.00**

Winchester Cartridges & Guns, sign, tin, pictures guns & dead birds hanging from moose antlers, by Alexander Pope, 36x30", NM, A 1,200.00

Winchester Cutlery Tools, sign, paper litho, split image of mother & daughter in kitchen, father & son in garage, sm water stain, 16x21", EX, A....................**240.00**

Winchester Repeating Arms Co, calendar, 1889, paper, grizzly attacks hunter, 12 months in 2 rows, missing overpad, rare, 28x20" overall, EX, A.................**1,000.00**

Winchester Repeating Arms Co, calendar, 1896, paper, hunter standing & 1 on bended knee aiming at moose, Cartridges, framed, 26x14", VG+, A......................**900.00**

Winchester Repeating Arms Co, calendar, 1897, paper, cowboy by horse aiming at deer, Cartridges, framed, 26x14", VG+, A......................**750.00**

Windisch-Muhlhauser Brewing Co, sign, die-cut tin, 3 gents around barrel having a beer, Lager Beers & company name below, scratches, rare, A...**1,600.00**

Wings King Size Cigarettes, sign, cardboard, lg plane & Piper Cub Given Away... at top, pack & more planes in center, 1950s, 30x20", EX, A..................**110.00**

Wings King Size Cigarettes, sign, paper, lg plane above row of 4 other planes, Free Piper Cub Airplane, product & ad copy below, 15x10", M, A......................**70.00**

Winner Cut Plug Tobacco, lunch box, tin, depicts racing cars, hinged lid & wire handle, good sheen, 4x8x5", EX, A.......................................**140.00**

Winslow, Rand & Watson's Teas & Coffees, sign, die-cut cardboard, mother watching her 2 children break a wishbone, If You Wish For The Best..., framed, 33x15", A...**625.00**

Winston Cigarettes, ash tray, embossed tin, D............**8.00**

Winston Cigarettes, playing cards, rodeo cowboy on bucking bronco in black on red & white Winston background, Rodeo Awards, complete, M, D.............**20.00**

Wish Bone Combination Coffee, tin, pictures wishbone & lettering on green background, Drip Grind, slip lid, 6x4" diameter, G, A..................................**15.00**

Wm C Davis Home Bakeries, tip tray, elegant woman with flowers in her hair, lists various breads on rim, 2 sm hanging holes, 16x13", EX+, A.......................**450.00**

Wm J Friday & Co Inc, pocket mirror, depicts smiling man & frowning man with same eyes, Fine Wines, Liquors, & Cigars, Pittsburgh, round, EX, A.....................**45.00**

Wm J Lemp Brewing Co, tray, man with beer & sandwich encircled by lettering & 2 logos, repeated logos on black surround rim, round, A.........**575.00**

Wm Peter Brewing Co, tray, depicts logoed star in center, Selected Malt & Hops Beer, Union Hill NJ, oval, 14x17", EX, A...**325.00**

Wm Younger & Co's Scotch Ale, sign, die-cut tin, depicts 5 animated gentlemen at bar, The 'Younger' Generation, scratches/rust, 15" long, G-, A.....................**225.00**

Wolf Co Flouring Mill Machinery, poster, paper, depicts Little Red Riding Hood & the wolf with inserts of machinery, matted & framed, 27x19", NM, A.......**500.00**

Wolf Co Flouring Mill Machinery, sign, paper, child in floppy hat & machinery below, Flouring Mill Machinery, original metal strip & frame, 21x13", EX, A...**175.00**

Wolf Co Flouring Mill Machinery, sign, paper, depicts night factory scene, Aug Wolf & Co Works, matted & framed, 27x37", EX, A..**300.00**

Wolf Co Flouring Mill Machinery, sign, paper, girl in wide-brimmed hat with inserts of machines & lettering, matted & framed, approx: 21x12", EX, A..............**225.00**

Wolf's Head Motor Oil, sign, 2-sided tin, flanged, Ask For above product name on red, white, & green background, 1960s, 22x17", EX, A.................................**65.00**

Wolf's Head Motor Oil, tin, product name on wide diagonal white stripe, oval logo with wolf head bottom right, ca 1931-35, 1-gal, VG+, A..**35.00**

Wolf's Schnapps, sign, cardboard, touring car outside of tavern with occupants enjoying schnapps, original frame, 22x28" overall, G, A.................................**150.00**

Wonder Enriched Bread, sign, embossed tin, depicts lg loaf of bread, Builds Strong Bodies 8 Ways, 12x20", EX, D..**95.00**

Wood Coffee, measure, brass, figural swami handle, D..**18.00**

Wood's Canadian Coffee, tin, souvenir can with multiple Canadian landmarks on insets, original slip lid, wood knob, 1-lb, 7x4" diameter, G-, A **35.00**

Woodlawn Mills, display case, tin, pictures man driving a shoe at Shoe Lace Station, original marque, 14x12x11", G, A...400.00

Woolsey's Varnishes, pocket mirror, celluloid mirror picturing paint can, minor spotting, 3x2", VG, A **45.00**

Woonsocket Rubber Boots & Shoes, sign, embossed tin, Woonsocket above Rubber, Boots, & Shoes lettered on the diagonal, Geo P Langford, 9x19", VG+, D **50.00**

WOW Motor Oil, tin, Waverly Oil Works banner among letters WOW, red top band, red & blue bottom band on yellow, ca 1935-45, 1-qt, EX, A................................**25.00**

Wright & Pitson Victor Corp, catalog, 1923, 64 pages of sporting supplies, 6x8", VG, A..............................**25.00**

Wright & Taylor Distillers, tray, elegant women seated in front of factory, Old Charter Distillery, 12" diameter, VG+, A **525.00**

Wright & Taylor Distillers, tray, factory on leaf flanked by logo, Fine Old Ky Taylor, Old Charter Whiskey on rim, 13" diameter, NM, A **450.00**

Wrigley's Double Mint, sign, tin, pack of gum on red background, The New & Better Peppermint Flavor, Be Sure It's..., line border, 6x13", VG, A **55.00**

Wrigley's Double Mint Gum, display, die-cut tin, Wrigley man holding 3 boxes of Double Mint gum, celluloid head intact, 1 box missing lid, rare, A **450.00**

Wrigley's Double Mint Gum, sign, cardboard stand-up, girl holding cigarette behind lg pack of gum, For White Teeth & Smooth Facial..., 14x8", VG, D.................**40.00**

Wrigley's Gum, display, die-cut tin, Wrigley man holding 4 boxes for different chewing gum, celluloid head intact, 14x14x7", VG, A 550.00

Wrigley's Gum, display, die-cut tin, Wrigley man pointing to slant-front case, Ask For Wrigley's, rare, vertical, 19x13x6", VG, A **700.00**

Wrigley's Gum, trolley sign, Wrigley figures flanked by packs of gum with Wrigley's on banner above, 1920s, 11x21", VG+, D **100.00**

Wrigley's Juicy Fruit, match holder, tin, rectangular, appears EX, A..**240.00**

Wrigley's Mineral Scouring Soap, sign, embossed tin, shows package, To Clean, Scour, Scrub, & Polish, Established 1870, wear, 14x20" without frame, G, A **140.00**

Wrigley's Soap, tip tray, black cat mascot sitting atop mineral scouring soap, C Shonk litho, ca 1905-10, 4" diameter, NM, A **150.00**

Wrigley's Spearmint Gum, display box & lid, cardboard, Mint Leaf Flavor, 1930s, 4x6", NM, D.....................**40.00**

Wrigley's Spearmint Gum, display box & lid, cardboard, Wrigley man on lid, Perfect Gum, Flavor Lasts, 1930s, 4x6", NM, D **50.00**

Wrigley's Spearmint Gum, sign, die-cut cardboard stand-up, girl encircled behind lg pack of gum, Sweetens The Breath, 14x10", VG, D **30.00**

Wrigley's Spearmint Gum, trolley sign, man in hat & suit projecting hand with lg pack of gum, Pure, Wholesome, Inexpensive, 1950s, 11x21", VG+, D............**50.00**

Wyandotte Clothing House, pocket mirror, picturing a lady, oval, stained, D **20.00**

Wynola Soda, sign, paper, depicts soda bottle cradled in 5¢ symbol, Drink Wynola, Good Anytime, 2 Glass Bottle, 1950s, 9x20", NM, D.....................................**22.00**

❦ **Y** ❧

Y-B Cigars, tin, colorful can picturing the Yocum Brothers, slip lid, good sheen, dents/chips/edge wear, 6x6x4", EX, A **95.00**

Yacht Cut Plug Tobacco, pocket tin, flat, ship & anchor logo, VG+, A...**150.00**

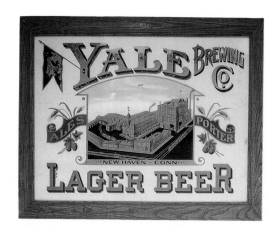

Yale Brewing Co Lager Beer, sign, reverse-painted glass, some flaking, 24x32", A.....................2,600.00

Yale Keys, sign, embossed tin, Stout Sign Co litho, St Louis, ca 1930s, NM, A...**160.00**

Yale Keys, sign, embossed tin, 1940, 17x36", VG, D....**100.00**

Yale Tires, sign, tin, white letters on navy-blue background with gold trim, ca 1930, 48x18", EX, A **60.00**

Yankee Boy Tobacco, pocket tin, boy with baseball bat on checkered background, slip lid, NM, A...........**590.00**

Yardley Talcum, tin, By Appt To HRH Prince Of Wales on front, chrome with Deco styling, ca 1930s, D **25.00**

Yardley's Old English Lavender, sign, canvas roll-down, woman & children on English street, lettering at right, Distilled From ..., 29x35", VG, A **30.00**

Yeast Foam, sign, product superimposed over woman showing her muscles, Keep Fit!, Eat...For Health, framed, 14x10", EX, A **200.00**

Yellow Daisy Long Cut Tobacco, lunch box, tin, shows 2 crossed yellow daisies, slip lid, wire handle, overall wear, G-, A **400.00**

Yellowstone Whiskey, tray, labeled bottle in front of a waterfall, Taylor & Williams Distillers of Louisville, 13x11", G+, A **65.00**

Yonkers Brewery, tip tray, logo on acorn, Y B Dry, rim chips, 4" diameter, EX, A **60.00**

York Brewing Co, tip tray, gold lettering on wood background, Katz's Export Lager, minor rim chips, 4" diameter, NM, A **130.00**

Yosemite Lager Beer, tip tray, Enterprise Brewing Co, VG+, A **800.00**

Your Friend Motor Oil, tin, silver with lg red hat at center, green bottom band with Motor Oil, ca 1955-65, rust/scratches, 2-gal, VG, A.....................................**35.00**

Yuengling's Brewing Co, tip tray, eagle & barrel logo, Beer, Porter, & Ale, slight discoloration/wear, 4" diameter, EX, A **45.00**

Yuengling's Brewing Co, tip tray, eagle & barrel logo, Beer, Porter, & Ale, 4" diameter, M, A **100.00**

Yuengling's Brewing Co, tip tray, pictures young girl in floppy hat, Bottled Beer, Porter, & Ale, 4" diameter, NM, A **140.00**

Yum Yum Smoking Tobacco, pail, tin, pictures boy smoking on blue background, Extra Sweet, Aug Beck & Co, slip lid & bail, some wear, 7x6", G, A............**100.00**

Z

Zane Liquor Co, shot glass, barrel shape, ...Wholesale & Retail Wines & Liquors, 631 Main Street, Zanesville Oh etched on 5 lines, M, D **18.00**

Zanol Baby Mine Talc, tin, pictures baby with blocks on both sides, rare, EX, A **140.00**

Zanol Military Foot Powder, tin, WWI soldier & sailor shaking hands, stars & stripes on lid, EX+, A.........**75.00**

Zatex Chocolate Billets, container, glass jar with embossed lettering, knob on lid, gold background faded, A **450.00**

Zenith Carburetor, sign, heavy metal, double-sided, man in winged hat, Service Station, 27x10", VG, A **375.00**

Zeno Chewing Gum, cabinet, oak with pressed marquee lettered Zeno over 3 shelves, mirrored back door, 19x11x8", NM, A...**400.00**

Zeno Chewing Gum, display box, tin, pictures boy climbing over brick wall to get a box of Zeno gum, A .**120.00**

Zeno Chewing Gum, vendor, 1¢, wood & iron, Choice Flavors, Zeno Mfg Co, original condition, plus key & instructions, 17x10", EX, A.........................**800.00**

Zeno Pepsin Chewing Gum, vendor, revolving pressed steel & mirrored case with cast base, decals on mirrors, some wear, 15x8" diameter, VG, A **175.00**

Zepp's For The Hair, banner, red & white on blue, horizontal oval flanked by barber poles featuring Noonan's & Slikum..., 28x68", EX, A **350.00**

Zepp's German Lustral, sign, wood with gesso frame, Our Price Lists, lists F Dashner's barber shop services, 1900-1910, gesso loss, 28x21", A............................**150.00**

Zeppelin Motor Oil, tin, photo offset of blimp for Fleete-Wing Corp, spout & handle, scratches/slight wear, 2-gal, 12x9x6", VG, A **200.00**

Zeppelin Motor Oil, tin, pictures zeppelin flying over sea in shades of blue, blue lettered band at bottom, ca 1925-45, 2-gal, 12x9", VG, A **195.00**

Zerolene Medium Motor Oil, tin, blue with lg blue & white circle behind polar bear, Standard Oil Co, 1915-25, 1-gal, 11", VG+, A..**250.00**

Zerolene Zero Cold Test Oil, tin, pictures polar bear on blue background, blue & white letters, Standard Oil Co, 1915-25, faded, 5-gal, 15x9", VG+, A **210.00**

Zett's, see Geo Zett's

Zig-Zag Cigarette Paper, dispenser with papers, tin, pictures bearded man in oval inset, scratches/worn lettering, 6", G, A **30.00**

Zingo Sweets, tin, pictures 2 seater open race car, black & gold, dents/chips/discoloration to gold, 10-lb, 9x10" diameter, G-, A **85.00**

Zipp's Cherri-O, dispenser, white ceramic barrel shape with gold banding, bird logo, white round knob on spigot, 16x8", A **1,200.00**

Zipp's Cherri-O, tray, HD Beach Co litho, ca 1920s, 12" diameter, M, A 650.00

Zira Cigarettes, sign, paper, somber-faced woman & package of cigarettes, Lorillard Co, 1912, matted & framed, 17x14", NM, A..**90.00**

Zonite Dandruff Shampoo, trolley sign, illustration of shampoo bottles, 11x21", VG+, D, ...**85.00**

Zu Zu Ginger Snaps, sign, paper litho, depicts clown with product & lettering below on light blue, The Snappiest Ginger..., 15x12", A **190.00**

7-Up, can, inflatable, 1970s, EX, D **$25.00**

7-Up, door plate, aluminum, 7-Up in oval, Come In, worn/faded, 9x4", G, D **$35.00**

7-Up, lighter, aluminum, approx: 2x1", EX, D............**$45.00**

7-Up, menu, chalkboard, slanted bottle & 7-Up logo atop board, rounded corners, vertical, NM, D..............**$45.00**

7-Up, playing cards, Fresh Up, D **$12.00**

7-Up, poster, cardboard, depicts plate of food & bottle of 7-Up, beef sandwich & Seven-Up, 1960, 10x17", EX+, D **$15.00**

7-Up, push bar, porcelain, Fresh Up With Seven-Up in exploding green letters flanked by logos, 3x30", NM, D **$45.00**

7-Up, push bar, porcelain, Fresh Up With Seven-Up in red flanked by logos, 3x30", EX, D **$45.00**

7-Up, sign, depicts bottle of 7-Up, Freshen Up, It Likes You, 17x6", EX, D **$50.00**

7-Up, sign, tin, colorful Pop Art depiction with logo under rainbow, 1974, 13x30", VG+, D..........................**$26.00**

7-Up, sign, tin, pictures a man's hand tipping a bottle of 7-Up, Your Fresh Up at upper left, horizontal, EX, A..**$95.00**

7-Up, sign, 1930s, tin, 7-Up logo with bubbles flanked by You Like It..., ...It Likes You, 11x28", VG+, D......**$25.00**

7-Up, sign, 1930s, 7-Up logo with bubbles at right of Fresh Up lettering, 2 horizontal lines & band at bottom, 11x18", EX, D **$32.00**

7-Up, sign, 1948, die-cut cardboard, smiling man displaying a case of 7-Up, Here's Your Family Fresh Up, 12x10", EX+, D..**$40.00**

7-Up, soda bottle, painted glass, bicentennial, 11", D $4.00

7-Up, thermometer, depicts bottle of 7-Up, The Fresh Up Family Drink, rounded corners, 15x6", EX, D......**$60.00**

7-Up, thermometer, porcelain, depicts bottle of 7-Up, lettered in French, rounded corners, 15x6", VG+, D **$50.00**

Index

Books on Antiques and Collectibles

Most of the following books are available from your local book seller or antique dealer, or on loan from your public library. If you are unable to locate certain titles in your area you may order by mail from COLLECTOR BOOKS, P.O. Box 3009, Paducah, KY 42002-3009. This is only a partial listing of the books on antiques that are available from Collector Books. All books are well illustrated and contain current values. Add $2.00 for postage for the first book ordered and $.30 for each additional book. Include item number, title and price when ordering. Allow 14 to 21 days for delivery.

BOOKS ON GLASS AND POTTERY

1810	American Art Glass, Shuman	$29.95
2016	Bedroom & Bathroom Glassware of the Depression Years	$19.95
1312	Blue & White Stoneware, McNerney	$9.95
1959	Blue Willow, 2nd Ed., Gaston	$14.95
2270	Collectible Glassware from the 40's, 50's, & 60's, Florence	$19.95
3311	Collecting Yellow Ware - Id. & Value Gd., McAllister	$16.95
2352	Collector's Ency. of Akro Agate Glassware, Florence	$14.95
1373	Collector's Ency. of American Dinnerware, Cunningham	$24.95
2272	Collector's Ency. of California Pottery, Chipman	$24.95
3312	Collector's Ency. of Children's Dishes, Whitmyer	$19.95
2133	Collector's Ency. of Cookie Jars, Roerig	$24.95
2273	Collector's Ency. of Depression Glass, 10th Ed., Florence	$19.95
2209	Collector's Ency. of Fiesta, 7th Ed., Huxford	$19.95
1439	Collector's Ency. of Flow Blue China, Gaston	$19.95
1915	Collector's Ency. of Hall China, 2nd Ed., Whitmyer	$19.95
2334	Collector's Ency. of Majolica Pottery, Katz-Marks	$19.95
1358	Collector's Ency. of McCoy Pottery, Huxford	$19.95
3313	Collector's Ency. of Niloak, Gifford	$19.95
1039	Collector's Ency. of Nippon Porcelain I, Van Patten	$19.95
2089	Collector's Ency. of Nippon Porcelain II, Van Patten	$24.95
1665	Collector's Ency. of Nippon Porcelain III, Van Patten	$24.95
1034	Collector's Ency. of Roseville Pottery, Huxford	$19.95
1035	Collector's Ency. of Roseville Pottery, 2nd Ed., Huxford	$19.95
3314	Collector's Ency. of Van Briggle Art Pottery, Sasicki	$24.95
2339	Collector's Guide to Shawnee Pottery, Vanderbilt	$19.95
1425	Cookie Jars, Westfall	$9.95
2275	Czechoslovakian Glass & Collectibles, Barta	$16.95
3315	Elegant Glassware of the Depression Era, 5th Ed., Florence	$19.95
3318	Glass Animals of the Depression Era, Garmon & Spencer	$19.95
2024	Kitchen Glassware of the Depression Years, 4th Ed., Florence	$19.95
2379	Lehner's Ency. of U.S. Marks on Pottery, Porcelain & Clay	$24.95
2394	Oil Lamps II, Thuro	$24.95
3322	Pocket Guide to Depression Glass, 8th Ed., Florence	$9.95
2345	Portland Glass, Ladd	$24.95
1670	Red Wing Collectibles, DePasquale	$9.95
1440	Red Wing Stoneware, DePasquale	$9.95
1958	So. Potteries Blue Ridge Dinnerware, 3rd Ed., Newbound	$14.95
2221	Standard Carnival Glass, 3rd Ed., Edwards	$24.95
1848	Very Rare Glassware of the Depression Years, Florence	$24.95
2140	Very Rare Glassware of the Depression Years, Second Series	$24.95
3326	Very Rare Glassware of the Depression Era, Third Series	$24.95
3327	Watt Pottery - Identification & Value Guide, Morris	$19.95
2224	World of Salt Shakers, 2nd Ed., Lechner	$24.95

BOOKS ON DOLLS & TOYS

2079	Barbie Fashion, Vol. 1, 1959-1967, Eames	$24.95
3310	Black Dolls - 1820-1991 - Id. & Value Guide, Perkins	$17.95
1514	Character Toys & Collectibles 1st Series, Longest	$19.95
1750	Character Toys & Collectibles, 2nd Series, Longest	$19.95
1529	Collector's Ency. of Barbie Dolls, DeWein	$19.95
2338	Collector's Ency. of Disneyana, Longest & Stern	$24.95
2342	Madame Alexander Price Guide #17, Smith	$9.95
1540	Modern Toys, 1930-1980, Baker	$19.95
2343	Patricia Smith's Doll Values Antique to Modern, 8th ed	$12.95
1886	Stern's Guide to Disney	$14.95

2139	Stern's Guide to Disney, 2nd Series	$14.95
1513	Teddy Bears & Steiff Animals, Mandel	$9.95
1817	Teddy Bears & Steiff Animals, 2nd, Mandel	$19.95
2084	Teddy Bears, Annalees & Steiff Animals, 3rd, Mandel	$19.95
2028	Toys, Antique & Collectible, Longest	$14.95
1808	Wonder of Barbie, Manos	$9.95
1430	World of Barbie Dolls, Manos	$9.95

OTHER COLLECTIBLES

1457	American Oak Furniture, McNerney	$9.95
2269	Antique Brass & Copper, Gaston	$16.95
2333	Antique & Collectible Marbles, 3rd Ed., Grist,	$9.95
1712	Antique & Collectible Thimbles, Mathis	$19.95
1748	Antique Purses, Holiner	$19.95
1868	Antique Tools, Our American Heritage, McNerney	$9.95
1426	Arrowheads & Projectile Points, Hothem	$7.95
1278	Art Nouveau & Art Deco Jewelry, Baker	$9.95
1714	Black Collectibles, Gibbs	$19.95
1128	Bottle Pricing Guide, 3rd Ed., Cleveland	$7.95
1751	Christmas Collectibles, Whitmyer	$19.95
1752	Christmas Ornaments, Johnston	$19.95
2132	Collector's Ency. of American Furniture, Vol. I, Swedberg	$24.95
2271	Collector's Ency. of American Furniture, Vol. II, Swedberg	$24.95
2018	Collector's Ency. of Graniteware, Greguire	$24.95
2083	Collector's Ency. of Russel Wright Designs, Kerr	$19.95
2337	Collector's Guide to Decoys, Book II, Huxford	$16.95
2340	Collector's Guide to Easter Collectibles, Burnett	$16.95
1441	Collector's Guide to Post Cards, Wood	$9.95
2276	Decoys, Kangas	$24.95
1629	Doorstops, Id. & Values, Bertoia	$9.95
1716	Fifty Years of Fashion Jewelry, Baker	$19.95
3316	Flea Market Trader, 8th Ed., Huxford	$9.95
3317	Florence's Standard Baseball Card Price Gd., 5th Ed.	$9.95
1755	Furniture of the Depression Era, Swedberg	$19.95
2278	Grist's Machine Made & Contemporary Marbles	$9.95
1424	Hatpins & Hatpin Holders, Baker	$9.95
3319	Huxford's Collectible Advertising - Id. & Value Gd.	$17.95
1181	100 Years of Collectible Jewelry, Baker	$9.95
2023	Keen Kutter Collectibles, 2nd Ed., Heuring	$14.95
2216	Kitchen Antiques - 1790-1940, McNerney	$14.95
3320	Modern Guns - Id. & Val. Gd., 9th Ed., Quertermous	$12.95
1965	Pine Furniture, Our Am. Heritage, McNerney	$14.95
3321	Ornamental & Figural Nutcrackers, Rittenhouse	$16.95
2026	Railroad Collectibles, 4th Ed., Baker	$14.95
1632	Salt & Pepper Shakers, Guarnaccia	$9.95
1888	Salt & Pepper Shakers II, Guarnaccia	$14.95
2220	Salt & Pepper Shakers III, Guarnaccia	$14.95
3323	Schroeder's Antique Price Guide, 11th Ed.	$12.95
3324	Schroeder's Antique & Coll. 1993 Engag. Calendar	$9.95
2346	Sheet Music Ref. & Price Guide, Pafik & Guiheen	$18.95
2096	Silverplated Flatware, 4th Ed., Hagan	$14.95
3325	Standard Knife Collector's Guide, Stewart	$12.95
2348	20th Century Fashionable Plastic Jewelry, Baker	$19.95
2349	Value Guide to Baseball Collectibles, Raycraft	$16.95

Schroeder's ANTIQUES Price Guide

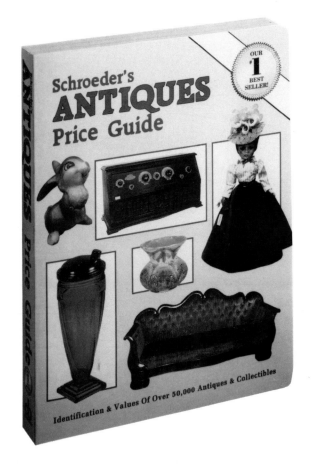

Schroeder's Antiques Price Guide is the #1 best-selling antiques & collectibles value guide on the market today, and here's why . . . More than 300 authors, well-known dealers, and top-notch collectors work together with our editors to bring you accurate information regarding pricing and identification. More than 45,000 items in almost 500 categories are listed along with hundreds of sharp original photos that illustrate not only the rare and unusual, but the common, popular collectibles as well. Each large close-up shot shows important details clearly. Every subject is represented with histories and background information, a feature not found in any of our competitors' publications. Our editors keep abreast of newly-developing trends, often adding several new categories a year as the need arises. If it merits the interest of today's collector, you'll find it in Schroeder's. And you can feel confident that the information we publish is up to date and accurate. Our advisors thoroughly check each category to spot inconsistencies, listings that may not be entirely reflective of market dealings, and lines too vague to be of merit. Only the best of the lot remains for publication. Without doubt, you'll find Schroeder's Antiques Price Guide the only one to buy for reliable information and values.

8½ x 11", 608 Pages   **$12.95**

COLLECTOR BOOKS
A Division of Schroeder Publishing Co., Inc.